E-Life after the Dot Com Bust

Brigitte Preissl · Harry Bouwman
Charles Steinfield
Editors

E-Life
after the Dot Com Bust

With 26 Figures
and 20 Tables

Physica-Verlag

A Springer-Verlag Company

Dr. Brigitte Preissl
German Institute for Economic Research (DIW)
Königin-Luise-Straße 5
14195 Berlin
Germany
bpreissl@diw.de

Prof. Harry Bouwman
Delft University of Technology
Faculty of Technology, Policy and Management
Section Technology and Innovation
Jaffalaan 5
2628 BX Delft
The Netherlands
w.a.g.a.bouwman@tbm.tudelft.nl

Professor Charles Steinfield
Michigan State University
Department of Telecommunication
East Lansing, MI 48824-1212
USA
steinfie@msu.edu

ISBN 978-3-7908-2453-7

Cataloging-in-Publication Data applied for
A catalog record for this book is available from the Library of Congress.
Bibliographic information published by Die Deutsche Bibliothek
Die Deutsche Bibliothek lists this publication in the Deutsche Nationalbibliografie; detailed bibliographic data is available in the Internet at <http://dnb.ddb.de>.

Physica-Verlag is a part of Springer Science+Business Media

springeronline.com

© Physica-Verlag Heidelberg 2010
Printed in Germany

Hardcover Design: Erich Kirchner, Heidelberg

Table of contents

Part 5: Policy challenges

Introduction

Brigitte Preissl[1]

German Institute for Economic Research (DIW), Berlin, Germany

After a period of astonishing growth of e-commerce markets in terms of suppliers and turnover, the rapid expansion came to an abrupt hold in the year 2000. This was marked by the failure of a number of promising Internet-only firms, also popularly called 'dot coms'. At the same time, stock markets showed a pronounced re-evaluation of dot coms and other Internet-related firms, which brought indices down from record heights to more 'normal' values. What had been seen by some observers as a 'New Economy', a frictionless growth regime with high productivity increases, no cyclical movements of the economy's course and high employment levels, now seemed just another peak in a continuing cycle. As enthusiastically as e-commerce and the related new ways to do business had been praised by some analysts, the proclamations of the end of the e-commerce expansion now seemed just as radical. Both the rocket-like upwards movement of market valuation of dot coms and their subsequent lack of sustainability call for a more sober and realistic analysis of past events and future perspectives.

The PLACE (*P*hysical Presence and *L*ocation *A*spects in Electronic *C*ommerce *E*nvironments) project, a joint initiative of Telematica Instituut Enschede, the Technical University of Delft, TNO Strategy Technology Policy (the Netherlands) and the University of Lansing (USA) seemed to be a good framework for promoting discussions of these issues. The German Institute for Economic Research (DIW) that had followed the PLACE project as an interested observer co-hosted a workshop, which took place in Berlin (Germany) in December 2001. A group of researchers from seven countries met to discuss various aspects of the impact of the dot com crisis on the future of e-commerce. Their contributions provide the basis for this publication.

The crisis that hit Internet-based firms so hard was induced by a number of factors which have all contributed to the severity of the phenomenon. It can be argued, however, that attaching too much significance to some prominent success stories in the beginning of the general e-commerce excitement was mirrored by an equally exaggerated overemphasis of some spectacular failures. Although these failures marked the end of a very dynamic expansion path and dragged down many firms that operated as intermediate service and goods suppliers, the long-term development of e-commerce scenarios might not have been dramatically affected. This is Peter Keen's central argument. He suggests looking at 'average' cases rather than extremes, both during the boom and during the sobering-up peri-

---

[1] E-mail: bpreissl@diw.de

ods. At the same time, he uses recent negative experiences to draw lessons for further e-commerce strategies. After the crash, commentators had extrapolated from individual disasters, and thus, again, they worked on exceptions and failed to find the core of e-commerce development patterns. While research concentrated on exceptional cases, e-business moved on in quite traditional patterns and can be seen as a well-established mainstream business practice. Whether explosive successes or dramatic failures, e-business initiatives launched a search for innovation that has led to a consolidation of experience and a platform for sustained e-business expansion. The next generation of innovation is well under way and benefits from a better understanding of basic patterns and trends. The two basic principles Keen lists as essential elements of this generation of innovations are clear lessons learnt from previous failures. (1) Technology architectures: the growth of e-business has paralleled, contributed to and benefited from technological innovations. Many of these have taken decades to evolve. Now, they have matured and provide an entirely new technology architecture for e-business, enterprise IT operations and interorganisational e-business "value networks". (2) Financial management: e-business is now more about financial management than technology: this involves capital efficiency, risk hedging, and targeting investments towards proven measures of e-business payoff.

Keen's approach, which discusses e-commerce development over the past few years from the perspective of a fairly 'normal' radical innovation cycle and emphasises the organisational and strategic challenges involved for companies, might lead to a better understanding of the significance of the crash than simply concentrating on the drama of success and failure. It might also imply a consolidation of research and practice in e-commerce.

The article thus provides a solid basis for the rationale behind most of the following articles. They concentrate on what Peter Keen calls 'new generation e-business', which is emerging from an analysis of past failures as well as new technologies and new innovation ideas. The challenges involved, both for enterprises and for society at large, are discussed from technological, organisational and socio-political perspectives.

The second article in this section focuses on a more theoretical discussion on the nature of online versus offline markets. Theoretically, electronic markets are a close approximation of frictionless perfect markets. Complete information accessible by all market participants and infinitesimally short reaction times seem to justify this hypothesis. In these perfect electronic markets, competition should generate its beneficial effects of ensuring high productivity levels, which are automatically transferred to customers, and fair conditions for all market participants. The supposed efficiency gains from more perfect markets were one of the arguments that led to the proclamation of a New Economy that would not be troubled by the side effects of 'distorted' market conditions. However, the short history of electronic markets did not show convincing evidence of this kind of improvement in the functioning of markets. An increase in transparency in some places (for example, easier comparison of prices for air traffic) has been accompanied by new sources of market dysfunctions (for example, dominance of certain providers in navigation systems). Consumers find it difficult to take advantage of increased transparency due to more and more readily available information and instead see themselves confronted with *information overflow*. Thus, only a very small portion of the information accessible via the Internet is actually used. Recently, the dot com bust of the past years has raised questions about the degree of competition achieved in business-to-consumer e-commerce markets, particularly when large companies and well-established brands have a comparative advantage.

Latzer and Schmitz discuss the widely held view that business-to-consumer e-commerce markets are, or at least tend to be, frictionless and approach the ideal-type market specified by microeconomic theory. The social consequences could be manifold, affecting consumers and respective government policies. Theoretical and empirical arguments for and against the assumption of frictionless, and, thus, highly competitive electronic markets are presented, and policy conclusions based on this analysis are discussed. The research conducted by Latzer and Schmitz suggests that – even though the arguments for a frictionless business-to-business e-commerce market are not dismissed – those against a frictionless market eventually prevail. Four arguments present a strong case against the assumption of perfect electronic markets: (1) Perfect markets require homogenous products, but it is one of the distinguishing features of electronic markets that they allow products and services to be shaped almost individually, which creates heterogeneity of supply, a phenomenon which has also been called *versioning*. Hence, homogeneity is the exception rather than the rule in online markets. (2) The concentration of attention of Internet users on a few web pages contradicts the full information hypothesis. Even if price comparisons are provided in automated systems and allow customers to obtain an overview of the market, the heterogeneity of commodities make it necessary to add quality as a additional dimension for which information is required. Hence automatic price comparisons only apply to markets with well-defined homogeneous goods, such as telephone calls. Learning about this kind of complexity might have diminished the enthusiasm of users after the initial phase of e-commerce. (3) Network effects and increasing returns to scale are inhibiting the realisation of full competition; the interaction of online and offline markets creates specific rules that make it doubtful whether competitive conditions in an electronic market can be considered as independent from those in the corresponding traditional market. (4) Last, but not least, contrary to theoretical expectations, prices in electronic markets are far from homogeneous. Instead of deducing theoretical claims of perfect markets from the technical conditions of online trade, the 'new generation' of electronic business *research* requires us to examine the specific rules that shape online market mechanisms. For this purpose, it might also be necessary to go beyond the toolbox of traditional market analysis and to introduce new features, such as network analysis or prosumer approaches.

Even if the 'crash' rhetoric is abandoned and gives way to a more long-term oriented analysis, it is worthwhile to examine the approaches that lie behind many past and present e-commerce ventures and to study the risks involved and their suitability for creating sustainable concepts. The second section of this book takes this perspective.

The business studies and consulting world has shaped the concept of 'business models' as a strategic tool for launching new products and services (mainly) in information technology and service-related activities. One of the obvious and immediate questions arising from the failure of prominent representatives of the dot com world is whether the business models underlying many e-commerce initiatives have been unrealistic, inconsistent or have not been properly implemented. This has led to an intensive discussion about the nature of e-commerce related business models, their specific features, risk implications and dominant patterns, as well as their perception and reflection in the academic and business world.

The first contribution in this section (written by Richard Hawkins) provides an analysis of the relationship between business model concepts, their actual implementation and the dot com crash. The term 'business model' itself can be seen as an outcome of recent debates and controversy about the future of e-commerce. As a result of the technical potential of electronic transactions, a new approach to selling goods and services had emerged with a strong impact on company strategies. This new approach has been reflected along strategic and normative as well as analytical and conceptual dimensions. However, as such, the term still has no standard definition or coherent conceptual basis in any intellectual discipline. The related theoretical concepts still seem rather premature and tentative, and there is no general understanding of the meaning and usefulness of the term. Nevertheless, the dot com crash that cast many doubts on the future of electronic commerce also highlighted the business model issue as containing potentially both a reason for the crash and a recipe for avoiding further shocks of this kind. Apart from the conceptual fogginess of the term, the dot com crash has, thus, led to a request for a revision of the approaches used to conduct business over global electronic networks. The models developed also hinted at problems that had emerged from business strategies characteristic of the initial phase of e-commerce enthusiasm which might have aggravated or even caused the crash. On the other hand, new variations of business models were advertised after the crash as a means to prevent future shocks and to re-establish confidence in e-commerce enterprises. One of the problems in creating sustainable business models in the recent past seems to be related to the fact that business models show two dimensions with possibly contradictory strategic implications. The components related to business functions affect financial aspects of the company, whereas industrial dynamics are related to productivity and profits. One explanation for the volatility among Internet-oriented enterprises might be found in this dichotomy in business models. The specific business models that constituted the basis of dot com firms in the boom years were relying on a particular functioning of capital markets. The readiness to finance high-tech related innovations and the flexibility of financial markets to nourish what seemed to be the basis of an unforeseen range of business opportunities distracted attention away from the production and efficiency aspects of the various business models. Obviously, companies often failed to establish the right balance between the two dimensions. Richard Hawkins critically examines these perspectives. His paper draws on three bodies of recent original research to examine these propositions. It begins by suggesting that the business model concept is essentially a different way of defining the various kinds of commercial relationships (involving production, distribution and revenue generation) that a company has with the products and/or services it provides to customers. A framework is developed for assessing business model evolution in this light. Electronic commerce may offer new opportunities for companies to experiment with new or different models, but it is likely that implementing new models will often require systemic change in the way a company operates. This may have different repercussions for existing traders than for entrepreneurial start-ups. The paper also examines the 'model as product' concept, suggesting that the business dynamics of business models (related to the financial aspects of the company) can be very different from the industrial dynamics (related to productivity and profits). This dichotomy is explored as an explanation for the recent volatility among Internet-oriented enterprises.

This chapter is followed by an extensive account of the current discussion on the nature, functions and components of business models presented by Harry Bouwman and Erik van Ham. Here, the debate moves on to more theoretical and analytical ground. The vast literature on conceptualising, organising, and managing business calls not only for a comprehensive overview of business models and their components, but also for the development of criteria to evaluate the superiority of one model over others. Hence, tools and concepts for the measurement of the efficiency of business models have to be developed. Bouwman and van Ham discuss the state of the art of the e-commerce business model literature. The popular notion of business models and its specific significance in an e-commerce environment are the subject of a critical analysis. Essential components and their interaction, functions and explanatory value of different approaches are presented, and, thus, important insights into the fundamental question of 'what is a business model' are gained. Business models are presented as abstract models of everyday practice. In theory, it is easy to classify and describe concepts and to arrive at consistent approaches, but these models remain of academic value only unless they are tested in real-world applications, i.e., they lead to a 'business case'. A second substantial part of this paper is dedicated to the performance of business models and the criteria for assessing it. Hence, the emphasis of the early days of e-commerce on having a business model is expanded towards an evaluation of how appropriate the model is. Even the most differentiated theoretical analyses of business models can therefore only make a significant contribution towards understanding e-commerce if the model is accompanied by empirical evidence of its viability, implementation patterns and the outcome over a period of time. Bouwman and van Ham extend the analysis of business cases to an empirical test of criteria and methods for a valuation and comparison of business models. The analysis of business cases takes us back to the question of what can be said, on the basis of empirical evidence, about the usefulness of business and revenue models on the one hand, and of the performance indicators used here, on the other hand. Whether this will lead to a 'new generation of business models' and new metrics that give more enlightened and more reliable support to e-commerce strategists remains to be seen.

The third paper in this section (written by Charles Steinfield) introduces business models that take advantage of synergies emerging from a combination of physical and virtual presence, discusses case studies of successful applications and presents the results of survey research. This contribution follows the general line of examining the less spectacular and more solidly grounded e-commerce activities. Indeed, it is not online-only firms as the essential model of New Economy actors that are likely to create fundamental changes in traditional markets, but hybrid firms that use electronic distribution channels along with physical channels to optimise their sales strategies. The second wave of electronic commerce is dominated by traditional firms who know how to successfully exploit the opportunities of online applications, capitalising on complementary physical assets.

With each new dot com failure reported, there is growing recognition that the Internet is unlikely to displace traditional channels in the near future, at least not in the world of business to consumer commerce. Rather, contrary to suggestions during the early euphoria that the Internet changed everything, it now appears that Web-based electronic commerce is playing a secondary role; one that mainly supplements brick and mortar retail channels. Indeed, the arrival of big retailers on the e-commerce scene may have contributed to the collapse of many struggling dot coms, while causing others to recognise that they need a physical outlet in order to survive. Electronic commerce researchers, using terms like "clicks and mortar," "bricks and clicks," "surf and turf," "cyber-enhanced retailing," and "hybrid e-commerce," now consider the combination of physical and web channels to be a distinct electronic commerce business model. In the first chapter of the second section, Steinfield explores the relationship between traditional and electronic channels through a series of case studies conducted in the Netherlands and the US between 1999 and 2001. His paper emphasises the continuous relevance of click and mortar strategies which had been neglected in the perception of e-commerce developments during the dot com boom. Based on these cases, Steinfield identifies the underlying dynamics of click and mortar business models, including the sources of potential synergies between physical and e-commerce channels, the management interventions necessary to avoid potential conflicts between channels, and the benefits that may result from a tight integration of physical and virtual strategies. There is ample evidence that hybrid strategies continue to be implemented, despite the end of e-commerce illusions. This marks a striking contrast with pure online adoptions where scepticism prevails and investment has dropped to very low levels. Without the pressure to react immediately to a hyper trend, companies that already have a stable offline presence seem to plan their online activities more carefully and integrate them more thoroughly with existing business strategies.

The third and fourth sections of the book discuss e-commerce related applications. For the most part, they have hardly been affected by the crash and continue to be a basis for further enhancement of this transaction mode. Nevertheless, the underlying technological, organisational and strategic concepts have not been developed independently of previous experience. They implicitly reflect the lessons learnt from past success and failure in suggesting new solutions. Section three presents two examples of electronic business that have developed in the shadow of the more visible events, the development of service concepts that include considerable consumer involvement and can be seen as the self-service equivalent of online markets, and the almost unnoticed, albeit dynamic evolution of business-to-business e-commerce. Section four is dedicated to mobile applications that will constitute the big technological and service challenge in the coming years. Given the vast amount of service opportunities provided by mobile technology, the adoptions selected can only hint at the potential that will be created, problems involved and at implementation risks. Three examples represent this vast field: location-based services, the community creating capabilities of wireless adoptions, and user-friendly mobile systems that account for SME concerns.

From a vendor's point of view, e-commerce can facilitate new models of division of labour, which typically encompass a higher level of involvement on the customer's, specifically the consumer's, end of transactions. In order to overcome shortcomings of computer-mediated communications, numerous individualization or personalization features have been added to e-commerce applications. In the telecommunication industry, as one prominent example, increasingly, self-service portals providing administrative functions such as billing status, change of tariff or billing address have been established. More advanced features such as unified messaging are even more customer specific and are beneficial inasmuch as they are regularly adapted to individual, situation-specific needs. These service features constitute a typical example of a 'new generation' adoption. The emphasis is on creating new services as a source of value added, as well as on ways to create more efficient business procedures, and not (as was typical of 'old generation' e-commerce) on making quick profits.

However, contrary to vendors' expectations and theoretical predictions, the new consumer participation options have not been well received and adopted by customers so far (for example, Yahoo's personalization features). The paper by Klein and Totz is based on several analyses of focal groups, combined with usability tests with mobile phone users. Two major shortcomings have emerged from this research: firstly, many functions were not known at all to potential customers, and, secondly, the usability of the Web portal was very limited. These findings must be a cause for concern for the vendors since ongoing innovations in the telecommunications industry are leading to a need for even more user involvement: for instance, location-based services require adaptable and regularly updated consumer profiles in order to provide satisfying results. Based on the dilemma between the limited success of self-service options to date and extended requirements in the near future, the paper reports on findings on the acceptance of customer self-service portals. It analyses and frames the trend towards increasing user participation in advanced telecommunication services, and discusses design options for G3 telecommunication solutions. The conclusions drawn are indicative of a new approach: more efforts are being made to shape products according to customer needs, and challenges deriving from a reluctance of customers to accept offers have to be taken seriously in order to prevent disappointment after the launch of new services.

Statistics on turnover in e-commerce reveal that the magnitude of business-to-business transactions is far more impressive than that of B2C sales. Despite more optimistic projections, electronic markets for end consumers do not seem to be able to expand beyond the 10% range of all retail transactions. Therefore, attention is increasingly shifting to the opportunities arising for business-to-business commerce. Whilst the business-to-consumer part of e-commerce underwent a profound shake-up, the impact on the business-to-business side was hardly noticeable.

This may be due to the fact that changes here were of a different nature. They often took the form of not much more than incremental process innovation characterised by the use of new modes of communication and the integration of logistics systems along the supply chain. Hence, transactions and, very often, supplier-customer relationships already existed; they were just handled differently after the introduction of electronic sales and procurement channels. In contrast, in business-to consumer e-commerce, often a customer base had to be created and new services launched. Therefore, investment in consumer-related online sales bears a greater risk. However, the impact of business-to business adoptions on productivity and the organisation of markets, as well as on parameters and mechanisms of competition, is probably much more profound than in the business-to-consumer world focused on in the first four papers. As Wigand points out in his paper, enterprises do not have much choice but to organise the links with their suppliers and customers in highly integrated networks. These networks have established a new transaction paradigm that is state of the art in organising procurement and sales procedures not only for the large players, but also for small and medium-sized players in most markets. The impact of electronic business between enterprises on the economy becomes beneficial through productivity effects to be gained from reducing transaction costs and streamlining procurement and marketing procedures. Electronic markets are, thus, a device allowing more complex developments of international markets for goods and services. Wigand argues that the emergence of global markets with new competitive configurations, increasing sophistication of customer demands and rising research and development costs are changing business processes and procedures. Electronic markets seem to be an appropriate tool for handling these challenges efficiently. These changes have little to do with the e-commerce hype generated by the mushrooming of dot coms; hence, the burst of the dot com bubble has shown little, if any, impact on developments on the business-to-business side of electronic commerce.

The business-to-business side has nevertheless been included in this volume, since it will be an essential part of 'new generation' e-commerce. Firms invest large sums of money in the reorganisation of their supply chains and distribution channels, and these investments are likely to result in new schemes of market organisation and in a substantial revision of patterns of competition and market power. Rolf Wigand's paper provides a discussion of options and challenges for firms. It analyses networked supply chains in which systems, processes and relationships (internal and external) are effectively integrated. His focus is on the adoptions that generate additional value and, thus, have the potential to lead to sustainable new practices. He assumes to find such adoptions in interconnected supply chains. Intensive collaboration and the increasing need to base supply chains on knowledge management systems have created 'intelligent supply chains' that constitute *value webs* consisting of what are known as value constellations, i.e., structured groups of cooperating partners that combine efforts to generate value added. Wigand concludes that advances in technology, competition and expectations from business partnerships force firms to rethink and restructure their supply chain relationships. These resulting challenges for supply chain management require substantive and extensive changes to existing practices.

While first generation e-commerce firms began to struggle, technological development moved on. It provided wireless solutions that form a basis for many e-commerce related applications. Mobile commerce seems to be a promising field, although the market has experienced its own crash. The key word here is 'UMTS'. Telecommunication service providers have purchased licences for the use of the radio spectrum required at an extraordinarily high price, and it is uncertain whether there will be a sufficiently large mass market to justify these investments. Any assessment of the situation today (after the initial launch of services was delayed for technical reasons) confirms the high risks involved, and it seems unlikely that license costs will be able to be covered before the targeted market is lost to yet another gadget from telecom labs. Although, here – as well as in wired online services – expectations had be revised, this does not reduce the potential of technology in general to generate a new innovation cycle. In a world of fascinating technological developments, it is the dynamics of technical progress that dictates new solutions and dominates the generation of new services. It is not always the case that the resulting systems respond to actual users' needs. This applies to the availability of certain features as well as to the user-friendliness of handling, maintaining and administrating systems. Mobile technology that explicitly targets a mass market in which not only technology experts but all groups of society are potential users is still at a stage where services can be shaped according to user needs. Maitland discusses these issues, emphasising the need to combine technological features with individuals' skill levels, organisational settings and managerial competencies.

Around the time of the dot com crash, another illusion around electronic markets had to be abandoned. In the early stages of e-commerce, many authors argued that the unique characteristic of electronic markets to simulate perfect market conditions provided an excellent opportunity for small and medium-sized enterprises to participate in markets without the usual handicaps deriving from size. After a few years of practical experience and some empirical evidence, there is still no simple answer to the question as to whether small-to-medium-sized enterprises (SME) can improve their competitive situation by integrating e-commerce in their strategies. On the one hand, electronic business seems to offer excellent opportunities for SMEs to overcome the comparative disadvantages they face with respect to their larger competitors. They gain relatively easy access to large customer groups, can step beyond local boundaries in the supply and marketing channels and economise in transaction costs to the same extent as big firms. On the other hand, economies of scale prevail with respect to the cost of establishing and running e-business systems, as well as with respect to the benefits to be gained from a large number of adoptions. They allow larger companies to exploit the productivity potential of e-commerce to a much greater extent than SMEs. Thus, it is no surprise that SMEs are rarely among intensive adopters of e-commerce. Maitland dedicates part of her chapter to SMEs as a specific group of users of wireless applications. She argues that new opportunities for SMEs to improve their competitive conditions might arise from mobile technologies with specific features that might help to overcome some of the difficulties inhibiting the competitiveness of SMEs. If suppliers of mobile technologies are able to provide services that take into account the specific needs of SMEs, this is another hint at the emergence of a 'new generation' in e-commerce, where disillusions of the past are used to take a step towards more advanced solutions.

Departing from the identification of the specific features of m-commerce as related to e-commerce, Maitland deduces the challenges emerging for the shaping of m-commerce systems and for users who want to integrate these systems efficiently into existing business routines. Maitland concludes that the new services emerging from recent advances in wireless and mobile technologies may present solutions for some problems faced by SMEs, although they belong to a group of users that is traditionally challenged in the adoption and exploitation of new communication technologies. Wireless technologies may enable SMEs to develop more advanced modes of managing both internal and external processes. Furthermore, mobile commerce may, along with traditional electronic commerce solutions, allow SMEs to pursue market expansion strategies. Given the broad potential these new technologies present to SMEs, this chapter examines the forces that will influence their adoption.

In the context of this book, Maitland's chapter offers a perspective on new generation e-commerce that concentrates on two aspects: (1) the dot com crash has not impeded the development of useful new technological solutions; technological innovation evolves almost independently of its economic exploitation. Thus, technological evolution did not directly reflect problems that occurred in its applications in business and might have been a reason for unsatisfactory business results. As such, technology seems to follow an autopoietic system and only few links are 'backwards', i.e., problems in adoption leading to the development of next generation technology. (2) In this context, it becomes more important for e-commerce strategies to place great emphasis on the user perspective and to reflect the acceptance of new services.

Mobile commerce scenarios do not suffer from the burden of a past failure. Despite the clearly more cautious approach (compared with early e-commerce enthusiasm) and dampened expectations following an ill-footed start with licensing agreements, mobile services are still presented as a future growth market with enormous potential.

In the mostly anonymous world of the Internet, a new form of personal contact has emerged: Internet communities. Not only do these communities serve a need for communication among people with overlapping interests, but they also help suppliers to create a sense of bonding and, thus, tie the groups to a certain site, its products and services. Internet communities also respond to the need to create trust, which is particularly difficult to achieve in a non-physical environment. Aschmoneit, Heitmann and Hummel adapt this concept to the world of wireless applications. Departing from a characterisation of virtual communities, the authors show how specific elements of these communities can be matched by mobile systems. They further discuss the particular contribution of 'mobility' to community formation and sustainability. Location awareness, ubiquity, identification and immediacy are identified as the essential characteristics of mobile environments, and their relation to community generating and operating features is analysed. The concept of mobile virtual communities is then also adopted in product-related community concepts, which creates a link to business applications of the community approach.

The success of Internet communities suggests two relevant factors: the potential for new and innovative service concepts given in a networked environment, and the significance of building trust and loyalty through peer communication in virtual systems. Furthermore, the discussion shows that electronic markets are likely to develop features that have little in common with the ideal of perfect markets where individuals make decisions independently of each other. The analysis also shows, however, that suppliers have to be well aware of the characteristics of online markets, and they should try to use their potential to be successful in e-commerce. Thus, in the future, online merchants might see themselves confronted with quite complex challenges with respect to customer loyalty and customer service techniques.

The truncation of a dynamic expansion path caused by the dot com bust had severe repercussions in many industrialised economies. The loss of confidence in stock markets and in the viability of e-commerce concepts intensified the beginning of economic recessions in many countries. Furthermore, the bust has cooled down expectations of politicians in almost the same way as those of the business world. However, the realisation of an economy that makes intensive use of the Internet and exploits the (sustained) potential it provides for growth and employment is still on the agenda of most governments in industrialised countries. Hence, decisive policies to promote the diffusion of Internet adoptions and thus to counterbalance the retardation of developments because of insecurity about the future expansion of markets are a core element of e-commerce policies. However, the bust has given rise to a new challenge: rapid technological development and radically new market conditions and customer-supplier relationships not only offer options for innovative business, but also create a set of challenges for suppliers as well as for economic policy and civil society. In the light of the dot com crash, these challenges need a thorough examination in order to identify the risks involved and the demand for policy action. Economic policy measures should aim at avoiding disruptive developments in the future and at re-establishing trust in electronic markets. Three papers discuss related issues: Internet access in the US and in Europe as a pre-requisite of the development of e-commerce markets is the topic of the first paper in this section. This is followed by a chapter discussing alternative policies for handling the large potential for privacy violations in an environment that is a perfect background for the commercial, political or criminal use of any private information. Finally, the third contribution presents local and regional e-commerce policies in Germany as an alternative to more globally oriented policies that were the focus of attention in pre-crash periods.

A wide diffusion of Internet access is not only a matter of social concern, but also of eminent economic importance, since in networked systems critical mass phenomena require the transgression of certain thresholds in usage to make services profitable and attractive for even more users. And 'always on' Internet access is a particularly important precondition for e-commerce. In the light of emerging global markets, a balanced diffusion of subsequent generations of access technologies among the most important trading partners is of crucial interest for all parties involved, because, almost paradoxically, the country with the more advanced diffusion cannot exploit this advantage if its main trading partners are lagging behind. Therefore, it is an important message that the gap in access to advanced communications infrastructure and services that has long existed between these regions is once again increasing, as new data suggests. However, Michael Berne's and Johannes Bauer's paper, which examines the effect of public policies in the US and in Europe towards communication infrastructures and their impact on Internet access and e-commerce, tells a more complex story. The analysis shows the importance of differentiating between fixed and mobile access and between narrowband and broadband solutions.

Berne and Bauer expand earlier research, in which they found significant effects of public policies on Internet access, and study the implications of these policies for e-commerce. Large differences in e-commerce patterns between the various European countries and the USA are identified. The differing policies towards the development of fixed broadband and mobile telecommunications (2.5 and 3G) result in a scenario which makes it likely that new ways to buy on-line will not be indiscriminately provided in each country. This will directly impact the evolution of e-commerce. In the wake of the European 3G licences and the collapse of major players in the broadband networking market, past policies have been questioned. Risks and benefits associated with these policies are examined in the paper, and the prospects for e-commerce in a medium-term perspective are discussed.

Privacy has emerged as one of the key public policy issues of the digital age. In times of high-flying expectations of the growth potential of electronic markets, the implicit assumption prevailed that either privacy questions were not of great relevance to potential customers, or that they could be resolved by technological or organisational means in a very short time. However, privacy concerns may well have been one of the reasons why demand was eventually less dynamic than many suppliers had assumed. The question of how to protect the right of individuals to control the use that is made of their personal data has long been discussed in relation to the vast potential for exploiting personal data for commercial or political purposes using modern communication technology. All too often, however, recent debates have focused narrowly on the privacy implications of the Internet and e-commerce. The chapter written by Bach and Newman situates current digital privacy challenges and privacy debates in a temporal context, looking back as well as forward. It outlines how digital technologies challenge privacy, what tools societies have developed in response to previous privacy challenges, and how these tools are mixed and deployed to master current ones. Three approaches to solving the privacy question are examined: technological devices, specific business models, and government regulation. Furthermore, interaction among these three solutions is discussed. This framework provides a lens through which to gauge temporal, sectoral and geographic variation in privacy regimes. The chapter contrasts the current state of privacy regulation in Europe with that in the US and points out the fundamentally different perspectives that lie behind each region's regulatory approaches. We do not really know exactly how privacy concerns contributed to the dot com crash, but undoubtedly, many consumers are concerned about the security of their data, not only for reasons of guaranteeing the protection of personal information, but also and predominantly for reasons of avoiding fraud. Hence, a more consistent and convincing regime for privacy regulation that also holds for international markets seems to be part of a 'new generation' e-commerce scenario that rests on more solid grounds than its predecessor.

Traditionally, the dot com world has been associated with global business transactions. The use of electronic connections in a local context has not gained much attention. Nevertheless, local policy makers are concerned about the participation of locally oriented companies in the new markets. The dot com bust also directed the focus in e-commerce policies away from Internet-only firms towards the use of electronic technologies in traditionally locally or regionally oriented firms. Fuchs's paper analyses options that regional intermediary actors of e-commerce have at hand or use to promote activities in the business-to-business sector. The research is based on empirical investigations in three different regions in the state of North Rhine Westphalia – Aachen, Dortmund and Bielefeld. Specific supportive strategies of local authorities in these three regions are analysed in detail, referring to intensive interviews and secondary data analyses. Interview partners comprise experts from institutions for the promotion of the local/regional economy and from chambers of commerce as well as chambers of artisans and selected managers responsible for decision making within enterprises of the manufacturing and information industries.

The chapters of this book point out a number of challenges and unresolved issues that should appear on the agenda of company managers as well as policy makers in the next wave of e-commerce evolution: business models that lay sufficient emphasis on revenue planning, responsiveness to consumer needs and the integration of new technological devices are to be considered on the business side. Taxation of virtual transactions, secure payment and the protection of information on individuals are only the most urgent topics that are already being discussed in politics, but universal solutions are still a long way away.

Part 1:
The phenomenon of the dot com crash

Building new generation e-business: exploiting the opportunities of today

Peter G. W. Keen[1]

Fairfax Station, Virginia, USA

Abstract

The crash that hit many dot com firms and resulted in an abrupt end of enthusiastic forecasts of e-commerce development should be seen as an opportunity to learn from the mistakes that have been made and to move on to more viable and sustainable business models. Using 'old generation' e-commerce experience as a huge laboratory directs attention towards general patterns and trends of a long-lasting development path in e-commerce. This approach proves to be more useful than concentrating on single exceptional cases and their dramatic failure in the crash. It will be argued that e-commerce is just about business, and its evolution, thus, follows the well-known rules of investment, financing and market reactions.

Overview: e-commerce is just business

The aim of this chapter is to provide practical guidelines for building effective business models and practices for new generation e-commerce. New generation here does not mean next generation innovations in either the electronic or commerce components of e-commerce. New generation refers to the plans made today to position for the markets and opportunities of the next 2-5 years. New "generation" implies an old generation. The simultaneous and interrelated crash of the NASDAQ, the collapse of the dot com boom and the recession that began in 2000 are the obvious marking of a shift that merits the term "generational". The relevance of the old generation is for taking stock and drawing lessons but only for the purpose of moving forward.

The analysis and guidelines in this chapter are based on what may be seen as an unusual or even provocative claim. This is that the dot com collapse is largely irrelevant to any discussion of e-commerce. The more interesting and useful per-

---

[1] E-mail: peter@peterkeen.com

spective is to view the old generation – Chapter 1 of a long story[2] – as a large-scale set of experiments from which no general extrapolations about e-commerce can be made. The dot com crash tells us little about e-commerce as a whole, for two reasons. The first is that e-commerce far predates the Web and the dynamics of e-commerce revenue and cost structures, consumer response, and patterns of innovation are very much the same for the pre-Web as for the Web era. The dot coms have always been a tiny fraction of total e-commerce. According to University of Texas reliable and non-hype annual review[3], they accounted for under ten percent of the total U.S. Internet economy, and between one and two percent of total business revenues at their peak in 2000.

What was truly new about Chapter 1 of Internet e-commerce, the dot com surge, was that it created a volatile, varied, risky and often exotic laboratory. Just about every experiment in market targeting, pricing strategies, partnerships, new technology, auctions, uses of technology, promotions, alliances, customer segmentation, financing, products and services that the human mind could articulate as a "business model" and convince someone to finance got its chance.

A laboratory provides lessons and insights from individual experiments but does not throw much light on general patterns and trends. The discussion in Chapter 1 of Internet business was thus basically all about outliers. In an immature field explicitly driven by radical innovation and search for "new" business models, there are few patterns, little trustable evidence of long-term trends, and no normal distribution of samples – companies, customers, costs, industry sectors – from which to derive reliable lessons from experience and hence make reliable recommendations for new action. There are no "averages", only individual cases. Striking instances then become the base for analysis and extrapolation. Because there is no normal distribution to compare against, it is completely unclear whether the companies will turn out to be just outliers, way off the scale, or represent a new average, a pacesetter or a soon-to-be mainstream.

In the euphoria of the dot com surge, commentators generated many assertions about the future of e-business from a small number of firms: Amazon, Ariba, Cisco, Priceline, Webvan, and the like. After the crash, the fashion shifted to extrapolation from disasters such as Boo, Exodus, Webvan and Ariba – often the very same companies but with opposite interpretations. Amazon remains a barometer for e-business as marking either sunny weather in store or storms on the horizon; assessments of its status and likely future are almost an e-commerce mood meter. The situation for the trade press has become analogous to the competition that the London Times newspaper held for its journalists in the 1930s: to create the world's most boring headline. The winner was "Small Earthquake in Chile: Not Many Hurt." It became boring to write a headline "Many Dot Coms Profitable." It is as boring to write one that states "eBay continues to do well" as it is to tell the world that "Wal-Mart continues to do well." As the fashion shifts, the headlines reverse the tone. Recently, the new headlines are largely about the successful embedding on the "e" in the "c" as more and more firms harmonize their

---

[2] See Keen 2000.
[3] University of Texas 2003. The latest figures available are for January, 2001.

channels, melding Internet, call center, physical locations and distribution services. There is still no statistical normal distribution and there remains a wide gap
between e-commerce leaders and laggards, but the news is that e-commerce is not
headline material for articles about dot bomb, dot con and Internet company
shares selling for less than their equivalent as paper to decorate a wall.

Headlines are not needed for new generation e-commerce to move ahead and
outliers should be treated as just that until there is a body of experience and stability to distinguish six-sigma special cases from one-sigma leaders and laggards
clustered around a meaningful average. We have such data for supply chain and
logistics, because this highly successful component of e-commerce reached momentum and payoff well before the Web. In the six-sigma headline mode of discussion, this precursor of what is now subsumed under the general label of B2B e-
commerce was initially seen as sure to change the entire nature of commerce, with
Cisco and Ariba two of the headline makers. Post-dot com collapse, it looks like a
disaster; Cisco plunged and Ariba still struggles to stay in business. Focus on the
history of supply chain management and the picture changes entirely: the University of Maryland's in-depth studies and surveys show that over the past decade –
pre- and post-Web – the percentage of U.S. GDP tied up in inventory and supply
chain management costs as dropped by 40 percent, that in any industry the top ten
leaders in the use of electronic SCM tools – including but not confined to the
Internet – use half the working capital per unit of sales than their median competitors, half the overhead and half the inventories.[4] Yet, B2B is in disfavor and, yes,
Ariba and Cisco moved from exemplar to cautionary tale. So?

There are plenty of useful lessons to learn from these and many other B2B fa-
bles – stories with messages – but they are more about business and organizational
issues for any high growth company in any volatile industry. Ariba did a great job
as did Cisco. They both misjudged some business trends that had little to do with
e-commerce and nothing to do with dot coms in general. Basically, Ariba did not
recognize the sensitivity of its business to the high tech market; when that
slumped, it was almost inevitable that any broker and intermediary whose revenues depended on their health would be caught up by the drop. Cisco misestimated
the telecommunications industry slump and mistimed its inventory cutbacks.

The second reason for ignoring the dot com collapse as the base for a guide to
new generation e-commerce strategies and opportunities is in the form of a decid-
edly non-boring headline: "What Collapse? It Was Just Business As Usual." The
crash of so many dot coms was not a collapse of e-commerce; the most striking
evidence for this is that the pattern of growth in e-retailing continued to be very
much the same in the recessionary period of 2001 and 2002 as it had been in the
two preceding boom years. Online business remained a small percent of the total
economy – around 1% in 2000 and on track for 2% by 2005, a figure far below the
exuberant forecasts of the boom period but still solid commercial growth and very
close to the (short) historical rate of increase since the launch of Amazon in late
1994. Online retailing grew faster than did non-online business, even though so
many big names like eToys had gone under and Toys"R"Us now relies on Ama-

---

[4] Boyson et al. 1999, pp 135-138.

zon as its service arm to help it survive. Amazon is in far better shape than Kmart. *Business Week* in mid-2003 reported that far from being "bubble-era hype" was "stronger than ever." Its special report includes the following claims: U.S. networked business-to-business transactions now amount to $2.4 trillion, consumer e-commerce was on track to reach close to $100 billion by the end of 2003, and that anyone who invested $1,000 in every single dot com e-retailer, would have earned a 35% return.[5]

The dot com phenomenon, in all its phases, should not be viewed as at all unique. The lead up to the crash followed the same pattern of previous business expansion and innovation generated by deregulation and globalization (a form of quasi-deregulation of supply sourcing and market barriers), which in so many ways is what the Web has added up to. The pattern is apparent in the history of the U.S. airline industry, telecommunications worldwide, PCs, and electrical utilities. The first phase is that nothing happens. The status quo holds. In telecommunications, five years after deregulation in the U.S. and UK, AT&T and British Telecom still maintained around a ninety percent share of the long distance phone market. The Internet had been in operation for well over a decade before the Web browser began the transformation of Internet operations from a domain limited to academic and technical professionals to a browser on every PC.

Then, often for no apparent reason, some new player does something interesting. In e-commerce the something interesting included Amazon's sudden success, Priceline's new slant on pricing and eBay's invention of the online yard sale. In the airlines, it was Southwest's bypassing of the basic and very successful business model of American Airlines and British Airways: hubbing. It built its strategy on highly selective point-to-point routing and a new style of financial operations and customer care. In telecommunications, MCI's launch of the first billion dollar telecommunications product, Friends and Family, began the breakdown of the telecommunications industry establishment's control of the industry through the strength of branding. In the utilities industry, Enron was just one of the many companies to view power supply as just another futures market.

Such innovations capture interest and imitation and there is a resulting explosion of new entrants challenging the status quo of the industry and often claiming a new edge – business model – in their thinking, organization and operations. In the airlines, thousands of startups bought second hand planes and competed on the basis of a flexibility and small-is-beautiful model that overlooked issues of branding and "distribution" – marketing and reservation systems. The Internet saw the same pattern except multiplied by thousands across all dimensions of industries, small and large firms, new and established entrants. E-retailing took off, online auctions were everywhere and travel became one of the main consumer e-commerce markets.

At some stage and for whatever reason, realities of commerce start showing up and relatively suddenly there is a shakeout followed by a massive and often long consolidation. In the airlines, the realities of scaling and marketing began to bite into the hopes and forecasts of the new players. In e-commerce even before the

---

[5] Business Week 2003, pp. 60-68.

dot com collapse, the dynamics of successful versus unsuccessful e-retailing were becoming very apparent – customer acquisition costs, process capabilities in distribution and order fulfillment, margins, etc. The shakeout was brutal and left many dot coms dead in the water, just as most airlines and telecommunications companies were left stranded well before the recession and 9/11 crashing of the airlines and the 2002 recognition of the overcapacity, misinvestment and accounting frauds and fiction of the leading telecommunications players. We do not label these as the dot jet collapse or the dot wire crash but as business failures. The dot com equivalents were business failures, often in business basics. After the shakeout, there is a long period of consolidation and a new establishment emerges. The airlines are back to a small number of megaplayers and consortia, with many well-known companies gone or likely to go. Obviously, Internet-based e-commerce is now in a post-shakeout consolidation phase. That consolidation often puts "innovation" and expansion on hold and looks for efficiencies, cost savings and rationalization: business basics.

Business basics are the issue. At some stage, the E of e-commerce will disappear, as it already has in banking and it will be integrated into everyday business and not seen as something distinct and often separate. The contrasts of clicks versus bricks and then clicks and bricks will become "what's the difference?" In the mid-1980s, ATMs, electronic cash management systems and financial EDI (electronic data interchange) were all "electronic banking"; now, they are just banking, to the degree that a major problem for startup online banks was their lack of physical ATMs. Technically, an ATM is a general purpose computer with the distinguishing feature that a card activates it. That terminal can increasingly link via standard servers and switches to a range of financial communication networks, but also to government social service payments systems and license renewal processing systems, and even university administration systems. (There are many case examples of the exploitation of the ATM as in effect a portal.)[6] Most ATM users do not think of it as a "computer" or anything special. It is just a service point.

We are not yet at the same stage in online business, but the question now is not if but when this will happen and how to prepare for it. E-commerce today is a matter of emphasis – literally so – and where policy makers and executives place the emphasis strongly influences just about every element of their strategies. In its early stages, e-commerce was very much Electronic commerce – big E and little C. The focus was on the technology as the driver of business: the Internet as infrastructure, the Web browser as link to customers, intermediaries and suppliers, and a host of new software and data management tools as the foundation for product and services design.

Even before the dot com shakeout, the recognized challenge had become how to mesh technology and business and move on to Electronic Commerce, Big E and Big C. The new priorities became to use the power of E to first build revenues (instead of just "hits"), and then to turn revenues into profits. Many companies could not make the transition, but far more did than most reports suggest. *Business Week* stated in mid-February 2003, that over 40 percent of the 208 publicly traded Inter-

---

[6] See Keen 1991, Chapter 3 for examples.

net companies are now profitable, up by almost double from a year earlier. It comments that "In key areas such as e-tailing and online finance, profitability has become the rule rather than the exception. And those profits are measured by generally accepted accounting principles – no "pro forma" tallies need apply."[7] Around the same time, *USA Today* reported that over half the companies on its Internet 50 list that mixes both large and small firms were profitable, up from half that number the year before. In other words, in one of the worst periods in recent business history and the worst for e-commerce, in the boring headline of the newspaper, "Profit possible in post-bubble tech world." (February 13, 2003) It is worth noting that both of these publications focus on averages not outliers; the data are now available and comparable. And it is the about EC, not e-commerce.

The routinization of the e-commerce technology base

Today, we are very much moving on to the era of little E and big C: electronic Commerce. It is commerce that motivates this shift, not because the technology is a secondary factor but because the IT base for e-commerce is moving rapidly to becoming the equivalent of electricity: a set of standard interfaces taken for granted by the user, a massive infrastructure of technology utilities that link automatically and directly from producer to distributor, a variable cost pricing scheme, and clear standards that enable product and service designs. Outside the mainstream of e-commerce are many developments that do not as yet fit into this emerging e-commerce base. These include advanced multi-media interface tools (such as Flash MX), many aspects of wireless services and proven applications and tools that demand too much telecommunications bandwidth or add too much "latency" – delay – in processing to be fully practical in everyday usage. But all these and any future innovations are *explicitly* being designed to fit into this electricity-like infrastructure base; they have to for them to be successful. In a sense, this move to technology as routine is the e-commerce supply side's basic business model. Even Microsoft is moving in this direction. Its packaging of its own Web services capabilities, .Net, is being marketed as the best way to achieve goals of modularity, integration and speed of development for Web-based initiatives, not as being a different direction and pathway. Similarly, IBM's strategy is explicitly committed to the very opposite of its previous history: on-demand, pay as you go services via "grid" computing – a deliberate equating of Web-based services with the electrical grid.[8]

These trends mark the increasing subordination of E to C in e-commerce planning, service design, delivery and operations. In terms of both the E and C of e-commerce, the hype is over. The initially underestimated difficulties of actually executing rather than announcing a business model are fully apparent. There will be no more grand multi-billion dollar experiments funded by naïve investors.

---

[7] Barnes 2003.

[8] For a succinct summary of Web Services and their use, see Fontana 2003,

While the technology continues to evolve and thus open up new e-commerce opportunities, it is now almost axiomatic that in and of itself successful innovations in technology do not directly lead to innovations in their use and impact. The most recent illustration of this point is mobile commerce. Here, the technology of 3G, WAP, and Web-enabled phones was predicted to create massive new markets. So far, they have not done so and much of the turmoil of the telecommunications industry comes from its repeating the big E, little C approach of most of the failed dot coms; the $200 billion spent in Europe alone on 3G licenses makes the dot com spending appear almost like petty cash. The industry has flailed in its search for effective business models; in the context of Web commerce, it is noteworthy that it typically calls these "revenue models."[9]

By contrast, the Web is now as routine in everyday life as the ATM. This is the first generation of business and society where the term "high tech" is a misnomer. The technology core of e-commerce is simply No Big Deal for most organizations and individuals, including in urban areas of countries that previously lacked telecommunications infrastructures and access to IT resources. There is no mystique left in "high tech" in an era of MP3, PDAs, Askjeeves, DSL, eBay, $300 full function desktops and $700 laptops, wi-fi and portable DVD players. Amazon.com is just another retailer. The IT hardware manufacturing industry is an extension of consumer electronics; PCs, laptops, mid-range servers and storage are globally sourced as components to be assembled and branded in the same way as televisions and camcorders. Dell now competes on its own terms with the branders of PDAs, storage, and servers. Companies like Sun Microsystems, EMC, and Compaq have lost much of their ability to set the terms of competition; their premium hardware has been commoditized and it has become harder and harder to find a new premium offer, through software, architecture and high- end product performance.

IT relatively suddenly became a mature industry at the very same time – mid-2000 onwards – that its stock market premiums collapsed. The PC industry is the leading example here: rapid market saturation, commoditization, overcapacity, and price erosion. In software, IT services and uses of IT in administrative functions, back office processes and call centers there is a rapidly growing emergence of global outsourcing and mega-utilities. 5-7 year deals in the $1-10 billion range are, if not commonplace, sufficiently frequent to merit little notice in the press. Many countries are joining the global outsourcing community. These are not casual deals.[10] Apart from being big in financial terms, they are a major organizational shift. They are a recognition that there is no reason to retain in-house the many standard functions that can be both *better* and more cheaply handled via the transportability of business processes and either their technology base or access to it via telecommunications links. They are a more implicit recognition that there is no reason to retain in-house IT resources that can be both *better* and more cheaply handled by specialist firms abroad. The main message from just about every study of back-office and business process outsourcing is that the skilled labor needed for

---

[9] See Keen and Mackintosh 2002.
[10] See Keen 2002.

new generation technology application is available in many regions of the world – including those of traditional IT but also in many countries that are categorized as "lesser" developed. The Philippines, India, Mauritius and Slovakia are examples of new e-commerce skill pools and service providers.[11]

IT is as a result of all the trends towards routinization moving from being a high upfront capital cost – with very high risk in terms of implementation, adoption and payoff – to a pay-as-you-go variable cost, including for many skills that in Chapter 1 of Internet e-commerce were very scarce but are now commodities. In 1998, anyone who could write HTML code for Web sites was a "Webmaster" and earned around $600 a day. Now, HTML is "Save As" in Microsoft Word. Today, XML skills are at a premium. Microsoft has announced that XML, too, will soon be a "Save As" option in Word. In 2000, no company could find enough Java programmers. Today, quite literally, it is hard to give them away; a number of software development and systems integration firms that tried to ride through the recession and retain this expensive talent found that clients would not pay for them even at cost. Mid-range skills are more and more being sourced globally; when you phone AOL for technical assistance, you get through to Makati in the Philippines. That is where the Love Bug virus came from – his fellows describe the student responsible for it as pretty average compared to the rest of his class.

More and more "development" activities, are being handled not just outside IT departments but by teams of business people supported by just a small number of IT specialists, mainly in the areas of data quality assurance (including security), integration and architecture – these are IT skills which will not rapidly commoditize. These teams deliver results in 90-180 day "ventures" rather than the large-scale, long schedule standard IS projects.[12] Examples are business process management (not at all the same thing as reengineering but with the same target, carried out more cautiously, in smaller increments, and with better process mapping and implementation tools), data mining, new generation e-commerce and Web-based services, and multi-media systems.

These are the new mainstream of IT application and thus of new generation e-commerce. They can only increase, not decrease and, correspondingly, reliance on traditional IT systems development staff for e-commerce service development can only decrease. One of the implications of this routinization, even commoditization, of the IT skill base is that any region or country can be a player in e-commerce as niche supplier. Slovenia, Hungary, Jamaica, Bermuda, India, the Philippines and Mexico are examples. In its short history, the Web takeover of e-commerce from EDI and industry-specific services (online banking, airline reservations, retailing procurement, etc.) was very much driven from centers of "advanced" skill resources, most obviously Silicon Valley. As that situation changes along with the changes in the nature and supply of the e-commerce technology

---

[11] In 2002, articles in the IT trade press abut global outsourcing were occasional and mainly centered on offshoring of programming. Now, every issue of the leading magazines contains multiple articles on the topic. They stress the skill premiums as well as the cost advantages. A representative summary is Hayes and McDougall 2003.

[12] For a detailed set of case analyses of eight such 90-120 ventures, see Keen 2003.

base, then obviously the options for supplying and obtaining the E also change rapidly. For chapter 1, technology and technical people were at a premium. They will both remain so in specific areas; end-to-end security and information assurance or RFID (radio frequency identification) applications in retailing are examples of today's premiums. But Chapter 2 of Web-based e-commerce is already being based on sourcing, not building, standard technology.

It will also benefit from the shift in development of applications and services that has been building up since the beginning of the Web explosion and is gathering increasing and continued momentum. In the technology itself, the Web is being augmented by standards and tools loosely termed Web services that facilitate this trend by making it more and more practical to build and integrate new services in small modules. While there are many gaps in what may be termed Transitional Web services – those that are clearly sure to become part of the enterprise- and interorganizational platforms of new generation e-commerce but are not yet fully stable, secure, and proven – Foundational Web services are well in place (the key acronyms here are XML, the enabler of total sharing of data and electronic documents, SOAP, http (the core substructure of the Web), and C++, Java and their progeny). After forty years of sustained effort, the software field is close to its goal of building large-scale applications out of self-integrating, reusable "objects", "components", "applets" and the like. The browser wars – Netscape versus Explorer – are long over, as are the operating systems battles. Windows of course owns the desktop but Linux and Unix now co-exist with it. The operating system is a commodity. More and more organizations speak of becoming "agnostic" in the areas of browsers, operating systems and data management platforms that previously dominated IT industry competition and large organizations' IT strategies.

This routinization of technology platforms has three major implications, all of them highly positive for new generation e-commerce. The first is that most of the infrastructures are in place and affordable across regions, markets and demographics. This obviously shifts the focus of e-commerce innovation from building technology capabilities and capacity to building business ones. The early e-commerce pacesetters uncovered many technology problems, such as scaling – being able to rapidly expand IT operations to handle often explosive increases in volumes of users and transactions and more recently decreases in them – security, privacy and protection against the almost open invitation to launch their viruses that hackers from many places and with many motives saw in the Internet. In general, the focus on IT-building got in the way of business management. In retrospect, it is obvious that many e-commerce players lacked basic skills and staffing in such areas as finance, human resources, and operations. In others, the primary of the technology imperative created cultures that neglected or even disdained general management skills and blocked the efforts of executives brought in to replace floundering founders.

The routinization of the e-commerce technology base thus frees up management attention, resources and skills. It makes absolutely no sense whatever for any company, except a few megaplayers in IT rather then just e-commerce, to build and maintain its own e-commerce technology operations. The second major implication of the routinization is that the shift from own and operate to rent and pay as you go is the guaranteed path for standard uses of IT. Had there been in place to-day's technology industry, set of basic Web-based standards and availability of skilled and reliable outsourcing firms, e-commerce would have followed an en-tirely different finance path than it did. Fundamentally, the entry fee for e-commerce was upfront capital to be invested in two main areas: IT and customer acquisition. These fixed costs are analogous to R&D: invested yesterday and a drain on today's cash flow and profits in the interests of profits tomorrow. As so often with IT, the full cost burden was underestimated by factors of 10-100. The Web site that could be built for, say, $100,000, cost millions to integrate and oper-ate as an e-commerce platform that must link to legacy systems, other partners' services and complex data base systems. In many ways, it has been the equally underestimated cost of customer acquisition that caused the crash of many online retailers and financial service firms.

The routinization of the technology platform transforms the upfront financial capital burden of e-commerce initiatives. It does not remove the burden of cus-tomer acquisition, however. This means that it increasingly routinizes technology costs and operations but not the commerce costs and operations. At the policy level of cities, regions and countries, the economic development issue here is whether these infrastructures will be publicly funded or left to the market. What-ever the answer, it is very clear that new generation e-commerce rents the E com-ponent rather than builds it.

Making sense of the e-commerce Chapter 1 laboratory

That means that the differentiator is commerce. At one level, that is common-sense. However, in the early surge of the dot coms the assumption was that this commonsense meant that new business models would be key to success – a differ-ent form of commerce. The evidence from the dot com laboratory is that it is more the execution of the model than the model itself that makes the difference. Each of the main innovators claimed some degree of uniqueness in its business model. But the patterns showed basically the same uniqueness just about everywhere. An in-sightful set of case studies edited by Stephen Elliot[13] shows that the dynamics of e-commerce innovation, including explanations of success and failure, are very similar across the countries studied: Hong Kong, Greece, Australia, Denmark and others. The choice of initial target markets – B2B in the business sphere and retail-ing, travel and basic financial services in the consumer arena – are almost identi-cal. The problems of management, scaling, and revenue-building are *structurally* the same, however much their situational differences.

Examples of situational differences that do have substantial impacts on e-commerce targeting and evolution are the relative costs of Internet telecommuni-cations access and ISP services, and the availability of consumer credit. The latter is a surprisingly understudied element in the e-commerce field, even though it

---

[13] Elliot 2002.

may well be the single most differentiating factor for new generation e-commerce as it spreads across the world and penetrates the SME (small and medium enterprise) markets, in terms of both e-commerce sellers and buyers. In the mobile phone market, consumer credit has led to the popularity – even necessity – of pre-paid phones in the UK and their almost complete absence in the U.S., where very few users would have a clue what a SIM and "top up" are. However, the same structural patterns of mobile phone adoption and usage are apparent worldwide, reinforcing the view stated here that e-commerce in general follows fairly common paths of both supply and adoption.

The increasing routinization of the e-commerce technology environment is encouraging for regions and economies that were situationally left behind in the early e-commerce surge, for whatever reasons: the high cost of Internet phone access and ISP services (Japan, France), lack of technology and telecommunications infrastructures (Africa, rural regions in developed as well as underdeveloped countries), monopolistic telecommunications regimes (India, Japan) or political restrictions (China, Singapore). The routinization of the e-commerce technology infrastructure is removing most of these constraints but more importantly for national and regional development, the commonality of patterns of e-commerce innovation identified by Elliott and others suggests that the lessons of the dot com era in the U.S. can be used to guide selective prioritization and investment, at both the policy and individual firm level.

If that first era is viewed as a giant laboratory, there are so many instructive lessons to be gained. The disasters are then actually of value; they moved e-commerce forward even though, of course, they decimated their investors' portfolios. The morality – even legality – of the financial dealings of the dot coms, VCs and Wall Street analysts with vested interests in the price of the stocks they analyzed obscures just how much of the dot com phenomenon was about e-commerce and how much was straight financial manipulation. In any case, outliers were the news for investors, analysts and business observers. In the early surge of dot com hype, hope and billion dollar gambles, wild extrapolations were made from individual cases to produce assertive claims about the death of bricks, then no – it's clicks *and* bricks, no – the bricks have won, Amazon is dead, no – it's on track, and the like. Forget the extrapolations. Even today, we lack the time series and sample size to make reliable statistical sense of e-commerce. There are few meaningful averages and standard deviations to guide future management and policy decisions. Yesterday, the extrapolations were very much made through rose-colored lenses. Every e-commerce "success" was to become the norm for entire industries. Today, the extrapolations are generally filtered through dark gray lenses that see individual disasters as the inevitability of the future.

Cases are just cases. Most of the first surge of e-commerce was the equivalent of a set of experiments in a high risk, high capital cost industry like pharmaceuticals. Most of them did not work out. That does not necessarily vitiate their messages. The explosion of B2B and subsequent crashing of the many B2B portals like Ariba, for example, highlights the complexity of process change in organizations; B2B relationships turned out to be highly dependent on existing processes, incentives, existing relationships, and internal systems. These eroded the value of software-based portal processes. The lesson should not be a dot com extrapolation but a recognition that business process management must be the driver of B2B. Similarly, the lesson from Priceline and others is that variable pricing does work, not that Priceline would or would not be a success.

Lessons from the Chapter 1 laboratory; the fundamental cost and profit structures of the firm

The start of Web e-commerce take-off can be appropriately marked by the late 1994 launch of the first version of Netscape's Navigator browser and Amazon's initiation of full operations. If there is just one lesson to take from the multiplicity of "experiments" between then and the April 10, 2000 crash of the NASDAQ that signaled the demise of the dot com era, it is that the fundamental issue for every single player in e-commerce was and remains the difference between the cost structures of the technology-dependent firm and the more typical organization. The diagram in Figure 1 below shows the difference in a schematic form.

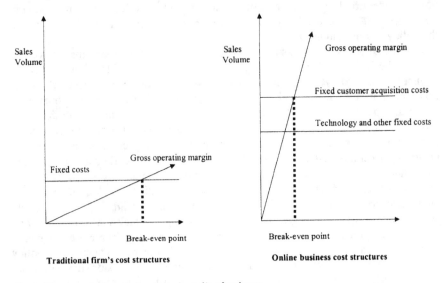

Fig. 1. The nature of cost structures in online business

The traditional firm has relatively low fixed costs and high variable costs (labor, inventories, operations support, etc.) This means that its gross margins are low. Below the break-even point shown in Figure 1, it loses money of course but can generally work its way through short periods of tough times, mainly by reducing its variable costs, especially labor. Above break-even, it makes money but in most industries net operating margins are well below 10 percent.[14] By contrast, gross margins for digital services are in the 85 percent range (eBay is an example). Fixed costs, however, are extremely large, as discussed below. Above the break-even point, the high margins lead to massive profits. Below break-even the losses are just as massive, with the fixed costs a burden that cannot be borne for long.

The stereotypical dot com was built on two high (often very high) largely fixed costs that demanded plenty of financial capital: IT platforms and customer acquisition.[15] Customer acquisition here relates to the marketing, advertising, promotion, discounts, commissions and referral fees that it must spend in advance in order to build its customer base. While figures vary, most analyses indicate that it costs around $50 in retailing and closer to $200 in financial services to get a new customer to make a first purchase. This is not out of line with the costs in traditional insurance and start up of magazines. What was new was the scale of the market needed to recover the costs of customer acquisition and technology platform. Building a customer base of 1 million meant spending at least $50 million and more often $100 million. The dot coms largely assumed that the percentage of "hits" – the number of customers who contact the site – that would turn into sales would be high. This was very much an e-commerce assumption, that the technology itself would generate the business. One typical study in 2000 showed that the average large-scale e-commerce Web site generated 1.8 million hits a month. 15% of these hits turned into transactions. But the number of repeat customers was just 24,000 or 1.3 percent. The average purchase transaction was around $30.

The math just could never work out into a profit. $50 to generate a gross revenue of $30. Up to $300 million to build and brand a household name (the estimate of Charles Schwab's head of advertising, who was a veteran of the comparable AT&T, MCI and Sprint long-distance phone service wars). In mid-2000, most dot com retailers were spending 65% of their revenues on marketing. The costs of building and operating a technology platform that could process 1.8 million accesses just to build a repeat customer base of 24,000 were in themselves bigger than the revenue base of most players. It is not surprising that so many dot coms could not sustain any growth.

Without going into details, this simple diagram explains so many of their failures. Even today, many online companies ignore the imperative of turning hits into transactions and transactions into repeat business. Many of them do not, for example, according to a 2000 survey respond to customer e-mails (40%) or even recognize that the customer is a repeat buyer (75%). Others do not track or re-

---

[14] The financial figures in this section have been taken from a wide range of sources. Three books by Peter Keen provide detailed references: From .Com to .Profit (2000), The Process Edge (1997) and The eProcess Edge (2000). References and additional data are available on www.peterkeen.com. Figures for 2002 onwards are highly suspect because of the instability of both the economy and Internet business, the many accounting tricks that have been revealed in the accounts of a number of online companies, and the lack of reliable categorizations and validations. Those presented here are well-grounded and still applicable.

[15] See Keen and Earle 2000; Keen and McDonald 2000 for detailed references.

spond to the customers who abandon their shopping cart – an indication of a strong interest in making a purchase but some glitch in completing it. Most companies' business models assumed that online advertising would generate a whole new industry and revenue base. Today, banner ads are just a way of filling up the screen with displays most of us ignore. All in all, too many dot com players had business models that were not profit models in definition and execution. At best, they were "hit" generator models.

Only a few firms – Amazon, AOL and Schwab are noted examples – recognized that e-commerce success in the consumer market rested on repeat business and on gradually reducing the high fixed cost burden of technology and acquisition outlays. Amazon's business model was based from the start on this target. Since, as stated earlier, there are so many problems in assessing dot com accounting figures, it is not clear if Amazon is really profitable for the long-term but its pro forma profitability in 2002-2003 was significantly affected by its reducing the percentage of its overall revenues it spent on these two capital investments. (Technically, most of these expenditures were expensed just as R&D is, but they were clearly capital rather than expense in that they provided no short-term payoff and were a high risk investment in the firm's future.)

But there is yet another catch hidden in the diagram above. The dot com, technology-dependent firm gains the benefit of very high operating margins that, if and only if it got above breakeven in recovering its programmed technology and customer acquisition costs. Then it made huge amounts of money. This was the case for AOL and Yahoo at their peak. AOL spent a decade and half a billion dollars in marketing before it broke even. It was able to generate $1.2 billions a year in cash flow on revenues of $6.5 billion (its "run rate" at its 2000 peak). Yahoo had gross operating margins of 80%. EBay's were 74%.[16]

The catch is that the cash flow machine that is operating above break even is a disaster when volumes slump. Schwab had dominated the online securities market through its customer service, customer retention and cross-selling of services from many other providers. It was able to charge $29.95 for a transaction that others provided for as little as $6. In a crowded competitive field, it achieved a 30% market share. Then the stock market crashed and the day traders fled. When high margin revenues disappear what is left in the dot com cost structure is all the high fixed costs, in Schwab's case mostly technology and staff costs. For AOL and Yahoo, what became apparent was how much of their revenue – and Amazon's, too – was based on the volumes of other e-commerce companies, either through fees they paid as commissions or for advertising or through often complex financial deals in which the companies took an equity position in other, smaller providers in return for payments they booked as revenues. The profit structures of the dot coms as a whole were highly sensitive to volumes. AOL derived much of its income from creative – and legal – accounting for business from its partners. It also failed and continues to fail to extend its income from its subscriber base. That base provides a monthly fixed flow of revenue but subscribers have shown little interest in paying for other services.

---

[16] Keen and McDonald 2000.

In many ways, the fundamental business issue for IT in general has always centered on the financial structures of the firm. IT has substituted fixed cost capital for variable cost labor, raising break even points, but raising variable margins. The diagram used to illustrate the discussion was introduced in the is author's 2000 book *From .Com to .Profit* – or so he thought. Skimming through his 1986 book *Competing in Time: Using Telecommunications for Competitive Advantage*, he found the very same diagram summarizing "The Impact of Electronic Delivery Base on Costs of Services." (Page 50)

Beyond showing the impact of age on loss of memory, there are several points relevant to the 2003 discussion here. The main one is that the *structural* issues remain the same but the situational ones have shifted. The business logic underlying the diagram has not changed, but the nature of telecommunications costs has and continues to change. For new generation e-commerce, the opportunity is to shift from fixed cost investment to variable cost contracting. In 1986, the fixed costs of telecommunications were very high indeed, with only large firms having the scale to lease expensive data lines, build global networks or even afford 800 numbers. This meant that only a relative few players exploited what remains the core of business-to-business e-commerce: electronic data interchange. The technology base needed to enter the e-commerce market was prohibitive through the mid-1990s, which is why, though accurate, the analysis in *Competing in Time* was mainly of interest to large banks, airlines, utilities, etc.

What changed the situation was not the Internet as such. It was really in the context of EDI and standard industry e-commerce just an alternative delivery infrastructure and even today pioneers like Wal-Mart and American Airlines still rely on their core "proprietary" systems that are optimized to their own business patterns, security needs and services. These are, of course, evolving towards Web services and already incorporate links to the Internet and use of the Web. The Web introduced two new elements to e-commerce, both of which relate to the cost structures of the firm. First, it reduced the e-commerce entry cost for midsize and small companies in terms of both building their own capabilities and services and reaching customers. Secondly, it lowered the fixed cost investment and time needed to build a large-scale e-commerce technology base. While the costs of building these turned out to be far heavier than the low cost of the front-end Web site made it appear, the Web still lowered the investment base. There is no way that a startup firm like Amazon or eBay could have built a capability to serve millions of customers through traditional methods – including methods of financing. The earlier e-commerce innovators paid for their infrastructures out of their operations and established sources of equity and loans. It was the new financing levers associated with the Web that made the investment difference.

For new generation e-commerce, this pattern of cost structures – fixed versus variable, steepness of the margin line, and sensitivity of payoff to volumes changes in a key new way: the fixed costs become more and more variable costs. Scale can be added in smaller increments. Here is a simple guideline for new generation e-commerce basics, for both policy makers, the e-commerce technology and services supply industry and e-commerce players, whether dot coms or established companies incorporating electronic channels and services in the same way that banks incorporated ATMs and cash management and made the "electronic" term redundant: *Think electricity*. This is the real business model for e-commerce – and for information technology in general. IT must become a variable cost for its users instead of an upfront risk capital investment. For its suppliers and users, it will become a utility for basic everyday operations. The utility blueprint is Web services as an evolution path. For investors, the business model credibility is in the C of e-commerce with the E assumed as being provided through external services. This is the new commonsense of both technology supply and business use.

Lessons from the Chapter 1 e-commerce laboratory about business targets

So far, the arguments of this chapter hide a major potential risk for new generation e-commerce that has to be recognized up front: competitive differentiation via electronic differentiation too often is not sustainable. Again, it is useful to look at e-commerce as pre-dating the dot coms. The classic e-commerce innovation was the ATM. Today, it is so embedded in the structures of everyday life that it is easy to overlook how risky and radical it was and the many parallels to today's e-commerce that bring forth the old adage that those who ignore history are doomed to repeat it. When Citibank launched its ATM initiatives, Bank of America was publicly alarmed not because it feared Citi's success but that its inevitable failure could put the entire U.S. banking industry at risk. Citi in turn saw the opportunity to create and maintain a proprietary competitive advantage. It built its own ATM network so that other banks could not piggyback on its innovation. It made several entrepreneurs very rich as Citibank grew to depend on their technology. Other banks came into the then electronic banking game with their own networks and technology standards. Increasingly, though, smaller players drew on the emerging ATM utilities like Cirrus and Most that offered shared infrastructures. Customers began to expect that they could use their bank's ATM card at any machine. The end of this more than a decade-long sequence was that the premium item that Citibank created had become a commodity and shared networks the norm and no bank had any competitive advantage. They had added to their own cost base and greatly benefited their customers but even Citibank had to surrender to the inevitable: the ATM card as an interface to any bank worldwide. Many commentators argue that the industry would have been best advised to accept this long-term reality and collaborate from the start to build shared networks and common interfaces.

In the Internet e-commerce era, the laboratory shows many examples of a similar loss of competitive differentiation, added cost base and increased price competition at the expense of the provider but very much to the benefit of the customer. The obvious examples are airline ticketing and car purchases. Historically, airlines, travel agents and car dealers had an information edge over buyers in their knowledge of prices, inventory and range of customer choices. They used this edge to optimize their margins and retain a strong degree of control over their marketplace. Internet e-commerce essentially gives away that edge. The customer can use the airlines' own Web sites, search engines and online intermediaries to locate the best deals. They often use this information to bypass the very providers who provide them with access to it. Here, the customer gains but the industry in many ways loses, analogous to the evolution of ATMs. Travel agents have been the main victims here; online e-commerce has contributed to a 20% decrease a year in the number of agencies in business as their services are commoditized, as airlines pressure the agents by reducing their commissions and providing financial incentives for passengers to book online and use their own reservation systems, and as intermediaries like Travelocity, Priceline and Expedia erode their prices. In the business market, travel departments are using the new openness of pricing and inventory information to negotiate deals with airlines that cut prices by as much as 80%. In the auto industry, while dealers still maintain control of sales outlets via distinctly non-competitive regulatory restrictions and while such Chapter 1 e-commerce stars as AutoByTel have not been able to move from dot com to dot profit, car buyers routinely use the Web to gather information about prices, options and promotions that they use to provide them with new bargaining power, bypassing the information provider who created that benefit for them.

Economists talk about asymmetry of information to capture the advantage that airlines, car dealers, brokers and distributors have historically used to leverage their own role and profits in industry value chains. Web e-commerce outliers looked like breaking that asymmetry and building customer power that would be rewarded by those customers gravitating to them. Many of these portals went under in the dot com crash. The laboratory experiment lesson is not that they failed but that they failed to build a W3 capability. Here, W3 does not stand for World Wide Web but Win-Win-Win relationships – a win for the provider of an e-commerce service, for its customers and for relevant business partners. Two out of three is not enough to ensure stability. This W3 principle underlies many of the successes of Chapter 1 to the degree that it must be an imperative in the design of new generation e-commerce services. Here are a few examples from the laboratory, again with the implicit statement that it is irrelevant whether or not they refer to a specific dot that thrived or died:

- Customer self-management underlies many of the successes in both consumer and business to business e-commerce. Basically, the art form is to make the provider's back office administrative expense the customer's valued front-office and to provide incentives for other online providers to help extend the provider's range of services and brand. Yahoo, Dell, Fedex, Cisco, Schwab and many airlines and banks are examples here. The economic driver is the cost difference between a customer handling a query or making a transaction at a cost to the provider of a few cents versus the typical $10 for call center response. Self-management shifts out many costs but it works only if customers gain, too, in terms of personalization, special deals and a level of convenience and responsiveness that goes beyond what they can get by picking up the phone and dialing 1-800 something. The scale of the self-management opportunity is indicated by Fedex's saving of $25 million a month from the 2.4 million daily tracks of packages that previously were handled via its 1-800 phone number. Its

CIO comments "And best of all, customers prefer doing business with us on the Internet."[17]

- Many B2B portals did not create a W3 situation. They and the customer gained, but dealers, brokers, and other intermediaries lost out or worried that they would lose something somewhere. The auto industry's ambitious Covisint portal was potentially a big win for the major manufacturers and their largest "Tier 1" suppliers, but the smaller players saw in advance that they would be sure losers and opted out.

- The complex issue of consumer trust, privacy and security is really a W3 agenda that was poorly handled by many Chapter 1 e-commerce players. They demanded and used – even misused – personal information mainly to maximize their selling opportunities. Consumers saw this as an intrusion and abandoned the site quickly. Others abandoned personalized Web site offers when they heard about the misuse of cookies, selling of email addresses and uses of software that captures information about customers to profile their behavior across many sites.

- In mobile commerce, the basic W3 challenge is that customers will not pay for services that are just conveniences. In standard Internet e-commerce, the same has long been the case. The old adage about the Internet, before it became a business services platform, was that "Information wants to be free." The (mainly strongly anti-business) Internet community used it to share information and ignored issues of security and in many instances of copyright. Information is a universal and common good. That viewpoint underlies what many adults see as immoral – Napster's enablement of a large-scale industry of downloading music for free (until it was legally forced to end the service) – but that a whole generation sees as perfectly reasonable. Perhaps information does want to be free; certainly, no company has as yet succeeded in building large-scale services where customers are willing to pay for information: online newspapers, search engines, or the many city and restaurant guides that can be accessed from a Web-enabled mobile phone.

- One of the world leaders in Internet and mobile banking, Nordea (which operates in the world's leading Internet and mobile communications societies in the world, Scandinavia) insists that giving away services has distorted the entire economics of e-commerce.[18] Doing this puts the provider into a lose-lose situation; if the customer values the service they will use it but insist it remain free. It will be very hard to charge for it later. If it begins by charging for the service, it comes up against the growing expectation of free information or the competition from providers who will give it away in order to attract customers. Mobile commerce has been badly blocked by its inability to create a revenue model for data services, beyond SMS.

In each of these and the many other Chapter 1 e-commerce examples, the business model of providers in one way succeeded. They offered something of interest

---

[17] Canabou 2003, p. 53.
[18] Keen and Mackintosh 2002, p. 43.

and value to customers. They assumed that the customer would create value for themselves, via sales or commissions from other companies for referrals. Many expected online ads to compensate for their free services. As mentioned earlier, even for the small numbers of branded portals such as AOL and Yahoo that did build a strong, high margin revenue base through ads, that base was highly sensitive to scale. The only major and successful brands in e-commerce information services have from the start accepted that information is free (Google, AskJeeves, Yahoo) or at the very least a free part of a paid subscription (AOL). Only the Wall Street Journal has built a critical mass of paid subscribers for its online newspaper and that is both small in volume and a special case. News is available everywhere via Yahoo, AOL, individual publications and search engines – for free.

W3 may well turn out to be the single key element in any effective business model for new generation e-commerce. The evidence favoring this view is apparent again across the Chapter 1 laboratory: the emergence over time of the concept of value networks. These may be often loose online collaborative arrangements in supply chain management where the technology is used to create flows of information for collaborative forecasting; reports show that this has reduced inventory levels along the supply chain by around 25% for all parties. The complexity and interdependencies of modern business increasingly make collaboration and alliances essential and obviously these will arrive at and maintain a stable equilibrium if, and only if, they are W3 in nature. It can be argued that many of the dot coms that crashed were a big success – for the customer. Others were a success for the provider and its customer base but a loss for many established intermediaries.

The design and maintenance of W3 value networks is the agenda for new generation e-commerce. Two out of three is just not enough.

Conclusion

The line of reasoning outlined in this chapter provides a way of thinking about new generation e-commerce. It does not point to specific actions or business targets but offers some simple guidelines for creating a clearing in the forest of muddle, claims, headlines, assertions and often intellectual undergrowth and vendor debris that so marks e-commerce discussion. The line of reasoning here is:

1. The underlying structural issue for e-commerce is the cost dynamics of the firm, with e-commerce pushing towards heavy investment in basically fixed or at least programmed costs in two areas: technology and customer acquisition.
2. Customer acquisition costs can be recovered only through repeat business (the cornerstone of Amazon and Schwab), cross-selling of other services (Yahoo, which "runs" well over 15,000 online stores – for commissions and advertising fees) and strong ongoing relationships (Cisco's online self-management services for established customers and Dell's customized Premium Page Web sites for its largest ones).
3. Technology fixed costs were a blockage to e-commerce diffusion in the pre-Internet e-commerce era and a massive burden for the fast startup, rapid expan-

sion dot coms. The routinization of the e-commerce Web-based technology infrastructure opens up growing opportunities to shift to technology as a variable cost and source services and skills globally and selectively. This opportunity cannot be missed and is surely the middle-term mainstream for IT in general – the equivalent of the electrical utility industry.

4. The commercial challenge for any e-commerce initiative is how to ensure it is W3. This applies whether the business model is focused on the consumer or business market, e-commerce, mobile commerce, clicks, bricks, clicks as part of bricks, portals, retailing, banking, healthcare, manufacturing or distribution.

E-commerce has too often been thought of in revolutionary terms. It is an evolutionary force, in terms of both business and technology. The word evolution is just one letter different from revolution, of course. The firms that focus their e-commerce initiatives to take advantage of the lessons from Chapter 1 on the online economy, especially concern cost structures, will be part of what historians will almost certainly label as the Something Revolution, with many companies out of business because they failed to treat e-commerce as commerce. Evolve or erode. What most stands out in 2003 about e-commerce is how robust in aggregate it has been, however volatile the fortunes of individual companies and most of the dot coms. E-commerce is everyday business, which makes it an everyday business management responsibility.

References

Barnes T J (2003) The Web is Finally Catching Profits. Business Week, February 17, p 88

Boyson S, Corsi TM, Dresner ME, Harrington LH (1999) Logistics And The Extended Enterprise: Benchmarks And Best Practices For The Manufacturing Professional. Wiley, New York

Business Week (2003) The E-Biz Surprise. May 12, pp 60–68

Canabou C (2003) The New IT Agenda. Fast Company, April, p 53

Dennis AR, George JF, Jessup LM, Nunamaker JF, Vogel DR (1988) Information Technology to Support Electronic Meetings. MIS Quarterly, vol 12, issue 4, pp 591–624

Elliot S (ed) (2002) Electronic Commerce: B2C Strategies and Models. John Wiley and Sons, New York

Fontana J (2003) Web Services Pioneers Report Minimal Pain, Plenty of Gain. Computerworld, March 10

Hammer M, Champy J (1993) Reengineering the Corporation: A Manifesto for Business Revolution. Harper Business, New York

Hayes M, McDougall P (2003) Gaining Ground. Information Week, March 31, pp 34–42

Hof RD (1998) Overview: The "click here" economy. Business week, june 22

Keen PGW (1991) Shaping the Future: Business Design Through Information Technology. Harvard Business School Press, Boston

Keen PGW (1997) The Process Edge: Creating Value Where it Counts. Harvard Business School Press, Boston

Keen PGW (2000) Competing in Chapter 2 of Internet business: Navigating in a new world. Eburon, Delft

Keen PGW (2002) Business Process Co-sourcing: Imperative, Historically Inevitable, and Ready To Go. CSC Index White Paper

Keen PGW (2003) A Recipe For Business Process Management: Slashing Cycle Time. Action Technology Executive Briefing Paper

Keen PGW, Earle N (2000) From .Com to .Profit, Inventing Business Models that deliver Value and Profit. Jossey Bass, San Fransisco

Keen PGW, Mackintosh R (2002) The Freedom Economy. McGraw-Hill, New York

Keen PGW, McDonald M (2000) The eProcess Edge. McGraw-Hill, New York

Keen PGW, Sol HG (2003) Rehearsing the Future (in manuscript)

Puttruck D, Pearce T (2000) Clicks and mortar: passion-driven growth in an Internet world. Jossey-Bass, San Francisco

University of Texas (2003), The Internet Economy Indicators. May 7, www.internetindicators.com

Washington Post (2000) A new economy nightmare: value America rode the Internet up like a rocket and came down like one. March 5, p H1

Winograd T, Flores F (1986) Understanding Computers And Cognition. Ablex, Norwood New Jersey

B2C e-commerce: a frictionless market is not in sight – arguments, empirics and policy implications

Michael Latzer[1], Stefan W. Schmitz[2]

Research Unit for Institutional Change and European Integration, Austrian Academy of Sciences, Vienna, Austria
Oesterreichische Nationalbank, Vienna, Austria

Abstract

In our paper we challenge the widely held view that B2C (Business-to-Consumer) e-commerce markets are or at least tend to be frictionless, approaching the ideal-type frictionless market in microeconomic theory. The social consequences would be numerous, affecting the impact on consumers and on respective state policies. We discuss arguments for and against the assumption of a frictionless, highly competitive B2C e-commerce market and present the results of an empirical study on success factors in B2C e-commerce. In addition we provide a survey of empirical studies of the intensity of competition in B2C e-commerce. We argue that the intensity of competition is lower than widely expected and that the dot com shakeout might further increase concentration in B2C e-commerce. Finally, we discuss policy implications based on the theoretical and empirical analysis. We conclude that the rather technology-centred arguments for a frictionless market are outweighed by arguments and by empirical evidence against a frictionless market based on industrial economic considerations.

Arguments for a frictionless e-commerce market

"One of the major features of the Internet revolution is its potential to make the whole economic system, nationally and internationally, more competitive by bringing markets closer to the economists' textbook model of perfect competition, characterized by large numbers of buyers and sellers bidding in a market with perfect information." (Litan and Rivlin 2001, 315)

"Lower search costs in digital markets will make it easier for buyers to find low-cost sellers, and thus will promote price competition among sellers." (Bakos 2001, 71)

---

[1] E-mail: michael.latzer@oeaw.ac.at
[2] E-mail: stefan.schmitz@oenb.at

The widely held view that B2C e-commerce markets are, or at least tend to be frictionless rests in essence on the following arguments:

- The abundance of information results in low search and information costs, so that prices can be compared at virtually no cost.
- Transaction costs are low and market transparency is high, as the goods sold in B2C e-commerce are essentially homogenous. The rising use of search engines and electronic price comparisons further decreases transaction costs and increases market transparency.
- High transparency of B2C e-commerce markets leads to a high intensity of competition and high contestability of B2C e-commerce markets:[3] technological barriers to entry are low; access to production and distribution capacities is fast and inexpensive; possibilities of "boundary crossing" for large companies are high.

We classify these arguments as widely technology centred, as they are based on options provided by internet technology, but fail duly to account for industrial economic considerations, changing business strategies and empirical evidence.

Arguments against a frictionless B2C e-commerce market

In the following we present a number of arguments against a frictionless B2C e-commerce market which have received little attention in the literature so far: heterogeneity of composite goods, limited market transparency, high endogenous sunk costs, network effects, increasing returns to scale and positive feedback loops. Further, we argue that some *business strategies* that are discussed more widely in the literature on B2C e-commerce limit the intensity of competition in B2C e-commerce: price discrimination, lock-in effects and bundling. Finally we provide empirical evidence based on our own surveys as well as on a review of empirical studies. Even though arguments for a frictionless B2C e-commerce market are not dismissed, we argue that those against a frictionless market eventually prevail.

Heterogeneity of composite goods and asymmetric information

The conditions for a frictionless market – including homogeneity of goods offered by a large number of sellers who are price takers, and fully informed buyers – are not reasonable assumptions in the analysis of B2C e-commerce markets.[4]

The utility derived from the purchase in B2C e-commerce depends on the quality attributes of the *composite good*, consisting of the product (e.g. book, CD) and of various complementary goods (e.g. consumer and privacy protection, transpar-

---

[3] See Mai and Oelmann 2001.
[4] For a general discussion of imperfect information in the product market see Stiglitz 1990.

ency of information, delivery service, payment procedure). While quality attributes of a particular book or CD can be assumed to be homogenous across B2C e-commerce companies, there is considerable heterogeneity with respect to the quality attributes of the complementary goods.[5] They are often experience goods. Hence, asymmetric information prevails in the B2C e-commerce market.[6] A first-time purchase at a hitherto unknown online store can be interpreted as an investment under uncertainty. A positive shopping experience with regard to the price/quality ratio of the composite good will reduce the inclination of an individual to risk the investment of a first-time purchase at another store, unless the expected price/quality differential compensates at least for the additional uncertainty involved at the margin.[7]

The options available to sellers of experience goods to (partly) overcome the related informational problems – advertising, certification, guarantees, previews, reviews, and reputation – affect market transparency, market structure and consumer behaviour.[8]

Market transparency

Market transparency in B2C e-commerce markets is lower than widely assumed. We present evidence that the amount of information provided on the web is huge, while consumers' resources to handle it are limited. Online consumers respond to abundance of information by restricting their attention to a very limited fraction of online shops. B2C e-commerce companies respond with high marketing and advertising expenditures and face high customer acquisition costs.

The following examples provide evidence for lower than expected market transparency:

- Search engines cover only a small fraction of web-sites (0.03%)[9] and e-commerce companies have the means to manipulate the perception of the search results.[10] Consequently, web-traffic is highly concentrated among the top web-sites, with the top 0.1% attracting one third of the total volume of web-site visits in the sample.[11]

---

[5] See Borenstein and Saloner 2001; Lucking-Reiley et al. 2000; Smith et al. 1999.

[6] See Bakos 1997, 2001.

[7] Rajgopal et al. (2000) find that positive online customer experience is viewed as sustainable comparative advantage by financial markets as revealed by market prices of e-commerce companies.

[8] Prices are above marginal costs in order to provide an incentive for the firm not to loose the marginal customer, hence the firm has market power. Consumers are skeptical to switch to new entrants (see Stiglitz 1990, p. 824).

[9] See Bergman 2000.

[10] See Lawrence and Gilles 1999; Sullivan 2001.

[11] See Adamic and Huberman 1999. Their sample consists of 60.000 users and 120.000 web-sites.

- We analysed the distribution of page views among the top 100 B2C e-commerce sites.[12] About 50% of the total page views on the top 100 sites are concentrated on 11 companies' sites, and about 75% of the page views on 38 companies' sites. Amazon.com holds a 21% share, while all other companies are under 5%, flattening out quickly from 4.7% to 0.6%. We excluded auction sites from these calculations, as they also cover C2C e-commerce. Nevertheless, the biggest auction site, ebay.com, had a 35% share among the top 100 e-commerce companies in the fourth quarter of 2000. Altogether, these data indicate low market transparency, as users concentrate on a few leading online web shops when (window-) shopping online.
- Although the number of e-commerce companies offering books, CDs and travel arrangements online is very high, consumers tend to search very few shopping sites and the proportion of shoppers who stop their search after the first site visited is high.[13]
- In a consumer survey[14] conducted in January and February 2000 in Austria, the most important criterion for consumer choice was the brand name of the B2C e-commerce company (very important/important for 49%), followed by the trade mark of the good under consideration (very important/important for 40%). Classical internet-based sources of information were ranked on places three to five: search engines (very important/important for 33%), portals (very important/important for 31%), and recommendations on the internet (very important/important for 30%). Finally, advertising and recommendations in traditional media (very important/important for 25%) also had some influence on consumer choice.
- Further empirical studies confirm these findings: often consumers do not shop at the lowest-priced shopping sites; branded retailers can charge a higher premium above the lowest price than unbranded ones can.[15]

Endogenous sunk costs

To some extent, sunk costs associated with market entry in B2C e-commerce are lower than in conventional retail markets, as the demand for the inputs personnel and outlet space is lower in online than in offline retail operations. However, endogenous sunk costs seem to be high in B2C e-commerce, leading to barriers to entry and market concentration – opposed to the ideal of a frictionless market. The evidence presented above shows that brand names play a crucial role in B2C e-commerce so that marketing and advertising expenditures are expected to be high.[16] These endogenous sunk costs affect the market structure: the concentration

---

[12] Data source: Alexa Research 2001.
[13] See Johnson et al. 2000.
[14] For details see Latzer and Schmitz 2000.
[15] See Brynjolfsson and Smith 2000b; Clay et al. 2000.
[16] Pure player in B2C e-commerce reported advertising and marketing costs of 76% of revenues in 1999 (Shop.org 1999). In the Austrian retail market SMEs spend less than

ratio in markets characterised by sunk costs does not converge to zero as the market size grows.[17] By limiting the number of competitors and the intensity of competition in the market, even in the presence of free entry, the long-run average prices can be sustained above marginal costs to recoup sunk costs.

The asymmetric information with respect to price/quality attributes and limited market transparency, in particular with respect to non-contractible characteristics of the composite goods, and the prominent role of reputation, mean that marketing and advertising expenditures play a crucial role in B2C e-commerce.[18] B2C e-commerce is characterised by network effects, increasing returns to scale and positive feedback loops. Since history matters in these markets,[19] marketing and advertising expenditures have a longer-lasting impact on these industries. These endogenous sunk costs are barriers to entry – eventually prices have to rise above marginal costs to recoup endogenous sunk costs, and the intensity of competition is lower than in the absence of endogenous sunk costs, *ceteris paribus*. Furthermore, even if the B2C e-commerce market expands, there is a positive lower limit for the concentration ratio even under free entry.

Network effects, increasing returns to scale and positive feedback loops

The existence of network effects, increasing returns to scale, and positive feedback loops[20] implies that larger B2C e-commerce companies will either sell at lower prices or have larger margins which enable them to invest more in non-price competition or simply generate higher profits. Minimum efficient scale is higher in the presence of positive feedback loops than in their absence so that the intensity of competition is likely to be lower.

B2C e-commerce is often interpreted as exhibiting network effects.[21] The literature on networks distinguishes between direct and indirect network effects.[22] Direct network effects arise as the marginal participant increases the value of the network for all other current and prospective participants as the number of individuals to communicate with increases. Direct network effects are mostly taken into account by network sponsors. Indirect network effects are the result of market interaction and, therefore, they are not considered externalities.

2% of revenues on marketing and advertising activities on average in the same year (Austrian Chamber of Commerce).

[17] See Sutton 1991.

[18] Most of the literature on the intensity of competition completely neglects this issue, exceptions are Schmitz (2000, 206), Schmitz and Latzer (2002). Borenstein and Saloner (2001, 11) mention endogenous sunk costs in passing only.

[19] See Katz and Shapiro 1985; Shapiro and Varian 1999.

[20] See Shapiro and Varian 1999.

[21] See Borenstein and Saloner 2001.

[22] See e.g. Katz and Shapiro 1985; Liebowitz and Margolis 1994, 1998.

Increasing returns play a more prominent role due to the cost structure of inventory management, in procurement, distribution and reputation.[23]

Price discrimination

In a frictionless market the law of one price prevails – there is no price discrimination, which is a common business strategy in B2C e-commerce to raise the price above marginal costs and to decrease the intensity of competition. A number of studies[24] argue that price discrimination is the explanation for the larger than expected price dispersion in B2C e-commerce, because the informational prerequisites can be obtained more easily in B2C e-commerce than in the traditional retail market. The argument presupposes that B2C e-commerce companies are not pure price takers – i.e. they must have some market power – and that arbitrage is not possible between different segments of the market. The segmentation of the market is usually assumed to be achieved by product differentiation, as it is relatively inexpensive to produce multiple versions of a digital good.

Price discrimination affects the intensity of competition *(i)* by reducing the transparency of the market and *(ii)* by reducing the number of buyers and sellers in each segment relative to the non-segmented relevant market.

The diffusion of online price comparison sites and shopbots is assumed to increase the intensity of competition. But B2C e-commerce companies react to technological advances in order to preserve profits and decrease the intensity of competition: since not all consumers engage in a costly search, B2C e-commerce may randomise prices to increase revenues without losing all the price-sensitive customers.[25] Shopbots may facilitate tacit collusion among B2C e-commerce companies.[26]

Lock-in effects and switching costs

Another business strategy that affects the intensity of competition in B2C e-commerce is the creation of lock-in effects and switching costs. They are the result of a previous investment that, if compatible with a current purchase, reduces the costs of the purchase (or increases the utility derived from it). The investment depreciates rapidly, if the consumer switches suppliers, unless the investment is perfectly compatible with the new supplier.

Marketing and advertising expenditures (incl. discounts) might be higher in B2C markets than in comparable offline markets in the early stages of market development. The existence of lock-in effects and switching costs makes current market shares more valuable in the future. Furthermore, the effects of marketing

---

[23] See Borenstein and Saloner 2001.
[24] See Baylis and Perloff 2001; Clay et al. 2000; Clemons et al. 2000; Clemons et al. 2001.
[25] See Varian 2001.
[26] See Varian 1999; Kauffman and Wood 2001.

and advertising expenditure are longer-lived when customers face switching costs. Once the market matures, companies charge higher prices in markets with switching costs than in markets without them, and companies with a larger market share charge higher prices than those with a smaller one.[27]

Lock-in effects in B2C e-commerce can be endogenous, i.e. strategic instruments of B2C e-commerce companies: e.g. loyalty programmes and customisation. But they can also be consequential on the nature of the composite goods, which is an experience good; learning about its quality is an informational investment under uncertain conditions. The subjective switching costs are equal to the maximum insurance premium the consumer is willing to pay, to be guaranteed a composite good that provides (at least) the same level of utility to him.[28] In short, bundling purchases at a single online store reduces non-pecuniary and pecuniary (e.g. per-item shipping costs) transaction costs associated with online shopping.[29]

Bundling

Bundling[30] is a business strategy that is considered to reduce the intensity of competition in markets for information goods in general and in B2C e-commerce in particular.[31] It is a strategy that focuses on the aggregation of large numbers of information goods so that the entire set (or bundle) of goods can be sold at a single price. The list of examples comprises online newspaper articles, music and software downloads, photographs and video clips.[32] In their model, Bakos and Brynjolfsson (1999a,b) show that:

- The seller of the larger bundle will always be willing to spend more for an additional good to add to the bundle. Thus the larger bundler will grow larger relative to the smaller one.

---

[27] See Klemperer 1995.

[28] See Klemperer 1995, p. 517. For empirical evidence of the significant role of lock-in effects and switching costs due to positive experience with the quality of composite goods see Brynjolfsson and Smith (2000b) and Chen and Hitt (2001). Johnson et al. (2000) find evidence for the role of cognitive switching costs in B2C e-commerce.

[29] Johnson et al. (2000) find evidence that a high fraction of B2C e-commerce customers is loyal to one book or CD shop only.

[30] Bundling has similar effects as price discrimination. As compared to first degree price discrimination the bundling strategy reduces the number of different prices to a uniform price for all consumers, and greatly reduces the information requirements and transaction costs while maximising seller's profits. For a discussion of bundling in the context of price discrimination see Varian 1990, p. 626.

[31] See Bakos and Brynjolfsson 1999a, 1999b. However, one has to bear in mind that the problem is structured as bundling versus selling all goods separately, i.e. mixed bundling is ruled out. Consequently, Bakos and Brynjolfsson cannot derive marginal conditions for the optimality of including an additional good in a bundle, or selling it separately.

[32] See Bakos et al. 2000 for different bundling strategies in the online brokerage market.

- In a slightly adapted model the bundler can attract more consumers, charge a higher price and achieve higher revenues from a single, specific good than the seller distributing the good's imperfect substitute on its own.
- A bundling strategy can make market entry unattractive for potential entrants, if their goods cannot be bundled.[33]

Empirical results on price levels and price dispersion

Many empirical studies concentrate on two criteria for market frictions: price levels and price dispersion. Empirical studies on price levels argue along the following lines: assuming that marginal costs are at least as low in B2C e-commerce as in traditional retailing, prices would be lower in the frictionless B2C e-commerce market than in traditional retailing.

Table 1. Empirical studies on price comparisons between B2C e-commerce and the comparable offline market

Higher prices in B2C e-commerce	Inconclusive results	Lower prices in B2C e-commerce
Arbeiterkammer Wien (1999); Bailey (1998); Clay et al. (2000); Frank and Hepperle (2001); Goldman Sachs (1997)*; Ward (2002)**	Repl and Huber (2001)***	Bakos et al. (2000); Brynjolfsson and Smith (2000a); Friberg et al. (2001)****; Lee (2000); Scott Morton et al. (2001a,b*****)

*Data reprinted in Bailey 1998, Appendix 2.
**Classification refers to findings with respect to pure B2C e-commerce suppliers (offline and multichannel suppliers which do not price in significantly different ways).
***The study finds higher prices in B2C e-commerce in 66% of the cases.
****Classification refers to total price on baskets of goods (online prices are not lower than offline prices for single items due to fixed transport costs).
*****Empirical results in the second study – using the same data set – refer to a subgroup of all consumers in the first one only (African-Americans and Hispanics).

The findings summarised in Table 1 justify a rejection of the joint hypothesis that the intensity of competition in B2C e-commerce is higher than in traditional retailing *and* that marginal costs are equal or lower at the relevant level of output. This may be due to a rejection of one or both of its components.[34] Six of the studies present evidence of higher, and six (two of them are based on the same data set) of lower prices in B2C e-commerce than in the comparable offline market.

---

[33] See also Nalebuff 2000.
[34] An empirical example is reported in Ward (2002) who suggests that marginal costs and the intensity of competition are higher online (i.e. pure internet grocery markets vs. hybrid and offline markets) than offline. The study is a fine example of the powerful combination of tests of price levels and price dispersion.

Empirical studies concentrating on price dispersion argue along the following lines: in a frictionless market the law of one price prevails – in practical circumstances the dispersion of prices tends to be very small.

Table 2. Empirical studies of price dispersion in B2C e-commerce

Large price dispersion in B2C e-commerce	Inconclusive results	Small price dispersion in B2C e-commerce
Bailey (1998) ; Bakos et al. (2000); Baye et al. (2001); Baylis and Perloff (2001); Brynjolfsson and Smith (2000a,b); Clay et al. (2000); Clay and Tay (2001); Clemons et al. (2000); Frank and Hepperle (2001); Pan et al. (2001); Tang and Xing (2000); Tang and Lu (2001)*	Lee (2000)	Ward (2002)

Note: There is no clear cut-off point to classify price dispersion as large or low in the literature. We base our classification on the judgement of the authors as expressed in the papers cited.

*Reported evidence of price dispersion is significantly higher for random titles and lower only for a subset of all titles (namely, popular ones).

Of the fifteen studies included in Table 2, thirteen report findings of a large price dispersion in B2C e-commerce. Only one yields inconclusive results and one reports findings of a low price dispersion. Consequently, the hypothesis that B2C e-commerce markets approach the ideal of a frictionless market (high market transparency, low transaction costs, homogenous goods) has to be rejected.[35]

Nevertheless, the empirical results have to be interpreted with care. (1) The "disequilibrium critique" stresses that the hypothesis of lower prices in B2C e-commerce and a low price dispersion in a frictionless market are theoretically valid only in market equilibrium.[36] High losses in B2C e-commerce indicate that it might not yet have reached a sustainable long-term equilibrium. (2) These hypothesis presuppose data sets and information which are very hard to collect – e.g. data on marginal costs, degree of homogeneity of goods in the sample – so they have to be considered as ideal-type formulations. (3) The interpretation of lower prices in B2C e-commerce and/or a low price dispersion as evidence of a high intensity of competition is a logical fallacy – "fallacy of affirming the consequent".[37]

---

[35] Among the studies in Table 2, 12 (80%) focus on search goods, 10 (67%) on low price goods (e.g. CDs or books) and 13 (87%) on physical goods.

[36] See Borenstein and Saloner 2001, p. 9.

[37] See Barker 1989, p. 69.

Empirical evidence on transparency, endogenous sunk costs and market structure

As argued above, low market transparency and high endogenous sunk costs are arguments against a tendency towards frictionless e-commerce markets. Two surveys[38] of Viennese B2C e-commerce companies in January/February 2001 and January/February 2002 provided empirical findings regarding these and various other indicators of the market structure in Viennese B2C e-commerce.

The surveys aimed at three interrelated objectives: (*i*) In the first survey the primary objective was to generate data on company strategies and characteristics in Viennese B2C e-commerce. (*ii*) The second survey aimed at empirical evidence of success and failure, respectively, among the participants of the first survey as well as their subjective explanations for their business situation. The second survey enables us to conduct a longitudinal analysis which links the findings of the first survey with those of the second, notably the realised growth rate of revenue amongst the participating B2C e-commerce companies.

The survey sample consisted of 179 companies.[39] The first standardised questionnaire was made up of 41 questions in three categories (status and dynamics of B2C e-commerce in Vienna, market structure, regional aspects). There was a 32% response rate.[40] The second standardised questionnaire was kept very short (four questions) in order to ensure a high response rate among the participants in the first survey – there was a 93% response rate. Both questionnaires involved questions concerning the provision of data (hard facts, e.g. revenue growth rate, number of customers) and questions calling for subjective interpretations and attitudes (e.g. success factors). The econometric and non-parametric analyses are based solely on the hard facts reported. However, we also show that the quantitative results are consistent with the results of the more subjective questions.

The *results of the econometric analysis* of the number of customers, employees and the rate of revenue growth in Viennese B2C e-commerce can be summarised along the following lines:[41]

- The number of customers in B2C e-commerce (January/February 2001) is a negative function of the number of customers in the traditional line of business and the customer acquisition costs in B2C e-commerce (relative to the traditional line of business), but a positive function of the interaction term of the

---

[38] See Latzer et al. 2002a.

[39] Although it is unlikely that this set of companies encompasses the entire population, we conjecture that those companies we could not identify, have a low visibility and are unlikely to attract a large number of customers.

[40] The sample is quite heterogeneous so that the differences in strategies, characteristics and performance are likely to be pronounced. The sample comprises of 58% of companies with up to 1000 customers/year (January/February 2001), 27% report between 1000 and 10.000 and a further 16% more than 10.000. Most companies had been active in retail-sales, whole-sale or catalogue-sales before they expanded into B2C e-commerce, only 7% followed a disintermediation strategy.

[41] See Schmitz and Sint 2003.

number of customers in the traditional business and the marketing investment relative to B2C e-commerce revenue. Further statistical tests (Pearson's correlation coefficient and non-parametric tests) cannot refute the econometric results. We interpret these findings as strong evidence that the size of the customer base and the size of the marketing investment play a crucial role in determining the number of customers in B2C e-commerce. Large multichannel companies with a high marketing budget have a comparative advantage over start-ups and SMEs (small and medium-sized enterprises). Nonetheless, the data also show that size on its own is not sufficient to attract customers in B2C e-commerce and that ineffective marketing (higher customer acquisition costs in B2C e-commerce than in the traditional line of business) has a negative effect on the number of B2C e-commerce customers.

- The number of employees in B2C e-commerce (January/February 2001) is strongly positively affected by the number of customers. The relationship is not linear, as it increases with the size of the marketing investment (relative to B2C e-commerce revenue). Further statistical tests (Pearson's correlation coefficient and non-parametric tests) cannot refute the econometric results.

- The growth rate of revenue in B2C e-commerce (in 2001) is negatively related to size (whether measured by the number of customers or proxied by the number of employees) and the customer acquisition costs in B2C e-commerce (relative to the traditional line of business), but strongly positively affected by the interaction term of size and marketing investment. As we measure the relative growth rate of revenue, large companies that grow rapidly in terms of absolute numbers, feature lower growth rates than small ones which are less successful in absolute terms (pure size effect). Once the pure size effect has been accounted for, the interaction term of size and marketing investment strongly positively affects the growth rate of revenue in B2C e-commerce. The non-parametric tests indicate a positive rank correlation between the growth rate of revenue and the interaction term of the size and marketing investment, albeit the significance level is slightly below 90%. We interpret these findings as evidence that large, multichannel companies that invest in effective marketing grow more rapidly, in addition to the fact that they already have a larger customer base.

The econometric and non-parametric results indicate a competitive advantage for multichannel companies, which is confirmed by the analysis of the questions in the two surveys that focused on subjective interpretation of, or attitude toward different issues rather than purely on data. In the first survey, 96% of the respondents argued that a modern image for their traditional business was also very important/important advantage for the multichannel companies. Furthermore, 92% indicated that multichannel companies profited from higher trustworthiness derived from their traditional business reputation. According to the second survey, the most important success factor in B2C e-commerce was "synergies with the traditional business" (74%). Only one fifth of the respondents reported a migration of revenues from their traditional business to their own B2C e-commerce activities, while one half of the respondents experienced extra revenue also in their traditional business. The remaining 40% argued that their expansion into B2C e-commerce did not affect their traditional business at all. At the same time, most of the companies had already been active in either retail or catalogue sales before they entered the B2C e-commerce market (93%) and most had a very positive attitude towards cross-promotion and regard the following marketing methods as very important: after-sales services in the local stores (83%), pick-up goods bought in B2C e-commerce at local store (67%), exchange goods at local stores (66%).

The econometric and non-parametric results further emphasise the crucial role of marketing investment in explaining the performance of B2C e-commerce companies. In the first survey, the respondents ranked a company's reputation in B2C e-commerce as the most important criterion in consumer choice among B2C e-commerce suppliers (71% very important/18% important criterion). A high reputation in the traditional business was the second most important criterion (with 67% very important/31% important). In the second survey, respondents ranked the reputation in their traditional business as the second most important success factor (72%). High marketing investment was regarded as a success factor in B2C e-commerce by 28%. At the same time, only 16% reported that lower prices were a success factor. This is not very surprising, as 90% reported similar prices in B2C e-commerce and in their traditional business (± 1.5% incl. p&p, VAT if applicable). On the other hand, 78% of respondents argued that problems with consumer- and privacy-protection were a barrier to consumers adopting B2C e-commerce. In addition, 75% believed that the market was intransparent with respect to products and prices, and 64% reported that it was intransparent with respect to suppliers and their business practices. Overall, these results refute the hypothesis that B2C e-commerce market is highly transparent, confirming the importance of marketing investment, i.e. endogenous sunk costs.[42]

Finally, we analysed the forecasts of companies regarding their revenue growth in B2C e-commerce. In the year 2000 the general expectations concerning the economic success and impact of B2C e-commerce changed dramatically in both financial markets and in the popular press. Between mid-March and end of May 2000 the Internet Stock Index (ISDEX) dropped by 55%.[43] We analysed whether the dot com shakeout was accompanied by high uncertainty with respect to the growth of B2C e-commerce in Vienna. We approached the question by comparing

[42] The conclusion, that the market is less transparent than widely expected, is also consistent with a survey among more than 1000 B2C e-commerce users in Austria in January/February 2000: The most important criteria users based their choice of B2C e-commerce company on, were the brand name of the B2C e-commerce company (49% very important/important) and the brand name of the company that produces the products offered (40% very important/important). The most important barriers to B2C e-commerce adoption were uncertainty with respect to data- and consumer-protection (75% very important/important), impossibility to examine products sufficiently before the purchase (74% very important/important) and uncertainty with respect to the payment mechanisms in B2C e-commerce (71% very important/important) (see Latzer and Schmitz 2000).

[43] See Keating et al. 2003.

forecasts and realisations of the revenue growth rates in B2C e-commerce in Vienna in 2001. Table 3 summarises the results of the first and the second survey concerning the forecasts (rows $E(\Delta ECOMREV)$) and the realisation (columns ($\Delta ECOMREV$) of the *growth rate of revenue* in B2C e-commerce in Vienna in 2001. The responses are grouped in 6 categories.

Table 3. Revenue growth rate in B2C e-commerce in Vienna 2001. Forecast and realisation (N=37)

		0%	<10%	<20%	<50%	<100	>=100%	Sum
	0%	2.7%	0.0%	0.0%	0.0%	0.0%	0.0%	2.7%
	<10%	2.7%	*10.8%*	5.4%	2.7%	2.7%	2.7%	27.0%
	<20%	0.0%	2.7%	*2.7%*	5.4%	5.4%	0.0%	16.2%
	<50%	2.7%	0.0%	2.7%	*8.1%*	0.0%	0.0%	13.5%
	<100%	2.7%	5.4%	2.7%	5.4%	*5.4%*	8.1%	29.7%
	>=100%	0.0%	0.0%	0.0%	0.0%	5.4%	*5.4%*	10.8%
	Sum	10.8%	18.9%	13.5%	21.6%	18.9%	16.2%	100.0%

Revenue growth rate in B2C e-commerce in Vienna 2001: *Realisation* (column header); row label: Revenue growth rate in B2C e-commerce in Vienna 2001: *Forecast*

- The interpretation, based on the six categories and 37 responses, shows that 35.1% of the respondents achieved their forecasts for 2001 exactly (*italics* in diagonal), 32.4% overestimated (below the diagonal), and 32.4% underestimated (above the diagonal) their revenue growth rate in 2001.
- The categories are relatively broad, so that the precision of the interpretation concerning the differences between the forecasts and realisations is smaller relative to a comparison of the individual responses. Instances of under- and overestimation that occur within the categories are not captured by category-based approach.
- Nevertheless, an analysis based on the exact values reported in the two surveys provides a similar picture: 10.8% of the 37 respondents achieved their forecasts exactly, 48.7% overestimated, and 40.5% underestimated their revenue growth rate in 2001. The pronounced reduction in the ratio of respondents achieving their forecasts exactly (from 35.1% to 10.8%) is in line with expectations, as the analysis is now based on exact values rather than on broad categories. While the analysis based on the first approach tends to underestimate differences between forecasts and realisations, the second approach tends to overestimate them, as it does not distinguish between minor and substantial differences between the two values.
- Nonetheless, the congruence of the interpretation of both approaches is striking: even though the number of companies achieving their forecasts exactly differs, it is still substantial. Furthermore, the two groups that either over- or underestimated their revenue growth rates are quite similar in both cases.
- In order to analyse the relative extent of over- and underestimation we conducted statistical tests of the equality of the means and variances of the two

subsamples of the absolute values of $E(\Delta ECOMREV) > \Delta ECOMREV$ and $E(\Delta ECOMREV) \leq \Delta ECOMREV$, respectively. Figure 1 (see appendix) shows the frequency distribution of the differences between forecasts and realisations. Table 4 (see appendix) provides the descriptive statistics of the entire data set of absolute values of over- and underestimation. (For the purpose of the statistical analysis the latter also includes the 10.8% of the companies that achieved their forecasts exactly. Although the means and the variances are not identical, the differences are not significant, as the test for equality of means of the subsample (Table 5, see appendix) clearly fails to refute the hypothesis of equal means. The Levene test for equality of variances cannot refute the hypothesis of equal variances of the two subsamples (Table 6, see appendix).

Based on the analysis of both, the number of companies that over- or underestimate the growth rate of revenue in B2C e-commerce and the extent of divergence between forecasts and realisations, we conclude that the Viennese B2C e-commerce companies did not systematically over-estimate growth rates despite the end of the B2C e-commerce hype.

Policy implications

A frictionless B2C e-commerce market would imply that there is no market failure and hence no need for market regulation. However, the results of our analysis – that there is no frictionless B2C e-commerce market in sight – lead to quite different policy implications regarding the need for government intervention in B2C e-commerce markets.

Market interventions are frequently justified by (potential) market failure and many of the above identified characteristics of B2C e-commerce – asymmetric information, lower than expected market transparency, network externalities and increasing returns – could lead to such a failure of market allocation.

Government intervention is usually considered the remedy for (potential) market failure. However, not only (potential) market failure, but also inefficiencies of regulatory policies should be taken into account. There are a number of potential sources of these inefficiencies that have to be considered (e.g. information deficits, rapid technological change, regulatory capture and principal-agent problems between politicians and officials). The B2C e-commerce market is evolving rapidly, and there is now widespread consensus, both in the US and the EU, that government regulation has to be reduced to a necessary minimum and that the regulatory framework has to be flexible.[44] Hence the analysis of B2C e-commerce regulation should be based on a cost-benefit analysis of different institutional arrangements. It has to take into account private sector efforts to cope with potential market fail-

---

[44] Currently, there is some consensus to minimise state intervention in B2C e-commerce albeit there are still substantial differences between the US, Japan and industry organisations, on the one hand, and the EU and Canada, on the other. See Mann 2000; Schmitz 2000.

ure, as well as the proper legal framework for B2C e-commerce, which includes the allocation and monitoring of property-rights.

Heterogeneity of complementary goods, their characteristics as experience goods and resulting asymmetric information in B2C e-commerce limit consumer sovereignty and provide a rationale for government intervention. A regulatory framework for consumer protection and the protection of privacy can reduce asymmetric information with respect to the composite goods and increase market transparency in B2C e-commerce. In addition, a proper legal framework can increase consumer trust in B2C e-commerce in general and enhance market growth. The transnational character of e-commerce complicates such regulations, and new forms of self- and co-regulation are being sought to solve these problems.[45]

Other potential sources of market failure are network externalities and increasing returns to scale. Network externalities (but not network effects) play an empirically minor role in B2C e-commerce as direct network effects are internalised by the B2C e-commerce companies, whereas indirect network effects are pecuniary effects and cannot be considered externalities. The necessary condition for a natural monopoly is subadditivity, which requires declining average incremental costs in each product line of a multiproduct firm and economies of scope at or below the relevant level of output.[46] However, network effects and increasing returns to scale do not necessarily imply that B2C e-commerce has a tendency towards natural monopoly: due to the heterogeneity of consumer preferences it is unlikely that network size is the only relevant factor in network choice, i.e. the B2C e-commerce company. In particular with regard to the social aspects (e.g. chat rooms) and consumer reviews, it is likely that the characteristics of other participants are an important factor. The fact that increasing returns to scale play a prominent role in B2C e-commerce does not necessarily imply that declining average incremental costs prevail at an output level at or below market volume. In this case, marginal costs increase with the volume of sales of a B2C e-commerce company after a certain threshold. If the production function of B2C e-commerce companies exhibits diminishing marginal productivity at output levels below market volume, more than one can exist in equilibrium. Limitations on the organisational and informational capacity are of special importance in B2C e-commerce.

The crash might further increase the tendency towards concentration in B2C e-commerce markets. Our results show that larger and more marketing savvy companies grew faster in 2001 and seemed less affected by the shakeout than their smaller competitors. As financial markets became less enthusiastic about B2C e-commerce, costs of refinancing increased sharply. Start-ups in particular experienced a sharp increase in financing costs. Hence, entry in the industry has become harder. At the same time a lot of companies have been forced to exit the industry, thus reducing the number of enterprises and increasing concentration. Only a few B2C e-commerce companies have positive operating cashflows, while the majority are hit much harder by increasing financing costs. Companies that have suc-

---

[45] For empirical evidence of self- and co-regulation and an analysis of its advantages and disadvantages compared to state regulation see Latzer et al. 2002b.

[46] See Panzar 1990, p. 27.

ceeded in establishing a strong brand name and a good reputation are less likely to see their positions contested, as the large marketing expenses are harder to finance now than during the boom. In 1999, financial markets reacted favourably to high cash-burn rates of B2C e-commerce companies that invested heavily in marketing. But in 2000 the markets became very critical with respect to high cash expenditure and in particular with respect to high marketing costs.[47] Furthermore, consumers whose confidence in B2C e-commerce is negatively affected by the shakeout might increasingly turn to the market leaders with a high reputation. Large B2C e-commerce companies frequently expand and diversify their product range in order to capitalise on their brand names. Consequently, for a growing number of products (books, toys, gardening equipment etc.) concentration tends to increase as companies diversify their product range and thereby expand their dominance from their core market into others.

Our arguments for low intensity of competition do not necessarily imply that anti-trust issues are becoming more important in B2C e-commerce: *(i)* Traditional retailing is a close substitute for large parts of B2C e-commerce, blurring the borders of relevant markets. *(ii)* The market is still growing and regulation in order to raise static efficiency can adversely affect dynamic efficiency.[48] *(iii)* Market structure in high-technology markets is less stable over time. In B2C e-commerce in particular, new business models, advances in technology (e.g. payment systems) and innovative marketing strategies could lead to rapid changes in market structure and limit market power. *(iv)* Although the growth rates of B2C e-commerce have been impressive in recent years, market volume is still relatively low relative to the traditional retail market, but also in relation to traditional catalogue sales.[49] Consequently, B2C e-commerce companies are still struggling to increase their customer base, so market power is still limited even for companies that dominate the market.

Although the abuse of market power in B2C e-commerce does not appear to be a pressing problem, size and endogenous barriers to entry are important. SMEs face barriers to adoption of B2C e-commerce so a policy that aims at the rapid diffusion of B2C e-commerce within SMEs needs to provide active support. Financial constraints in particular have risen as a result of the dot com crash and the general economic downturn. However, due to the shakeout and the tendency to concentration, it is questionable whether economic policy should aim at a higher diffusion of B2C e-commerce among SMEs in the first place.

Conclusions

In this paper we challenge the widely held view that B2C e-commerce markets are, or at least tend to be frictionless. We summarise and classify the common ar-

---

[47] See Demers and Baruch 2001.

[48] See Klodt 2001, p. 44.

[49] See Latzer and Schmitz 2000.

guments for frictionless e-commerce markets as largely technology centred, as they are based on options provided by internet technology, but duly fail to account for industrial economic considerations and empirical evidence: heterogeneity of composite goods, limited market transparency, endogenous sunk costs, network effects, increasing returns to scale and positive feedback loops. Further, we argue that some business strategies limit the intensity of competition in B2C e-commerce: price discrimination, lock-in effects and bundling. Even though the arguments for a frictionless B2C e-commerce market are not dismissed, we argue that those against a frictionless market eventually prevail. The econometric and non-parametric evidence, based on our two surveys of the Viennese B2C e-commerce market, suggests that large, marketing savvy companies keep growing relative to their smaller, less marketing savvy competitors. The positive effects of size on growth indicate a concentration process in the B2C e-commerce market. Furthermore, the empirical analysis highlights the crucial role of marketing investment in B2C e-commerce, so the analysis of market structure has to account for the significance of endogenous sunk costs, which constitute barriers to entry and limit the intensity of competition. The dot com crash may further increase the tendency towards concentration in B2C e-commerce markets as higher financing costs increase market exits and decrease market entry.

Although some of the characteristics emphasised lead to (potential) market failure, we argue for a sensible use of government intervention, taking into account possible inefficiencies of regulatory policies due to rapidly changing technology and business strategies. Nevertheless, heterogeneity of composite goods and asymmetric information limit consumer sovereignty and provide a rationale for consumer and data protection regulation. Furthermore, size plays a crucial role in B2C e-commerce, which – together with endogenous barriers to entry – limits the potential benefits SMEs may derive from adopting B2C e-commerce.

Finally, we analysed the forecasts and the realisations of the growth rate rates of B2C e-commerce revenue in Vienna in 2001. The data has not revealed any systematic bias towards over- or underestimation of expectations despite the considerable changes of attitude towards the New Economy in public opinion and, in particular, the worsening sentiment of investors as mirrored in the development of financial markets during 2000.

References

Adamic LA, Huberman BA (1999) The nature of markets in the World Wide Web. Xerox Palo Alto Research Center, Palo Alto

Alexa Research (2001) E-Commerce report Q 4 2000. http://www.alexaresearch.com (January 2001)

Arbeiterkammer Wien (1999) Erhebung Internetshopping. Wien

Bailey JP (1998) Electronic commerce: prices and consumer issues for three products: books, compact discs, and software. OECD DSTI/ICCP/IE(98)4/FINAL, Paris

Bakos Y (1997) Reducing buyer search costs: implications for electronic marketplaces. Management Science 43. http://www.stern.nyu.edu/~bakos (8. Juni 2001)

Bakos Y (2001) The emerging landscape for retail E-Commerce. Journal of Economic Perspectives 15:69–80

Bakos Y, Brynjolfsson E (1999a) Bundling information goods: pricing, profits and efficiency. Working paper. Sloan School of Management MIT, Cambridge, MA

Bakos Y, Brynjolfsson E (1999b) Bundling and competition on the internet. Working Paper. Sloan School of Management MIT, Cambridge, MA

Bakos Y, Lucas HC, Oh W, Simon G, Viswanathan S, Weber B (2000). The impact of electronic commerce on the retail brokerage industry. Working paper. Stern School of Business, New York University, New York

Barker SF (1989) The elements of logic. McGraw Hill, New York

Baye MR, Morgan J, Scholten P (2001) Price dispersion in the small and in the large: evidence from an internet price comparison site. Working paper, Indiana University

Baylis K, Perloff JM (2001) Price dispersion on the internet: good firms and bad firms. Department of Agricultural & Resource Economics, University of California, Berkeley, CA

Bergman MK (2000) The deep web: surfacing hidden value. White paper, Brightplanet. http://www.brightplanet.com (March 2001)

Borenstein S, Saloner G (2001) Economics and electronic commerce. Journal of Economic Perspectives 15:3–12

Brynjolfsson E, Smith MD (2000a) Frictionless commerce? A comparison of internet and conventional retailers. Management Science 46:563–585

Brynjolfsson E, Smith MD (2000b) The great equalizer? Consumer choice behavior at internet shopbots. Working paper, MIT Sloan School of Management, Cambridge, MA. http://ecommerce.mit.edu/papers/ude (May 2000)

Chen PY, Hitt LM (2001) Measuring the determinants of switching costs: a study of the online brokerage industry. Proceedings of the International Conference on Information Systems

Clay K, Krishnan R, Wolff E, Fernandes D (2000) Retail strategies on the web: price and non-price competition in the online book industry. Working paper, Heinz School of Public Policy and Management, Pittsburgh

Clay K, Tay CH (2001) Cross-country price differentials in the online textbook market. Working paper, Heinz School of Public Policy and Management, Pittsburgh

Clemons EK, Hann I, Hitt LM (2000) The nature of competition among online travel agents: an empirical investigation. Working paper, Department of Operations and Information Management, The Wharton School, University of Pennsylvania

Clemons EK, Hitt LM, Gu B, Thatcher ME, Weber BW (2001) Impacts of the internet on financial services: a quantitative analysis of transparency, differential pricing and disintermediation. Paper prepared for the conference "Financial Ecommerce", Federal Reserve Bank of New York, New York

Demers E, Baruch L (2001) A rude awakening: internet shakeout in 2000. Working paper, Simon School of Business, University of Rochester, Rochester

Frank B, Hepperle G (2001) The internet's impact on the market for antiquarian books: some unexpected empirical results. Unpublished manuscript, University of Hohenheim, Hohenheim

Friberg R, Ganslandt M, Sandström M (2001) E-commerce and prices – theory and evidence. Paper presented at the workshop "Network Economics", IAS 16/17 May, Vienna

Johnson EJ, Moe W, Fader P, Bellman S, Lohse J (2000) On the depth and dynamics of World Wide Web shopping behavior. Working paper, Department of Marketing, Columbia Business School, New York

Katz ML, Shapiro C (1985) Network externalities, competition, and compatibility. American Economic Review 75:424–440

Kauffman RJ, Wood CA (2001) Analysing competition and collusion strategies in electronic marketplaces with information asymmetry. Department of Information and Decision Sciences, University of Minnesota, Minneapolis

Keating EK, Lys TZ, Magee RP (2003) The internet downturn: finding valuation factors in spring 2000. Journal of Accounting and Economics 34:189–236

Klemperer P (1995) Competition when consumers have switching costs: an overview with applications to industrial organization, macroeconomics, and international trade. Review of Economic Studies 62:515–540

Klodt H (2001) Und sie fliegen doch: Wettbewerbstrategien für die Neue Ökonomie. In: Donges JB, Mai S (eds) E-Commerce und Wirtschaftspolitik. Schriften zur Wirtschaftspolitik. Lucius & Lucius, Stuttgart, pp 31–48

Latzer M, Schmitz SW (2000) Business-to-Consumer e-commerce in Österreich: Eine empirische Untersuchung. In: Latzer M (ed) Mediamatikpolitik für die Digitale Ökonomie. Studienverlag, Innsbruck, pp 286–306

Latzer M, Schmitz SW (2002) Die Ökonomie des e-commerce – New Economy, Digitale Ökonomie und realwirtschaftliche Auswirkungen. Metropolis Verlag, Marburg

Latzer M, Bauer J, Fuchs G, Just N, Purtsche I, Schmitz SW, Sint PP, Teutsch B (2002a) Status und Dynamik des Business-to-Consumer e-commerce in Wien. Forschungsbericht im Auftrag der Stadt Wien. IWE-ÖAW, Wien

Latzer M, Just N, Saurwein F, Slominiski P (2002b) Selbst- und Ko-Regulierung im Mediamatiksektor. Alternative Regulierungsformen zwischen Staat und Markt. Westdeutscher Verlag, Wiesbaden

Lawrence S, Gilles CL (1999) Accessibility of information on the web. Nature 400:107–109

Lee MJ (2000) A comparative analysis of pharmaceutical pricing. Department of Economics, University of Illinois, Urbana-Champaign

Liebowitz SJ, Margolis SE (1994) Network externality: the uncommon tragedy. Journal of Economic Perspectives 8:133–150

Liebowitz SJ, Margolis SE (1998) Network externalities (effects). The New Palgrave Dictionary of Economics and the Law. MacMillan, London

Litan RE, Rivlin AM (2001) Projecting the economic impact of the internet. The American Economic Review Papers and Proceedings 91(2):313–317

Lucking-Reiley D, Bryan D, Prasad N, Reeves D (2000) Pennies from eBay: the determinants of price in online auction. Working paper, Vanderbilt University, Nashville

Mai S, Oelmann M (2001) Elektronischer Handel im Lichte der Bestreitbarkeit der Märkte. In: Donges JB, Mai S (eds) E-Commerce und Wirtschaftspolitik. Schriften zur Wirtschaftspolitik. Lucius & Lucius, Stuttgart, pp 49–92

Mann C (2000) Transatlantic issues in electronic commerce. Working paper 7/2000, Institute for International Economics, Washington, D.C.

Nalebuff B (2000) Competing against bundles. Working paper series H, Working paper 7, Yale School of Management, Yale

Pan X, Ratchford BT, Shankar V (2001) Why aren't prices of the same item the same at me.com and you.com? Drivers of price dispersion among e-tailers Working paper, Sloan School of Management, MIT Boston

Panzar JC (1990) Technological determinants of firm and industry structure. In: Schmalensee R, Willig R (eds) Handbook of industrial organization. Amsterdam, pp 3–60

Rajgopal S, Venkatachalam M, Kotha S (2000) Does quality of online customer experience create a sustainable competitive advantage for e-commerce firms? Working paper, University of Washington, Seattle

Repl J, Huber R (2001) Hotelbuchungen in Europa: Ein Preisvergleich zwischen verschiedenen Buchungsmedien. Katalog-, Internet- und Direktbuchung. Erhebung November 2000. Arbeiterkammer Wien, Viennna

Schmitz SW (2000) Die Förderung des B2C e-commerce. In: Latzer M (ed), Mediamatikpolitik für die Digitale Ökonomie. Innsbruck, Studienverlag, pp 62–219

Schmitz SW, Latzer M (2002) Competition in B2C e-commerce: analytical issues and empirical evidence. Electronic Markets 12(3):163–174

Schmitz SW, Sint PP (2003) B2C e-commerce strategy and market structure: the survey based approach. Discussion paper 323, DIW Berlin, Berlin

Scott Morton F, Zettelmeyer F, Silva-Risso J (2001a) Internet car retailing. Journal of Industrial Economics 49:501–519

Scott Morton F, Zettelmeyer F, Silva-Risso J (2001b) Consumer information and price discrimination: does the internet affect the pricing of new cars to women and minorities? Working paper no ES-15, Yale School of Management, Yale University

Shapiro C, Varian H (1999) Information rules – a strategic guide to the network economy. Harvard Business School Press, Harvard

Shop.org (1999) State of online retailing 2.0. http://www.shop.org (May 2000)

Smith MD, Bailey J, Brynjolfsson E (1999) Understanding digital markets: review and assessment. Boston. http://ecommerce.mit.edu/papers/ude (October 2001)

Stiglitz JE (1990) Imperfect information in the product market. In: Schmalensee R, Willig R (eds) Handbook of industrial organization. Amsterdam, pp 769–847

Sullivan D (2001) Buying your way in to search engines. SearchEngineWatch.com, 2 May 2001. http://www.searchenginewatch.com/webmasters/paid.html (May 2001)

Sutton J (1991) Sunk costs and market structure. MIT Press, Cambridge, MA

Tang FF, Xing X (2000) An empirical study on pricing differences between dot coms and hybrids in the online video market. Working paper AE-WP2000-06, Nanyang Business School, Singapore. http://www.ntu.edu.sg/nbs/ae/Working-Papers.htm (December 2001)

Tang FF, Lu D (2001) Pricing patterns in the online CD market: an empirical study. Electronic Markets 11 (Lee JK, Schmid BF, Buchet B (eds) Special issue ICEC 2000)

Varian HR (1990) Price discrimination. In: Schmalensee R, Willig R (eds) Handbook of industrial organization. Amsterdam, pp 597–654

Varian HR (1999) Market structure in the network age. Berkeley. http://www.sims.berkeley. edu/~hal/people/hal/papers (June 2000)

Varian HR (2001) High-technology industries and market structure. Paper prepared for the symposium on "Economic Policy for the Information Economy", Federal Reserve Bank of Kansas City, Jackson Hole, WY

Ward, MR (2002) Inferring competition from prices: Evidence from online grocery markets. Working paper, Department of Economics, University of Illinois, Urbana-Campaign

Ward MR, Lee MJ (1999) Internet shopping, consumer search and product branding. Department of Economics, University of Illinois, Urbana-Champaign

Data appendix

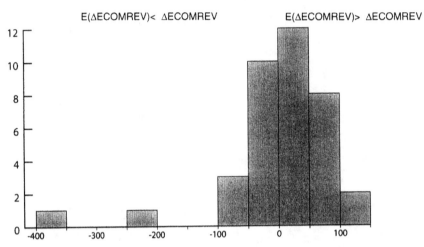

Fig. 1. Histogram of differences between expected and realised revenue growth in B2C e-commerce in 2001: [$E(\Delta ECOMREV) \leq \Delta ECOMREV$] under- and [$E(\Delta ECOMREV) > \Delta ECOMREV$] overestimation of revenue growth rate in 2001; [$E(\Delta ECOMREV) \leq \Delta ECOMREV$] underestimation of revenue growth rate in 2001

Table 4. Descriptive statistics of absolute values of differences between expected and realised growth rate of B2C e-commerce revenue in 2001, of the absolute values of subsamples of under- [$E(\Delta ECOMREV) \leq \Delta ECOMREV$] and overestimation [$E(\Delta ECOMREV) > \Delta ECOMREV$]

	Total	$E(\Delta ECOMREV) \leq$ $\Delta ECOMREV$	$E(\Delta ECOMREV) >$ $\Delta ECOMREV$
Mean	53.5	57.7	49.1
St. Dev.	75.4	99.7	38.4
St. Error	12.4	22.9	9.0

Table 5. Test for equality of means of total sample and subsamples: H_0 cannot be rejected

H_0	t	df	Sign	mean$_{E(\Delta ECOMREV) \leq \Delta ECOMREV}$ – mean$_{E(\Delta ECOMREV) > \Delta ECOMREV}$
$E[E(\Delta ECOMREV) \leq \Delta ECOMREV] =$ $E[E(\Delta ECOMREV) > \Delta ECOMREV]$	-0.342	35	0.734	-8.6

Table 6. Levene test for equality of variances of total sample and subsamples: H_0 cannot be rejected

H_0	F	Prob
Var[E(ΔECOMREV) $\leq$ ΔECOMREV] = Var[E(ΔECOMREV) > ΔECOMREV]	1.828	0.185

Part 2:
Business models

Looking beyond the dot com bubble: exploring the form and function of business models in the electronic marketplace

Richard Hawkins[1]

TNO, Institute for Strategy, Technology and Policy, Delft, The Netherlands

Abstract

The recent so-called dot com crash cast many doubts on the future of electronic commerce, but it also highlighted business models as an issue. This paper begins by assessing the dot com crash critically, suggesting that e-commerce came through the crash in a much better condition than often is supposed. It then defines business modelling in terms of the amalgamation or integration of various economic processes, process and organisational models with technological architectures. Drawing upon recent original research, the paper then examines the role of business models in the electronic marketplace. It proposes that business models play a complex range of roles and that they can even become products in their own right, often creating or transforming markets, but at the same time increasing investment risks. The case is made that developing a better understanding of business model dynamics may help to moderate investment volatility in Internet-enterprises as well as provide new avenues for commercial activity.

Introduction

In many respects, the business model is an artefact of the e-commerce euphoria that emerged in the 1990s. Prior to this period, few comments about business models could be found even in the popular business press, let alone in the learned literatures of business, management, economics and their like. The perceived champions of e-commerce during the 1990s were the so-called dot com companies. However, as the new millennium dawned the dot coms began to look less like a commercial revolution and more like a bubble getting ready to burst.

As the bubble grew, the market filled up with books and articles about business models, ranging from the mildly analytical to the *quasi* instructional – how to con-

---

[1] E-mail: hawkins@stb.tno.nl

struct viable models and how to avoid lemons. Their timing was propitious. If the bubble did not burst, guiding concepts would still be sought as to how to compete in this flourishing environment. If the bubble did burst, firms (not to mention the economy as a whole) would need handy frameworks within which to explain failures and restructure for future success. Either way, the business model seemed to fill a niche even if nobody could explain exactly what it was.

Problematically, most of what was being discussed in this new business model context had been discussed already with far more rigour in other more securely established contexts. Indeed, at first sight, business model concepts (and there were many) appeared to be little more than random amalgamations of business plans, business cases, process and organisational models, price and revenue models, and systems architectures. Individually, all of these subjects have voluminous literatures supported by extensive research. What possible purpose was being served by adding yet another flavour to this already rich broth?

It would be easy just to dismiss the business model discussion outright as *merely* an artifact of the dot com boom. Certainly, the concept is rooted almost exclusively in the electronic trading environment. But actually, the most intriguing aspects of this discussion only started to clarify as it appeared that the boom might be turning to bust. Even before it was obvious that market confidence in the dot coms was being severely shaken, significant intellectual movement had became discernible away from the emphasis on new technology as a driver of new business models (e.g. Kraemer et al. 2000; Kern et al. 2000; Jutla et al. 1999), and towards the idea that that technological capabilities had to be exploited in a more balanced relationship with the strategic and organisational capabilities of companies (Ballon and Arbanowski 2002; Mahadevan 2000; Afuah and Tucci 2001; Timmers 1999). In other words, the business model idea began to be linked with a renewed recognition that you can't build new markets, much less a whole new economy, on capital investment alone. Common sense, you might think, but anathema for many 'new economy' prophets throughout most of the 1990s.

We are now perhaps at the cusp of a neo-orthodoxy that calls into question assumptions that buyers and sellers will respond positively to new technology in the marketplace just because new it may offer increased convenience and efficiency and/or lower costs. Indeed, on the whole, the emergence of the business model issue has had the general positive effect of focussing attention away from technology as such and towards the interaction of technology with the complex social and economic milieu to which we refer loosely as 'the market'. Provided we define the 'business model' – or more accurately, a process which we can call business modelling – in this broad context, the concept is relevant and useful in explaining some of the origins and consequences of the extreme technological optimism we witnessed in the previous decade and also for describing the contemporary dynamics of the electronic marketplace.

However, if we accept the 'business model' as an operational concept, it stands to reason that we should be able to identify and compare critically the various characteristics and outcomes of individual business models. It is at this point that some intriguing new questions emerge. How do markets perceive and absorb business models? How much variety is possible? Is it necessary for each individual enterprise to develop new or unique models? What is the relationship between business models and product/service characteristics? Do business models have collective dimensions – perhaps profiting from positive network externalities? The list goes on.

Most business model discussions still focus on what seem to be the most obvious reasons for doing business electronically, namely, efficiency and cost minimisation. While not underestimating the importance of these factors, I will argue below that business modelling plays a crucial role also in what we might call the social psychology of markets – the various individual and collective factors that induce firms and individuals to participate in different markets in different ways. This latter element may be key to explaining the role of business models in recent bubble phenomena and to assessing the future impacts of these phenomena.

The argument has several facets. As business models are inevitably linked to the dot com phenomenon, the first concern is to determine whether or not there was actually a dot com crash – a question that is far more open than many presume. Once this is out of the way, a case must be made that we can define the business modelling process in terms that add to our understanding of how companies actually do business in an electronic environment. Finally, we have to look at the role of business models in the electronic marketplace. I will propose that business models play a complex range of roles, not all of them related necessarily to the production and distribution of goods and services in the first instance. I will suggest that *business models can become products in their own right*; moreover, that this has been the main aspect of business models that has been visible to most investors up to this point, thus being at the root of the most obvious recent consequences in the market.

To support these arguments, I will draw upon several bodies of original research in which colleagues and I have been involved during the past 5–6 years.[2] As the scope and extent of this research is quite broad relative to the space available in this Chapter, I will refer to it collectively, giving some general references within which various findings are contained. Where I call upon supporting published statistics, I will refer mainly to recent figures from the US Census Bureau.[3]

---

[2] This research trajectory began in 1996. Main completed projects have been funded by the FAIR Consortium, European Commission Fourth Framework Advanced Communication Technologies and Services (ACTS) Programme (1996–98), the STAR Consortium, European Union Fifth Framework Programme (2000–2001), the Electronic Commerce Business Impacts Project (EBIP), funded by the OECD, the Telematica Instituut and the Dutch Ministry of Economic Affairs (1998–2002), and Business Models for Innovative Telmatics Applications (BITA), funded by the Telematica Instituut.

[3] The US Census Bureau acknowledges that their statistics on intermediate goods have limitations and inconsistencies. Furthermore, they refer only to the US. Nevertheless, given the serious doubts about the reliability of (particularly proprietary) cross sectional data, the US data are at the moment the most extensive available longitudinal statistics to have been gathered according to a verifiable methodology.

Was there a dot com crash? – exploding the dot com mythology

In assessing business model issues, sharp distinctions must be made between entrepreneurial start-up firms geared mainly or solely to the e-commerce and established firms who also engage in various forms of electronic trading. Importantly, distinctions must also be made between total e-commerce activity as a proportion of total sales and the rate of growth in e-commerce from year to year. The growth rate is by far the more interesting figure, provided that it is considered in an appropriate context.

We can begin discussion of the dot com crash by getting rid of some obvious excess baggage about dot com companies. First is the common association of dot com registration with on-line trading. With hindsight, we can see that during the 1990s, a crescendo of e-commerce expectations for dot coms was generated by the overactive imaginations of market researchers and securities analysts. This despite the fact that by far the majority of dot coms are conventional companies with established shares of mature markets – most blue-chip industrial multinationals are also dot coms.

There was never any necessary link between the dot com rubric and online trading. Indeed, as the Electronic-commerce Business Impacts Project (EBIP) shows, is probably safe to say that to this day most firms who have a web presence do not actually trade electronically to any significant extent, confining their online activities to advertising, corporate advocacy, general communications and the like (TNO 2003). Furthermore, of the firms that do trade online, there is little if any evidence to show that they are concentrated among the entrepreneurial start-ups.

The second piece of baggage is that dot coms (particularly the start-ups) are more technically advanced than other companies. Many companies with dot com registrations are among the most technically advanced in the world, irrespective of their online trading profiles. However, this technical advancement may be concentrated far away from any trading interface as such – typically in the back office or on the shop floor. By contrast, the technology base of a dot com start-up can be (and often is) no more complex or advanced than a proprietary software package oriented to a PC or workstation. Moreover, even high profile dot com start-ups sometimes persist with otherwise antiquated business processes in the back office (Amazon, for example, still uses distribution buffers – anathema to modern supply chain management principles).

The third piece of baggage is that consumer sales were somehow major drivers and/or significant indicators of growth in the electronic marketplace. Certainly the business-to-consumer (B2C) paradigm may have been an important psychological factor driving the surge in market capitalisation for many dot com start-ups throughout the 1990s. In reality, however, all but a tiny percentage of the total actual value traded electronically is traded between companies (US 2001). Indeed, despite almost universal projections of exponential B2C growth, the figures suggest that B2C popularity in the 1990s peaked early and at a rather low level. By most reasonable estimates, online retailing stands currently at probably an all time high of maybe 1.5% of retail sales world wide, although, intriguingly, the growth rate is now starting to pick up (see below).

The fourth piece of baggage is that intangibles drive the electronic marketplace. The future of e-commerce and therefore the requirement for new business models has been described mostly in terms of shifts in value production from tangibles to intangibles. But it is widely acknowledged that the relationship between tangibles and intangibles must be considered in a far more complex framework than mere substitution (Hawkins et al. 1999; Stabell and Fjeldstad 1998; Bailey and Bakos 1997). Steinfield et al. (2001) show that e-commerce activities in many industries are predominantly undertaken by firms that maintain also a conventional physical presence. To the extent that we have figures, they tend to back up this observation. US Census Bureau data indicate that in 1999 (the most recent available data year) some 90% of electronic transactions that occurred in the US occurred between manufacturing firms or otherwise through wholesale merchant sales – both modalities strongly oriented to conventional, mostly tangible products (US 2001). Recent European figures (from a much smaller sample) appear to allocate more activity specifically to services, but actually they show much the same bias towards tangibles once allowances are made for differences in statistical categories (Diess 2002).[4]

A final piece of baggage is the assumption that e-commerce was a driver of growth. But we must be careful here. This assumption is 'baggage' not because we can disprove it, but because we cannot show anything one way or the other. As at least a few observers persisted in noting both during and after the Internet boom, there is no simple one-way relationship between IT investment (in this case in e-commerce) and growth (Baily 2002, van Ark 2002, OECD 2001). Quite simply, the degree to which IT investment stimulates growth and productivity and the degree to which growth and productivity stimulates the demand for IT, are open (if perhaps reciprocal) questions. In other words, IT investment could be either an independent or a dependent variable, or both, depending upon the circumstances!

So, did the dot coms ever play a major economic role, was there a bubble and did the bubble explode? To the first part of the question, it depends upon how narrowly you define dot coms. Certainly, established firms continued to contribute to growth throughout the 1990s and many of these engaged in electronic trading (Baily 2002). The role specifically of e-commerce in their performance has not been measured satisfactorily and, indeed, the methodological problems are non-trivial. Likewise, although surely it appears that the super-active investment interest in entrepreneurial start-ups stimulated capital markets in the 1990s, the actual

---

[4] These figures from Eurostat show that most of the e-commerce activity is occurring in the areas of 'business services', 'distribution' and 'transport and communication'. Allowing also for the imprecision in these categories in a services context, it is clear that most of the activities are related in some respect to the range of activities included under the 'manufacturing shipments' designation as used for the US data. The conclusion is much the same – e-commerce is probably most significant in supply chains for manufactured goods.

effects on growth during this period are difficult to demonstrate, especially given the recent rapid decline in shareholder value (OECD 2001).

Was there a bubble and did it explode? Again, it depends on how you want to interpret the evidence. But if there was a crash, certainly it is curious that e-commerce activity actually appears to be increasing in spite of it. Indeed, it was after the supposed crash that the beleaguered B2C sector appears to have begun growing significantly for the very first time. Recent official statistical estimates from the US (covering 1999 to the third quarter of 2002) indicate that the B2C transactions total has risen quite dramatically from 0.7 % of retail sales by the end of 1999 (US$ 5,481 billion), to 1.3 % at the end of the third quarter of 2002 (US$ 11.061 billion) – roughly a 100% increase in two of supposedly the most difficult years for B2C enterprises in terms of investor confidence (US 2002). If these figures do not suggest an immanent major upsurge, neither do they support perceptions that e-commerce is in serious trouble following a dot com crash.

Certainly billions of dollars have been wiped off shareholder value for over-hyped start-ups that showed little apparent basis for holding their value in the first place (Senn 2000). But huge amounts of value were removed likewise from the stock of perfectly viable firms with enviable track records for innovation, growth and high profit levels. For a time at least, the whole IT industry took a plunge. Ridiculous capitalisation levels for junk firms may have been partly responsible, but certainly this was not the only explanation. There was also a general downturn in several high-growth, high-profit markets for applied technology and services. For example, the huge markets for telecom equipment began to dry up at roughly the same time as confidence in the dot coms started to crumble, probably due as much to having reached a ceiling in investment potential for key telecom goods and services (particularly on the mobile front) as to any fall-out from a dot com bubble.

It appears most likely that the coincidence of a host of factors contributed to a collapse of confidence in high-technology markets at then end of the 1990s. But what was the role of business models in this debacle? Was it simply that companies got their business models wrong? If so, is it possible to identify what might be the 'right' models in future? To explore this, we first need a more systematic description of what a business model is and how it functions in real markets.

What is a business model and how does it function in an enterprise?

There is now a burgeoning literature with many opinions as to what business models are, how they work and what their strategic importance might be. Most of this work seeks to instruct firms in the arts of business model development rather than to worry overly much about whether or how business modelling differs from the normal run of activities involved in strategic and organisational planning. Nevertheless, two basic observations generally stand out:

- the business model concept is inherently oriented to the process of *linking* new technological environments to business strategies;
- the logic of business model development is linked closely to perceptions of *value* and especially to how new customer value can be created by trading in an electronic milieu.

New technological possibilities pose fundamental questions about the ways enterprises operate, how they are positioned in the market, how they extract revenues, how they realise profits and how they structure relationships with suppliers and customers. Ballon and Arbanowski (2002) propose that it is the integration of commercial and technological factors – often between firms as well as within them – that distinguishes *business* models from other types of organisational and financial models. This leads them to define the business model as a description of how a company or set of companies intend to create value with a product or service.

Perhaps the missing element in this definition is the 'capture' of value. In principle, electronic trading creates opportunities to capture value that might be lost using conventional market interfaces. This can occur through more efficient commercial processes (i.e. lower costs and higher income retention), or by means of enhanced relationships with buyers and sellers – increased customisation, complementary services and so forth. The effects show up in revenues, which can be affected not just by price levels and market conditions, but by how, as well as how efficiently, a firm extracts income form the products and services it purveys (Hawkins 2002, Mahadevan 2000). Indeed, technical change in the e-commerce context is often associated specifically with the actual process of value capture, whether in the form of business substitution, or new income at the margin.

Thus, we could propose extending the above definition – a business model is a description of how a company or set of companies intend to create *and capture* value with a product or service. In other words, *business modelling is about the amalgamation or integration of various economic, process and organisational models with technological architectures*. In practical terms, it is about *minimising randomness* in the process of integrating new business ideas with new and/or existing technological capabilities. This kind of definition carves out a distinctive niche for business modelling and focuses analytical attention upon a relationship between technological and commercial logic that heretofore has been confined largely to a 'black box'.

In this scenario, choosing an available business model, or developing a new one, becomes an exercise in finding new ways, through new technology (i.e. capital investment), of co-ordinating business relationships and functions in the creation of value. Ideally, in order to sustain growth, this investment would be aimed at creating *new value* – i.e. at the margin – rather than, for example, just substituting online for offline sales. It is nevertheless probably atypical for this process to unfold entirely within a single firm. An entrepreneurial enterprise anticipates demand, but usually this involves the co-ordination of various productive resources. This requires complex organisation and it is unusual for a single entrepreneur (be it an individual or corporation) to be able to provide all of the requirements to float an enterprise in the market.

Problematically, most of the theory surrounding enterpreneurship is focussed upon the discrete firm. Schumpeter (1934, 1939) first characterised the process in terms mostly of how the individual entrepreneur exerted a disruptive force that led to change and growth. Subsequent thinking added more of an emphasis on the technological and economic conditions for enterprise, focussing particularly on the problem of paradigmatic change in technology and organisation (Freeman 1982; Dosi 1982). The implications of paradigm change are many, but a major implication is that the main reason for the failure of new enterprises can be that the entrepreneur fails to cope with the systemic relations between various forces in the market. To create a viable enterprise, various factors of production, distribution and consumption have to be brought into alignment in order to form a critical mass.

The networking characteristics of enterprise generate an essential question regarding the role of business models in the creation and distribution of new value; namely 'What are the determinants and boundaries of collective behaviour in creating business models?'. Although transaction cost economics has become one of the most influential explanations for these kinds of dynamics, this is essentially an approach to explaining the boundaries of the firm in terms of make or buy decisions (Coase 1937; Commons 1950). Transaction cost analysis tends to focus on single transactions between discrete firms rather than on complex transaction structures within networks of firms. It tends also to view collective behaviour only in terms of 'hierarchies' formed for the purpose of controlling prices (see Williamson 1975). As such, it tends to polarise the debate, virtually ignoring the ground between these extremes which is actually where most transactions are conducted (Ghoshal and Moran 1996; Ring and van de Ven 1992).

Other arguments that focus specifically on organisational dynamics are perhaps more enlightening. Powell (1990) interprets the great variety of co-operative and alliance structures in the economy as evidence in itself that the network dynamic is key to understanding the ways in which enterprise boundaries are created. Ghoshal and Moran (1996) argue that the organisational forms within (and presumably between) firms are not simply envelopes for maximising transaction efficiency, but essential mechanisms for isolating firms from the market so that they can plan and innovate. The foundation of these views is the observation that firms do not form relationships only in order to buy and sell. They also form them in order learn from each other by acquiring new technological capabilities and working practices, or by gaining experience in markets that otherwise they would not exploit (Hakansson 1987; Granovetter 1973).

In such situations, value is actually produced *through* an alliance. However, choices regarding economic and organisational structures may be limited. Granovetter (1985) and Gulati (1995a, 1995b) imply that decisions to structure market relationships in various ways are not simply available to firms as more-or-less instrumental alternatives. Rather, the choices are governed by social and institutional circumstances that can vary according to the characteristics of different markets.

These organisational dynamics generate fundamental questions about the exclusivity of any putative business model. Basically, there are two strong hypotheses:

- *Business models are specific.* Firms compete on the strengths of discrete business models. This entails developing new models to exploit new commercial opportunities.
- *Business models are generic.* Firms can compete in various ways within the boundaries of similar or identical models. This entails that the scope for new models is limited and that new commercial opportunities do not require new models necessarily.

By no means is the evidence clear cut, but much of it does rather appear to favour the latter hypothesis. Many of the earliest discussions of business models were entirely indiscriminate – identifying practically every on-line trading activity in terms of a new model. Even here, however, a primary objective was to inspire all firms to emulate the models of early e-commerce adopters, hardly implying exclusivity. Moreover, once removed from the e-commerce context, virtually all of these presumed 'new' business models could be condensed into a few generic trading mechanisms, all of which existed also in conventional trading environments. Despite the bells and whistles, high-profile outfits like Amazon or Dell are functionally little more than mail-order retailers. Both have redesigned much of the ordering and fulfilment structure, but neither has married new technology to a substantially new economic relationship with a product or service.

Research undertaken between 1996 and 2000 in the FAIR and STAR programmes looked specifically at the issue of whether firms could make money in an electronic market environment that they could not make (at least to the same extent) in a conventional environment (Hawkins 1998, 2001a, 2001b, 2002; Hawkins et al. 2001). To do this, the technology aspects of business modelling were marginalised in order to focus in on the income issue. It was reasoned that if the expectations of increased income through new technology adoption could not be articulated *a priori*, there would be limited incentive to explore e-commerce and no need to look at business models. From this revenue-biased perspective, three essential modes were identified that would have to operate in any business model:

- *A transaction mode* – This defines the basic structure of the transaction in terms of whether it is conducted directly between buyer and seller, or via intermediaries who enhance the transaction in specific ways (excluding generic service providers like banks or public telecom operators).
- *A revenue mode* – This defines how income actually is generated from the production and/or distribution of goods and services. Specifically, it identifies the relationship with a product or service upon which the revenue stream is based. For example, a retailer earns income from an item in a different way than the producer does, or than a provider of support services might do.
- *An exchange mode* – This defines the actual mechanism through which income is collected, similar to a price or revenue model. These mechanisms range from

simple cash and carry wholesaling and retailing to complex commercial con-
structions involving the sale of commercial rights, dynamic pricing etc.

Although the technological dimensions of these modes were not examined in
great detail, the assumption was that each could be mediated with technology.
What was interesting in the empirical research was that in practice there appeared
to be a limited number of variations within each mode and rather few permutations of all three modes that were appropriate or workable in any given market.
Moreover, no variations and permutations were found among successful e-
commerce adopters that were not found also in conventional transaction environments. STAR research suggested that the dynamics of business modelling had less
to do with model selection or development as such, but rather with the practical
availability of different broadly generic models (most not at all new) in different
circumstances.

Little evidence was found that successful e-commerce adoption required original or unique business models, but substantial evidence was found that e-
commerce provided adopters with opportunities to deploy models that heretofore
had not been common in their particular markets but which nevertheless were
common in markets for other types of goods and services. Much of this model
'drift' between market sectors occurred because of increased opportunities to supplement product sales with special features or complementary services. The general conclusion was that in practice there are relatively few viable business models, that they have many generic characteristics and that their success depends
upon how well they are matched to the requirements and expectations of buyers
and sellers in specific markets.

However, this conclusion need not mean that all elements of the first hypothesis
(exclusivity) can be eliminated. EBIP research examined strategic behaviours of
successful implementers in several industry supply chain contexts across eleven
countries (TNO 2003). Although not specifically focussed on business models, the
research yielded many indications about the kinds of business model choices that
are available to firms depending upon the positions they hold in various supply
chains. In particular, the research showed that strategic dependencies do not disappear in electronic trading and are often reinforced. Moreover, it was evident that
open technological architectures like the Internet had little direct bearing upon the
openness of markets. All of this tended to suggest that although in principle any
firm could enjoy greater freedom in the selection and deployment of business
models in an e-commerce setting, choices were limited in practice by established
market structures. These did not appear to change radically in most industries
mainly or solely as a consequence of e-commerce.

On balance the evidence indicates that although it is important for firms to consider their business models carefully, the model as such may not confer any special strategic advantage. Unless of course a firm is in a position to control the access of other firms to the same model – for example, by imposing rents on access
to key back office or trading interface software. The key requirement is to get a
model, or indeed several different models, established in a market. Different models have characteristics that may fit one market and not another. Determining

which is which involves close interaction between buyer and seller, guided to a large extent by perceptions of product value and how it can be exchanged. But the whole process must take account of all of the complementarities and dependencies that characterise a typical marketplace. In practice, this may limit the choice of models available to a given firm, causing it to focus strategy on how the model is applied rather than on what it is.

Business models and the creation of new value in the marketplace

If business modelling forges a union between technology and commerce in the creation of value, how in practice can the result be interpreted and absorbed by the market? Although research on this question is still relatively scarce, we can engage at least in some informed speculation. As background, however, consider Veblen's proposition made a century ago that 'industry', which he saw in terms of production and distribution, is not the same as 'business', which he saw in terms of buying and selling the many intangible interests and rights that were associated with industrial activity (Veblen 1904).

Although made with reference to an industrial landscape that was different from our own in many ways, Veblen's dichotomy remains worthy of attention. Essentially, he is drawing attention to the differences between *actual* (i.e. realisable) value, as embodied in goods or services in the form of measurable inputs and outputs, and *perceived* value, which is abstract and not necessarily reflective of actual value. His point was that business might well be sustained, at least for a time, solely by perceptions of value, but that there are dangers in interpreting these perceptions as sufficient for assessing the productive potential of an enterprise.

The observation is useful in considering business models because, clearly, they can have substantial perceptual elements. Arguably, a business model that succeeds in increasing the economic gain from a good or service has some very concrete or 'actual' value for the traders who employ it. On the other hand, business models also might create general perceptions that gain is being maximised, or eventually will be maximised (thus creating a 'futures' market), when this may not be the case. This is a risk especially if the nature of the technological dimension is misunderstood or its extent overestimated.

It has become common in connection with business models to express linkage between actual and perceived value elements as a 'value proposition'. This concept is rooted in conventional economic theories of markets in which demands are issued based mainly upon customer understanding of product or service utility. These signals trigger a response from product and service originators who can fulfil this demand. They in turn respond with a 'proposition' to the market that (a) value exists in the particular goods or services being offered (b) that this value can be exchanged optimally in a specific way. In principle, these relations are embodied in the price. To give an example, the value proposition of the supermarket concept is that convenience, quality, variety and the lowest price is provided to the consumer most optimally via bulk buying and large scale distribution at central-ised outlets. E-commerce enhances the proposition by adding the convenience of having goods delivered to the door.

But the whole value proposition idea is rather linear and one-dimensional – hardly a suitable basis upon which to build business models. Creating value is an intensely dynamic and interactive social process. Beyond simple economic signals lie the complex social functions of the market. As various studies of the social psychology of markets have shown there can be considerable tension between 'demand pull' and 'supply push' dynamics in the market (Niece 1998; Lane 1992; Liess 1988; Scitovsky 1976). Moreover, markets can behave in not totally rational ways, especially if rationality assumptions are linked mainly to utility (Khaneman 1994; Khaneman and Tversky 1982). For example, customers can respond to status claims for particular goods and services that raise expectations as to the 'correct' price (i.e. luxury goods). Or, producers can create artificial scarcity by restricting production and distribution of certain types of goods.

Such complex social dynamics imply that buyer and seller communities can have very different perceptions of the value that is created and exchanged in a par-ticular transaction context. Returning to the supermarket example, customers can socialise this environment, endowing it with attributes of the high street or neighbourhood shop and perhaps taking this ambience into consideration in pur-chase decisions. By going online, a company must compensate for any risk of change in customer behaviour in this different milieu, or for segmentation in the customer base.

All of this further undermines the value proposition concept, which essentially is a statement that a particular product, sold in a particular way at a particular price will meet a demand. In particular, acceptance or rejection of a new proposition may be influenced by more than just price. For example, Lane (1991) points to the "experience" of specific kinds of markets as being also a significant factor. This experience is partly a function of institutional legitimacy – creating confidence that the market will operate honestly and efficiently. But it is also a matter of achieving symmetry between the characteristics of the market environment and those of the specific products and services exchanged in them – i.e. ensuring that the look-and-feel of the marketplace matches the characteristics of the products and conforms to the social patterns and expectations of the customers.

If indeed the process of value determination is interactive in this way, its terms must be accepted by both buyers and sellers in order for it to function. This im-plies a kind of (perhaps implicit) contract based on information symmetry between buyer and seller. But herein lies the problem. Even if symmetry could be estab-lished at a fixed point in time, the relationship of customers to many products is neither static nor predictable over time. Users can invent ways to create value with goods or services which were not envisaged by the product originator. For exam-ple, SMS messaging was offered originally as a low value supplementary service for digital mobile telephones. Over time, however, users developed preferences for communicating by SMS rather than by voice alone, thus creating a very sub-stantial new market for mobile services without demanding substantial change in the technology as such.

The idea that producers propose value suggests that relations of supply and demand have fixed elements on the supply side. Instead, we could consider that information symmetry is never perfect and this uncertainty creates tensions in the market. Suppliers nevertheless *must* make assumptions that customer value can be created in specific ways – in the present context through new technologies – and these can be worked out in business models. But the *supplier value assumptions* the upon which the model is based can be countered over time by *customer value preferences* which emerge as customers gain experience with products and services and socialise them into the conditions of everyday use.

Although some information always flows back and forth between supplier and customer – i.e. the supplier understands a range of customer preferences and the customer has knowledge of a range of available goods and services – no supplier can achieve complete flexibility in meeting customer preferences. For one thing, production requires the commitment of substantial resources over time based upon supplier assumptions of customer value (ideally reflecting the best information available to the producer at a given time). Investments in product trajectories must be compensated and this restricts producer choice in responding to changes in demand which can evolve extremely quickly. Moreover, customers can express *strong* preferences that signal needs for new products and services or *weak* preferences that signal only the need for incremental improvements. Alternatively, they can learn to use existing products in different ways, adapting them to preferences rather than issuing new demand as such.

The idea that there is enhanced customer value should an acquisition be made in a particular way – e.g. in an online rather than an offline environment – can create different perspectives on where the value in a particular business model might lie. In the first instance, there are always questions about whether electronic trades merely substitute a portion of normal sales volumes, or otherwise generate new sales at the margin. Accordingly, the need for business modelling can arise for three basic reasons:

- *substitution* – an existing type of business is transferred in whole or in part to an electronic environment
- *supplementation* – an existing type of business develops new elements that are available only in an electronic environment
- *novelty* – a wholly new type of enterprise is floated that is oriented exclusively to an electronic environment.

In the first case, the gains might be realised only through substitution. The market could perceive that the business was using electronics simply to do the same things more efficiently. The online business model might not be substantially different from the offline model. At a very basic level, the performance of this company could be assessed using conventional productivity and quality criteria. The second case offers more obvious scope to supplement efficiency gains with the creation of entirely new value. But business model performance becomes somewhat harder to assess. Gains might be attributed to a new model, but likely also to factors such as existing market strength or brand recognition. In the last case, however, by definition, all gains are made at the margin. Thus, the enterprise can be defined largely in terms of its business model and more performance aspects might be attributed directly to this model.

Buyers and sellers could perceive any model in these scenarios in various ways. But if a model seems obviously the most efficient way to vend a product or service, or if it defines an essentially new economic relationship with products or services, *investor interest* can be created also. Recalling Veblen, investor interest goes beyond the practical utility of the business model and imbues it with a futures orientation. Irrespective of the current levels of business performance, it seems obvious that online distribution is the most optimal way to vend software or games, that as the number of web sites grows there will be profits to be made from search engines, that Amazon is a far more efficient way to acquire books (most of which increasingly have to be back ordered anyway), or that e-Bay will organise a parallel economy to that of the high street.

The business models of enterprises like these can themselves become very attractive to investors. Basically, investors place bets that future earnings will reflect the obvious superiority of the models. If other investors come to the same conclusion in sufficient numbers, capitalisation can quickly outstrip book value. Thus, the business model becomes a product on its own. Indeed, as optimism for the potential of new business models grows in general, it may be possible for firms to start up with the objective of proposing a particular model solely in order to attract investment.

Final thoughts

With hindsight, it seems clear that the dot com boom was driven at least partly by dynamics as described above. But does this mean that all of the business models that once attracted so much enthusiasm turned out to be worthless? In some cases, probably yes, but certainly not in all and maybe not in most. Recall the figures given above indicating that performance in B2C e-commerce may only now be starting to live up to expectations. Many on-line start ups still trade despite the evaporation of their share price. And remember that in any case, most e-commerce activity has yet even to touch the B2C interface directly.

The lesson may be that 1990s optimism over the future of e-commerce and the dot coms may have been misplaced rather than mistaken. Certainly more attention was paid by analysts to the individual rather than the collective dimensions of developing business models and establishing them in markets. Even on the limited evidence presented above, this appears to have been wrong-headed. The degree of variation that is possible in business models such that a substantial strategic advantage is gained appears to be limited for most companies for a variety of institutional and structural reasons. The pattern, even with the most high profile start ups of the past few years, has been incremental rather than radical innovation.

Perhaps more importantly still, investment decisions ignored the complexity of customer/supplier interactions over time. The assumption (whether understood in precisely these terms or not) was that a new business model was the operational expression of a new value proposition. But from what we are beginning to understand about the social dynamics of the marketplace, it is unlikely that such a proposition simply can be exchanged between suppliers and customers for the simple reason that customers also create their own value in goods and services. Value can't be a proposition because it is reciprocal.

If considered in isolation, history indicates that business models can cloud investor perceptions of company value, potentially leading to volatility in securities markets and knock-on effects for both information technology producers and users. On the other hand, a better understanding of the business modelling process may focus both investor and industry attention back towards fundamentals, thus blunting the impacts of speculation and clearing a path for further innovation in the electronic marketplace.

References

Afuah A, Tucci C (2001) Internet Business Models and Strategies. McGraw-Hill Irwin, Boston

van Ark B (2002) Measuring the New Economy: An International Comparative Perspective. The Review of Income and Wealth 48 (1):1–14

Baily MN (2002) Distinguished lecture on economics in government: The new economy, post mortem or second wind? Journal of Economic Perspectives 16 (2) Spring:3–22

Bailey JP, Bakos Y (1997) An exploratory study of the emerging role of electronic intermediaries. International Journal of Electronic Commerce 1 (3) Spring:7–20

Ballon P, Arbanowski S (2002) Business models in the future wireless world. Wireless World Research Forum (White Paper)

Coase R (1937) The nature of the firm. Economica 4:386–405

Commons JR (1950) Institutional Economics. Univ. of Wisconsin Press, Madison

Diess R (2002) E-commerce in Europe. Statistics in Focus, Industry, Trade and Services, EUROSTAT, December, Luxembourg

Dosi G (1982) Technological paradigms and technological trajectories: a suggested interpretation of the determinants and directions of technical change. Research Policy 11 (3):147–62

Freeman C (1982) The Economics of Industrial Innovation. Frances Pinter, London

Ghoshal S, Moran P (1996) Bad for practice: a critique of the transaction cost theory. Academy of Management Review 21 (1):13–47

Granovetter M (1973) The strength of weak ties. American Journal of Sociology 78 (6):1360–1380

Granovetter M (1985) Economic action and social structure: the problem of embeddedness. American Journal of Sociology 91 (3):481–510

Gulati R (1995a) Social structure and alliance formation patterns: a longitudinal analysis. Administrative Science Quarterly 40 (4):619–652

Gulati R (1995b) Does familiarity breed trust? The implications of repeated ties for contractual choice in alliances. Academy of Management Journal 38 (1):85–112

Hakansson H (1987) Industrial Technological Development: A Network Approach. Croom Helm, London

Hawkins R (2002) The Phantom of the Marketplace: Searching for New E-Commerce Business Models. Communications & Strategies 46 (2):297–329

Hawkins R (2001a) The Business Model as a Research Problem in Electronic Commerce. Issue Report No. 4, STAR project (Socio-Economic Trends Assessment for the Digital Revolution), European Union 5th Framework Programme, July

Hawkins R (2001b) Electronic Commerce and Business Model Evolution: an Exploratory Study of Experience and Practice in European Firms. Issue Report No. 5, STAR project (Socio-Economic Trends Assessment for the Digital Revolution), European Union 5th Framework Programme, July

Hawkins R (1998) Creating a Positive Environment for Electronic Commerce in Europe. Working Paper No. 36, FAIR Consortium, European Commission 4th Framework Advanced Communication Technologies and Services (ACTS) Programme, February, SPRU, Brighton

Hawkins R, Mansell R, Steinmueller WE (2001) Controlling Electronic Commerce Transactions. Co-authored chapter in Mansell R, Steinmueller WE, Mobilizing the Information Society: Strategies for Growth and Opportunity, Oxford University Press, Oxford, pp 196–239

Hawkins R, Mansell R, Steinmueller WE (1999) Towards Digital Intermediation in the Information Society. Journal of Economic Issues XXXIII (2), 1999:383–391

Jutla D, Bodorik P, Wang Y (1999) Developing Internet E-Commerce Benchmarks. Information Systems, vol 24, 6:475–493

Kahneman D, Tversky A (1982) The psychology of preferences. Scientific American 246:160–173

Kahneman D (1994) New challenges to the rationality assumption. Journal of Institutional and Theoretical Economics 150:8–36

Kern C, Braynard R, Hoffman T, Azam MD, Lim B (2000) On Developing a Barter E-Commerce Application. Journal of Computer Information Systems, Summer:77–83

Kraemer KL, Dedrick J, Yamashiro S (2000) Redefining and extending the Business Model with Information Technology: Dell Computer Corporation. The Information Society, vol 16:5–21

Lane RE (1991) The Market Experience. Cambridge University Press, Cambridge

Leiss W (1988) The Limits to Satisfaction. McGill-Queen's University Press, Kingston and Montreal

Mahadevan B (2000) Business Models for Internet-Based E-Commerce: An Anatomy. California Management Review 42 (4):55–69

Neice DC (1998) ICT and Dematerialisation: Some Implications for Status Differentiation in Advanced Market Societies. FAIR Working Paper No. 43, March, SPRU, Brighton

OECD (2001) The New Economy: Beyond the Hype. The OECD Growth Project. Organisation for Economic Co-operation and Development, Paris

Powell WW (1990) Neither market nor hierarchy: network forms of organization. Research in Organisational Behaviour 12:295–336

Ring PS, Van de Ven AH (1992) Structuring co-operative relationships between organisations. Strategic Management Journal 13:483–498

Schumpeter J (1934) The Theory of Economic Development. Harvard University Press, Cambridge Mass.

Schumpeter J (1939) Business Cycles: A Theoretical, Historical and Statistical Analysis of the Capitalist Process, McGraw-Hill, New York

Scitovsky T (1976) The joyless economy: an inquiry into human satisfaction and consumer dissatisfaction. Oxford University Press, Oxford

Senn JA (2000) Electronic commerce beyond the 'dot com' boom. National Tax Journal LIII (3, part 1) September:373–383

Stabell CB, Fjeldstad ØD (1998) Configuring value for competitive advantage: on chains, shops, and networks. Strategic Management Journal 19 (5):413–437

Steinfield C, de Wit D, Adelaar T, Bruins A, Fielt E, Hoefsloot M, Smit A, Bouwman H (2001) Pillars of virtual enterprise: Leveraging physical assets in the new economy. Info 3 (3) June:203–213

Timmers P (1999) Electronic Commerce Strategies and Models for Business-to-Business Trading. John Wiley, Chichester

TNO (2003) The Electronic Commerce Business Impacts Project: Final Report. Paris: Organisation for Economic Co-operation and Development, and Delft: Netherlands Organisation for Applied Scientific Research, forthcoming

US (2002) Department of Commerce, Economics and Statistics Administration, US Census Bureau. US Department of Commerce News, 22 November

US (2001) Department of Commerce, Economics and Statistics Administration, US Census Bureau. E-Stats, March 7

Verhoest P, Hawkins R, Desruelle P et al. (2003) Electronic Business Networks: An assessment of the dynamics of business-to-business electronic commerce in eleven OECD countries. Report prepared for the OECD, Directorate for Science, Technology and Industry (DSTI), Committee for Information, Computer and Communication Policy, Working Party on the Information Economy. TNO-STB, Delft

Veblen T (1965) The theory of business enterprise. Np: Kelley 1965 (first published in 1904)

Williamson O (1975) Markets and Hierarchies: Analysis and Antitrust Implications. Free Press, New York

Business models and e-metrics, a state of the art[1]

Harry Bouwman[2], Erik van den Ham

Information and Communication Technology, Faculty of Technology, Policy and Management, Delft University of Technology, The Netherlands

Abstract

In this paper we will discuss the state of the art of the e-commerce business model as presented in the relevant literature. We address the following questions: What business models are being distinguished? What exactly is a business model? What are the criteria on the basis of which the performance of business models can be assessed? Business models are often abstract models of everyday practice. In theory it is easy to classify and describe them, but until a model is tested at the level of a business case its true value remains academic. A business model can be ever so useful for a company, a certain economic sector, industry or branch, or a certain geographical market, and at the same time be utterly useless in a different context. We describe a business case as the specific application of a (combination of) business model(s) by an individual company in a specific context. To assess the value of a business case we need metrics. In this paper we therefore also deal with a second set of questions, i.e. how can we measure the performance of business cases and what are relevant performance indicators? An analysis of individual business cases can offer insight into the relevance of the more generic business model concept.

Introduction

In the spring of the year 2000, high expectations with regard to the so-called new economy were tempered. The negative feelings were based on stock exchange de-

---

[1] This paper is a result of two research projects. The first of these, which was funded by ECP.NL, discussed emerging business models. In this project we collaborated with Dialogic innovation and Interaction. Work on Business Models has been continued in the BITA (Business Models for Innovative Telematics Applications) project of the Telematica Instituut, KPN Research, IBM, ING Bank, TNO-STB, and Delft University of Technology.
[2] E-mail: H.Bouwman@tbm.tudelft.nl

velopments surrounding technology funds. Many dot coms went bankrupt; others scaled down their activities considerably or changed their business models. There is talk of dot.bombs, dot.gones and dot.cons. The reaction in the public and business media is disproportionate. In our view there is an undeserved negative and unrealistic perception surrounding the possibilities of e-commerce and e-business. Careful analyses of developments are hard to find, with few exceptions (Castells 2001). Developments in the domain of e-commerce and e-business outside the over-hyped world of virtual Internet companies deserve attention. Traditional companies are increasingly aware that Internet-technology enables business processes (e-business), for instance in the *pre-sales, sales* and *after sales* transaction phases, where Internet is combined with other physical channels. We describe e-commerce as the actual transaction between a customer and an organization, taking place through an electronic interface (or being initiated that way, for example by making an appointment with a representative of the company or organization[3]). In our view, e-business is the support of company processes through Internet-technology (and related information and communication technology). Weill and Vitale (2001) describe e-business as doing business in an electronic way by completing processes through open networks, whereby parts of the physical process are replaced by the electronic exchange of information. The use of Internet-technology for e-business activities by more traditional companies is sometimes called *the second wave of e-business.*

The discussion about the impact of e-commerce and e-business on individual companies, as well as on the economy as a whole is often obscured by the lack of proper data and indicators. There is a clear parallel with discussions regarding the economic impact and effects of information and communication technology. In this context people often refer to the productivity paradox. The increasing importance of information and communication technology (ICT), and the accompanying investments, are being observed, as is the case with e-commerce and e-business, but the economic impact remains unclear. In this context we would like to point to a number of findings by Brynjolfsson and Hitt (1995, 1996), who argue that there certainly is a connection between ICT and productivity. Haltiwanger and Jarmin (2000) suggest that standard statistics do not consider the output, quality and cost reductions associated with information and communication technology. The role of information flows and the reduction in transaction costs are hard to quantify. David (2000) argues that there are three reasons why the effect of ICT on productivity is hard to demonstrate. Firstly, productivity measurements are artefacts of an inadequate measuring instrument, and therefore do not highlight the real economic performance. Secondly, investments in computer hardware are being overrated, partly as a result of the over-enthusiasm and management of expectations by the industry (Bouwman and de Jong 1996). Finally, too little attention is paid to costs associated with the transition phase in which 'new' technologies are being implemented. Experiments cost money, implementations hardly ever go as planned, etc. In other words, lessons are often learned at a cost.

---

[3] This definition is based on the one used by the Central Statistics Agency in the Netherlands

What holds true for the productivity paradox also goes for the demonstration of the impact of e-commerce and e-business. We are dealing with a transitional phase. The use of Internet-technology in business processes is a process of innovation and learning. These processes take time and cost money, as became apparent during the dot com crisis. Nevertheless, the scarce figures on e-commerce and e-business still show an increase. For the Netherlands an increase of the financial volume of the B2C e-commerce market from € 426 million to € 888 million in 2002 was reported (CBS 2002). The question that remains is whether the impact of e-commerce and e-business can be measured, and, if so, how? At macro-level we have provided an impulse by developing an e-commerce monitor for the Netherlands, in co-operation with the Ministry for Economic Affairs and ECP.nl (Hertog et al. 1999; Bouwman et al. 2000). The Dutch Central Statistics Agency (CBS) is implementing this monitor (CBS 2001, 2002). This paper is intended as a second step towards the development of measuring tools at a micro-level, i.e. the level at which the actual new services are enabled by e-business technologies. Our focus is on the assessment of business and revenue models based on the analysis of business cases, while taking into account both tangible and intangible benefits.

The object of this paper is to provide insight into the ways companies can use e-business-technology and organize business processes to offer customer value and generate income. Implicitly this means examining the business models that are being used by companies, in relation to the costumer value that is being offered. Slywotsky (1996) describes a business model (or 'design', to use his terminology) as *"the totality of how a company selects its customers, defines and differentiates its offerings (or responses), defines the tasks it will perform itself and those it will outsource, configures its resources, goes to the markets, creates utility for customers and captures profits"*. Timmers (1998, 1999) talks of *"an architecture for the product, service, information flows, including a description of various business actors and their roles, a description of potential benefits for the various actors, and a description of the sources of revenue"*. Weill and Vitale (2001, p. 34) provide the following definition of a business model: *"a description of the roles and relationships among a firm's consumers, customers, allies and suppliers that identifies the major flows of products, information and money, and the major benefits to participants."* In these definitions we find the various elements we have formulated in our objective. For the sake of convenience we shall interpret our objective in terms of providing insight into which business models are worth being pursued by companies. What is the use of e-commerce and e-business? Or to put it more bluntly: how can a company make use of e-business technology including Internet, middleware and services technologies to offer value to its customers and thus make a profit?

Business models: research questions

To realize our objective it is useful to formulate a number of concrete research questions. We will not discuss the question as to why business models are important. In his article in this volume Hawkins addresses this question extensively. In the present contribution we take a more pragmatic look at business models. The research focus of this paper will be on:

- What business models are being distinguished?
- What exactly is a business model?
- What are the criteria on the basis of which the performance of business models can be assessed?
- How can we measure the performance of business cases, the specific application of a (set of) business model(s)?
- What are relevant indicators on the basis of which the performance of business models can be assessed?

We will answer these questions by outlining the 'state of the art'. This outline is based on literature studies and an Internet search. Relevant entries have been selected using a number or key words such as e-commerce, e-business, business model, business modelling – names of specific business models we are interested in- performance indicators, revenue models, tangible and intangible costs and benefits, etc. Literature research included scientific journals from various files, such as Pica. The Internet search was conducted using Google and other search engines. The period during which the literature and Internet search was conducted is 1996-2002. Literature and Internet research alone, however, is not sufficient. The problem will have to be made more concrete by discussing the concepts and elements that constitute a business model and the analyses of business models at case level. In this paper we will first discuss the literature on business models and then present our view on these models and on the underlying concepts. Next we will discuss literature focusing on the financial aspects and other metrics of business models. We will present the outlines of a measuring instrument and some of the first experiences with this instrument in case studies. We will only discuss these case studies very briefly.

Business models

Business models are often abstract models of everyday practice, they do not exist in a pure form. Often a company will combine a number of business models within a specific business case. In theory it is easy to classify and describe business models, but until a model is tested at the level of a business case its true value remains academic. At the level of a business case it is possible to draw conclusions with regard to the more abstract general concept of a business model such as that of a content or a full service provider. A business model can be ever so useful for a company, a certain economic sector, industry or branch, or a certain geographical market, and at the same time be utterly useless elsewhere. We describe a business case as the specific application of a (combination of) business model(s) by an individual company in a specific situation.

In various taxonomies a large number of business models are mentioned (Timmers 1998, 1999; Money Magazine 1999; Rayport 1999; IBM 2000; Madehevan 2000; Rappa 2003; Turban, Lee, King and Chung 2000; Afuah and Tucci 2001; Deitel et al. 2001; Deitel et al. 2001; Raessens 2001; Rayport and Jaworksi 2001). The basis for these classifications varies. Some classifications are based on developments in the area of technology, others on marketing concepts or product types. In some classifications elements like value creation or strategy play a role. Classifications tend to be based on new opportunities offered by the Internet. Some classifications pop up in a number of places, sometimes in slightly modified or more detailed versions. Basically the business models discussed in these taxonomies are applications of what Weill and Vitale (2001) call *Atomic* business models, to wit *Content Provider, Direct to Customer, Full Service Provider, Intermediary, Shared Infrastructure, Value Net Integrator, Virtual Community* and *Whole-of-Enterprise/Government* models. Most taxonomies can be brought back to these eight basic models. Using these atomic business models one could present a complete overview of business models at a rather abstract level. However, few of the authors who present these taxonomies discuss the constructs and elements that constitute their models. They merely identify the empirical business models that are found in the e-commerce and e-business domain.

The concept of business model and its elements; state of the art

In the 1970's the concept of business model was used to describe and map business processes, information and communication patterns within a company in order to build an IT-system (Stähler 2001). More recently business models are related to market structures and the place of individual companies within those structures. Sometimes the concept is used to describe co-ordination mechanism in economic processes i.e. markets or hierarchies, or to discuss intermediation or disintermediation trends. In other studies the implementation of a specific market model, for example the English auction, is discussed in terms of business models. Very often only one aspect is emphasized in discussions of business models, for example the B2C-model for the retail sector. Furthermore, the concept of business models is used as a synonym for business modelling: the modelling of organization processes with the use of Unified Modelling Language (UML), an object-oriented modelling language. It is clear that the concept business model is widely used but hardly ever clearly defined. Alt and Zimmerman (2001) argue that the concept is a *common sense* term, which is to say that a generally accepted definition of a classification of business models is missing. Both in scientific circles and in the business community the term business model is often used without providing a clear indication of what the term is supposed to mean. On the basis of their review Alt and Zimmerman (2001) suggest that there are some common elements that turn up in business models:

- Mission: determining the overall vision, the strategic objectives and the value proposition, but also the basic features of a product or service.

- Structure: this has to do with the actors and their role within a specific business environment (a value chain or web), the specific sector, customers and products that the company targets.
- Process: the concrete translation of the mission and the structure of the business model into more operational terms.
- Revenues: the investments needed in the medium and long term and the revenues that are generated.

Afuah and Tucci (2001) focus more specifically on Internet business models. In their view, the method that companies use to make money in the long term by using the Internet is of central importance. What is important is a system of components (value, revenue sources, price, related activities, implementation, capabilities and sustainability), relationships and interrelated technology, which determine what a business model is. Focusing on the various basic elements of Internet business models, Afuah and Tucci (2001) formulate a large number of operational questions. The central question with regard to customer value, for instance, is phrased as follows: does the company offer something special to its customers or for a lower price than its competitors? Specified for an Internet model the question sounds: In what way does the Internet enable the company to offer something special? Can the Internet help solve customer problems? Other elements are scope, price, income sources, related activities, implementation, capabilities and sustainability. Afuah and Tucci's approach is centred on customer value, without being explicit as to what this concept means.

Mahadevan (2000) emphasizes value creation, revenues and logistics. *A business model is a unique blend of three streams that are critical to the business. These include the value stream for the business partners and the buyers, the revenue stream, and the logistical stream.* The success of a business model, according to Mahadevan, depends on the robustness of the value stream. Value creation as far as the buyer is concerned means a reduction in searching and transaction costs. The seller can reduce the costs associated with customer tracing, promotion and transaction and benefit from a shorter turnover rate. The introduction of all sorts of intermediary parties on the Internet would only increase the value stream both for the supply and the demand side. According to Mahadevan this will lead to a virtuous cycle, which will finally materialize in Virtual Communities. These communities offer benefits to all parties concerned: companies, customers, market makers and portals. Examples mentioned are VerticalNet and WebMD/Healtheon. The value being created in Virtual Communities depends on the contribution of the individual parties involved. Virtual Communities often imply high switching costs.

Osterwalder (2002, also Osterwalder and Pigneur 2002) is far more systematic in his approach to the concept of business models. Based on the questions *what* a company has to offer, *who* it targets, *how* this can be realized and *how much* can be earned, he discuss four basic elements of a business model, i.e.:

- product innovation and the implicit value proposition,
- customer management, including the description of the target customer, channels, customer relations,

- infrastructure management, the capabilities and resources, value configuration, web or network, partnerships
- financial aspects, the revenue models, cost structure and profit.

In our view an increasingly important element with regard to business models for new innovative e-business products and services is the complex network, which is necessary to produce these new e-commerce services. In essence we hold the opinion that services offered via the (mobile) Internet cannot be produced by a single business unit but are more and more produced within a complex value system in which business units within and between several organizations have to work together to share necessary resources and capabilities. To a certain degree the collaboration between cross-firm and cross-business units is strategic in nature. Furthermore, there has to be some common understanding as to what kind of product or services is going to be delivered, who has to contribute what, what kind of resources should be in place and what kind of capabilities are necessary (see also Hedman and Kalling 2002).

Business models: our view

In our vision the discussion surrounding business models can be reduced to a model with at the top the business strategy of a company (or set of companies). The strategy has to do with the overall vision, i.e. the implementation of one or a combination of several business models at the level of a business case, the decision of which business units inter- and cross firm have to collaborate within a value web, and the way the market for a specific product or service and the assumed customer value of this product or service is defined. The strategy focuses on the way new possibilities offered by the Internet, e-business and e-commerce can be incorporated in a new and creative manner. This goes beyond the basic technology, hardware and/or software and has to do with new business concepts and cases.

To a large extent the strategy depends on the competitive environment in which the company operates. It has to do with actors and their role within a specific business environment, i.e. a complex value system, the specific sector, customers and products the company focuses on, and the changes brought about by new technologies such as the Internet. The strategy largely determines the processes that lie at the basis of the business case. It is the concrete implementation of the business case in operational terms, centring around the organizational processes, alignment of business processes, of business processes and IT operations, interconnection and interoperability of systems, etcetera. This is required for the e-business solution to become operational. Concrete processes are being described (the domain of business modelling and UML, see Oude Luttinghuis 2000) and it is determined what e-business software applications are needed (Jansen and Van der Stappen 2000). The bottom line with regard to ICT and Internet technology is that the economic value of e-business and e-commerce depends on the capabilities of a (network of) companies to align technology with offering services or products through electronic means.

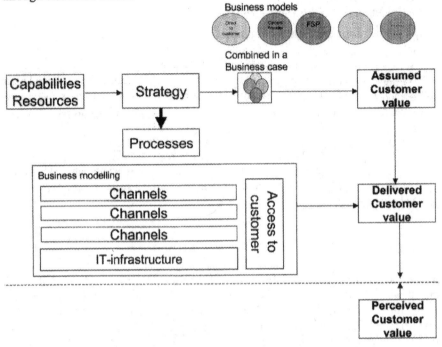

Fig. 1. Representation of the relationship between model, revenue model and business cases

With regard to customer value we want to note that in most cases the assumed customer value, as defined in strategic plans, is not the value that will be ultimately delivered to the customer, due to all kinds of organizational, technical and operational problems, and even then is not the value that will be perceived by the end user. In many cases the customer value as perceived by the end user is hardly related to the assumed customer value as proposed in the initial business plans. Rogers (1983) calls this reinvention.

Revenue streams and models: state of the art

One thing we failed to point out sufficiently is the financial argumentation: the revenue streams between supplier and demand, but also between partners within value-creating networks such as the specific revenue models. Financial and performance indicators, both tangible and intangible, have to be taken into account. Only a broad set of indicators can provide insight into the value of a particular business case and at a more conceptual level the underlying (combination of) business models. Different approaches can be discerned, discussing investment decisions, revenue models, or the performance of businesses.

Investment decisions

When it comes to investment decisions there are many surveys available (Demkes 1999; Renkema 1996; Oirsouw 1993). The authors of these surveys describe a large number of methods that are predominantly based on financial criteria. They discuss general financial methods as well as multi-criteria, ratio and portfolio approaches (Renkema 1996). Financial methods are aimed at average cost-effectiveness, net cash worth, and internal return. Multi-criteria methods are those found in *Information Economic*, Kobler Unit Framework and the Siesta-method, which is partly based on the *Strategic Alignment* model. The ratio-methods are those found in *Return-on-management* and *IT-assessment*. Portfolio-methods are found in Bedell, investment portfolio and investment mapping (see Renkema 1996, and Demkes 1999). Some methods go beyond the purely financial considerations, for example the *balanced score cards* (Kaplan and Norton 1992, 1996) and the option theory, a more detailed elaboration of the net cash worth concept (Renkema 1996; Demkes 1999). Demkes (1999, p. 91) does point out that decision-makers hardly ever use these kinds of methods. Generally speaking the cost side is reasonably well-charted. As far as the revenue side is concerned, which, from our point of view includes realizing cost reductions but also long term advantages that stem from intangibles, literature is less uniform.

Revenue models

Revenue models indicate what methods of payment are used, what is being paid for, and thus in what way income is generated. The thinking about models for income generation is less articulated than that with regard to business models. Furthermore, the distinction between the two is often vague. Mahadevan (2000), when talking about revenue models, distinguishes, for example, subscriptions, shopping mall operations, advertisements, computer services, general services, time usage and sponsoring (or free services). Weill and Vitale (2001) distinguish between (1) payments for transactions, (2) payments for information and advice, (3) payments for services and commissions and (4) advertisement-generated income and payments for referrals. Their distinctions are elaborated in little detail and seem fairly random. Grimshaw et al. (2000) mix up business models, value propositions and revenue models. They apply the following distinction:

- *add value*: add value at transactions between sellers and buyers,
- *alliances*: especially associated partners selling products and services,
- *arcade*: charging micro-payments for content,
- *brand*: a unique market proposition,
- *custom made*: online sale followed by production,

- *integrate*: integration of e-business and other business activities,
- *membership club*: an (annual) contribution for access to content,
- *price*: price fluctuations based on variations in supply and demand,
- *service*: bundling a unique set of services.

It is not hard to understand the confusion: in some cases business models and revenue models are identical, and some business models contain several revenue models. In the media industry (and therefore the Internet-world) this is the case with the sale of magazines to subscribers or of advertisement space to companies. As a rule a business model contains more than one form of income generation. At the business case level it becomes more apparent in what way companies expect to earn money. Afuah and Tucci (2001) emphasize that it is important to have good insight into revenue models, especially since there is often some form of mediation (who gets paid by whom) especially in those cases where more parties are involved in the production of a specific service sold over the (mobile) Internet and where there are network externalities.

Another complicating factor is the domain to which the revenue models refer. Chen's (2001) division is based on the complete Internet value chain, whereby suppliers of infrastructure, suppliers of Internet applications, and the intermediary and commerce levels play an important role (see also Holland et al. 2000, p. 14/15; Story et al. 2000). Chen lists revenue models on the basis of five and eight C's respectively. In his view, the five most important revenue models are based on: *connection*, offering access to the Internet, *commercials*, *commerce*, *content* and *community*. Additional income can be generated by *consulting*, *contracting* (in the case of activities being outsourced) and *controlling* (for example Internet-site maintenance by third parties). Applegate (2001) and Rayport and Jaworski (2001) use a similar division.

Performance indicators

The third school of thought deals with performance indicators. Performance indicators for organizations have long ago ceased being determined solely on the basis of solid economic assets. In 1981 the book value of a company was equal to its market value. In the year 2000 the average market value was 4.2 times the book value. In other words, the value of a company is determined not only by its *tangible* assets, but by its *intangible* assets, such as goodwill, as well (Boulton et al. 2001), which include, for example, marketing costs for branding, patents, etc. There have been various attempts to quantify these assets by means of performance scales and indices, such as the Value Creation Index, Value on Investment[TM], the Performance Measurement Matrix, Smart Pyramid, the Macro Process Model, the Balanced Score Card, the Performance Dashboard and the Customer Value Index (this list was partly based on Marr and Neely 2001).

These indices are partly directed towards determining the stock market value of a company (see also Sawhney et al. 2001) and therefore are of less value to our approach. As an example we will discuss the Value Creation Index (Low and

Kalafut 2002). This index contains five elements to do with the creation of value, namely: alliances, innovation, *eyeballs* (user traffic), investments in brand name, and *stickiness* (defined as the time people spend at a particular website, see www.forbes.com/asap/2000/0403/140.html   and   www.cbi.cgey.com/pub/docs/-New_VCI.pdf.) The index is based on data gathered through an Internet survey and a subsequent statistical analysis of these data. The analysis shows that the first three factors are especially important. Investments in marketing campaigns add little to the value of a company. The number of alliances a company has with other companies: joint ventures, marketing and co-production and other forms of co-operation, has a considerable predictive value with regard to the stock exchange value of a company. Network companies as a centre in the network economy appear to do better at the stock exchange (see also Selz 1999; Earle and Keen 2000). Innovation indexed as budget spent on R&D and investment in capital goods also correlates strongly with the value determination. User traffic is the third explanatory factor. We do want to point out that this research was conducted early in the year 2000 (the start of the downfall of the dot coms) and that its findings include both dot coms and *click and mortar* companies. Comparable to this approach is a study conducted by Barua, Konana, Whinston and Yin (2001), which establishes a relationship between business drivers and measurements for operational excellence and financial success.

Of greater interest are models that measure the performance of an organization. In the Value on InvestmentTM (VOI) approach a relationship is established between strategy, business models and modelling on the one hand, and implementation and innovation (Davies 2001). The approach is based on the balanced score card (Kaplan and Norton 1992, 1996). In addition to the financial performance, which is usually referred to in terms of Return on Investment (ROI), other ways to measure success are elaborated on the basis of internal work processes, performance of systems and infrastructure, productivity of employees and customer satisfaction. Wherever possible these value drivers are 'dollarized', i.e. expressed in monetary terms. A measure for customer satisfaction can be the number of repeat visits to a website (retention).

Rayport and Jaworski (2001) also base their approach on the balanced score card, which in their view has a number of limitations. According to Rayport and Jaworski (p. 263), the balanced score card cannot be used to evaluate business models.. They argue that there is no clear definition of strategy (or business models), no clear location of organizational capabilities or resources and no clear identification of strategic partners. Rayport and Jaworski have developed an alternative method. This method, the so-called performance dashboard, is equipped with a set of concrete indicators. They are:

- measures for market opportunities, including market size and competitive environment,
- business model measures, the unique value proposition, capabilities and resources, exclusive partnerships, investment in technology
- measures for branding and implementation, brand awareness, but also indicators for system uptime, number of IT staff and % inaccurate orders.

- measures for customer acquisition, customer share, purchases, service requests.
- financial measures, such as revenues, profits, earnings per share and debt to equity ratio.

Business models and metrics

Many of the elements we have discussed above can also be found in the model that Afuah and Tucci (2001) use for assessing business models. They recognize three levels, going from the specific to the general, from revenue models to business models. At this point we refer to their measurement of indicators in general terms only. Level 1 has to do with profitability: income and cash flow. Although income and cash flow are ultimately important indicators, private, but also public companies will rarely publish this information. Afuah and Tucci therefore suggest a number of possible proxy-indicators at Level 2. These indicators predict profitability: Profit Margin, Market Share and Growth Ratio of income. Level 3: characteristics of the business model elements: customer value, scope, price, income sources, related business activities, implementation, capabilities and sustainability. For each element at Level 3 Afuah and Tucci suggest benchmark questions.

The approaches we have discussed so far are all concerned with rendering the new value that e-business can generate measurable. The main factor is creating value for visitors. More operational indicators are therefore also relevant in mapping the performance of business and revenue models. Operational indicators at the level of websites are usually referred to as webmetrics. The search for reliable and valid indicators for webvisits is still going on – although there appears to be a growing consensus that simply counting the number of hits or pageviews is of little value. Stray visitors and one-time surfers are not very interesting, what is important are meaningful contacts and user interaction. Reach is extremely relevant as a condition (without reach there is no effectiveness), but we have to determine more accurately to what the term reach refers. Ultimately, the question is whether contact with a visitor (customer) actually leads to transactions. Retention and conversion are the relevant terms in this respect. The nature of the transactions can vary enormously (depending on the business case). The most widely-used measures are hits, pageviews, number of visits, duration of sessions, click through rate, conversion rate, reach, and unique visitors.

Outline of a measuring instrument

To summarize, there is a broad range of concepts and methods for analysing business models and their components, and for measuring their performance. Concepts refer to the strategic level, the more operational and financial-economic level of revenue models, but also to the level of the website itself or the traffic on or use of that website. The objective of this paper is not (yet) to develop a model by which we can understand the factors behind value creation of e-business, but merely to develop a measurement tool to analyse the performance of business cases. Conclusions based on this analysis can be generalised to business models. The measurement instrument is still under construction. Nevertheless, we will present the central foci of the instrument by drawing a distinction between the concepts we want to 'measure' (1) at the business case or strategic level, (2) at the revenue level and (3) at the level of the website. Along with Afuah and Tucci (2001, but also Rayport and Jaworski 2001), we propose to look both at more qualitative and at more quantitative indicators.

At a strategic level the indicators are, seen the more intangible nature of the issues, more qualitative in nature, such as:

- Customer value and scope:
  - what is the value proposition for the customer and by what is it determined, what are the value drivers,
  - who are the customers, what can be said about market scale and scope, market reach and scalability?
- Capabilities: what are the assets, resources, capabilities, etc. of the organization (or complex value web) needed to generate customer value? Important questions are for instance: who has access to infrastructure, specific middleware necessary for a specific type of service, such as location-based technology, customers, customer information, billing and accounting: how are these critical assets and resources distributed within the value web?
- Sustainability (degree to which the business model is based on the transportation of bits, money, logistics) and copyability (entry barriers, closed loop solutions). With regard to sustainability it is assumed that a business case that is based on information (bits) only is more vulnerable and copyable, while business models where all kinds of arrangements, such as payment systems or extensive logistic operations, have been put in place, are less vulnerable for imitation. Copyability of a business model has more to do with the ease with which another actor can imitate a specific business case. This is especially the case when entry barriers are low and there are no interdependencies between supply and demand.
- Flexibility is viewed from the company's or complex value web's point of view, and relates to the question whether it is easy for a provider to change the business case, – not only in terms of scalability but also in terms of customization and switching costs. Business cases are not static and they develop over time, new versions of products and services can be developed or bundling of offerings can take place (Shapiro and Varian 1999). However, if the development of new versions or bundling of existing products and services are hindered, for instance by the limited capabilities of legacy systems, changing business cases becomes less easy.

At the level of revenue models we propose to look at a qualitative level at motivations for investment decisions, methodology being used to assess costs, tangible and intangible (more strategic) benefits and risk, and participants in the decision–making process. What are the non-material resources, i.e. leadership, alliances, networks, human, intellectual and social capital, and benefits: at a strategic level, i.e. competitive advantage, response, brand name, reputation.

At a more quantitative level issues like income, cash flow, and price (development) are important. On the cost side we propose to look at investment, fixed and variable costs, cost structure and operational costs for organization, technology and marketing, depreciations in relation to time, but also cross-subsidization. Personnel-related costs are an important component. Finally, we can assess the potential profit (income minus costs).

At the level of websites the important factors are the average number of daily page-views, unique visitors, reach, conversion rate and their development over time. A more qualitative assessment relating assumed customer value to the experience of visiting a website can also be made (Bouwman et al. 2001).

At present we are still developing a concise measuring instrument to deal with the various concepts underlying business cases. In ongoing research we used some of the qualitative and quantitative indicators discussed above. So far, the use of concepts and indicators in our analysis is driven largely by the mere availability of data and the cooperation of e-commerce managers of specific business cases in providing the necessary data. We will therefore only discuss the results of business cases in general terms.

An initial assessment of some business cases

Based on these elements we have been engaged in a number of case-studies assessing the value of business cases in the domain of e-Tailing i.e. CD-Now, Free Record Shop, Plato; B-2-B market places i.e. WebMD, VerticalNet, Chemdex, DSM, and application service providers, i.e. Mysap, Entreprise Business Solutions, Siennax (for a more detailed discussion see Holland et al. 2000, 2001). When we look at these business cases, the following stands out. The e-Tailing model is the most telling example of the inevitability of the 'bricks and clicks' or 'clicks and mortar' strategy, in view of the lack of success of CDnow in contrast to the other cases that have successfully integrated their online business and their offline activities. Without a physical presence most e-Tail cases do not work, as many successful click and mortar business cases and the failure of many dot coms have proven (http://place.telin.nl, see also Steinfield in this volume). There are opprtunities here for established companies whose reputations will allow them to translate confidence into market share and who can link their physical distribution and fulfilment channels to an additional sales channel. Synergy is above all to be found in consumer trust, the possibility to offer new services and, of course, efficiency and cost-effectiveness. We have seen that B2B market places come in various shapes and sizes, which can to a large extent be explained by differences in product and market types, and that market places can offer a varied spectrum of services. As far as these B2B market places are concerned the shake-out is in progress (it is expected that only a few will survive in each market segment), as is the quest for interesting income sources, but at the same time the prospects at macro-level are favourable. As far as the ASP model is concerned, the macro-figures are also expected to be favourable. The benefits of outsourcing ICT-functionalities are clear, and the promises great – especially in segments of large data-processing companies such as financial institutions – but the bottleneck is trust. There is as yet little awareness among customers that the ASP formula may offer benefits, and the main obstacle is and will remain operational security (Holland et al. 2001).

If we look beyond the business models we see that those models that can be expected to be relatively successful (e-Tail companies with a 'click and mortar' strategy, closed B2B market places and ASP), have in common that there are more or less steady customer relationships, that consumer confidence is a very important driver for success, that the copyability of the formula is limited and the scalability large – and that there is a recognisable value proposition. Companies are more successful when they succeed in translating the knowledge regarding their customers into added value for those customers. What is ultimately important is to offer added value for which customers are willing to pay. Naturally, with each of these models existing companies have an advantage. As far as existing companies are concerned the incorporation of the Internet into their strategy leads above all to process and service innovations (improving existing activities) and to a lesser extent to product innovations (embarking on new activities). This turns the Internet into an additional channel, albeit with a number of specific characteristics and associated new forms of added value. Another lesson to be drawn from the first wave of e-business is that entry barriers do play a significant part. Information on the Internet is not merely the oxygen that provides transparent markets and limited margins, it is the glue that binds customers and thus leaves dominant market structures intact. This is another aspect from which existing companies will benefit.

When we draw a conclusion, we presuppose that the bandwidth of strategic indicators, financial performances and webmetrics provide a fair approximation of the matter and performance at the level of individual company's cases. However, our experience is that it is problematic to get access to the proper quantitative information. In many cases the figures provided are not the figures we were after, but rather the figures that happened to be available. Companies are loath to share experiences with others. At the same time we have had to recognize that traditional indicators, which are often qualitative and output-oriented, do little justice to the complexity of the phenomena we are dealing with. The measuring instrument we propose tries to remove as much of that complexity as possible, but there is still plenty of room for improvement. We have to continue to bridge the gap between what we see as the reality of e-business and our model of that reality. Customer value, for example, is increasingly added in networks of actors (communities) rather than individual companies. But how does a network of companies become the analytical unit? In addition, there are advantages and benefits for companies that cannot be expressed in straightforward financial terms. How can we develop reliable and valid indicators to measure those? These are some of the basic questions we will have to deal with to better understand the value of business case. Furthermore, we have to be aware that business models are not static, but change over time. As a result, drawing conclusions at the level of business models even becomes more complicated.

References

Adams C, Neely A (2000) The Performance Prism can boost M&A Success. http://www.som.cranfield.ac.uk/som/cbp/mergers.pdf

Adams C, Kapashi N, Neely A, Marr B (2001) Managing the Measures. Measuring e-business Performance. Accenture, Cranfield School of Management

Afuah A, Tucci C (2001) Internet Business Models and Strategies. McGraw-Hill, Irwin Boston

Alt R, Zimmerman HD (2001) Introduction to Special Section: Business Models. Electronic Markets 11 (1):3–9

Applegate LM (2001) Emerging e-business models: lessons from the field. Harvard Business School, Boston, July 26

Barua, A, Konana P, Whinston A, Yin F (2001) Measures for e-business Value Assessment. IT Pro.January, February, pp 35–39

Boulton R, Elliott T, Libert B, Samek S (2001) Beyond e-business. What is creating Value today. An Arthur Andersen White paper

Bouwman H, de Jong A (1996) Predicting Consumer Adoption of Information Technologies (160-172). In: Jankowski N, Hansen L (eds) Multimedia: A Critical Review of the Technology and its Applications. John Libbey, London

Bouwman H, den Hertog P, Holland C (2000) Measuring E-commerce. Trends in Communication 6, pp 13–35

Bouwman H, Staal M, Steinfield C (2001) Klantenervaring en Internet concepten. Management and Informatie, vol 9 (6):52–60

Brynjolffsonn E, Smith M, Bailey J (1999) Understanding digital markets, review and assessment. MIT

Brynjolfsson E, Hitt L (1996) Paradox Lost? Firm-level Evidence on the Returns to Information Systems Spending. Management Science 42 (4):541–558

Brynjolfsson E, Hitt L (1995) Computers as a Factor of Production: The role of Differences Among Firms. Economics of Innovation and New Technology 3, pp 183–199

Brynjolfsson E, Smith MD (1999) Frictionless Commerce? A comparison of internet and Conventional Retailers. MIT Sloan School of Management

Cap Gemini Ernst & Young (2000) Measuring the Future. The Value Creation Index. (www.businessinnovation.ey.com)

Castells, M. (2001) The Internet Galaxy. Reflections on the Internet, Business and Society. Oxford University Press, Oxford

CBS (2001) De Digitale Economie, 2001 (The Digital Economy, 2001, in dutch). Voorburg: CBS, Ministerie van Economische Zaken

CBS (2002) De Digitale Economie, 2002 (The Digital Economy, 2002, in dutch). Voorburg: CBS, Ministerie van Economische Zaken

Chen S (2001) Strategic Management of e-Business. Chichester: John Wiley & Sons

David P (2000) Understanding Digital Technology's evolution and the Path of Measured Productivity Growth: Present and Future in the Mirror of the Past. In: Brynjolffsonn E, Smith M, Bailey J (1999) Understanding digital markets, review and assessment. MIT

Davies T (2001) E-Gov planning and the value of investment. Presentatie Booz Allen & Hamilton. E-gov 2001, 9 July 2001

Deitel HM, Deitel PJ, Steinbuhler K (2001) E-Business & e-Commerce for Managers. Prentice Hall, Upper Saddle River

Deitel HM, Deitel PJ, Nieto T (2001) E-Business & e-commerce. How to program. Prentice Hall, Upper Saddle River

Demkes R (1999) COMET: A comprehensive methodology for supporting telematics investment decisions. Telematica Instituut, Enschede

Earle N, Keen P (2000) From .com to .profit: inventing business models that deliver value and profit. Jossey-Bass Inc, San Francisco

Grimshaw D, Breu K, Myers A (2000) Exploiting e-business. A survey of UK Industry. Cranfield: Information Systems Research Centre, School of management. Cranfield University

Haltiwanger J, Jarmin R (2000) Measuring the Digital Economy. In Brynjolffsonn E, Smith M, Bailey J (eds) Understanding digital markets, review and assessment. MIT

Hedman J, Kalling T (2002) The Business model: A means to Comprehend the Management and Business Context of Information and Communication Technology. ECIS Proceedings, 2002, June 6-8, Gdansk, Poland, pp 148–162

den Hertog P, Holland C, Bouwman H (1999) E-commerce de maat genomen. Ministerie van Economische Zaken

Holland Ch, Bouwman H, Smidts M (2000) Back to the Bottom Line. Onderzoek naar succesvolle e-Businessmodellen. ECP NL, Leidschendam

Holland Ch, Bouwman H, Smidts M (2000) Return to the Bottom Line. ECP NL, Leidschendam

Jansen W, van der Stappen P (2000) State of the art in e-business services and components. Telematica Instituut, Enschede, GIGA-TS

Kalakota R, Whinston AB (1997) Electronic Commerce, A Manager's Guide. Addison Wesley Longman Inc, Reading, Massachusetts

Kaplan R, Norton D (1992) The balanced scorecard: measures that drive performance. Harvard Business Review, January-February, pp 71–79

Kaplan R, Norton D (1996) Using the balanced scorecard as a strategic management system. Harvard Business Review, January-February, pp 75–85

Low J, Cohen Kalafut P (2002) Invisible Advantage. How Intangibles Are Driving Business Performance. Perseus Publishing, Cambridge (Ma)

Mahadevan B (2000) Business models for internet- Based E-commerce. California Management Review 42 (4):55–69

Marr B, Neely A (2001) Measuring E-business Performance. Papers presented to the 12th Annual Conference of the Production and Operations Management Society, POM-2001, March 30-April 2, Orlando Fl.

Neely A, Adams C, Kennerley M (2002) The Performance Prism. The Scorecard for Measuring and Managing Business Success. London: Prentic Hall/Financial Times See also: Http://www.cranfield.ac.uk/som/cbp/prism.htm

NetGenesis & Target Marketing (2000) E-metrics. Business Metrics for the New Economy. Cambridge MA & Santa Barbara CA: NetGenesis & Target Marketing

van Oirsouw R, Spaanderman J, de Vries H (1993) Informatie-economie. Investeringsstrategie voor de informatievoorziening. Academic Service, Schoonhoven

Osterwalder A (2002) Business Models and their Elements. Position Paper presented to the International BITA B4U workshop, Business Models for Innovative Mobile Services. Delft, The Netherlands, 15-16 November

Osterwalder A, Pigneur Y (2002) An e-business Model Ontology for Modelling e-business. In: Loebbecke C, Wigand R, Gricar J, Puchicar A, Lenart G (eds) Ereality: constructing the eEconomy. Proceedings 15th Beld Electronic Commerce Conference. Bled Slovenai June 17-19, 2002

Oude Luttighuis P (2000) A Survey of Networked Enterprises.: Telematica Instituut, Enschede, GIGA-TS

Porter M (2001) Strategy and the internet. Harvard Business Review. March 2001, pp 63–78

Raessens B (2001) E-business Your Business. Over de effectiviteit van E-commerce. Lemma, Utrecht

Rappa M (2003) Business models on the web. http://digitalenterprise.org/models/models.html

Rayport FJ, Jaworski BJ (2001) e-Commerce. McGraw Hill/Irwin, Boston

Rayport FJ (1999) The truth about Business internet Business Models. Harvard Business Reviews Briefs

Renkema T (1996) Investeren in de informatie-infrastructuur. Richtlijnen voor besluitvorming in organisaties. Kluwer Bedrijfsinformatie, Deventer

Rogers E (1983) Diffusion of Innovation. The Free Press, New York

Sawhney M, Gulati R, Paoni A, The Kelogg TechVenture Team (2001) TechVenture. New Rules on Value and Profit from Silicon Valley. John Wiley & Sons. Inc, New York

Selz D (1999) Value Webs. Emerging forms of fluid and flexible organisations. Thinking, organising, communicating and delivering value on the internet. Dissertation St. Gallen

Slywotzky AJ (1996) Value Migration. How to think several moves ahead of the competition. Harvard Business Press, Boston

Shapiro C, Varian H (1999) Information Rules. A Strategic Guide to the Networked Economy. Harvard Business School Press, Boston Ma

Stähler P (2001) Geschäftsmodelle in der digitalen Ökonomie. Merkmale, Strategien und Auswirkungen. Josef Eul Verlag, Köln

Story V, Straub D, Stewart K, Welke R (2000) A Conceptual Investigation of the E-commerce industry. Classifying structures for providing products and services in the electronic marketplace. Communications of the ACM, vol 43, no 7, pp 117–123

Tapscott, D, Ticoll D, Lowy A (2000) Digital Capital: Harnessing the Power of Business Webs. Harvard Business School, Boston

Timmers P (1998) Business models for E-commerce. Electronic Markets, 8 (2):3–7 (wwww.electronicmarkets.org)

Timmers P (1999) Electronic Commerce Strategies and models for business-to-business trading. John Wiley publisher, Chichester

Turban E, Lee J, King D, Chung HM (2000) Electronic Commerce A managerial perspective. Prentice Hall, Upper Saddle River

Weill P, Vitale MR (2001) Place to Space. Migrating to e-business Models. Harvard Business School Press, Boston

Click and brick electronic commerce

Charles Steinfield[1]

Department of Telecommunication, Michigan State University, East Lansing, USA

Abstract

In this chapter an overview of the click and brick approach to electronic commerce is provided. This approach involves the integrated use of traditional and Internet based sales channels. The chapter introduces the basic motivations behind a click and brick model, identifying sources of synergy between physical and virtual operations. Management strategies that can help to alleviate channel conflicts are described. The chapter also highlights the types of benefits that can accrue to companies that successfully integrate the Internet with existing physical operations. Several example cases are provided to illustrate the basic framework.

Introduction

Despite the early fascination with dot com companies, there is a growing recognition that the Internet is unlikely to displace traditional channels anytime soon, at least in the world of business to consumer (B2C) commerce. Rather, many traditional enterprises have moved to integrate e-commerce into their channel mix, using the Internet to supplement existing brick and mortar retail channels (Steinfield 2002). Electronic commerce researchers now consider the combination of physical and web channels to be a distinct electronic commerce business model, most commonly referring to it as a "click and brick" or "click and mortar" approach (Timmer 1998).

In this chapter, a broad overview of the click and brick approach to e-commerce is provided. In the first section, a brief look at the current e-commerce situation highlights the overall importance of taking an integrated brick and click approach to e-commerce development. In the second section, a detailed examination of the sources of synergy between traditional and Internet-based channels is provided. The third section introduces the dangers of channel conflict, and points out possible management strategies to improve channel integration. The fourth

---

[1] E-mail: steinfie@msu.edu

section highlights the potential benefits that firms may reap when pursuing a more integrated approach to e-commerce. Section five introduces three brief cases that give concrete examples of click and brick strategies. Section six discusses a few critical factors that may inhibit firms' attempts to more tightly integrate physical and Internet sales channels. Finally, the chapter closes with several conclusions regarding the importance of the click and brick approach in electronic commerce research and practice.

Click and brick e-commerce overview

Click and brick firms have both Internet and physical outlets, and seek synergies between them in order to reduce costs, differentiate products and services, and find new sources of revenue. In the business-to-consumer area, electronic commerce can be considered as a marketing channel, which can be defined as a means to interact with end-consumers. Many firms rely on a mix of different channels such as physical stores, catalogue sales, and e-commerce. Firms pursuing channel integration attempt to tightly coordinate the use of channels, even within a single sales activity, in order to improve their profitability (Friedman and Furey 1999). Therefore it is helpful to distinguish the truly integrated click and brick approaches from those that treat electronic commerce more as a separate and parallel channel. The difference is illustrated in Figure 1. In the parallel case, customers are not able to easily move between electronic commerce and traditional channels. For example, many firms require that goods ordered online be returned directly to the e-commerce subsidiary, rather than through physical retail outlets. In the integrated, or synergy approach, customers are able to seamlessly move between channels as they interact with a firm. For example, a customer may do product research and initiate an order online, but pickup the merchandise and obtain after-sales service in a physical outlet.

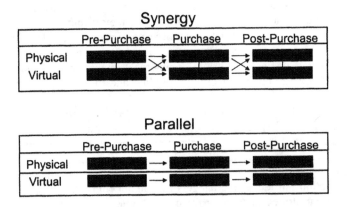

Fig. 1. Contrasting synergy with parallel approaches to click and brick e-commerce

In the early years of electronic commerce, many in the industry felt that pure Internet firms (the dot com's) had significant economic advantages over traditional firms. As a result, many traditional firms chose a parallel approach to the Internet in an attempt to avoid saddling e-commerce divisions with the burdens of higher costs and reduced innovativeness they felt characterized physical stores. The widespread failure of dot com firms, however, forced traditional retailers to re-think this approach and seek out synergies. Today, it appears that the electronic commerce activities of traditional retailers have helped to maintain a steady growth in online sales during the period in which large numbers of dot com enter-prises have failed. The US Commerce Department estimates that the number of people who have purchased a product or engaged in banking online more than doubled between 2000 and 2001, growing from 13.3% of the US population in August, 2000 to more than 29% in September, 2001 (NTIA 2002). Additionally, the NTIA (2002) reports that more than a third of Americans, and fully two-thirds of the Internet users, now use the Internet to obtain product information. Not sur-prisingly, despite the economic slowdown in 2001 and 2002, this increased e-commerce activity has translated in growing online sales revenue. Fourth quarter, 2001 e-commerce sales increased by 13.1% over fourth quarter, 2000, reaching more than $10 billion (US Census Bureau 2002).[2] Total retail sales only increased by 5.3% during the same period.

Sources of synergy between traditional and e-commerce channels

Click and mortar firms have a number potential sources of synergy not necessarily available to pure Internet firms or traditional firms without an e-commerce chan-nel. Borrowing from classic competitive advantage theory (see Porter 1985), such sources of synergy include common infrastructures, common operations, common marketing, common customers, and other complementary assets that can be shared between e-commerce and physical outlets (see Figure 2).

---

[2] Note that this underestimates total consumer-oriented e-commerce activity, since the Census does not include online travel, financial services, and ticket agencies in their re-tail sample.

Adapted from Steinfield et al. 2002

Fig. 2. Sources of synergy in an integrated click and brick approach

Common infrastructures

E-commerce channels can make use of a variety of existing infrastructures such as logistics or IT systems in order to reduce costs or offer capabilities that would be hard for dot com firms to match. An example of the use of a common logistics infrastructure would be when a firm relies on the same warehouses and trucks for handling the distribution of goods for e-commerce activities as it does for delivery to its own retail outlets. Likewise, if a firm has a capable IT infrastructure, including product and customer databases, inventory systems, and a high speed IP network with high bandwidth connections to the Internet, the adoption and use of Internet-based commerce can be enhanced.

Common operations

Existing retail operations can also be put to good use in support of e-commerce, permitting integrated applications to emerge. For example, an order processing system shared between e-commerce and physical channels may enable improved tracking of customers' movements between channels, in addition to potential cost savings.

Common marketing

E-commerce and physical channels may also share common marketing and sales assets, such as a common product catalogue, a sales force that understands the products and customer needs and directs potential buyers to each channel, or advertisements and promotions that draw attention to both channels.

Common buyers

Instead of competing with each other, or pursuing different target markets, e-commerce channels and physical outlets in click and mortar firms often target the same potential buyers. This enables a click and mortar firm to be able to meet customers' needs for both convenience and immediacy, enhancing customer service and improving retention.

Other complementary assets

There are many other types of complementary assets that click and mortar firms possess that purely Internet firms may not. The management literature, for example, notes such additional complementary assets as existing supplier and distributor relationships and experience in the market. As with the other sources of synergy, to the extent firms are able to share these assets across channels, they will be better able them to take advantage of an innovation like e-commerce (Teece 1986; Afuah and Tucci 2001).

Managing channel conflict in multi-channel firms

The integration of e-commerce with existing physical channels is a challenging undertaking that can create problems for management. More specifically, firms with multiple channels may fall prey to channel conflict. Channel conflicts can occur when the alternative means of reaching customers (e.g. a Web-based store) implicitly or explicitly competes with or bypasses existing physical channels, and are nothing new to e-commerce (Stern and Ansary 1992). One danger is that these conflicts result in one channel simply cannibalizing sales from the other. Perceived threats caused by competition and conflict across channels can have other harmful effects, including limited cooperation across the channels, confusion when customers attempt to engage in transactions using the two uncoordinated channels, and even sabotage of one channel by the other (Friedman and Furey 1999). Management must act to diffuse conflicts and ensure the necessary alignment of goals, coordination and control, and development of capabilities to achieve synergy benefits (Steinfield et al. 2002) (see Figure 3).

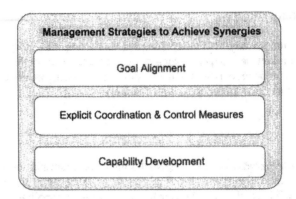

Adapted from Steinfield et al. 2002

Fig. 3. Categories of management strategies used to avoid channel conflicts and achieve synergy benefits

Goal alignment

One of the first tasks for managers of click and brick firms is to ensure that all employees agree that an e-commerce channel is needed, and that they will support it. This represents a process of goal alignment. Aligning goals across physical and virtual channels implies that all employees involved realize that the parent firm benefits from sales originating in either channel. One problem faced by click and brick firms is that the contributions made by the Internet channel may be intangible and hard to measure. Managers have to be open to such intangible benefits and not, for example, evaluate e-commerce divisions purely on the basis of online-only sales and profitability. Moreover, there must be agreement as to what types of customers (e.g. existing vs. new) are to be targeted by the new e-commerce channel. In essence, to avoid channel conflict, management must be proactive in obtaining the support of all employees, building consensus about the goals, methods of evaluating success, and targets for e-commerce. If management simply puts an e-commerce division into place without this goal alignment step, existing employees may feel threatened and may be uncooperative.

Coordination and control measures

In addition to obtaining consensus on goals, explicit coordination and control mechanisms are needed to move a click and brick firm more in the direction of integrated, rather than parallel channels. First, it is important for click and brick firms to design for interoperability across channels, so that customers may move freely between online and physical retail outlets. For example, customers make want to search a particular store's inventory from their own home computer to see if a specific item is in stock or not. They may want the store to hold the item for them to pick up on their way home, rather than have it delivered. This implies that the online system connects and interoperates with the store system.

Another example of explicit coordination is the use of each channel to promote the other. For example, an online visitor may be informed about various in-store special sales, just as an in-store customer may be told about particular complementary services found on the click and brick firm's Web site. Cross-promotions enhance the perception that all the arms of the click and brick business are working together to add value for customers. They also create payoffs from e-commerce that can reduce resistance, such as when online promotions generate greater in-store traffic.

One of the most critical management issues for click and brick firms is to pro-vide real incentives to employees to encourage cross-channel cooperation. Imag-ine a situation where store managers know that any time a customer buys some-thing online instead of in the store, it represents lost revenue and lower compensation. Store personnel will invariably encourage customers to buy in the store, since this provides employees with real income. E-commerce sales may help improve customer relations, but no rational sales person will knowingly direct cus-tomers to sales channel that only ends up reducing his or her income. In many successful click and brick firms, efforts have been made to allocate online sales to particular establishments, so that e-commerce does not succeed at the expense of physical outlets. This often is possible when customers have accounts tied to a particular establishment, and online sales from specific accounts are credited to the home establishment. Another way of allocating online sales to a physical out-let is to use the address of the customer.

Finally, click and brick firms often find that they are able to capitalize on the unique strengths of each sales channel, affording the possibility for some degree of channel specialization (Steinfield et al. 2002). For example, costs for certain types of transactions may indeed be cheaper in an online environment, suggesting that companies should encourage customers to use more efficient channels when possible. Banks, for example, have long attempted to persuade customers to use ATMs for routine cash transactions, rather than coming to a branch and occupying the services of a teller. On the other hand, many financial transactions require ex-pert advice and counseling, and are best done in-person at a branch. Hence, click and brick banks following a channel specialization strategy might offer customers incentives such as better interest rates or lower fees in return for the use more effi-cient online channels for routine transactions like money transfers or bill pay-ments. When more "advice-sensitive" transactions are sought, customers would be directed to their local physical bank branch (Steinfield et al. 2002).

Capability development

In many situations, traditional firms may lack important competencies needed to achieve synergy benefits with e-commerce. For example, traditional firms may lack Web development skills, or logistics skills needed to serve distant markets. In these situations, alliances may be more useful than attempting to develop a virtual channel in-house. Managers must recognize whether the requisite competencies are present in the existing traditional company, and if a partner is needed, must carefully construct an alliance that ensures that their e-commerce partner is not simply siphoning off business from physical retail outlets.

Potential benefits of an integrated channel approach

Once click and brick companies recognize the various sources of synergy across channels, and develop management strategies to avoid conflicts and encourage cooperation across channels, numerous benefits may result. Four broad areas of benefit include: 1) lower costs, 2) increased differentiation through value-added services, 3) improved trust, and 4) geographic and product market extension. The potential benefits from physical and virtual integration are depicted in Figure 4 and discussed in this section.

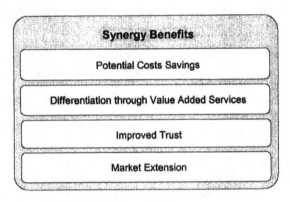

Adapted from Steinfield et al. 2002

Fig. 4. Categories of potential benefits from an integrated click and brick approach

Lower costs: Cost savings may occur in a number of areas, including labor, inventory, marketing/promotion, and distribution. Labor savings result when costs are switched to consumers for such activities as looking up product information, filling out forms, and relying on online technical assistance for after-sales service. Inventory savings arise when firms find that they can avoid having to stock infrequently purchased goods at local outlets, while still offering the full range of choices to consumers via the Internet. Marketing and promotion efficiencies are garnered when each channel is used to inform consumers about services and products available in the other. Delivery savings may result from using the physical outlet as the pick-up location for online purchases, or as the initiation point for local deliveries.

Differentiation through value-added services: Physical and virtual channel synergies can be exploited at various stages in a transaction in order to help differentiate products and add value. Examples of pre-purchase services include various online information aids to help assess needs and select appropriate targets, or, conversely, opportunities in the physical environment to test out products. Examples of purchase services include ordering, customization, and reservation services, as well as easy access to complementary products and services. Post-purchase services include online account management, social community support, loyalty programs and various after-sales activities that may be provided either online or in the physical store. Typical opportunities are in the areas of installation, repair, service reminders and training. Although many of these value-added services are potentially available to single-channel vendors, combined deployment of such services (e.g. online purchase of computer with in-store repair or training) can enhance differentiation and lock-in effects (Shapiro and Varian 1999).

Improved trust: Three reasons for improved trust, relative to pure Internet firms, derive from the physical presence of click and mortar firms, including reduced consumer risk, affiliation with and embeddedness in recognized local social and business networks, and the ability to leverage brand awareness. Lower perceived risk results from the fact that there is an accessible location to which goods can be returned or complaints can be registered. Affiliation and embeddedness in a variety of social networks may facilitate the substitution of social and reputational governance for expensive contracts or legal fees (Granovetter 1985). For example, an online customer may be more prone to trust the Web site of a business when the store manager is a member of his or her church, or when the customer's business and the online vendor are both members of the same chamber of commerce. Such ties are more likely to exist between geographically proximate buyers and sellers, suggesting that there may indeed be a preference for doing business with firms that are already physically present in the local market. Finally, marketing theorists have long recognized the power of branding as a means of building consumer confidence and trust in a product (Kotler 1999). Established firms are able to leverage their familiar name to make it easier for consumers to find and trust their affiliated online services.

Geographic and product market extension: Adding a virtual channel can help extend the reach of a firm beyond its traditional physical outlets, addressing new geographic markets, new product markets, and new types of buyers. Those in other geographic markets may be new or former customers who have moved away. Virtual channels can also extend the product scope and product depth of physical channels by enabling firms to offer new products that they do not have to physically stock locally. Moreover, firms may add new revenue generating information services online that would not be feasible to offer in physical outlets. Finally, the Internet may help reach customers within an existing market who may not have visited the physical outlet, but are otherwise attracted to the virtual channel due to its special characteristics.

Summary of the click and brick framework

The click and brick framework elements can be assembled into the summary framework portrayed in Figure 5. The framework directs our attention to the sources of synergy, the need for management strategies to capitalize on click and brick applications, and the potential benefits that can result.

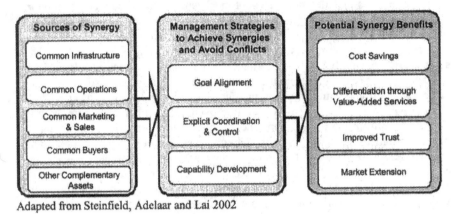

Adapted from Steinfield, Adelaar and Lai 2002

Fig. 5. A comprehensive click and brick model

Exploring the framework with several click and brick cases[3]

The framework is best illustrated by describing several cases of click and brick firms. These examples were selected from a series of click and brick cases developed by Steinfield, Adelaar and Lai (2002). Among their cases (the actual firm names were not reported based on the wishes of the interviewed companies), were a specialty retailer, a B2B building materials supplier, and an automobile manufacturer selling through dealerships. Each represents a different basic business arrangement - a multichannel retailer operating in the B2C arena, a B2B wholesaler, and a manufacturer promoting sales to consumers through an affiliated, but independently owned network of dealerships. They nicely illustrate the robustness of the click and brick approach.

---

[3] These cases are adapted from Steinfield et al. 2002.

An electronics retailer

This company is one of the largest specialty retailers of consumer electronics, personal computers, entertainment software and appliances with over 400 stores. The firm recently rolled out a new e-commerce site that featured both a deeper selection of products and a tighter integration with its traditional physical stores. The click and mortar design strategy enables the firm to benefit from a range of synergies between their virtual and physical channels. The goal is to be "channel agnostic," letting customers choose whatever channel or combination of channels best suits their needs.

A number of sources of synergy are available to the firm. One key source is the firm's exploitation of a common IT infrastructure between their e-commerce and store channels. They accomplished this by tightly integrating the Internet operations with existing databases and other legacy systems. The firm also consciously capitalized on common operations, especially in terms of purchasing, inventory management, and order processing. That common marketing and common buyers were a source of synergy is evident in their emphasis on replicating and leveraging the store brand in their online services.

Among the services enabled by the tight IT integration allows online customers to check out the inventory of individual stores, so that they might order merchandise for immediate pickup in the nearest store. In order to achieve this value-added service and derive the differentiation benefit from it, the service had to be supported by a change in business processes that ensured interoperability across the two channels. For example, if only one or two items desired by an online purchaser are in stock, in-store customers might claim them by the time the Web customer arrived for pickup. To avoid this situation, store personnel must be notified that an online customer has requested an item for pickup. Then employees remove the item from the shelf, and send an email confirmation to the online customer. In order to ensure that stores cooperated with this new capability, management incentives were also considered to avoid or diffuse potential channel conflicts. In particular, the company included performance in fulfilling online orders as one of the parameters influencing store manager compensation.

This seemingly simple service thus reflects the main components of the framework. Several sources of synergy come into play. First, the firm built the service by tying the Internet to a common, integrated IT infrastructure. Second, it supports the service by utilizing existing store inventory that was warehoused and delivered using common logistics infrastructure. Third, the shoppers can provide payment that is credited to the store, using existing operational systems such as credit card verification and approval systems already in place. Finally, the service targets common buyers – that is people living in near existing physical stores.

Management initiatives to achieve synergy and avoid conflict are also evident in this simple example. The online service depended upon the cooperation of store personnel, reflecting a need for goal alignment. This was achieved by developing a service that brought traffic into the store, rather than simply bypassing it altogether. Moreover, management recognized that the Internet could assist in pre-purchase activities, even if the eventual sale was consummated in the store. They did not require the e-commerce channel to generate its own profits. Additionally, they attended to the need for explicit coordination and control by developing a business process that ensured cross-channel interoperability. Finally, they created an incentive system that rewarded store personnel for their cooperation with the e-commerce channel.

Finally, the benefits of this one service are also captured well by the framework. Consider the cost savings in labor that stores accrue when customers search for products online, conduct research, order the product, and even make payment ahead of time, all without needing the assistance of a single employee. In terms of differentiation, this is represents a pre-purchase and purchase service that would be difficult for a non-click and mortar firm to offer. Because of the tie-in to the local store, which is also part of a well-known national chain, customers perceive much lower risk than they would if ordering from a less familiar, non-local Internet business.

The tight integration between the e-commerce and existing retail infrastructure offers this firm many other advantages that are derived from the same sources of synergy and enabled by many of the same management strategies. For example, because of their integrated approach, customers who order products online with home delivery are able to return products to their local store, enhancing trust and reducing perceived risk. Moreover, the integration of IT systems enabled store employees to access customer and order data to improve customer assistance, such as finding complementary goods.

Channel cooperation extends in both directions. In-store customers who are unable to find a product on the shelf can search the firm's online site through kiosks available in the store. Because of the integrated approach to marketing, the firm is also able to undertake promotional campaigns, such as sales and contests that customers can access in the store and on the Web. In addition of the Web channel also enabled value added services geared towards improving customer relationship management. In particular, the Web site allowed customers to store items under consideration in a 'Think About' folder. This provides useful marketing information to the firm, as they can provide more targeted promotions related to desired products.

A building material supplier

The building materials supply company has a double-pronged approach to e-commerce. First, they maintain their own Web site offering rich information services to their primary customer base – the professional builder. Second, they have an alliance with a building supply portal that allows them to offer e-commerce transactions to their existing client base as well as to new customer segments.

Professional builders are provided with an account that allows them to use the e-commerce site. They can login directly from the builder supply firm's home page. Orders are fulfilled by the local lumberyard where the builder has an account. Essentially, each lumberyard caters to the market located within a radius of

100 miles. Prices are individualized, encouraging builders to consolidate their purchases for volume discounts.

The building supply portal works with other suppliers, but is tightly coupled with the case study firm due to both firms having the same principle stockholder. In addition to providing online supply ordering services to builders, it also enables the firm to offer value added services, extend in to the consumer home improvement market, and provide customers goods not carried by the local lumberyard. Among the value-added services are a variety of accounting and management options that builders can use. These include maintaining an online ledger for a project – for example a house – that can be used as a template for the next project, saving builders time on order entry. Each builder can have his own personal Web page, including a personal product usage and construction plan folder. Builders can also check the status of their orders on a daily basis and order material outside the regular store hours, This is helpful because many builders do their administrative task at home in the evening. The personal pages include information on activities and promotions occurring at the local branch.

By outsourcing consumer e-commerce transactions to the online portal, the company now has a presence in the growing home-improvement market now dominated by such superstores as Home Depot. Because of the other partners who participate in the portal, the company is able to offer their existing customers one-stop shopping services, even for goods they do not themselves carry.

Individual stores receive all orders placed on the portal for their products electronically, and fulfill them through their normal supply chain and existing fleet of delivery trucks. New professional clients are first encouraged to setup a new account at a local branch, where local employees negotiate individual pricing arrangements..

The Web-based service supports standard orders. However, the company still maintains outside sales representatives (OSRs) who visit with builders on job sites to maintain good customer relations. The increased use of online ordering by builders allows OSRs to pay less attention to administrative tasks and to focus on selling value added services, giving advice, educating the client about the online channels, and strengthening customer relationships.

Through its online partner, the firm also completed a successful mobile service pilot using Palm Pilots. Builders were able to make on-site purchases for critical materials needed immediately. Materials were then brought out to the job by the local delivery truck. One interesting impact of this service is that it encouraged builders to wait until the last minute for some orders, and to make orders in smaller quantities than they would through normal channels. This is, of course, less efficient for the supply firm, creating some challenges for their delivery system. However, it is a new value-added service that strengthens their relationship to their core clients.

An automobile manufacturer

All automobile manufacturers realize that car shoppers are able to conduct extensive research online prior to buying a car. Carmakers have well-developed web sites providing rich information about their models, but for a variety of reasons are not able to sell cars directly to end customers through the web. Hence, they must work with traditional dealers to offer a click and brick experience. In one carmaker's e-commerce service, customers can configure their desired car online, obtain a fixed price quote, and choose a local dealer from whom they wish to take delivery. The application locates the matching car from dealer inventories, and if in stock at a different dealer from the one chosen by the customer, the dealers will swap cars with each other. The chosen dealer then gets full credit for the sale of the online-configured car, as well as the continuing service relationship to the customer. At the Web site, customers can also research cars and check the inventory of local dealers online. In addition, customers can apply online for credit and insurance, which is also submitted to local dealer.

This approach helps the manufacturer sell more cars without alienating their existing dealer network. The company realizes that in the car market, due to the logistics of delivery and the need for a physical presence for service and warranty work, bypassing dealers will not work. In fact, in many states, it is illegal for car manufacturers to sell directly to end consumers. To secure support from dealers for the initiative an e-dealer advisory board was created. The manufacturer has also introduced features such as online scheduling for maintenance and repair, and an ownership Web site where customers can find accessories that go with their car and receive maintenance service reminders.

Other electronic services initiatives include the introduction of mobile in-car services for safety, security and information. They are exploring the combination of GPS with wireless technology to deliver emergency roadside assistance, stolen vehicle tracking, navigation aids, and other travel related services. These in-car wireless services would be activated by the selling dealer, who would provide training to customers.

Conclusions

This chapter has provided a broad overview of the click and brick business approach. It introduced a framework to help understand the dynamics of managing a click and brick enterprise. The framework begins by identifying potential sources of synergy available to firms that choose to integrate e-commerce with traditional forms of business. It further emphasizes the many actions that firms can take to minimize channel conflicts and help achieve the benefits of synergy. And it describes four categories of synergy-related benefits from the integration of e-commerce with traditional businesses, including potential cost savings, gains due to enhanced differentiation, improved trust, and potential extensions into new markets. A few examples were described to provide a concrete illustration of the approaches taken by click and brick firms.

References

Afuah A, Tucci C (2001) Internet business models and strategies: Text and cases. McGraw-Hill Irwin, New York, NY

Friedman LG, Furey TR (1999) The channel advantage: Going to market with multiple sales channels to reach more customers, sell more products, make more profit. Butterworth Heinemann, Boston

Granovetter M (1985) Economic action and social structure: The problem of embeddedness. American Journal of Sociology 91 (3):481–510.

Kotler P (1999) Marketing Management, 10th Edition. Prentice Hall, Upper Saddle River, NJ

NTIA (2002) A nation online: How Americans are expanding their use of the Internet. National Telecommunications and Information Administration, Washington, DC

Porter ME (1985) Competitive advantage : creating and sustaining superior performance. Free Press, New York

Shapiro C, Varian HR (1999) Information rules: a strategic guide to the network economy. Harvard Business School Press, Boston, Mass.

Steinfield C, Adelaar T, Lai Y-j (2002) Integrating Brick and Mortar Locations with E-Commerce: Understanding Synergy Opportunities. Hawaii International Conference on Systems Sciences, Big Island, Hawaii, January 7-10

Steinfield C, Bouwman H, Adelaar T (2002) The Dynamics of Click and Mortar E-commerce: Opportunities and Management Strategies. International Journal of Electronic Commerce, forthcoming

Stern LW, Ansary AI (1992) Marketing channels. Prentice Hall, Englewood Cliffs, NJ

Teece DJ (1986) Profiting from technological innovation: Implications for integration, collaboration, licensing and public policy. Research Policy 15:285–306

Timmer P (1998) Business models for electronic markets. Electronic Markets 8 (2):3–8. http://www.electronicmarkets.org/netacademy/publications.nsf/all_pk/949

US Census Bureau (2002, February 20) Retail e-commerce sales in fourth quarter 2001 were $10.0 billion, up 13.1 percent from fourth quarter, 2000, Census Bureau reports. U.S. Department of Commerce News. Available from http://www.census.gov/mrts/www/current.html

Glossary

Channel: A means by which a seller interacts with end-consumers. Many firms rely on a mix of different channels such as physical stores, catalogue sales, and e-commerce. Firms pursuing *channel integration* attempt to tightly coordinate the use of channels, even within a single sales activity, in order to improve their profitability.

Channel conflict: Channel conflicts occur when an alternative means of reaching customers (e.g. a Web-based store) implicitly or explicitly competes with or bypasses existing physical channels. Perceived threats caused by competition and conflict across channels can have other harmful effects, including limited cooperation across the channels, confusion when customers attempt to engage in transactions using the two uncoordinated channels, and even sabotage of one channel by the other.

Channel specialization: Click and brick firms that attempt to direct customers to the most appropriate channel (e.g. one that is the lowest cost, or one that offers the requisite capabilities) are pursuing a channel specialization approach. It allows firms to capitalize on the unique strengths of each sales channel.

Complementary assets: Assets possessed by a firm, such as as existing supplier and distributor relationships and experience in the market, that help the firm take advantage of innovations such as e-commerce.

Differentiation: A competitive approach used by companies to set themselves apart from competitors through higher quality products and better customer services. Click and brick firms hope that they can use their combined channels to differentiate themselves from competitors.

Synergy: When the combined effect of two actions is greater than the sum of the individual effects. Click and brick firms hope that by combining traditional and online services, they can offer an experience to customers that is greater than possible through each channel by itself.

Part 3:
The challenge of new applications

Prosumers as service configurators – vision, status and future requirements[1]

Stefan Klein[2], Carsten Totz[3]

MIS Department, University College Dublin, Ireland
Department of Information Systems, University of Muenster, Germany

Abstract

From a vendor's point of view, e-commerce can facilitate new models of division of labor, which typically encompass a higher level of involvement on the customer's, specifically consumer's, end. In order to overcome shortcomings in computer-mediated communications, numerous individualization or personalization features have been added to e-commerce applications. In the telecommunication industry, as one prominent example, increasingly self-service portals have been established which provide administrative functions such as billing status, change of tariff or billing address. More advanced features such as unified messaging are even more customer specific and are beneficial inasmuch as they are regularly adapted to the individual, situation specific needs.

However, in contrast to the vendor's expectations, these features have not been well received and adopted by customers so far (e.g. Yahoo's personalization features (Manber et al. 2000)). We have conducted several experiments with mobile phone users, which showed two major shortcomings: firstly, many functions were not known at all and, secondly, the usability of the Web portal was very limited.

These findings must be quite troubling for the vendors as ongoing innovations in the telecommunications industry are leading to a need for even more user involvement: e.g. location based services require adaptable and regularly updated consumer profiles in order to provide satisfying results.

---

[1] Research for this paper has been funded by the Deutsche Forschungsgemeinschaft (DFG): PROSUMER is a joint research project between the IOS research group at the Department of Information Systems (University of Muenster) and the Sociological Research Center (SOFI) at University Goettingen. The experiments were designed and executed jointly. We gratefully acknowledge the support of our Goettingen colleagues Heidi Hanekop, Andreas Tasch and Volker Wittke in setting up the experiments and providing helpful insights.
[2] E-mail: stefan.klein@ucd.ie
[3] E-mail: wicato@wi.uni-muenster.de

Based on the dilemma between the limited success of self-service offerings to date and extended requirements in the near future, the paper will

- report on findings about the acceptance of customer self service portals,
- analyze and frame the trend towards increasing user participation in advanced telecommunication services, and
- discuss implications for service providers.

The vision: The Prosumer as configurator

The Prosumer

Economic value generation has been closely linked with varying models of division of labor within and across firms (Smith 1776). The emergence of a service society has coincided with extended consumer self-service (e.g. Bell 1974; Gershuny 1978). Authors like Toffler (1972) have extended this notion to include the consumer as part of the value chain and introduced the idea of consumers as co-producers, the so-called "Prosumer" (see also Tapscott 1996). In a related view, the economic analysis of households (Becker 1976; Lehmer 1993) has shown that household production is quite significant, and moreover the patterns of division of labor within households and more importantly between household and the official economy are changing, depending on factors like household income, cost of labor (including taxes) etc.

Given the increasing level of price competition in almost every part of retail operations, companies have explored models of "mobilizing the customer" (Normann and Ramirez 1993), i.e. enabling consumers to voluntarily take over parts of the value generation – such as picking, transporting and assembling furniture – in return for price incentives. The Swedish furniture chain IKEA is one of the most prominent and successful examples for this idea. Retail banks where customers get their cash at automatic teller machines and print their account statements at printer terminals are another example of extended self-service functions.

The proliferation of the Web has opened up a rich new field of consumer self-service support (Hanekop et al. 2001). The almost universal access to the Web in homes, offices, cafes, and increasingly in mobile environments combined with the browser as uniform, easy-to-use interface and assumed customer benefits, such as extended availability, control, and documentation, have encouraged and enabled companies to put functions like

- home banking (major banks),
- administration of customer profiles (airlines),
- access to the current billing status (telecommunication companies),
- ticket printing (Deutsche Bundesbahn), and
- customer decision support systems (McEachern and O'Keefe 1998)

online. One lesson that companies have learnt, however, is that as some parts of their administrative functions are shifted to the consumer, specific incentives, such as frequent flyer miles or Webmiles, are needed to compensate the Prosumer for her extra work. Overall, Web-based self-service support has become widely available as one way of increasing the frequency of customers' visits to suppliers' Websites. Implementation costs are fairly low and companies benefit from extended possibilities to track customers' online behavior. In most cases, self-service support reflects a specific click & brick scenario (Gulati and Garino 2000; Steinfield et al. 2001): traditional (brick) services like air transportation or telecommunications are administered online (click).

Product and service configuration

However, the vision of configuration tasks carried out in a Prosuming mode is far more extensive. It may even become the litmus test for future success of electronic commerce: only if companies succeed to find new forms of division of tasks with their customers will they be able to develop more advanced and complex online services (cf. Wittke 1997). At the same time, careful customer segmentation is needed in order to separate "power users" with a high level of involvement and commitment from those who just care for plain and simple online services.

The vision of configuration covers different aspects of consumer participation throughout the product and service life cycle (Kleinaltenkamp et al. 1996), e.g.

- in the innovation or design process, e.g. in consumer labs, (Hippel 1988),
- in market research (Leenders and Blenkhorn 1988),
- in the selection and combination of components (customization) as part of the requirements specification process (Pine 1993), as well as
- in an ongoing selection and combination of product or service properties, in order to adjust the systems properties to environmental parameters, contingencies or customer's preference (personalization or individualization)) or intentions. As far as the supplier is involved in this process, the customer relationship turns into a (mutual) learning relationship (Quinn 1992). Suppliers learn from customers' requirements, preferences, willingness to pay and involve them as co-designers. Customers are instructed by the suppliers to better understand and to make better use of their products and services.

The examples reflect a mature form of electronic commerce, which requires a high quality of Web design next to well established customer relations and advanced customer segmentation. The level of consumer involvement varies significantly across different customer groups.

In our research we have focused on the latter type of consumer configuration. It reflects the increasing complexity and versatility of products and services, such as intelligent homes or advanced telecommunication services (e.g. unified messaging), for which an initial configuration (customization, setting of defaults) is not sufficient, because it would limit the scope of functionality. Further, we are assuming that neither the producer (service provider) nor the product or service themselves are in a position to fulfill the configuration task without the consumer's participation. Even though intelligent systems can sense environmental conditions or mobile services can determine a consumer's location, they are not in a position to anticipate customers' intentions, plans and wishes. In this scenario, the Prosumer can only individualize and appropriate increasingly complex and versatile service through the execution of configuration tasks. At the same time, consumer configuration becomes a precondition for the suppliers and service providers to make the full potential of their services available.

The reasons for the observed trend towards increasingly complex services are manifold. While technology has enabled the feasibility of service production and configuration, the transformation of telecommunication markets has functioned as a driver. Figure 1 gives a summary of drivers of service individualization and hence emerging configuration needs in the telecommunication industry.

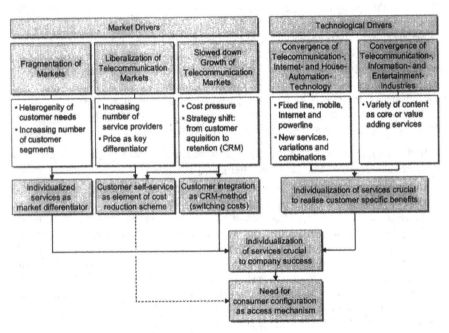

Fig. 1. Drivers of service configuration

For the purpose of this paper we will focus on "Web-based consumer configuration", i.e. the selection and combination of features as well as parameter setting in a Web-based environment (platform) made available by the service provider.

The challenge framed

As the proliferation of the Web has enabled extended configuration potential, and many e-commerce players have started to integrate self-service and configuration functions into their offerings (Hanekop et al. 2001), the question becomes pressing, of whether consumers are willing and able to accept and fulfill a role that is increasingly assigned to them (Wittke 1997; Heuser 1999). Figure 2 summarizes general driving and impeding factors that determine the Prosumer's decision parameters and trade-offs to be calculated.

We hypothesize that a close link exists between the Prosumer's disposition in terms of motivation and capabilities and configuration related cost/benefit deliberations and trade-offs. Accepting a configuration role can be seen as an investment decision: payments in terms of learning and risk taking have to be made initially before the returns in terms of configuration benefits can be reaped. Hence, the service properties (including the provider), the respective configuration options and the configuration environment need to be considered as input (or decision parameters) into the Prosumer's deliberations (see Table 1).

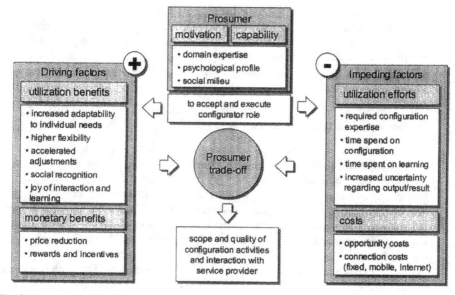

Fig. 2. Prosumer trade-offs

Table 1: Determinants of Prosumer acceptance

Determinants	Example	Impact on Prosumer
Service properties: – functional scope – core vs. peripheral functionality – reputation of the service provider	Call availability management	Perceived benefits, relevance of service elements, relation to the service provider
Configuration options: – scale and scope of configuration, – configuration leverage	Call forwarding and filtering	Configuration costs and benefits and process uncertainty
Configuration environment: – Interface and interaction design – Availability of alternatives to self-configuration	Web interface, PDA or mobile device, call center as alternative	Configuration efficiency (reasonable defaults, adaptability of the system) and benefits opportunity costs

Hypothesis 1: A Prosumer's disposition (motivation and capabilities) determines the perception of service properties and configuration tasks.

Even though the service properties, the configuration options, and the configuration environment can be analytically separated, they are evaluated in an integrated manner. The configuration environment is the medium for the Prosumer's access to configuration options, which – in the chosen setting of advanced telco services – are a precondition to use specific, individualized service properties. We hypothesize that the determinants together, even as they can be discerned, are necessary preconditions for the Prosumer's acceptance of a specific configuration role.

Hypothesis 2: The service properties are embedded in configuration options and the configuration environment.

Hypothesis 3: In her perception the Prosumer distinguishes between specific configuration tasks and service properties.

The Web as configuration environment is crucial for the overall quality perception of the customers and hence their inclination to accept a Prosumer role: The Web site is a surrogate for brick-and-mortar stores, sales personnel and tangible product-samples - communicating the service operators capabilities, their empathy and responsiveness towards customer problems, needs and desires, as well as the expected service quality. The Web interface accumulates several moments-of-truth incidents that decide on the success of a service provider. The Web site is the virtual touchpoint

- where company, product and service presentation determine the customer's purchase decision;
- where customers have to be convinced to invest in a relationship, although it is uncertain if it will prove beneficial for them;
- where poor configuration processes let customers drop out before placing an order;

- where information provided to and gathered from customers during interaction processes determines the expectations regarding quality as well as the quality level of the finished product or service;
- where after-sales communication affirms/approves customers in their purchase decision and supports customer satisfaction and loyalty.

In order to evaluate the configuration environment regarding usability and customers' quality assessment, it is essential to identify and consider its relevant determinants. Figure 3 illustrates the Web interaction as an encounter between the consumer with capabilities, motivation, expectations and involvement and the service provider with capabilities, goals and intentions.

We hypothesize that the consumer's quality perception of the configuration environment is critical for her evaluation of configuration tasks. In some cases we have a Web-only configuration environment while there is a multi-channel environment in others. The availability of communication options is expected to have an impact on the consumer's perception.

Hypothesis 4: The Prosumer's perception of specific configuration tasks is determined by the quality perception of the provider's configuration environment.

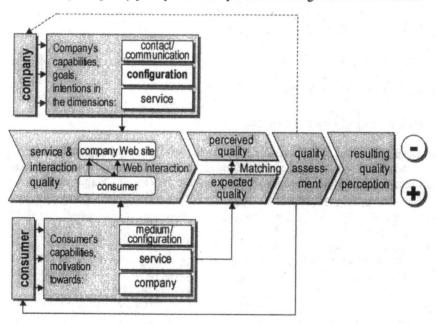

Fig. 3. Web quality assessment (adapted from Totz and Riemer 2001)

While we assume an analytical distinction in the perception of service properties and configuration, the decision to accept the Prosumer role is based on the service properties embedded in the configuration environment and the trade-off between functionality (service properties) and the price to get access to it (configuration).

Hypothesis 5: The Prosumer's acceptance of a concrete configuration role is determined by a combination of the service properties and configuration task evaluation.

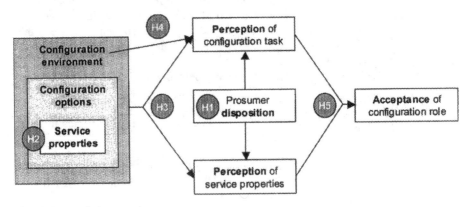

Fig. 4. Research framework

Empirical examination

Research design and experiments

In order to test our hypothesis we collaborated with a telecommunication service provider (telco) and designed an experiment with a real-world scenario and actual customers of telco. For the experiments, the test persons got mobile devices and test accounts and were assigned a number of practical self-service and configuration tasks (Table 2). The tasks were presented to the customers as realistic scenarios, integrating motives or obligations that might occur in their daily lives. E.g. the task "configuration of a call management module" was not presented as "please configure the call management module named XY on the self-service portal" but embedded in a narrative about reasonable customer motive: "It's Thursday night. On Friday, you are leaving the city for a weekend by the sea. The area at the seaside is not covered very well for receiving mobile phone calls. From Friday 9am to 3pm all calls to your mobile phone should be routed to your office number and from Friday 8pm to Sunday 8pm all calls should be routed to the number at your house at the seaside." We decided to assign all tasks in similarly indirect ways for two reasons: a) We regard the transfer of the real-world motive into specific self-service options as relevant because the customer has to accomplish the transfer during real interaction with the web-interface. Therefore, the evaluation of the interface usability and the acceptance of the self-service portal are influenced by aspects of process evidence and guidance by the system. b) By assigning contextually embedded tasks, we were able to gain information from the customer's point-of-view on alternative ways of obtaining the service.

Table 2. Experimental tasks

Tasks assigned to customers with pre-paid card	Increasing level of task complexity	Tasks assigned to customers with two-year contract
1.) Log-in to self-service portal (initial registration, password sent via sms, log-in)		1.) Log-in to self-service portal (initial registration, password sent via SMS, log-in)
2.) Change of customer address		2.) Change of customer address
3.) Credit check		3.) Check of billing status since last invoice
4.) Change of tariff		4.) Analysis of call volume (most frequent numbers) and change of tariff
5.) Configuration and test of web-based quick dial service "voice dial"		5.) Configuration and test of web-based quick dial service "voice dial"
		6.) Configuration of call-management service

To accomplish their tasks the test persons used the telco's Web-based self-service portal.

The experiments were conducted in October 2001 with a total of 36 test persons, 11 of them used a pre-paid card, 25 a two-year contract. Different service offerings and tasks were attached to the different contracts. Pretests were conducted to validate questionnaires and to ensure comprehensibility of the presented scenarios for the experimental usability examination. The data collection was done in three ways: During the experiments the test persons were observed, they had to fill out a questionnaire about their perception of the quality of the Web site (i.e. the configuration environment) after the experiments and were asked to discuss their impressions, interpretations and assumptions in focus groups of 4-6 participants. For the usability assessment of the Web portal – conceptually based on the Web quality assessment framework (Figure 3) – the critical incident method was adapted in order to map the consumer's interaction with the Web application. We decided to deploy the critical incident method as we wanted to gain information on the usability of the self-service portal in terms of interaction process quality. The critical incident method is well suited as it analyzes problems in the customer-driven interaction process. Information on the "most favorable font-size or colors" was not regarded as as relevant as information on the quality of the interaction process. Therefore, traditional Web-design aspects as e.g. font-size, navigational structure, colors etc. were not assessed in a separate way but are taken into consideration as they determine the usability in terms of process evidence. Preparing the tests, the structures of the different service processes were analyzed and modeled as observation "checklists". These checklists were used during the actual usability tests by the observers to mark actual problems and critical incidents during certain task execution. The test persons were briefed to "think aloud", to articulate their problems and to communicate when they thought they would terminate the interaction in a non-experimental setting.

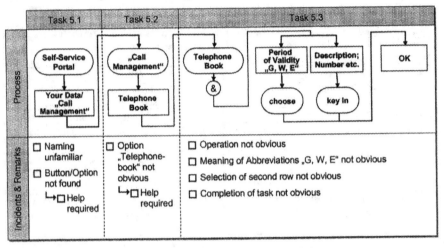

Fig. 5. Observation "checklist" with interaction process model

The design of the experiments reflects a difficult trade-off decision. The chosen self-service portal presented a state-of-the-art implementation. While we would have preferred more advanced configuration tasks, we wanted a realistic rather than an artificial configuration task environment. Therefore, even typical configuration tasks had to be reduced and simplified. The call management option for example embodies functionalities of time- and priority-sensitive call routing ("First, route the call to my mobile phone to phone number XY. If I do not pick up the phone, hold the call and route it to number YZ. If I do not pick up the phone, hold the call and route it to ..."). Pretests showed that this kind of extensive service functionality was difficult to communicate and not regarded as a relevant functionality by the majority of the customers. Furthermore, asking the test persons to "think aloud" and to communicate problems and moments of process termination should provide insight into their mental models and level of frustration. Our goal was to create an almost realistic situation for the test persons, avoiding tasks that would take longer and would require more attention than a real-world setting.

Table 3. Data Collection Methods

Method of Data Collection	Focus of collected Data	Data provides information on ...
Usability Tests of self-service portal – Critical Incident Method	Process clarity (process evidence), drop-out ratios, expressed likes and dislikes during interaction processes	H2, H4, H5
Questionnaires	Readiness/willingness to perform self-service-tasks online, experience of online- and mobile-usage, evaluation of perceived interaction-quality	H3, H4, H1, H5
Focus Group Discussions (recorded on video-tape)	Preferred Service-Channels, evaluation of service-quality, Motivation and capabilities for online-consulting and –prosuming, drivers of online-usage	H1, H3, H5

Findings and discussion

In the examined case, the customers have a choice between three service channels: calling the hotline, visiting the store and asking the staff to carry out the task or doing it autonomously via the Web-interface. The results of our focus group discussions showed clearly, that the hotline (call center) is not only preferred over visiting a store (major reasons: 24*7 availability, convenience, competence of call agents) but also over executing the tasks via the Web-interface (even though the initial interactive-voice-response system and queue times on the hotline are regarded as annoying). Although a significant number of customers tries to choose the fastest alternative to execute their concerns and regards the Web-based self-service portal as potentially suitable, a lack of process governance/ownership prevents the Web-interface from being accepted as an alternative to the hotline in practice. The test persons expressed that calling the hotline or visiting a store, they are the ones who "decide what to say and what to do" – on the Web-Interface, it is perceived to be the contrary. Furthermore, a (verbal) confirmation of the task assignment and its execution seems essential and unconsidered on the Web-interface.

Customer statement: "Yes, I want to determine the way to go. I say what I want and the agent answers if it'll be possible or not. If it's possible, I'll have the execution right away. Here (Web-interface) I do not decide on the way, I have to act upon predetermined processes."

Hypothesis 1: A Prosumer's disposition (motivation and capabilities) determines the balanced evaluation of service properties and configuration tasks.

We found some evidence for the validity of hypothesis 1 by analyzing the records of our focus group discussions. The evaluation of service properties and configuration tasks seems to relate less to demographic criteria than to personal characteristics. Neither the age of the customers nor their level of education allowed us to draw conclusions on attitudes towards service properties or disposition to configure the service via the Web-Interface. A 70 year old customer proved to be extremely interested in using a variety of services and their Web-based configuration, whereas test persons aged 25 and younger (although familiar with using the Internet) turned out to be less motivated. For the older person, Web-based self-service options were an opportunity to save time he could spend at home looking after his wife who was in need of care. For the youngsters, most of the service properties were of no use at all or occurred too infrequently to be considered as relevant.

A group of "expert users", who were employed in IT-related fields and were using the Internet for a variety of daily routines and tasks, appeared – as expected – very open-minded towards the configuration of services via a Web-interface. Their overall strong disposition to execute self-administrative and service configuration tasks was well-founded by their rich experience of what is possible on the Web and what is not.

Hypothesis 2: The service properties are embedded in configuration options and the configuration environment.

This hypothesis proves valid for services that substantially require a customer-specific ex-ante configuration. In our study the nature of the quick dial service function called "voice-dial" and the call management service support our position: both services have to be activated and personalized before customers are able to make use of them. The utilization of the quick dial service requires a detailed online-compilation of a system-based phone book (name, number, home vs. office vs. mobile). Similar embedded in configuration options and the configuration environment are the properties of the call management service. Although basic call redirection functionality might be configured via the mobile phone, the more sophisticated call management options require their configuration via the Web-interface. The customers have to define target numbers to which incoming calls are going to be routed, decide on routing sequences and assign periods of validity for target numbers and routing sequences. If the customer is not willing or able to configure the service via the Web-interface (configuration environment), she will not be able to use it.

Hypothesis 3: In her perception the Prosumer distinguishes between specific configuration tasks and service properties.

The quick dial service "voice-dial" was regarded as beneficial by 36% of the test persons. Due to profound problems during the configuration process (service option not found on Web-portal: 60%; configuration of service/service set-up murky or impenetrable: 70%; usage of service after Web-based configuration via mobile phone failed: 44%), the configuration effort was regarded as too high compared to the perceived usefulness of the service. Test persons professed that they would tend to buy a new mobile phone providing voice-dialing functionality instead of using the short-dial service to be configured via the self-service portal.

The general utility of the call management functionality was – at 78 % – even higher than the quick dial service. The majority of test persons clearly expressed their appreciation of the service. The highest drop-out-rate of all examined configuration- and self-administration-processes explains the poor evaluation of the service experience, whereas the test persons solely put the blame on the Web-interface for causing the interaction problems.

Hypothesis 4: The Prosumer's perception of specific configuration tasks is determined by the quality perception of the provider's configuration environment.

The test persons generally agreed on choosing the service channel that seems most convenient to them. For almost all our test persons this is the mobile phone, respectively calling the hotline. If calling the hotline does not prove convenient due to irritating interactive-voice-response systems or overlong queue times, other service channels are taken into consideration. Customers who do not have permanent Internet access avoid the Web-interface as they perceive the process from starting the PC to logging-in to the self-service portal as too time consuming – risking a waste of time, as test persons rarely claimed to be confident of being able to settle their matters online.

Furthermore, the evaluation of the configuration of the call management and the quick dial service "voice-dial" support hypothesis 4 as the test persons take alternative options to obtain the services into consideration. A Web-interface is basically regarded as a suitable and convenient configuration solution. The experienced configuration task fell short of acceptance as 91% of all test persons failed to commence the configuration process due to the fact that they were not able to find the right option on the Website. Being guided into the process by the observers, 68% of the customers complained about an opaque process and terminated the service configuration frequently. A similar evaluation resulted for the configuration and testing of the quick dial service: the test persons explicitly expressed a preference for being able to compile and organize phone books online but were disappointed with the corresponding options on the Website. For half the test persons, the purchase of a new mobile phone that would provide voice-dial functionality appeared more advantageous and straight forward than configuring the alternative quick dial service via the Web-interface and using it afterwards with their current mobile phone.

For the "expert users" the Internet is the preferred service channel for all kinds of administrative tasks. Furthermore, the option to configure certain services via a Web-interface is not only accepted but expected. The satisfaction voiced with the tested service properties and configuration tasks proved low as the quality of the interface fell short of the user's expectations.

Hypothesis 5: The Prosumer's acceptance of a concrete configuration role is determined by a combination of the service properties and configuration task evaluation.

A significant number of customers explicitly expressed their general disposition to accept the role as a service-configurator. The option to configure personal computers, clothes or even telecommunication-services online did not turn out to be an unrealistic scenario. A substantial number of test persons pointed out their familiarity with online self-services such as online-banking; a couple of them did already use Web-based configurators, e.g. for PCs or cars. Although the general disposition turned out to be higher than expected, customers seem to decide on whether to accept or reject the assigned configuration task in two phases: 1.) balancing their expected utility and effort before trying to configure a service; 2.) evaluating the perceived utility and effort after the configuration to decide on their disposition for recurring configuration tasks.

Table 4 summarizes the task related utility perceptions and the drop out ratios. As the values for the perceived utility cannot be related directly to the drop-out ratios, they disprove the assumption that high drop-out ratios might bear on poor incentives for the test persons due to a perceived lack of service utility.

Table 4. Task related findings

Task No.	Task Description	Perceived utility (high & rather high)	Drop-out ratio - Pre-paid	Drop-out ratio - 2yr contract
1	Log-in to self-service portal (initial registration, password sent via SMS, log-in)	---	0%	4%
2	Change of customer address	89%	0%	4%
3	Credit check/check of billing status since last invoice	98%	0%	12%
4	Change of tariff/analysis of call volume and responding change of tariff	92%	0%	Analysis 8%; change 20%
5	Configuration and test of web-based quick dial service "voice dial"	36%	config. 9% test 82%	config. 25% test 44%
6	Configuration of call management service	72%	---	68%

Conclusions

We observe a trend towards customization, individualization and personalization offerings in many online retail environments (Luedi 1997; Pepers, Rogers 1999). Embedded in a broader trend towards increasing complexity and versatility of consumer services - especially in the telecommunications industry - service configuration as a mode of Prosuming is introduced. Based on the conceptualization of service configuration, the paper develops a framework to explain the level of acceptance of the configuration role, a precondition of the success of suppliers' service design strategies.

While service configuration is popular among service providers and rationalization, our experiments are indicating a huge implementation and (related?) acceptance gap. The obvious explanation for this gap is insufficient design and implementation of the Web-based self-service portal. However, the focus group discussions indicated that even beyond the perceived deficits of the configuration environment (and the availability of a functionally superior alternative, i.e. the call center), the awareness of advanced service properties and configuration options was very limited. Based on our research we conjecture that consumers are far less prepared (in both senses of the word) to accept a configurator's role then service providers assume and wish. On the other hand, the service providers do not seem prepared either to walk their talk or to do what it takes to mobilize their customers to take on that role.

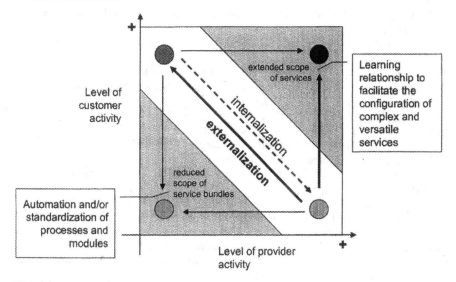

Fig. 6. Strategic options in service design

The research framework (Figure 4) describes the embeddedness of service properties in a configuration environment: they only become visible through the interface of the configuration environment. Moreover, we have observed a close coupling between the perception of the configuration task and service properties. The empirical findings are inconclusive regarding a distinction between the acceptance of the configuration task and the perception of service properties. The poor quality of the studied Web portals distorted more precise analyses of service properties and their perceptions.

Even though configuration is mainly framed as part of Prosumer's self service and hence an instance of task externalization, complex and versatile services call for – as Figure 6 illustrates – a high level of both provider and customer activity. Providers have to develop, monitor and maintain the configuration environments, customers have to configure. Configuration requires – beyond the externalization-internalization dichotomy – a transformation of the customer-supplier relationship towards a mutual learning relationship.

References

Becker GS (1976) The Economic Approach to Human Behavior. University of Chicago Press, Chicago, London

Bell D (1974) The Coming of Post-Industrial Society. A Venture in Social Forecasting. Basic Books, New York

Gershuny J (1978) After Industrial Society? The Emerging Self-service Economy. Prometheus Books, London

Gulati R., Garino J (2000) Get the Right Mix of Bricks & Clicks. Harvard Business Review May-June:107-114

Hanekop H, Tasch A, Wittke V (2001) "New Economy" und Dienstleistungsqualität: Verschiebung der Produzenten- und Konsumentenrolle bei digitalen Dienstleistungen. SOFI Mitteilungen 9:73-91 (in German)

Heuser, UJ (1999) Armer Home Oeconomicus. Die ZEIT 02/25:47

Hippel E von (1988) The Sources of Innovation. Oxford University Press, Oxford

Kleinaltenkamp M, Fließ S, Jacob F (ed) (1996) Customer Integration: von der Kundenorientierung zur Kundenintegration Gabler, Wiesbaden

Leenders MR, Blenkhorn DL (1988) Reverse Marketing - The New Buyer-Supplier Relationship. Free Press, New York

Lehmer G (1993) Theorie des wirtschaftlichen Handelns der privaten Haushalte - Haushaltsproduktion und Informationstechnik im Wechselspiel. Josef Eul, Bergisch Gladbach

Luedi FA (1997) Personalize or Perish. Electronic Markets 7 (3):22-25

Manber U, Patel A, Robinson J (2000) Experience with Personalization on Yahoo! Communications of the ACM 43(8):35-39

McEachern T, O'Keefe B (1998) Re-Wiring Business - Uniting Management and the Web. Wiley, New York

Normann R, Ramirez R (1993) From Value Chain to Value Constellation: Designing Interactive Strategy, HBR, July-August:65-77

Peppers D, Rogers M, Dorf B (1999) Is Your Computer Ready for One-to-one Marketing? Harvard Business Review January-February: 151-160

Pine BJ II (1993) Mass Customization - The New Frontier in Business Competition. Harvard Business School Press, Boston, MA

Quinn JB (1992) Intelligent Enterprise - A Knowledge and Service Based Paradigm for Industry. Free Press, New York

Smith A (1776) The Wealth of Nations, (originally published in 1776, reference based on: Penguin, Harmondsworth 1981)

Steinfield, C., Bouwman, H., Adelaar, T. (2001) Combining physical and virtual channels: Opportunities, imperatives and challenges. Proceedings of the 14th Bled Electronic Commerce Conference, Bled, Slovenia, June 25-26, 2001.

Tapscott D (1996) The Digital Economy. Promise and Peril in the Age of Networked Intelligence. New York

Toffler A (1972) The Futurist. Random House, New York.

Totz C, Riemer K (2001) The effect of interface quality on success - an integrative approach on mass customization design. Proceedings of the 1st World Congress on Mass Customization and Personalization, Hong-Kong, 2001

Wittke V (1997) Online in die Do-it-yourself-Gesellschaft? - Zu Widersprüchlichkeiten in der Entwicklung von Online-Diensten und denkbaren Lösungsformen. In: Werle R, Lang C (eds.) Modell Internet? Campus, Frankfurt/Main: pp 93-112

Business-to-business electronic commerce: the convergence of relationships, networked supply chains and value webs[1][2]

Rolf T. Wigand[3]

Department of Information Science, CyberCollege, University of Arkansas at Little Rock, USA

Abstract

Global competition, ever-increasing customer demands and rising development costs are altering the way business is being conducted. The dot com bubble burst has shown little if any impact on developments on the business-to-business side of electronic commerce. Firms are aware that they have no choice but to develop stronger and closer ties with suppliers on the buy-side and with their business customers on the sell-side of the extended enterprise. Massive investments are made in this area of electronic commerce and these efforts are happening rather quietly, almost in the background. This implies that every part of the supply chain is being challenged, from sourcing to procurement and from order fulfillment to customer service.

What is emerging from these developments is the networked supply chain in which systems, processes and relationships (internal and external) are effectively integrated. In turn, these efforts constitute the very essence of adding value in the interconnected supply chain which has become intelligent with its emphasis on collaboration, visibility, real-time information and knowledge management. Through networked supply chain management participants can operate within value webs as a unified entity, enabling them to share actions that were previously isolated activities. The resulting integration, coupled with ensuring real-time, accurate and accessible information between supply chain planning and execution systems, reduces redundancy and improves efficiency. Moreover, this permits firms within the chain to communicate information about market demand directly,

---

[1] This chapter benefited from a research study conducted for the Giga Information Group, Cambridge, MA, in 2002 for which the author expresses his gratitude.

[2] The author gratefully acknowledges the insight and comments received from Dr. Kurt Sundermeyer, Research and Technology (RIC/EN), Manufacturing and Supply Nets, DaimlerChrysler AG, Berlin, Germany.

[3] E-mail: rtwigand@ualr.edu

resulting in minimizing inventory buildup, sustaining quality and building profitable operations.

Moreover, networked supply chains speed time to market through collaboration with suppliers and customers.

These advances in technology, competition and relationship expectations force firms to rethink and restructure their supply chain relationships and demonstrate how business strategy and technology are converging. Whether firms want to or not, they will need to form alliances (value constellations) enabling, but also forcing them to collaborate closely and continually to serve the targeted customer base. These supply chain management challenges facing firms are formidable and they require substantive and extensive changes to existing practices. Future business-to-business electronic commerce will be enabled across a network of enterprises collaborating closely and continually.

Introduction

All chapters in this book focus on various aspects of electronic commerce electronic commerce since the dot com bubble burst. Just reading the popular press reflecting the current economic malaise, slow economic growth and stock market doldrums, appear to have triggered for many people a somewhat negative outlook on electronic commerce. This is, however, a rather illogical conclusion. There is no question that many casualties have littered the dot com landscape, but we should also examine these casualties' underlying business models. Maybe they were doomed in the first place no matter if they would have been traditional or dot com businesses. Some may also have been ahead of their time and just because they failed this does not necessarily preclude the possibility of future success. Moreover, Manyika and Nevens (2002) argue that many companies spent heavily on information technology (IT) during the pre-dot com bubble years, but did not gain the hoped for benefits, because they tackled IT and business levers that did not count.

Maybe one may argue that the dot com crash had a negative impact on certain Internet applications and technologies, but the underlying concept of electronic commerce, specifically leveraging the Internet and WWW to improve business continues to be as sound as before the dot com bubble burst. We are arguing below that firms do not have a choice but to embrace electronic commerce if they want to stay competitive and gain strategic advantage. Increasingly we realize that business-to-business (B2B) electronic commerce must be an essential component of any business strategy. Electronic commerce applications in the area of supply chain management have enjoyed considerable growth since the dot com bubble burst. Actually, we can observe massive investments on the buy- or downstream-side (supply chain management, logistics), as well as the sell- or upstream-side (customer relationships) of focal firms. These developments are observable along the entire value chain, ranging from potentially third-tier suppliers to a focal firm's customers' customers' customer. Forrester Research (2002) estimates that the U. S. investments alone spent on supply chain management (SCM) software purchases and rental fees will rise from $5.54 billion in 2002 to $5.98 billion in 2003, $ 6.16 billion in 2004 and $ 6.18 billion in 2005, respectively. One should examine this progression of spending considering that the corresponding figure for 2000 was merely $3.85 billion, followed by $4.80 billion in 2001. From manufacturers to retailers current supply chain developments are driven by the search for ways to keep inventory levels down and production levels up while realizing just-in-time delivery relationships. Supply planning and optimization efforts may help achieve those goals.

Broadly speaking, firms are facing three sets of challenges in the twenty-first century:

1. An *e*-economy reflective of the broad business environment in which global commerce is being conducted,
2. An *e*-business enterprise with the capability to exchange value (money, goods, services and information) electronically, effortlessly and without friction, and
3. Challenges to distinct competencies resulting in new types of competition.

Sooner or later something fundamental in a firm's or industry's business world will change and a new type of competition will emerge. This has been observed with the advent of electronic commerce for ten years or longer and the various forms of disintermediation (Benjamin and Wigand 1995; Wigand and Benjamin 1996; Wigand 1997) are examples of this. Although a segment in a value chain may be disintermediated or *leapfrogged*, the subsequent reintermediaries are typically different players and thus new competitors and a new type of competition have surfaced. When envisioning a business' evolutionary trajectory over time a challenge to distinct competencies may be depicted as an inflection point at which the trajectory bifurcates: (a) the trajectory for the traditional business moves downward, i.e. the business declines or discontinues to exist, or (b) the business moves on to new heights. Although it is difficult, if not impossible, to make predictions about point 3 in our dynamic and fast moving world of electronic commerce, this chapter addresses points 1 and 2 in particular.

In many ways, firms have no choice but invest in their relationships on both sides, i.e. with suppliers and with customers. In order to stay competitive and to develop just-in-time supply and delivery concepts, firms have no choice but to embrace these ever-tighter relationships. These relationships, in turn, can only be realized if they are conducted electronically, resulting in challenging questions with regard to trust, as well as boundaries of the firm. It is becoming increasingly difficult today to clearly delineate where a firm's "boundary" actually is, as these described relationships and underlying mutual trust create increasingly an operating environment of a *family of firms* (see Figure 1).

No doubt these developments have been massively shaped and challenged by the Internet and the World Wide Web (WWW). We must realize that these challenges should be seen in light of ever-ongoing traditional challenges that manufacturers face: Cost reduction efforts, service and customer focus, quality improvement, labor efficiency and unions, inventory and warehousing issues, run lengths and manufacturing flexibility, design for manufacturability, product reliability and others.

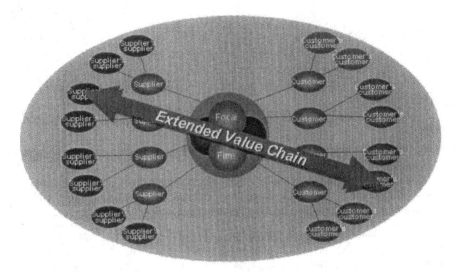

Fig. 1. Value creation has shifted to the entire extended value chain

In a way, we could argue that the Internet has indeed turned segments of the economy upside down. Especially with regard to supply chains, accounting for much of the industrial world's economic output, greater efficiencies and effectiveness have been achieved and the shape of these supply chains are changing drastically. Broadly speaking, we observe that vertically linked chains tying manufacturers, wholesalers and retailers together (Benjamin and Wigand 1995; Wigand 1996, 1997) via well-established, long-term and continuous supply contracts are gradually being replaced by more horizontal structures, especially as buyers gain access electronically to a wider choice of suppliers. Underlying these developments is the recognition that largely supply chains are being re-configured into *demand chains* (see Figure 2). Supply usually is driven by forecasts that are notoriously weak and unreliable predictors of demand. Demand chains are viewed as a set of links in that chain through which materials flow as a pipeline and that this pipeline can be managed and regulated at several strategic control points based on actual consumption (rather than forecasts). We also should note that with ever-increasing supply/demand chains being interconnected, actually creating a network, a firm may be a customer at one moment and a supplier (to the firm they bought from) the next. Being able to develop such a network and use it effectively, is becoming of increasing importance to firms and industries, but we must realize that the need and very existence of these networks is created by this *duality in relationships*.

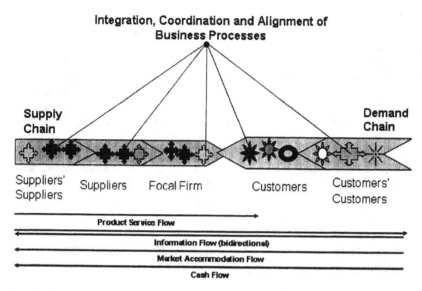

Fig. 2. The interfacing of the supply and demand chains

This, in turn, forces firms to literally rethink all features of their business models, including logistics, just-in-time delivery, inventory management systems, warehousing, marketing and pricing strategies. Extrapolating these developments to the level of the worldwide market one must recognize that this process may have massive and far-reaching implications. In this context we are analogously reminded of Archimedes who reportedly claimed, "Give me a lever long enough and a fulcrum on which to place it, and I shall move the world." Today global firms and manufacturers are attempting to reconceptualize and redefine their relationships with suppliers in an effort to lower costs, work closer together, increase speed and agility, reduce risk, raise quality and to become jointly more competitive. In the global market context these firms seem to apply Archimedian thinking as they are moving beyond the tactical sphere of procurement, purchasing and sourcing into the strategic realm of global supply management. We know that about 22 percent of the world economy's gross domestic product is comprised of manufacturing-materials procurement and when applying these efficiency gains to the global economy deep effects (including labor and inflation) are likely to be realized.

Given these developments, we define supply chain management as follows: Supply Chain Management (SCM) encompasses the activities of networks of businesses involved in the extraction of raw materials, transformation into tangible finished goods and delivery with any complementary services to the end consumer. SCM is the execution of firms' operations such as managing warehouses, inventory supplies and distribution channels. This may be broken down into two types of SCM: execution and planning. Execution tracks the storage and movement of products, as well as the demand and management of materials, information and financial data among suppliers, manufacturing, distribution and customers. Planning, including planning applications, addresses how to find the best way to fill an order on a set of operating constraints and may utilize, e.g., optimization software. Supply chain optimization is about finding bottle-necks in a firm's operations and how to eliminate these. How to fill an unexpected large order, e.g., is a decision to be made in which application software may provide solutions. One should note though that software is only part of the SCM battle, i.e. much human coordination and communication is required to make the systems work. One of the main challenges today is the merger and blending between planning systems and message information technology, a prerequisite and requirement for keeping people along the supply chain on the same page. This will make supply chains transparent and visible and allow users to open their planning systems to suppliers and customers over extranets (Wigand et al. 2002).

Current evolution of and key ingredients in electronic supply chain management

Current challenges in electronic supply chain management (eSCM) center around four areas: (1) Visibility, (2) integration, (3) real-time information operations, and (4) collaboration. These four areas may also be viewed as today's key ingredients in successful eSCM. The 'visibility' feature is already being offered by some software vendors today. 'Integration' and 'real-time information operations' are necessary prerequisites for the *royal discipline* of 'collaboration'. It is being labeled *royal* here in that 'collaboration' may be viewed as enabling highly desirable organization-spanning and yet self-sufficient, as well as self-sustaining planning. These topics are frequently identified in the SCM literature, especially in the field's leading journal *Supply Chain Management Review*. Moreover, these topics emerged as well in a recent study of 50 eSCM software application users from various industries in a study conducted for the Giga Information Group (Wigand et al. 2002).

Visibility

Supply chain visibility (SCV) solutions are designed to improve the flow of information among parties at all levels of the supply chain. SCV gives a unified view of complex, multi-process operations. Simply put it is about making information visible to the right people in the right way at the right time.

Definition. Supply Chain Visibility is the ability to see what is going on in a firm's supply base, from the raw materials end of the supply chain all the way out into the firm's demand chain and the needs of customers, possibly the customers' customers.

For a chief purchasing officer and others on the production side, having visibility probably means knowing inventory levels at the firm's suppliers and the suppliers' manufacturing schedules and capacities. Marketing chiefs and their sell-side colleagues want visibility into the demand chain: what do the company's customers want, how much of it do they want, where do they want it and what sales channel is most appropriate for that customer? Transportation managers and those on the fulfillment and execution side want to have a clear picture of where the company's inbound and outbound shipments are at any given moment. For all these supply chain stakeholders, the benefits come down to faster time-to-market, reduced inventories (and therefore lower costs), higher quality and greater customer satisfaction.

Scope: Ideally, the concept of visibility should encompass all the parties involved in supply chain activities.

Key concepts: Conceptually speaking, when a consumer buys a roll of paper towels, the forest products company should immediately know that they need to cut another tree to send to the pulp maker who supplies Procter & Gamble (P&G) so that P&G can make another roll of towels to send to the retailer.

Traditionally, a small, select group of individuals responsible for supply chain planning would provide the "magic" answers about the predictability of the supply chain. Visibility implies that people beyond these experts have a view of the activities and metrics that help measure the supply chain's effectiveness. These metrics are critical for optimizing customer relationship life-cycle models and increasing financial profitability. Furthermore, supply chain visibility enables the collaboration that can optimize these business processes.

Barriers. The biggest bottleneck to enabling visibility is that there are no common data standards or systems across the supply chain. Also, the technical and cultural obstacles to greater supply chain visibility remain significant. The technical challenges to a clear view into a firm's supply chain include both data and content issues. Data are critical because visibility assumes a smooth flow of accurate information among trading partners. The problem is not just moving data from one computer system to another. Rather, it is moving information through multiple systems both within an enterprise and among partners. Even when partners do establish bidirectional connections, they must ensure the information they are transmitting to each other is mutually intelligible, requiring the adoption of common standards and nomenclature.

At a more fundamental level, real-time visibility assumes a high level of automation among all partners in a supply chain and a continuous (or at least near-continuous) data flow, something that might not be possible for companies using the type of batch processing typically associated with electronic data interchange (EDI).

The cultural obstacles are believed to be even more daunting than the technical issues. For example, buying organizations looking to gain greater visibility into their suppliers' inventories may encounter resistance among suppliers reluctant to take on any additional expense or work that might be required. Going after information about a supplier's suppliers could raise the specter of disintermediation or, should the buyer take an interest in the supplier's cost structure, a price squeeze. On the other hand, the buying organization might hesitate to share proprietary information relating to demand or planned products, and purchasers may find it difficult to move from the traditionally antagonistic buyer-supplier relationship to one that is more collaborative with the value shared among partners.

In order for a supply chain visibility effort to be successful, it is essential that it makes the required information (forecasts, capacity, sales, inventory, etc.) visible only to authorized parties as designated by the information owner with clear restrictions on what is visible based on the user and company looking at the data.

Future. Despite the obstacles, changing market dynamics continue to push increasing numbers of companies toward greater supply chain visibility. In a consumer-driven economy, the time-to-market and cost reductions that greater visibility affords are compelling competitive advantages. No enterprise has reached the Holy Grail of 360-degree visibility, but many companies are spending considerable sums of money and endeavoring to gain a better view of at least part of their supply chain. They realize that the information flowing in this pipeline replaces physical assets and features with information. Goods flow in such a pipeline system just like the FedEx package flows in its pipeline and the package is trackable at all stages until it is delivered to the customer. In the long-run this supply chain, in accordance with our discussion on visibility, must resemble a *glass pipeline* linking the entire supply chain and enabling all partners to share, see, manage and control critical information pertaining to suppliers (forecasting, advanced planning, Manufacturing Resources Planning (MRPII), value sourcing), manufacturing [Enterprise Resource Planning (ERP), Collaborative Planning, Forecasting and Replenishment (CPFR), Materials Requirements Planning (MRP) and MRPII], advance planning, logistics (logistics software, forecasting), distribution (warehousing software, operations logistics), services (sales force automation, customer leadership operations), sales (sales force automation, customer leadership) and marketing (ERP, forecasting, advance planning, customer leadership operations). Such a *glass pipeline* not only delivers higher quality systems faster and cheaper among the above mentioned participating entities, the shared information among them can process customer feedback, identify problems and solutions, iterate and improve, streamline the entire process and share and distribute risks. When the glass pipeline is connected as a value chain to the WWW it becomes a two-way, real-time pipeline providing both flexibility and customer-based efficiency that were previously unattainable. This is also highly desirable for special event supply chain management when, e.g., a supplier is unable to deliver due to extreme weather conditions and other suppliers fill in the slack. Electronic commerce clearly is the most cost-effective way to link these segments allowing all partners to generate value from the information flow.

Integration

Supply Chain Integration (SCI) refers to a state where relevant information is transmitted quickly among trading partners, and where the partners are able to readily adjust their activities based on changes in requirements for material, production and delivery schedules. The information flow in a supply chain affects the timeliness of delivery to market. Hence it is extremely important to have proper communications in order to reduce inventory and increase inventory turns thereby reducing inventory holding cost. In a nutshell proper coordination is essential as information substitutes for material in a supply chain.

Today's firms face new opportunities to reduce cycle times, increase customer service, improve just-in-time delivery, develop tighter linkages with suppliers and customers, and further globalize supply chains. To achieve this, firms must address an array of issues addressing the concept of integration in supply chain management, including their customers, suppliers, as well as partners.

Definition. Integration is the collective incorporation and assimilation of processes that fit a focal company's size, structure (including the technological infrastructure), industry, and business model, ensuring an end-to-end process capable of delivering improved decisions and desired results of value to customers. Integration in the supply chain context includes all of the above considerations, as well this focal company's interfaces with its suppliers and customers.

Scope. Integration in supply chains not only includes a focal company, but also incorporates this focal company's suppliers and customers. Given how tightly interconnected firms are today to enable just-in-time delivery, focused attention on integration also requires such tight linkages with suppliers on the buy-side two or three tiers down the supply chain. Similar linkages over several tiers may extend on the sell-side to the customers as well (see Figure 1).

Key Concepts. Research has demonstrated that value is created through the integration, synchronization and coordination across four critical supply chain flows (see Figure 2):

1. *Product service flow,* representing the value-added movement of goods and services from the raw material provider to end customer.
2. *Market accommodation flow,* providing supply chain participants with visibility regarding timing and location of product consumption.
3. *Information flow,* the bi-directional exchange of transaction data and inventory status among supply chain partners.
4. *Cash flow,* which tends to move in the reverse direction of value-added activities, although it may flow in the same direction when promotions and rebates are involved.

These four flows occur in all supply chains. Researchers found that when coordination and integration were lacking in these flows, delays, redundancy and inefficiency resulted. To improve flows across a supply chain, individual competencies related to operations, planning and control, and behavioral dimensions of SCM must be integrated.

A firm's operational context within which SCM occurs is an important element and predictor of eSCM success. Operations integrates internal order fulfillment and replenishment processes with external work performed by the material and service providers and the distribution networks responsible for delivering products and services to customers. One may identify two types of operational integration: (1) internal and (2) external integration.

1. *Internal Integration:* Internal logistics integration focuses on the activities that link sourcing, production and replenishment into a seamless process capable of supporting end-customer requirements. The goal here is to achieve a high level of basic service at the lowest total cost. Many concepts have been mentioned in this context, but the three most important ones are: simplification, consolidation and internal "buy-ins".

2. *External Integration:* External integration links internal operations with both material and service providers and with customers. The goal is to create a seamless, synchronized supply chain that can more effectively respond to end-customer demand at the lowest total cost. Trade-offs occur among supply chain members to achieve the desired service/cost mix. Managing these trade-offs while sharing the risks and rewards calls for creative solutions to the cost-to-serve challenge. Here industry leaders strive for win-win outcomes to achieve long-term gains for the entire supply chain. One may identify four broad approaches to effective external integration: Resource focus, responsibility alignment, strategic compensation, and cooperative planning.

The Planning and Control Context: Integration in the planning and control context refers to the design, application and coordination of information technology and measurement systems to facilitate monitor and control the performance of purchasing, manufacturing, customer order fulfillment and resource planning. One may identify two types of planning and control integration: (1) technology and planning, (2) measurement.

1. *Technology and Planning Integration:* Integrated information processes and systems provide the input needed for plans that translate strategic goals into action and guide the activities of multiple supply chain participants. This task has become rather complex with the increasing flows of product, cash and information. Two concepts related to advanced technology and planning approaches are scan-based trading (SBT) (e.g., when a manufacturer assumes responsibility for store-shelf replenishment and "consigns" inventory to a retailer) and collaborative planning, forecasting and replenishment (CPFR). CPFR enables manufacturers and retailers to concentrate on improving sales, reducing waste and inefficiencies in the system, eliminating duplicate work activities and improving financial performance. Benefits of CPFR include: increased category sales and service levels, reduced inventory levels and shrinkage, improved forecast accuracy, enhanced ease-fill performance, higher profit and fewer forecast changes.

2. *Measurement Integration:* Integrated measurement systems are needed to create competitive advantage through high-performance logistics and supply chain capabilities. These systems must track operations both internally and externally among the supply chain participants. They must also reflect the operational performance of the overall supply chain, as well as the financial performance of individual companies. Integrated measurement systems are the basis for calibrating the many parts of the supply chain engine. Such measurement system can provide good metrics and strong measurement can provide timely feedback such that management can take corrective action and ensure superior results.

Research in this area suggests that the benefits of integrated measurement systems are:

- A cross-functional, multiorganizational measurement vision.
- Accurate performance data shared regularly with all members of the supply chain.
- Multiple, cascading measures that capture cross-functional and multiorganizational performance of supply chain processes.
- Performance measures aligned with internal budget allocation processes and internal and external reward structures.
- A focus on providing end-customer value.

Barriers. There are several barriers to SCM integration that can be identified:

- Lack of visibility of SCM activities
- Lack of internal support
- Misaligned measures, rewards and allocation processes
- Short-term performance focus
- Commingled product requirements
- Poor use of technology
- Lack of trust

At the behavioral level, one may also identify a number of barriers, including:

- Relationship integration
- Perception and recognition of value
- Trust

Future. Integration will continue to be an essential issue as eSCM will grow in importance for firms seeking to reduce costs, delays, redundancy and inefficiency; improve customer service and increase competitive differentiation. In these efforts processes requiring integration will extend past a focal firm's walls to embrace collaborative SCM and will face network scenarios. In years to come, most likely many solutions will be offered by vendors to manage this "messy middle," concerned with the aggregation, coordination and negotiation of multiple trading partners, all of which requiring the integration of their respective processes. Multiple model solutions are likely to suggest themselves, including many-to-many, one-to-many and one-to-one configurations. Firms undoubtedly will be challenged to sort through the resulting proliferation of solutions. Major players in this setting will attempt to architect a collaborative commerce strategy while focusing on the extended supply chain.

Real-time information operations

From a technology perspective, for many years there have been just three basic ways to communicate and collaborate electronically: by fax, e-mail or via electronic data interchange. All of these communication means have built-in delays.

Connecting front- and back-office functions with external supply-chain partners can dramatically improve the efficiency of manufacturing and distribution. Real-time event coordination allows contract, configuration, inventory, purchasing, and distribution systems to seamlessly interact using a rules-based event architecture.

The real time supply chain model combines the Internet's power with old business configurations and processes to remove old corporate confines and geographical limitations. It helps create a flawless path of information and communication flow among partners, suppliers, manufacturers, retailers and customers. Often manufacturers receive individual queries from customers about specific requests and it becomes imperative to respond within a very short time frame (such as for DaimlerChrysler AG being able to produce the so-called *5-day car* after an order has been received).

Definition. A real-time environment entails enterprise systems that talk to each other in real time and span from planning to execution. Real-time information flows accurately when and where needed in the electronic supply chain and is visible and retrievable by all partners.

Scope. Real Time Supply chains encompass all associations between a company and its customers, suppliers, and partners, such as business transactions, information sharing, and communications.

Key concepts. An appropriate network architecture helps provide total network integration, strengthens supplier and partner networks and resources. Security is a major consideration here.

The network application should be flawlessly integrated with the supply chain applications and other business processes.

Barriers. One major barrier will be overall acquisition and implementation costs.

Future. In a typical order fulfillment process in a real-time supply chain, a customer orders and chooses products online using graphical Web-based forms. Based on manufacturing specifications a configuration agent is made to make sure that the customer's order is producible. Subsequently, a globally accessible promise engine validates production slots based on customer orders and global execution standards. Consumer order information passes automatically through the real-time supply chain. The supplier's supplier obtains direct access to actionable requests as well as business data. This is made possible by the forecast and other information flowing between the customer's customer and the supplier's supplier. Consequently, the supplier's supplier is able to make the best decision for the customer's customer.

Collaboration

Collaboration or collaborative commerce is viewed by many authors in the field as an all-embracing philosophy. It requires companies to look beyond their four walls and join together to fulfill the ever-increasing demands and expectations of customers. It forces companies to foster new relationships, leading to better understanding of processes beyond normal traditions. In few words, collaboration then is viewed as an umbrella philosophy for a high speed, relationship-driven future.

Definition. Electronic collaboration (e-collaboration) is a set of electronically enabled interactions between and among enterprises, customers, suppliers and their employees to enhance value to customers. E-collaboration implies alignment of activities within an electronic medium driven by the need for mass customization (GartnerGroup 2000).

Scope. In terms of participation and benefits, there is considerable scope for every player. No matter if the company is big or small, it has a chance to play a role in the process of delivering goods or services to the customer. This brings in value to each and every participant, including the customer. The scope for more benefits is immense (e.g., lower inventory cost, increased productivity, better time to market).

Key concepts. For electronic collaboration (e-collaboration) to take place and be successful there are a few concepts and rules to consider:

1. E-collaboration requires people to work toward a *common goal* for the success of the entire chain. This may include, e.g., satisfying customer needs, producing better quality products or services or producing better collaboratively, as well as working on a very specific product specification from a customer.
2. *Sharing* of certain resources becomes inevitable. If two manufacturing companies are collaborating and one company is buying some products from a specific source and has extra space for other goods to be loaded on a truck, sharing this truck is an obvious example. This sharing may occur electronically through logistics programs
3. Companies need to *align or sacrifice some of their individual goals* in order to participate in a collaborative chain.
4. Companies must address *issues like:* change management, level-of sharing (need for protecting factors such as competitive edge, trade secrets, business model and more), organization politics, technology issues, and visibility.
5. *Effective interaction* with all third party supply partners, from independent sales agent to parts and service providers is essential.
6. *Sophisticated interaction* with the customer or customer base to define current and future demand in a real-time and ongoing basis.

Barriers. We identify a number of barriers to collaboration efforts in SCM:

- *Integration of business processes* to meet the needs of the collaborative chain. It is a collective planning and integration of process components that fits the company's size, structure, industry, and business model, ensuring an end-to-end process that's capable of delivering improved decisions and the desired results. The importance is the need for accommodating processes and functionalities, which ensure the smooth and effective functioning of the collaborative chain. In all this is a very complex process.
- *Monitoring the performance of the chain* is a very vital issue that needs to be addressed if this collaboration has to work. We need to make sure, all participants do their jobs and accomplish their tasks on time. This requires better visi-

bility, deep into the functional operations of the participating partners. More of an end-to-end monitoring and visibility of the entire chain is needed. Tools need to be developed for achieving these efficiencies, which, in turn, is very complex.

- *Organizational issues* are critical opponents to this philosophy. Organizations need to sacrifice their traditional business model and imbibe the philosophy of collaboration. This is a risky and critical situation and careful decisions need to be made on issues like: How much can we share? What is, the level of openness and visibility of the business functionalities and supply chain be offered to other partners? What are the core-functionalities of the firm? What is the cost of integrating the processes? Numerous other issues could be addressed in this area as well.
- *Understanding partners and confidence building measures* takes much time. It is very difficult to bring in two competing partners and ask them to open up and collaborate. This is a Herculean task and sometimes might lead to disastrous situations.
- *Security issues and technology reliability.* These two barriers alone are major undertakings in their own right. They are never-ending issues and addressing them makes collaboration very difficult.

The list of barriers does not end here, as one may think of many others. Although overcoming these barriers is difficult, it is possible, as firms become aware of the benefits of collaborating on the virtual medium.

Future. There will be a certain level of e-collaboration taking place due to the drive from the technology side and the availability of the virtual medium. Indeed, there are opportunities for companies to leverage these benefits and bring in more value to the firm. But the success of achieving total collaboration is very slim due to the very nature of human beings. People are initially hesitant to share and change things. At some point, there will be misunderstandings which might hinder the collaborative process or might indeed break the relationship in the chain. This will lead to a whole new world of issues, which in turn is very complex and chaotic. There are other issues like technology, global politics and economics that are very volatile and dynamic with time. These will definitely affect collaborative processes.

We have shown how the above four ingredients, i.e. visibility, integration, real-time information operations and collaboration, are key elements in the proposed *glass pipeline* and how such a pipeline adds value to all participants and entities within the supply chain.

The following section elevates this discussion to a conceptually higher level by showing how we may extend the current view of value chains in a supply chain to value-adding networks and value webs.

Leveraging the power of the WWW: from value-added chains to value networks and value webs

In the past the value chain has been viewed traditionally as a linear, step-wise and linked phenomenon (e.g., Porter 1985; Porter and Millar 1985). Each link in the supply chain may be viewed as such a linear value chain component. When links are added up or viewed in their entirety we may then speak of the entire value chain (embedded within the supply chain). Accordingly, the concept of the value chain divides a firm's activities into technologically and economically distinct activities it performs to do business. In their entirety these are viewed as "value activities." The actual value generated is measured by the amount that buyers are willing to pay for a product or service. A firm is profitable when the value created exceeds the costs of performing the value activities. This perspective, however, i.e. reflective of a linear, step-wise view, is no longer adequate and correct when viewing value chains, especially in the e-business realm. The linear steps "plan + buy + make + move + sell" are no longer appropriate and this is no longer how the supply chain function works. SCM systems of the 1990s and earlier were typically implemented accordingly, i.e. one point-to-point or hub-and-spoke basis. The linear chain however has evolved into a networked value chain with everyone being connected.

Recognizing the above developments, Rayport and Sviokla (1994, 1995) differentiate between the physical and virtual value chain and refer to the latter as *marketspace*, denoting that there has been a move from the marketplace to the marketspace. This perspective is reflected in Figure 3 below.

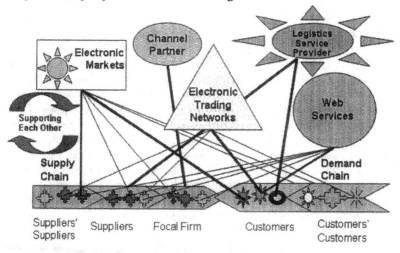

Fig. 3. The marketspace structure and its connections to supply and demand chains

Observing the above developments, however, we may recognize yet another conceptual level, i.e. the value matrix or value web.

A virtual value chain, however, may be more linked to a matrix (e.g., see Rayport and Sviokla 1995) or web, more appropriately labeled the *Value Web* (Wigand 1998) that is accessible at each point and freely configurable.

A *Value Web* (see Figure 4) is a permanent or temporary web of independent companies, has no hierarchy, no vertical integration, and enjoys fluid, flexible, and dynamic relationships (Wigand 1998; see also, Riemer et al. 2001; Selz 1999).

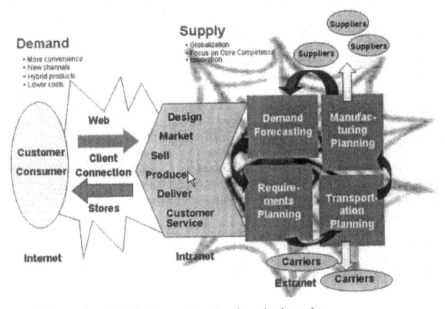

Fig. 4. From value-added chains to value networks and value webs

Before this model of a Web-based, networked value chain can be implemented, firms must work through a profound transition, starting with full support at the top and such a transition will permeate the firm and its processes inside and out. Key requirements for success are that everyone in the chain is linked (integration) and that information is available so that all participants are aware of the requirements and can act upon events as needed (collaboration). Moreover, additional key requirements are to have visibility of where the product is, its status and get alerts when expected events are not occurring. All of this should occur in real-time such that participants can be proactive in making sure that the product gets delivered.

Once a firm has gone through the initial steps of implementation, network-based SCM applications need to be implemented to improve, e.g., production processes or demand planning internally. Next these applications need to be rolled out down the chain such that true integration can occur and making possible that the firm can coordinate its supply chain activities in real-time with trading partners. This may sound very straight-forward, but as always the devil is in the details. Although integration is essential, networks can be fickle and tricky mechanisms. It is not uncommon that fixing one problem reveals another that must be addressed immediately. Similarly, improving internal processes often requires the examination of relationships in greater detail with what we previously called "outsiders."

Although the benefits of integrated eSCM are widely accepted and the resulting strengthened relationships are welcomed, the depth of the desired and needed integration may be questioned. Quickly squabbles and disagreement may surface when firms need to agree how deep they should or must go into their respective systems and databases. A jointly agreeable level of "visibility" must be found that the partners share. At times key bits of information need to be extracted rather than entire files. It can be seen that integration depth is likely to vary depending on the solution desired and level of pain the partners are willing to live with. Firms have sprung up offering integration services, often in an outsourced relationship, offering multi-tier process integration permitting firms to gain greater, deeper visibility and offering adaptive mechanisms for greater flexibility as the trading environment might change. Widespread integration is not possible without standardized software such as XML and variations thereof.

Several examples exist where such value webs are in operation today. ChemConnect Inc. of San Francisco, e.g., matches prospective buyers with sellers in cyberspace. ChemConnect developed a global market for numerous chemical products essential for the plastics and other industries. Manufacturing plants that in the past relied on one or two suppliers of hard to find products such as trichloroethylene or ferro silicon may now shop around globally for the best price and deal.

The author was involved in a project for PowerGasSmart, a company in central New York, offering firms in New York to subscribe to an electricity supply service that hourly (almost dynamically) checked for the best electricity rate among 26 approved electricity suppliers. Among those suppliers is Florida Power & Light, a major player at the national electricity wholesale level, which can produce electricity in Florida, ship that electricity to New York and sell it cheaper than any New York-based electricity producer is able to. As can be seen, among the 26 suppliers instant competition existed from the beginning. Subscribers to PowerGasSmart were able to find the cheapest electricity supplier each hour and then switch from one cheapest supplier to the next cheapest each hour, etc. Carrier, the air conditioning company in Syracuse, NY, had at the time a monthly electricity bill of over $450,000. We calculated for a given month that if Carrier would have been a subscriber, Carrier could have saved itself about $150,000/month. PowerGasSmart then could be seen as a value web or matrix that a buyer took advantage of each hour and then pulled out, yet revisited that value web in 60 minutes around the clock.

FreeMarkets Inc. of Pittsburgh By seamlessly facilitates the connection of the processes, people and information required in global supply management initiatives. The company can organize online auctions for suppliers bidding on purchaser contracts for industrial parts, raw materials and commodities. Several thousand suppliers from almost 50 countries have participated in its auctions. The request for quote (RFQ) process typically involves reams of paperwork and hours or days spent inputting information. This process is rife with errors, lost time and missed savings opportunities. Via systems like FreeMarkets, all potential or invited bidders receive the same RFQ at the same time electronically, and at a predetermined date and hour bidding for the components, products or services can determined date and hour bidding for the components, products or services can start. FreeMarkets provides firms with the ability to gain significant reductions in total cost of ownership (TCO) of goods and services, and to realize more seamless cross-functional collaboration between sourcing and supply chain management. Moreover, this standardizes supply management processes and gains control, accelerates knowledge capture, transfer, and sharing while creating sourcing intelligence, as well as gain greater real-time results visibility across the global supply management organization.

Yet other models follow the "industrial communities" paradigm such as VerticalNet Inc. of Horsham, PA serving a wide cross-section of industry. Others permit the bidding on such items as biological matter or office supplies.

These developments and opportunities suggest that we are moving toward a buyer- or consumer-centric situation, in which even a single transaction by a consumer may trigger multiple transactions across the supply chain. In order to be successful in this setting, firms need to learn how to take control over the changes in their supply chains. In turn, this suggests that firms need to become even more agile and flexible. The concept of flow manufacturing, i.e. products are made only as orders are received (as perfected by, e.g., Dell), is of even greater importance today. To eliminate bottle-necks, flow-based production lines are designed so that each step in the manufacturing process takes roughly the same amount of time. Potential benefits include lower inventory costs and fewer defective products. Granted, not all manufacturing situations and industries lend themselves for applying this concept, but there is plenty of room across many industries and products.

Flow manufacturing, in turn, also helps inventory management which by itself has made great strides over the last 15 years. Many examples may be cited in which inventory management allows firms to run down their large, expensive stockpiles, making possible lower consumer prices and increasing a firm's competitiveness. One should realize though that these gains were largely achieved through expensive electronic data interchange systems (EDI) (Wigand 1994) physically linking firms' inventory databases and were limited to firms wealthy enough to afford them. This is one reason why Wal-mart Stores, Inc. was able to expand its dominance during the last decade.

It seems that with the opportunities of the WWW (see Figure 4) one may expect a level playing field to form. Flexible application systems can link firms' databases via the Internet at much lower cost and with greater precision through the use of ERP, as well as data mining applications. This potentially makes the small retailer, e.g., a player in this environment reducing stockpiling costs (by enabling continuous replenishment) and, by linking to Web-based customer sales systems, allowing for more accurate control of the flow of goods in and out of their stores.

References

Benjamin R, Wigand RT (1995) Electronic Markets and Virtual Value Chains on the Information Superhighway. Sloan Management Review 36(2):62–72

Forrester Research (2002) SCM Software Purchases and Rental Fees (U. S. Market). Cambridge, MA

GartnerGroup (2000) The Evolving New Economy. Gartner Special Report, Stamford, CT, The GartnerGroup

Manyika JM, Nevens TM (2002) Technology after the Bubble: IT will rise again—but only if the providers learn how to help their customers make money. The McKinsey Quarterly, 4, Technology

Porter ME (1985) Competitive Advantage. Free Press, New York

Porter ME, Millar VE (1985) How Information Gives You Competitive Advantage. Harvard Business Review, July-August:149–160

Rayport JF, Sviokla JJ (1994) Managing in the Marketspace. Harvard Business Review, November-December:141–150

Rayport JF, Sviokla JJ (1995) Exploiting the Virtual Value Chain. Harvard Business Review, November-December:75–85

Riemer K, Klein S, Selz D (2001) Classification of Dynamic Organizational Forms and Coordination Roles. Unpublished paper. Retrievable at: http://www.wi.uni-muenster. de/wi/literatur/e2001/Riemer_et_al-classification.pdf

Selz D (1999) Value Webs: Emerging Forms of Fluid and Flexible Organizations. Dissertation St. Gallen, # 2310, Difo-Druck, Bamberg

Wigand RT (1997) Electronic Commerce: Definition, Theory and Context. The Information Society 13 (3):1–16

Wigand RT (1994) Electronic Data Interchange in the United States of America: Selected Issues and Trends. In Kilian W et al. Electronic Date Interchange aus ökonomischer und juristischer Sicht: Forschungsbericht zu dem von der Volkswagenstiftung geförderten Forschungsprojekt ELTRADO (Elektronische Transaktionen von Dokumenten zwischen Organisationen) - mit Beiträgen von Amelia H. Boss und Rolf T. Wigand zur Situation von EDI in den USA. Nomos Verlagsgesellschaft, Baden-Baden, pp 369–391

Wigand RT (1998) Emerging Value Webs: A New Business Model? Unpublished Paper

Wigand RT, Benjamin RI (1996) Electronic Commerce: Effects on Electronic Markets. Journal of Computer-Mediated Communication 1 (3)

Wigand RT, Picot A, Reichwald R (1997) Information, Organization and Management: Expanding Markets and Corporate Boundaries. Wiley, Chichester

Wigand RT, Lakshminarayan K, Siow J, Ghadiali Y (2002) Metrics and Measurement in Supply Chain Management (SCM). A Report Submitted to the Giga Information Group, Little Rock, AR: Department of Information Science, University of Arkansas at Little Rock

Part 4:
Mobile technology moves on

Mobile commerce technologies and services: a SME user's perspective

Carleen F. Maitland[1]

School of Information Sciences and Technology, The Pennsylvania State
University, University Park, USA

Abstract

Despite recent declines in the expectations for information and communications
technologies, advances in mobile and wireless technologies continue, particularly
at the organizational level. The use of these technologies and the services they deliver will be shaped by a variety of factors, both technical and managerial. In addition to recent advances in access technologies, advances in organizational and
mobile computing technologies will shape the nature of mobile commerce services. The acceptance of these services will be determined by the relative advantages they present as well as their ability to match the skills and needs of users.
Small-to-medium sized enterprises (SMEs) and individuals (or employees) em-
body unique combinations of skills and needs. Skills that enable these users to
take advantage of mobile commerce services are shaped primarily by previous experience with the Internet, e-commerce and mobile telephony. Furthermore, needs
of SMEs, including minimization of network management requirements related to
security, backup and data integrity, as well as ease of integration with existing systems and mediation services that make explicit the benefits of the technology and
service, will inform their adoption decisions. Although recent experience has
demonstrated that the market acceptance of ICT services has many uncertainties,
if these user skills and needs are taken into account in the design of mobile commerce technologies and services, they may provide SMEs with information processing and communication technologies that help them compete successfully.

---

[1] E-mail: cmaitland@ist.psu.edu

Introduction

During the late 1990s the rapid growth of electronic commerce markets and services provided motivation for technology developers, managers and researchers alike to focus attention on organizational uses of information and communication technologies (ICTs). Despite the recent decline in the perceived importance of these technologies for achieving organizational goals, the search for productivity enhancing ICT-based technologies continues. One area ripe with innovations is that of mobile and wireless technologies.

While skeptics view the development of mobile commerce and its underlying technologies as old wine in new bottles, others claim that mobile and wireless technologies provide communication channels that create the potential for new and exciting services. Characteristics such as increased ubiquity, accessibility, reachability, localization and personalization, serve as new bases for value (Baldi and Thaung 2002). In addition to these characteristics, it is expected that new bases for value are also created by the diversity of contexts in which mobile commerce will take place. For example, value creation can be based on time-critical arrangements, spontaneous decision needs, entertainment needs, efficiency ambitions and mobile situations (Anckar and D'Incau 2002). Furthermore, services are expected to be both passive, where the transfer of data occurs without action on the part of the end user (such as email receipt, status monitoring, and automatic updates) and active (such as shopping, information gathering, and appliance management) (Senn 2000). Finally, perhaps one of the most important characteristics of mobile commerce is that it resolves what has been a difficult issue for electronic commerce: payment.

Whether or not mobile commerce ventures will be able to make profitable services from these potential sources of value, the basic platform for the services, mobile/wireless access and computing technologies, are being deployed. The provision of services over these networks is likely to require a broad set of actors, with increased importance for the role of middleware providers (Maitland et al. 2003; Varshney et al. 2000). Although consumer services will also rely on middleware, as in e-commerce the m-commerce market segment where these services are likely to be most critical is the business services market. As consumers of mobile commerce services, organizations will only adopt those technologies and services that match critical organizational needs (improved efficiency, productivity and coordination) and that can be adopted easily by employees given their current skill sets.

In this chapter the potential for mobile commerce services are assessed by first examining the advances of mobile/wireless access technologies and mobile computing, particularly in the context of organizational computing. With this discussion as a basis, attention is then turned to the users' perspective. Although technological advances create the possibility for mobile commerce, the skills and needs of the users will also play a role in determining which services will succeed. Both individual employees and small-to-medium sized enterprises (SMEs) are examined. Considering mobile commerce from the user's perspective makes explicit the diversity of skills and needs, which in turn may provide the basis for a broader range of services.

From e- to m-commerce technologies

The meaning of the term m-commerce, similar to its predecessor e-commerce, is likely to evolve as experience with the medium grows. The evolution may lead, as it did with e-commerce, to a differentiation between transactions with consumers and transactions within and between firms (i.e. e-business versus e-commerce). Similar to e-commerce, m-commerce or m-business will rely on advances in middleware and other computing technologies, which are referred to by developers as *mobile commerce systems* (Lee and Ke 2001). Expanding this concept, if such 'systems' are provided through an application service provider, they could be referred to as *mobile commerce services*. Thus, as referred to here mobile commerce services are a sub-section of the broader m-commerce universe, and are likely to have organizations as their primary clients.

Considering organizations and their employees as potential users of mobile commerce services raises several questions. First, how will the adoption of mobile commerce services be influenced by advances in access technologies? Second, how well do changes in access technologies support or undermine advances in organizational computing and mobile computing? And finally, what do we currently know about the likely use of m-commerce services in organizations and can a consideration of the technologies provide a more nuanced view? Each of these questions is addressed in turn.

Mobile/wireless access technologies

The access technologies through which mobile or wireless users connect to a network are the foundation for high quality mobile commerce services. Recent advances in three types of access technologies (mobile telecommunication network infrastructure, wireless local and wide area networks, and Bluetooth technology) have provided optimism for the potential wide-spread deployment of advanced mobile and wireless services. While the individual characteristics of each of these technologies are significant on their own, a crucial and more complicated factor will be their interoperability.

Key characteristics in the mobile telecommunications network infrastructure are the trends such as decreasing cell sizes, decreasing power requirements for handsets, a migration to packet switching and increased channel bandwidth. For the user these developments have resulted in smaller handsets, a packet switched connection that is 'always on' (similar to a dedicated Internet connection), and the possibility to transfer large files such as pictures and video. The roll out of new network infrastructure is in many cases occurring in phases, starting with various second generation (2G) digital technologies (GSM, TDMA), moving to 2.5G technologies (GPRS, EDGE) and then on to a version of one of three third generation (3G) technologies. The three 3G standards accepted by the International Telecommunication Union are wideband CDMA, CDMA 2000 and the Chinese standard TD-SCDMA. The available bandwidth from these new technologies will vary depending on the network infrastructure, the network design, and the management of the data channels. The type of network infrastructure available to users will depend on a variety of factors, including the existing network infrastructure, the strategies employed by network operators, and whether or not the national government has made spectrum available. To date, users in Europe and parts of Asia are the most likely to have access to advanced mobile network technologies.

Advances in access technologies have also occurred in the area of wireless networks. The most popular wireless local area network technology is IEEE 802.11b (also known as Wi-Fi). The 802.11b technology allows for wireless transmission at approximately 11 Mbps for indoor distances up to several hundred feet and outdoor distances up to several miles (assuming line of sight and other transmission criteria) as an unlicensed use of the 2.4 GHz band. The deployment of 802.11b technology is growing rapidly, which creates a variety of advantages such as lower costs, a knowledgeable user base, and advanced applications. Furthermore, the technology is also being tested for use as a wireless wide area network. Proponents of this 'expanded use' of 802.11b envision a series of interconnected wireless networks that could serve as the basis for extremely wide area (even at the national scale) coverage in an unlicensed spectrum band.

An alternative network technology, 802.11a, transmits at up to 54 Mbps at typically shorter distances. The advantages of 802.11a are its larger bandwidth and ease of system design due to the larger number of channels, however it is slightly more expensive than 802.11b. A third standard 802.11g, which combines the best of 11a and b, is expected to be available in 2003 (Molta 2002).

A third wireless access technology is Bluetooth. Bluetooth was developed through a special interest group (SIG) consortium that includes 3Com, Agere, Ericsson, IBM, Intel, Microsoft, Motorola, Nokia, and Toshiba. The Bluetooth transceiver transmits over a maximum range of 10 meters at up to 1Mbps. The second generation of the technology will allow up to 2 Mbps. The technology includes a frequency hop scheme that allows devices to communicate in areas with high levels of electromagnetic interference as well as built-in encryption and verification. Bluetooth connections can be point-to-point or multipoint.

Convergence between the three access technologies is planned. Within the 802.11 technologies it is expected that network interface cards (NICs) will be deployed that support all three (a,b and g) technologies and automatically select the best system available. Also, NICs that combine the 802.11 wireless with mobile radio GPRS technology are expected. Chip designs that combine 802.11 and Bluetooth technology are also being refined for mass distribution. Although Bluetooth has significant implications as a stand alone technology, when combined with wireless LANs it represents an important bridge between computers and devices that were once connected through network cables. The 802.11 and Bluetooth combinations take advantage of the fact that the center transmit frequency for both technologies is the same, 2.4GHz.

Needless to say, the management of these different access modes and seamless interconnection and roaming between networks present some major hurdles. Until widespread adoption occurs it will be difficult to assess how well they work together and how complicated configuring multiple devices will be. Furthermore, it might be some time before applications are able to operate on multiple platforms. For example, while checking 'mobile email' on a mobile handset may be easy, accessing that same email via a wireless network through the Internet may be more challenging.

In assessing the potential of these various access technologies one cannot ignore the widely varying economics behind them. While mobile network technologies require licenses, and, hence, hefty fees to operate, a wireless network provider makes use of unlicensed (no fee required) spectrum. Thus, mobile network operators may have economic disincentives to allow users to access content through means other than their mobile network. These economic differences combined with concerns over transmission interference in the unlicensed spectrum have led governments to reassess their spectrum management policies (see Commission of the European Communities 2003; Australian Communications Commission 2003; FCC 2002).

Organizational computing and m-commerce

The success of mobile commerce services will depend partly on the ways these mobile/wireless access technologies are deployed in organizations. This deployment, in turn, will be shaped by the organization's particular computing arrangements. The interaction between these computing arrangements and access technologies will also be affected by trends in mobile computing, which requires consideration of the relationship between the user and their environment as well as that between the user and the access network.

Organizational computing arrangements have undergone a transition in the last 10 to 15 years. Currently, the dominant form of organizational computing is the client/server model where clients (desktop computers) are connected through a fixed network to a central server. This arrangement is a hybrid of pure centralized or decentralized network architectures. In such a network the server manages network traffic, provides a central storage facility and a centralized mechanism for handling security issues. Security features include virus blocking and enterprise firewall provision.

The server also makes centralized applications possible. The advantages of this configuration are savings on deployment to large numbers of end users and reduced storage requirements for end users, particularly when large, critical but infrequently used applications are involved. The disadvantages are that use of the application depends on network connectivity, whose quality may vary, and system-wide implications of poor server performance and outages.

In addition to the transformation to the client/server model, organizational computing has also faced the Internet innovation. This required a transition from stand alone dial up access to networked desktop access. This naturally brought computing and telecommunications staffs closer together, often leading to a merger of the two. This transition to desktop access was in some cases facilitated by the simultaneous trend toward a client/server model as Internet access became a centralized service within the organization.

Organizational and mobile computing

Given this fixed client-server network architecture found in many organizations, one must consider how it will serve the needs of mobile users. Thus, researchers in mobile computing are studying the extent to which our computing facilities for the fixed environment can be transferred to a mobile environment, or whether mobile applications require fundamental changes in the way computing is organized and managed. At its core mobile computing is concerned with increasing our capability to physically move computing services with us. As we take our computing services with us, it is naturally of interest to have these computing devices function in a variety of environments. From here it is possible to adjust the focus from one of pure mobility to one that accepts mobility constraints for increased interaction between computing devices and the environment. This is the area of focus in pervasive computing, where researchers assume the computer has the capability to obtain information from the environment in which it is embedded. The computer utilizes the information to dynamically build models of computing, and in an intelligent environment computing and communicating are reciprocal processes. The next stage of innovation is to combine mobile and pervasive computing, which is referred to as ubiquitous computing. Ultimately, ubiquitous computing means any computing device, while moving with us, can build incrementally dynamic models of its various environments and configure its services accordingly. In ubiquitous computing computers will be embedded in our natural movements and interactions with our environments – both physical and social. To differentiate between the three genres of computing (mobile, pervasive and ubiquitous) it is possible to plot them along continua of mobility and embeddedness (Lyytinen and Yoo 2002).

In addition to considering issues of the mobile user's relationship to his or her environment, the relationship of the user to the network must also be considered. Similar to the client/server model in fixed networks, mobile computing considers the mobile terminal a client with a particular relationship to the network and the server. The design of the client must take into account a variety of factors including battery life, storage and processing capacity, communication link and the realities of everyday use in a mobile, hence changing, and sometimes unfriendly environment.

Given these design parameters some argue for a 'thin client' model of mobile computing. In the extreme sense a thin client would represent a mobile terminal with little more than basic input and output functionality with all processing and storage managed by a central entity. This concept takes advantage of new computing innovations such as web services. Use of web services to extend applications to mobile devices would allow masking of operating system differences and would provide translation functions. Such a system would allow a mobile user to access applications quickly with little or no download time and little or no invest-ment. It also allows for rapid testing and customization (Starner 2002).

An alternate perspective argues, based on several points, for the deployment of thick clients. The first point can be summarized as 'the inevitability of thick cli-ents.' In this line of reasoning proponents of thick clients argue that end users with thin clients will eventually become frustrated by their lack of functionality. Slowly the thin clients will have increased disk storage, RAM, and a more powerful CPU, making them in essence a thick client. In addition to this inevitability argument, thick client advocates point to network performance as another reason to support their position. A truly thin client could not operate during a network outage or when the client is out of range and even a thin client that could operate independ-ent of the network connection will still rely on one for important functions. A third argument is aimed at debunking the expectation that clients will not be able to store large files such as movies. Thick client advocates point out that disk capacity has grown even faster than CPU speed and available RAM, and that in five years a mobile device may provide more than a terabyte of storage. The thick client advo-cates hence conclude that the real limiting factors for mobile client design are wireless transfer rates and battery-energy density (Starner 2002).

It is difficult to say which model will dominate. It is likely that a hybrid thin/thick client will emerge, similar to the current hybrid centralized/decentralized configuration of many organizational client/server computing arrangements. Simi-lar to these networks, the degree of centralization/decentralization in mobile com-puting is likely to depend on a variety of factors including the particular applica-tion, the needs of users and the local network characteristics such as reliability. However, unlike with fixed networks, mobile computing should allow users to travel beyond the networks configured by an organization's network administra-tors, and so the degree of centralization or decentralization may also depend on configurations adopted by other organizations, such as public wireless or mobile network operators.

Organizational mobile computing and m-commerce

Although these technologies present many theoretical advantages, as with any in-novation the key to diffusion of mobile computing technologies in organizations is the relative advantages of the applications they deliver. Currently these technolo-gies and their applications present advantages related to productivity and connec-tivity. However, the level of complexity of deployment can serve to reduce the overall assessment of relative advantage.

The relative advantages most commonly touted for organizational mobile com-puting is that it frees employees from the confines of their desks and makes possi-ble the use of what otherwise would be considered 'downtime' such as travel be-tween meetings, commuting, etc. These 'productivity enhancing' features are key as market research has found firms are unlikely to adopt ICTs that do not contrib-ute to increased efficiency of business processes (Frontline Solutions 2002). This explains why the diffusion of laptops has continued despite significant price dif-ferences compared with desktops. In addition to laptops, organizations have also been deploying mobile handheld devices (wait staff at outdoor cafes; delivery persons).

One of the most successful devices for mobile organizational computing is the personal digital assistant (PDA) and similar task-specific handheld devices. Although these devices may increase efficiency of business processes, this must be weighed against the total cost of ownership, which includes everything from software and batteries to replacement of lost devices. Estimating the benefits of mobile devices also requires consideration of the use environment. Although standard consumer-oriented devices may be attractive for their easy-to-use features and low costs, when use of the devices will occur in a hostile environment 'ruggedized' versions of the less expensive consumer devices may be a worthwhile investment (Albright 2002b). Furthermore, the value of PDAs has increased as the market for PDA software has expanded. For example, for sales representatives there now exist over 100 PDA applications, such as time and expense tracking and reporting programs (Gizon 2002).

Although PDAs have provided many organizations with valuable experience in deploying mobile devices, when handheld devices are network devices the complexity of deployment increases significantly. Having every mobile handheld device acting as a network node creates a variety of issues. First, just the increase in the number of network users creates extra demands on network capacity and the likelihood of conflicting requests for resources increases. For example, when multiple remote users query and make changes to a database and store information locally on their handhelds how can they be sure they are viewing the most up-to-date version? Albright (2002a) cautions organizations to carefully analyze the work flow of mobile users to solve these types of problems. Furthermore, deployment requires software that resolves issues such as authentification, conflict resolution processes, server failover and recovery processes, and alerts and conflict logging. In addition to these process and data issues, the organization must also consider whether to use real-time connectivity or synchronization. This decision is related to the thin/thick client issue discussed above. Real-time connectivity can use thin clients with reliable network connections whereas synchronization uses occasional transfers of data to a thick client, where processing and storage occur.

As the functionality of mobile devices and the variety of access modes increases, so do the number of security concerns. Although developments in technologies such as the IEEE 802.11i and Wi-Fi Alliance's Wi-Fi Protected Access (WPA) should help shore up the security of wireless LANs, they are seen as only temporary solutions (Molta 2002). Access technologies such as public mobile networks and Bluetooth provide greater security. In GSM security these features include authentication and encryption, and in 3G these services will be expanded to include data integrity, secure services and applications, as well as fraud detection. Security in Bluetooth derives primarily from its much shorter operating distances, which make sniffing unlikely, as well as its frequency hopping mechanism.

Whichever access mechanism is used there are a number of actions that can be taken to secure networks when mobile access is implemented. Organizations must consider that their users will be accessing the corporate network from a variety of locations, including work, home and the local café, and thus users, not administrators, must take responsibility for secure access. Other issues to consider are strong password requirements and the privacy and security threats resulting from lost mobile/wireless devices. Organizations must also be cognizant of regulatory requirements for privacy and security when transmitting identification information or health records (Shaw 2002).

In addition to security issues, mobile computing and mobile commerce services may require significant degrees of systems integration (Raisinghani 2002; Lee and Ke 2001). Integration may be an issue both within and beyond the firm's boundaries. Taking lessons from electronic commerce, research found that small firms often used web-based transactions to purchase goods and provide information long before employing the technology to sell their own goods and services (Sadowski et al. 2002). If organizations allow purchases from mobile devices the need for both intra and inter-organizational systems integration could come relatively early in the adoption of mobile commerce services. The challenges of integration in the mobile realm are reflected in a scenario presented by Kazi (2002) whereby solutions for the provision of customer support services by mobile network operators in the era of m-commerce are discussed. One suggested solution was that operators employ a mobile customer support system where customer service representatives (CSRs), working at a place of their choice, act as independent agents and bid to provide service. Such a system would require the operator to manage the remote data processing and data related to decisions made by the mobile CSRs. However, by using the technology the firm is trying to sell, the operator may benefit from knowledge gained about the strengths and weaknesses of its own services.

Mobile/wireless access technologies and mobile organizational computing provides the platform upon which mobile commerce and mobile commerce services will be built. As suggested above, the technologies create the possibility for a wide variety of services. At the organizational level, which of these services make it to market will depend on applications' relative advantages in terms of efficiency gains. This may convince managers to deploy a technology or service, however continued use will depend on performance quality and ease of use for both network administrators as well as end users. These important considerations are the next topic of discussion.

M-commerce technologies and services: the users' perspective

Up to this point m-commerce has been discussed from a supply-side perspective, where the issues described are predominantly those of firms deploying technologies and services. A broad understanding of m-commerce should also consider the users' perspectives. Examining the users' perspective provides a more holistic assessment of the potential of the technology. It also helps anticipate problems while simultaneously providing a better understanding of what users value and in turn the potential for new products and services.

As implied above, users can be conceptualized at several levels including the individual and the organization. Here the discussion is first concerned with individual user skills and needs, and then the focus is turned to the skills and needs of a particular class of organization: small-to-medium sized enterprises (SMEs). SMEs represent an interesting group of users in that their network needs are typically more complex than individual users and yet they often lack IT staff that provide larger firms with the expertise needed to manage complex systems. Furthermore, much of what has been written about mobile commerce and computing from the organizational perspective assumes those organizations are large, resource-rich firms. Furthermore, considering the experiences of SMEs as small organizations with networking needs may provide insights to needs of households adopting WLANs or, further in the future, the needs of individuals in the adoption of personal area networks (PANs), which are the hallmark of pervasive computing.

Individuals' skills and needs

The adoption of mobile commerce at all levels will depend on user's comfort with and subsequent acceptance of the technology, including device functions and features, the interface and service characteristics. This level of comfort will be partially determined by the skills users bring to mobile commerce, which are determined by previous experience with mobile and Internet technologies. For some, these skills have become nearly second nature and thus it can be easy to underestimate the range of skills they have developed. This range is much more obvious to primary school and occupational re-training professionals who provide the uninitiated with basic Internet skills, such as navigating and evaluating information from a variety of sources. For some the same can be said of skills necessary to manage and use a mobile phone. Even some avid mobile phone users continue to struggle with keeping the device charged. To highlight the differences in skill sets that different levels of experience (defined by prior Internet and mobile use) provide, Table 1 catalogs the skills of potential m-commerce service users. The lists of skills associated with the use of these media reflect basic usage and – depending on the level of use – the lists could be significantly expanded, adding skills such as chat room etiquette, web design or the composition of an SMS message.

In addition to individual user skills, their needs must also be considered. Extensive research to assess these needs, more specifically user willingness-to-pay, has been performed by mobile equipment manufacturers, which has been passed on to operators who design and provide services (see Nokia 2000, 2001). These studies have shown that among consumers who are interested in advanced mobile services, communication and information services such as email, ticket booking, banking, maps, and weather updates are likely to be the most popular. Experience in offering services over GPRS networks in Japan has shown that indeed communication is an important part of the mix of services, and surprisingly so have ringtones. Studies have also shown that users prefer to pay for these services through flat rate or standard (fixed plus usage-sensitive) tariff packages. In 2G users globally have taken control of their mobile charges through the use of prepaid plans, and this popularity is expected to continue.

Table 1. User skill heterogeneity

<table>
<tr><td rowspan="2"></td><td rowspan="2">User experience</td><td colspan="2">Mobile Telephone</td></tr>
<tr><td>Yes</td><td>No</td></tr>
<tr><td rowspan="4">Internet</td><td>Yes</td><td>1. e-mail management (sorting, use of listservs, spam)
2. information retrieval
3. connection
4. up and downloading files
5. navigation (back, double click)
6. e-commerce (carts, paypal)
7. management of mobile device (safeguarding, charging)
8. use of mobile devices (dropped calls, reception variability)</td><td>1. e-mail management (sorting, use of listservs, spam)
2. information retrieval
3. connection
4. up and downloading files
5. navigation (back, double click)
9. e-commerce (carts, paypal)</td></tr>
<tr><td>No</td><td>1. management of mobile device (safeguarding, charging)
2. use of mobile devices (dropped calls, reception variability)</td><td>NA</td></tr>
</table>

SME skills and needs

For organizations, individual user skills and needs are the baseline of employee skills and needs. However, organizations may also have developed a collective set of skills and needs that are related to managing the technology in the organizational context. As with individual users, these skills and needs will be shaped by the organization's previous experience with ICTs. In terms of SME skills, SMEs bring to m-commerce a variety of experiences with information and communication technologies (ICTs). Research has shown that although SMEs are a heterogeneous group, spanning a large range of sizes (1-499 employees), industries and organizational arrangements, which have implications for the ways in which they adopt ICTs (Martin and Matlay 2001), the majority of SMEs are much less likely to adopt ICT technologies than large firms (Gibbs and Tanner 1997). When SMEs do adopt ICTs, they often lack the resources, both in time and finances, to create the necessary conditions to fully integrate the ICTs into their business processes. Furthermore, they lack the resources to identify, examine, and possibly re-engineer these processes to make them more efficient, a pre-requisite to ICT integration (Chappell and Feindt 1999). It should be noted, however, that not all large firms who have the resources have made good use of the Internet (Dutta and Segev 1999).

SMEs' approach to integrating the Internet into their organizational computing practices was originally cautious. It developed at the same time as the transition from a stand alone to a networked computing environment and this transformation was non-trivial for some small firms. Originally the driver for network implementation was shared use of peripherals such as the company printer. However, with the advent of the Internet efficient provision of desktop access also required network access. Because Internet access was frequently first provisioned through dial-up access from a stand-alone computer, even for firms with an existing network the transition to desktop Internet access could be a significant transformation. First, networked Internet access requires much greater attention to security issues. Second, it can reduce management control since working at one's computer may no longer signal productive activity. Despite these negative aspects, desktop access allows SMEs a deeper integration of Internet use in business processes, an important benefit (Maitland 2001).

Research on SMEs' experience with more extensive Internet use and e-commerce reveal a sequential pattern of adoption. Earliest adoptions were frequently motivated by communication requirements, with use slowly moving to more advanced applications such as web surfing, making Internet purchases, and finally establishing a website for informational or selling purposes. Firms making the step to establish a website often do so as a response to environmental context, as opposed to being used for growth or strategic advantage (Sadowski et al. 2002; Raymond 2001).

Thus, from their experience with organizational computing and e-commerce SMEs bring some skills to the world of m-commerce. They are likely to have organizational networks and an established relationship with an Internet Service Provider (ISP). This relationship may be limited to Internet access, but also many small firms use ISPs for website hosting. Outsourcing what some may see as a crucial function such as the corporate website, may make SMEs predisposed to outsourcing arrangements for the management of mobile devices and their resulting networking needs.

This conjecture highlights the relationship between skills and needs, and raises an important point. Although an organization's needs in m-commerce services may arise due to adoption of the technology, a more fundamental consideration of needs should first be considered. This raises the following question: which, if any, fundamental SME communication and computing needs can be met through the mobile/wireless channel?

Although certainly not true of all SMEs, these organizations can be seen in aggregate as late adopters of information and communication technologies. Also, given the likelihood of incremental adoption their needs must be met with technologies they are capable of implementing. Thus, for many SMEs the concepts of pervasive or ubiquitous computing are a number of years away. However, it is possible that a number of their needs can be met through recent advances that have broad public appeal such as wireless LANs and mobile data. A study of SME needs as regards mobile data found that interest in mobile data services was shaped by previous ICT experience. The study began by identifying 4 general barriers to mobile data adoption: slow transmission speeds, a lack of standards, variability in the quality of the mobile channel, and handset characteristics. Given these limitations, interest in mobile data services was assessed through the use of focus groups that divided SME managers into three groups (full IT adopter, partial IT adopter, and IT non-adopters). The groups included representatives from a variety of industries including beauty, real estate, health, manufacturing, construction, retail, couriers, and tourism. For full adopters and non adopters the most popular mobile data service was a 2-way communication service that integrates video, voice and voice recognition. For partial adopters the favored service was remote access and security (for example being able to monitor one's home via a mobile handset). The second choice for full adopters is a service that prioritizes and screens messages, reflecting their understanding of the burden of this task when connected to a group of similarly avid users. This service did not register in the top choices of either partial adopters or non-adopters. Partial and non-adopters were also interested in navigation services (Harker and Van Akkeren 2002). Thus, these SME managers are interested in a variety of basic mobile data services, particularly those for communication and those that provide greater connectivity while helping manage the requisite tasks associated with increased connectivity.

In addition to mobile data services, SMEs are seen as a potential market for the exploitation of wireless LANs. For example, WLAN hot-spot aggregators are aligning with WLAN access point vendors to enable the connection of small businesses to a larger chain of nationwide access points. Also manufacturers have created wireless LAN systems that make it easier for proprietors of small shops to authenticate and charge users for wireless LAN access. Recognizing the lack of IT expertise of many small shop managers, service providers are also now offering to install, manage and run the service based on a revenue sharing agreement between the small shop owner and the IT firm. These firms are also trying to bundle value-added services, which in the case of retail includes wireless surveillance cameras and monitors with advertising (Kenedy 2003).

For SMEs with complex networking and communication needs, mobile operators are offering new solutions, such as mobile Centrex and mobile virtual private networks (VPNs). In a fixed environment Centrex services provided small firms with some of the advantages of a PBX without requiring in-house PBX management and maintenance skills or the capital to invest in equipment. For small firms trying to integrate mobile phones into their communication systems mobile Centrex service allows for integration, providing mobile handsets with the same dialing capabilities as the fixed networks. Mobile operators are also hoping to convince small firms, through aggressive price reductions, to abandon their fixed lines altogether. Such marketing strategies are based on data that show a higher percentage of small firm employees are mobile as compared with their larger counterparts. There are also mobile VPN services that provide secure access to corporate networks by mobile workers. As with fixed line Centrex, these services are attractive to SMEs because the operator maintains the systems and organizational investments in application-specific software are less burdensome.

The research on the skills, needs and services for SMEs highlights several important points. First, SMEs are a heterogeneous group and they vary significantly in their previous ICT experience and hence skills. Second, if one extrapolates from e-commerce experience, SMEs are likely to adopt m-commerce technologies and services gradually. Initially, their needs are likely to focus on communication services with data and information-based service demands possibly developing thereafter. Third, to take advantage of mobile/wireless technologies SMEs may need greater levels of service, particularly in the management of networks. Fourth, mobile/wireless technologies such as mobile Centrex and mobile VPNs may help SMEs overcome issues that were presented by their highly mobile workforces but that were unresolved by wireline networking technologies.

Users and mobile commerce services

Given the trends in mobile/wireless access technologies and organizational mobile computing, coupled with user skills and needs, what can we conclude about the use of mobile commerce services by SMEs? To understand how SME needs create implications for mobile commerce let us first consider the issue of thin and thick clients in mobile computing.

In the discussion of mobile computing trends two views were presented. One favors the use of thin clients whereby relatively dumb mobile terminals are deployed with the intelligence, storage and processing handled by the server or network switch. The alternative perspective is one that advocates use of a thick client, whereby the reliance of the mobile terminal on the quality and reliability of the mobile network channel is reduced by adding functionality to the mobile terminal. The arguments for each device focus on the capabilities of the technology, either the computing technology necessary for intelligent handsets or the network technology necessary for the mobile/wireless connection.

From a users' perspective, and in particular a SME user perspective, the pros and cons of thick and thin clients should be viewed in light of SME skills and needs. These skills and needs will be both those of the individual SME employees as well as those of the organization, incorporating skills related to use as well as management of the technologies.

From a SME perspective, arguments in favor of the centralization of services, and hence the use of thin clients, are based on security, structural characteristics and data management, as well as network management. Network security in both fixed and mobile/wireless environments is becoming increasingly difficult to manage. Frequent updates are required to ensure the integrity of the enterprise network. Managing security in a 'thick client' world requires that updates be transmitted to mobile handsets. Accepting patches and other security upgrades can be made mandatory upon connection however their receipt is not guaranteed. With thin clients security features can be managed centrally providing a greater level of control, and their reduced functionality and data storage reduces risk. A second factor in support of thin clients is related to SME organizational structure. SMEs typically have flatter hierarchies and less clearly defined competencies of individual employees, which result in high staff involvement in all business processes (Chappell and Feindt 1999). Given this high level of interdependency, employing thin clients, which require centralized storage, reduces the potential that valuable data will be unavailable to those who need it. As noted by Lee and Ke (2001), managing which version of the data one is working with is expected to present a significant challenge for mobile computing. Third, in the discussion of mobile computing and organizational deployment a variety of network management issues were raised. Among the concerns that must be addressed by the organization are authentification, conflict resolution processes, server failover and recovery processes, and alerts and conflict logging. Furthermore, the organization must manage password use in addition to managing the risks of privacy and security threats resulting from lost mobile/wireless devices. Given the typical SMEs' lack of available IT management resources, these issues will present challenges to the use of either thick or thin mobile clients. However, the reduced functionality of thin clients reduces the consequences of their loss or malfunction.

In assessing the benefits of centralization and thin client use individual user perspectives must also be taken into account. As with any organization, the individual employee's desires may coincide with or contradict those of managers. In terms of mobile commerce technologies and services individual user's perceptions will be partly determined by their experience with other ICT technologies. Internet use reveals that with decentralization comes greater responsibility. For those unintimidated by mobile and Internet technology the possibility of greater control over a terminal is liberating. However, for those with limited knowledge or resources the technology might be more accessible if the system design requires less control / responsibility. Hence, a knowledgeable employee working for a SME using thin clients may be frustrated by the lack of functionality of a device as well as the lack of control. Inexperienced users on the other hand may welcome a simpler device. Furthermore, whereas large organizations may be able to spend time and money training employees on the use of mobile/wireless devices, SMEs are more likely to have to rely on existing employee skills or self-learning.

There are also arguments that can be made from the SME perspective for the use of thick clients. Thick clients with their greater independence from network data transfers can save money on communication costs compared with their thin client rivals. Also, arguments in favor of thin clients were partially based on the assumption of low-levels of organizational and employee IT skills. However, this may change through further diffusion among the general public of desktop computers and wireless networks. As the number of households (i.e. families or groups of college students) with multiple computers increases, and hence the demand for Internet connectivity increases, households will find that, as opposed to multiple stand-alone connections, network-based Internet access via DSL or cable modem is economical and efficient. This trend will drive manufacturers to make network administration easier and will increase the general availability of network management skills. These skills will probably find their way into the labor force of SMEs, and with greater network management skills the need to centralize computing control will perhaps decrease.

As previously concluded it is unlikely that one network architecture will dominate and, given the heterogeneity of SMEs, services targeting small firms seem to be oriented toward both thin and thick client architectures. Furthermore, these services are likely to appear at every level of the mobile commerce value chain, whether they are offered as bundled services with wireless LANs or as packages available from the mobile network operator.

The presence of such entities is predicted if one applies Greenstein's (2001) concept of technological mediation to the mobile commerce industry. The concept, which was developed to explain the value of ISPs in the market for Internet services, predicts that mediation will occur when there is a mismatch between the technical possibilities offered by a frontier technology and user skills. The Internet presented a series of frontier or innovative and unknown technologies for which the uses were not always clear. The same is likely to be true for mobile/wireless technologies, as the service providers of WLAN access points suggest. Given the relatively low level of SME skills, the acceptance of mobile commerce technologies and services will likely require mediation to be successful.

For SMEs the combination of mobile/wireless technologies and the presence of mediators who translate the possibilities of the technology into concrete user applications could be very powerful. Aspects of IT that were once troublesome such as wiring and network administration, could potentially be outsourced allowing these firms to focus on their core competencies. Also, a centralized approach to organizational computing where even the server and network administrator are virtual entities may allow firms to better take advantage of their lack of embedded technological base and reduce investments required to take advantage of the benefits mobile/wireless technologies present.

Conclusions

Recently, expectations for the impact of information and communication technologies have diminished, perhaps creating a more realistic perspective. However, despite this dampening enthusiasm for ICTs in general, the development of organizational applications continues. In particular as advanced mobile and wireless access technologies are deployed, organizational uses of them are pursued. Globally, the growth of these access technologies are uneven with some areas embracing wireless LANs, while others experience growth in advanced mobile services. And although demand for them is still uncertain, these new access technologies make possible a wide range of mobile commerce services.

The deployment of these services will occur in the context of existing organizational computing arrangements, namely client-server architecture. Furthermore, mobile computing trends, such as the acceptance of thin or thick clients and the degrees of mobility and embeddedness of computing, will also shape the types of services that develop. Important considerations for organizational adoption will include the relative advantage of the service, security issues and integration of mobile commerce services into existing computing infrastructure.

However, not all organizations or users are alike. By examining the skills and needs of individuals and organizations the affect of their individual circumstances are highlighted. Individual skills, or those of employees, are likely to vary based on previous experience with both the Internet and mobile telephony. Similar to organizations, individuals also require a high degree of control over expenses incurred in the use of mobile services. Small-to-medium sized enterprises also have unique skills and needs. Experience with e-commerce shows that SMEs are slower to adopt ICTs, and when they do, adoption is in stages with context and communication playing important roles. Due to their small size and limited resources management of IT can present challenges and thus SMEs may be more likely to outsource IT management functions through the use of services such as mobile Centrex.

Mobile and wireless technologies and services may present SMEs with important solutions to long term problems. If services are appropriately designed, SMEs may be able to overcome existing network management problems. This would require mediation services that make explicit the potential of the technology while minimizing network management requirements. Integration of a variety of mobile/wireless terminals and applications must also be considered. Furthermore, mobile/wireless technologies may help SMEs leapfrog over fixed telecommunications and computing networks into more flexible wireless and mobile systems. These systems may reduce equipment start-up costs, allowing firms to better use their sparse capital resources.

References

Albrigth B (2002a) Mobile users not in sync? Frontline Solutions. June:17–20. www.frontlinetoday.com

Albright B (2002b) What are your mobile needs? Frontline Solutions. July. www.frontlinetoday.com

Anckar B, D'Incau D (2002) Value-added services in mobile commerce: An analytical framework and empirical findings from a national consumer survey. Proceedings of the 35th Hawaii International Conference on System Science

Australian Communications Authority (2003) Report from ACA workshop on spectrum licensing issues. March. Downloaded 4/21/03 from http://auction.aca.gov.au/current_projects/workshop_report.pdf

Baldi S, Thaung HP-P (2002) The entertaining way to m-commerce: Japan's approach to the Mobile Internet – A model for Europe? Electronic Markets 12:6–13

Chappell C, Feindt S (1999) Analysis of E-commerce practice in SMEs. European Union ESPRIT. Brussels January

Commission of the European Communities (2003) Commission recommendation on the harmonization of the provision of public R-LAN access to public electronic communications networks and services in the community. (2003/203/EC) March 20. Downloaded 4/21/2003 http://europe.eu.int/eur-lex/

Dutta S, Segev A (1999) Business transformation on the Internet. European Management Journal. 17:466–476

FCC 2002 "Spectrum Policy Task Force Report" U.S. Federal Communications Commission, ET Docket No. 02-135, November. Downloaded 2/13/03 http://www.fcc.gov/sptf/

Frontline Solutions (2002) April:50

Gibbs D, Tanner K (1997) Information and Communication Technologies and Local Economic Development Policies: The British Case. Regional Studies 31:765–774

Gizon K (2002) Mobile Computing Trends. Agency Sales Magazine. December

Greenstein S (2001) Technological mediation and commercial development in the early Internet access market. California Management Review 43:75–94

Harker D, Van Akkeren J (2002) Exploring the needs of SMEs for mobile data technologies: the role of qualitative research techniques. Qualitative Market Research 5:199–209

Kazi S (2002) Mobile commerce and the contact center. Customer Inter@ction Solutions November:54–57

Kenedy K (2003) Small businesses tune in to hot spots CRN, January 13:10a

Lee C, Ke C-H (2001) A prediction-based query processing strategy in mobile commerce systems. Journal of Database Management July-Sept:14

Lyytinen K, Yoo Y (2002) Issues and challenges in ubiquitous computing. Communications of the ACM. 45:63–65

Maitland CF, Bauer JM, Westerveld JR (2002) The European Market for Mobile Data: Evolving Value Chains and Industry Structure. Telecommunications Policy 26:485–504

Maitland CF (2001) Institutional assets: Shaping the potential for electronic commerce in developing countries. Unpublished dissertation. Delft University of Technology, The Netherlands

Martin LM, Matlay H (2001) 'Blanket' approaches to promoting ICT in small firms: some lessons from the DTI ladder adoption model in the UK. Internet Research 11:399–410

Molta D (2002) Mobile and Wireless Technology. Network Computing December 15:32–40.

Nokia (2000) Make Money with 3G Services. Espoo Finland

Nokia (2001) 3G Market Research: 3G Tariffing End User Study Global Findings. Nokia 3G Market Research Center. Espoo, Finland. April 10

Raisinghani M (2002) Mobile Commerce: Transforming the vision into reality. Information Resources Management Journal. 15:3–4.

Raymond L (2001) Determinants of Web site implementation in small businesses. Internet Research 11:411–422

Starner T (2002) Thick clients for personal wireless devices. Computer 35:133–135

Sadowski BM, Maitland CF, van Dongen J (2002) Strategic Use of the Internet by Small-and-Medium-Sized Firms: An Exploratory Study. Information Economics and Policy 14:75–93

Senn JA (2000) The emergence of m-commerce. Computer December:148–150

Shaw R (2002) Wireless Risks: Agents Beware! National Underwriter July 8:6, 8

Varshney U, Vetter R J, Kalakota R (2000) Mobile Commerce: A new frontier. Computer October:32–38

The development of location based services in mobile commerce

Charles Steinfield[1]

Department of Telecommunication, Michigan State University, East Lansing, USA

Abstract

With the more than one billion cellular phones in the world in 2002, joined by other wireless handheld computing devices like personal digital assistants (PDAs) and pocket PCs, there are significant opportunities for mobile commerce growth. Although mobile commerce enables access to goods and services regardless of the location of either buyer or seller, in many situations the specific location of the buyer and seller is critical to the transaction. A host of new *location-aware* applications and services are emerging with significant implications for the future of e-commerce. Much like the experience with the dot com era, however, the development of location-based services has fallen somewhat short of expectations. In this chapter, we attempt to provide a realistic assessment of the potential for location-based services, examining the market opportunity, technological origins, likely services, emerging policy issues, and potential future directions.

Introduction

Since the dawn of the Web, online shoppers have mainly experienced electronic commerce through personal computers connected to the Internet via some form of fixed line. In the near future this may change, as many e-commerce transactions are expected to occur via a wide assortment of wireless and handheld devices (Economist Intelligence Unit, October 15, 2001). Wireless e-commerce is more commonly known as mobile or m-commerce, and, as noted in other chapters in this volume, is expected to develop into a significant market opportunity in the coming years throughout the world. Mobile operators in particular view m-commerce as a critical means of increasing average revenue per user (ARPU), since increasing competition has driven down prices for voice services at the same

---

[1] E-mail: steinfie@msu.edu

time that costs related to the transition to the next generation digital wireless infra-structure have risen (D'Roza and Bilchev 2003).

Just as with e-commerce, m-commerce can be defined narrowly or broadly. Narrow definitions focus on the ability to complete transactions involving the ex-change of monetary value through wireless telecommunications networks (Barnes 2002; Clark 2001). Broader definitions, on the other hand, point to "the emerging set of applications and services people can access from their Internet-enabled mo-bile devices" (Sadeh 2002, p. 5). The more inclusive definition incorporates a wide range of communication, information, and entertainment, services, as well as alternative business models (e.g. advertising) that do not fit the narrow, transac-tion-dependent view. Within this set of emerging applications and services is a type of m-commerce that many in the industry feel represents the "killer" applica-tion: applications that take the user's location into account in order to deliver a service (VanderMeer 2001). Examples of such "location-based services" (LBS) include those that identify nearby options, such as when a cellular telephone user seeking information about restaurants is provided only the set of choices in the immediate vicinity. In the next stage of e-commerce and m-commerce develop-ment, location-based services (LBS) are expected to play an increasingly impor-tant role in helping to differentiate one service provider from another ((Fielt et al. 2000; Van de Kar and Bouwman 2001). For this reason, this chapter provides an overview of this emerging class of mobile services, examining the LBS market potential, its technological bases, the potential services, the industry value chain and likely business models, significant policy issues, and potential future direc-tions.

Among the conclusions we draw from a review of recent work on LBS, is that while the market potential is great, there are significant barriers to overcome. Technological barriers result from the diversity and cost of approaches to location determination, creating a complex set of choices for operators and a potential in-teroperability problem that can limit users. The lack of any standard approach to location determination and provision of location data to service providers may hinder market development, especially in the United States. We further find that, despite the promise of LBS for consumers, high costs, standards problems, and privacy concerns may limit the near term market to internal business applications among larger firms. LBS standards, privacy protection, quality of service, and conditions by which third party service providers access location information rep-resent several of the more critical policy issues to be resolved. Finally, in the area of potential future directions, it is evident that location is merely a starting point for personalization and context-aware services that use other relevant information when constructing service offers. Moreover, the rapid deployment of alternative wireless technologies, such as Wireless Fidelity (WiFi or 802.11) is both a threat and an opportunity for cellular operators, and will likely shape the future devel-opment of LBS.

Contrasting location awareness with the anytime anyplace view of m-commerce

Researchers exploring m-commerce often point to its ubiquity and convenience as the primary sources of subscriber value (Anckar and D'Incau 2002). The stationary nature of PC and Internet based e-commerce connections limits usage to those moments when a consumer is at home or at work in front of their PC. Potential buyers who are away from their PCs are unable to access information and services, or complete transactions. The anytime-anyplace potential of commerce through wireless devices can overcome this limitation, allowing information to be disseminated and transactions completed when the need or desire arises, even when buyers are in transit and away from their desks or home PC connections. In this conception of m-commerce, the location of buyers and sellers is irrelevant. Rather, a key motivation is to enable access to goods and service *regardless* of the location of either buyer or seller. Indeed, providing access to distant sellers has often been heralded as an important benefit of e-commerce. The lower search costs and electronic access afforded by the network allow connections to non-local sellers as easily as to local ones, giving rise to such clichés as the 'death of distance' (Bakos 1997; Cairncross 1997).

Contradicting to this common conception of e-commerce in general, and m-commerce in particular, is the view that in most economic transactions, the location of the buying and selling parties are relevant. In most traditional business-to-consumer (B2C) transactions, for example, buyers normally only consider purchasing goods at retail outlets that are within driving distance of their homes or offices. Even for catalog and network-based transactions, the concept of the location has meaning for at least some aspects of the transaction (Steinfield and Klein 1999). Obviously, location is required for physical goods delivery, and may influence such transaction elements as the choice of source of supply and delivery mode, shipping costs, relevant taxes, the language for associated information services, available promotions, after-sales service considerations, and so forth. The importance of location in e-commerce has been linked to the relative success of click and mortar e-commerce business models compared to digital pure plays (Steinfield et al. 2002; Steinfield et al. 2002b). Clearly for m-commerce, there are many types of services, such as those providing navigation, directory search, and ticketing/permission for entry, where the location of the consumer is of prime importance. Hence, localization and personalization are additional dimensions of m-commerce value creation (Anckar and D'Incau 2002).

The emerging LBS market

As with the early years of Internet-based e-commerce, the initial experiences with m-commerce were somewhat disappointing. This was particularly true in Europe where the first generation of Wireless Application Protocol (WAP) telephones and services did not meet with much success in the marketplace. Slow connection speeds, high airtime charges, poor quality screens, awkward user interfaces, and limited content and services all were likely contributors to the lower than anticipated usage of such services. Nonetheless, interest in m-commerce remains strong, due to 1) the sheer number of mobile subscribers worldwide, and 2) the increasing proportion of mobile users with mobile data capability. Worldwide there are far more cellular telephones than personal computers in service. The ITU estimates that there were more than 1.1 billion cellular subscribers in 2002 compared to 615 million personal computers. Moreover, the ITU estimates that the number of cellular subscribers surpassed the number of fixed lines for the first time in history in 2002 (ITU 2003). Increasingly, these cellular handsets are capable of connecting to the Internet, and in some countries such as Japan and South Korea, mobile Internet use is growing rapidly. NTT Docomo reports, for example, that the number of i-mode subscribers now exceeds 38 million, which is nearly half of all cellular phone subscribers in Japan (NTT Docomo 2003). The i-mode service is NTT Docomo's cellular service that incorporates wireless packet-switched connections for data services, including mobile Internet access. The Korean Network Information Center (KRNIC 2003) reports that nearly a third of the more than 32 million cellular subscribers in South Korea are mobile Internet users. Meanwhile, European cellular subscribers have demonstrated amply that SMS messages can enable many forms of m-commerce, and both i-mode and second generation WAP services have been introduced. One consulting report pegged the global number of wireless data subscribers at 170 million in 2000, with a forecast for this number to rise to 1.3 billion by 2004 (Wireless Today 2001).

Market estimates and forecasts specifically for location-based services have also been provided. A forecast from the ITU suggested worldwide revenues from LBS would exceed $2.6 billion in 2005, and reach $9.9 billion by 2010 (Leite and Pereira 2001). A recent report on the CyberAtlas Web site refers to an ARC Group study indicating that LBS will account for over 40 percent of mobile data revenues worldwide by 2007 (Greenspan 2002). This optimistic forecast further goes on to predict that there will be 748 million worldwide users of LBS as early 2004, up from an estimated 72 million in 2001. The ARC Group believes that by the end of 2004, nearly all wireless-enabled computing devices will use some form of location service. The same article also describes another marketing study by Ovum predicting that the Western European market for LBS will reach $6.6 billion by 2006, and that as much as 44 percent of cellular subscribers will be using LBS (Greenspan 2002).

Although these projections seem overly optimistic, there is some reason to expect that even without an explicit subscription to a location service, most cellular subscribers in the near future will unwittingly be using a location determination technology. This is due to the fact that regulators in most industrialized countries have initiated rules requiring cellular operators to deliver information about the location of a subscriber to public safety answering points in the event of an emergency. In the United States, the Federal Communications Commission issued the E911 mandate requiring every cellular operator to be able to detect the location of subscribers within 50 meters for 67 percent of emergency calls and 150 meters for 95 percent of calls (Federal Communications Commission 2003; Millar 2003).

This requirement is being implemented in a phased process that began in October 1, 2001 and is to be completed by December 31, 2005. Although virtually all operators have received extensions to their required implementation dates due to technical difficulties, the process is still ongoing. The European Union is similarly developing requirements for cellular operators for their e112 emergency services (D'Roza and Bilchev 2003). These are not meant to be e-commerce services per se, but have had the effect of pushing mobile network operators to build out the location detection infrastructure which can then be exploited for other commercial purposes.

Approaches to determining location

In wireline-based e-commerce, users are normally asked to input their location (e.g. in the form of a postal code) in order to filter service options based on the users' whereabouts. In the more current conception of wireless LBS, the user's location is determined automatically, without requiring him or her to explicitly provide it. There are many different techniques that have been developed for automatic location identification: some more appropriate for outdoor environments, and some better for indoor locations. In this section, we first overview the major technical approaches to determining location, and then review a taxonomy of LBS technology characteristics.

Most discussions of positioning technology focus on the task of locating users in outdoor environments, and can be divided into three broad categories: those where the mobile unit calculates its own location, approaches where the cellular network calculates the location, and hybrid approaches that combine two or more techniques (Djuknic and Richton 2002; D'Roza and Bilchev 2003; Levijoki 2000; Millar 2003). The basic attributes of these approaches, including strengths and weaknesses are summarized in Table 1.

Other than GPS, most of the techniques depicted in Table 1 are not yet widely implemented and require significant investment by either network operators, mobile subscribers or both. Moreover, GPS-bases solutions do not work in indoor settings, as there is no line of sight with satellites. A number of quite different techniques for the provision of location specific services to users in indoor environments have been studied. These indoor techniques are more rooted in the work on pervasive computing than cellular telephony, and are more likely to target users with laptops and personal digital assistants than cellular telephones. In general, most indoor approaches determine a users location simply by virtue of the fact that a device is within range of a low power transmitter or receiver (e.g. a wireless LAN base station), making them conceptually similar to a cell of origin approach in a GSM network. Table 2 lists the primary indoor LBS technologies.

Table 1. Alternative positioning technologies for location based services

	Basic positioning approach	Strengths	Weaknesses
Handset Based			
GPS	Triangulation method using timing signals from 4 satellites out of a system of 24 satellites.	• highly accurate • no new network infrastructure required • enhanced privacy for user	• no indoor service, poor coverage in urban "canyons" • new handsets required • power requirements • bulky size of receivers • delay in calculating location
Forward Link Trilateration	The mobile unit times the arrival of signals from multiple base stations, but sends the time differences to a location processor to determine location through triangulation	• reduced complexity, and cost for handset	• some modification to handset • network investment required
Observed Time Difference and Enhanced Observed Time Difference	Timing signals are sent from multiple base stations and software in the handset performs triangulation calculations to determine location	• enhanced privacy for user	• some modification to handset • some network investment
Cellular Network-Based			
Cell ID (also called Cell of Origin)	Uses the location of the base station currently handling a call to represent the subscribers location. Accuracy can be increased by sectorization (using directional antennas at the base station)	• available now • no handset modifications • low cost	• lower accuracy, especially in large rural cells • loss of privacy for user
Time of Arrival (TOA) and Time Difference of Arrival (TDOA)	Triangulates the location of the subscriber using timing of signals sent from the mobile unit to at least three different cell sites. TDOA requires synchronization among base stations and uses differences in arrival time.	• greater accuracy than Cell ID • can determine velocity and heading in addition to position • TOA does not require any handset modifications	• inferior accuracy for TDOA in analog and narrowband digital systems • new equipment needed at base stations • TDOA requires modification to handset • loss of privacy for user
Angle of Arrival (AOA)	Calculates the position of the subscriber based upon the direction (angle) of the arriving signal into two or more base stations	• no handset modifications	• problems caused by multipath reception • special antennas and receivers needed at base stations • loss of privacy for user
Multipath analysis	Determines location by comparing pattern of reception from subscriber with previous reception patterns stored in a database	• no handset modifications	• new receiving equipment needed at base stations • development and updating of database • loss of privacy for user
Hybrid Approaches			
Assisted GPS	GPS receivers are embedded in the cellular network which assist a partial GPS receiver in the handset, reducing the calculation burden	• eliminates many of costs imposed by GPS on handsets (e.g. can be smaller, longer battery life, etc.) • reduces the delay in calculating location • offers some control to user	• new handsets required
Other combinations, e.g. TDOA/AOA	use multiple techniques to extend coverage and improve accuracy	• increased accuracy • more robust	• cost of network infrastructure needed • loss of privacy for user

Table 2. Indoor techniques for location specific services

Technical Approach	Description
Infrared	Infrared sensors placed in throughout a building (e.g. in the ceilings) can be used to detect a person wearing a device (e.g. a badge), that periodically emits an ID code via an infrared transmitter (Want et al. 1992). The location of the badge wearer is determined by proximity to the sensor receiving the badge ID. It requires visual line of sight to function, and normally does not have very high accuracy (known as resolution). Moreover, it cannot work when the device (e.g. a PDA) is in a user's pocket.
Ultrasound	Ultrasound transmitters known as beacons send signals to a receiver, allowing the device to calculate its location based on proximity. These systems also send reference radio signals, and using timing differences between the ultrasound and radio signals to achieve very high accuracy, even to the point of determining the orientation of the target (Harter et al. 1999; Priyantha et al. 2000).
Radio Frequency (RF)	A target with a reflector or transmitter emitting a low power radio frequency signal can be detected by receivers strategically placed around a building. The target normally transmits some sort of ID information, and its location is determined either by proximity to a receiver or triangulation from received signal strengths to multiple receivers (Levijoki 2000). It doesn't require line of sight, but signal strengths are very sensitive to conditions (e.g. furniture, people) and so resolution is limited. RF tags known as RFIDs are being widely implemented for asset tracking in warehouses as a replacement for bar coded tags, and so costs of such systems are dropping.
Wireless LAN (WiFi)	Although primarily used to provide Ethernet connections and Internet access to laptop computers equipped with wireless LAN cards, such systems can provide gross location information simply by virtue of determining which users are being served by a particular base station. Given that such stations have ranges of roughly 50 meters, this provides some degree of location information. As more mobile devices such as Pocket PCS and other PDAs support the 802.11b standard, it is possible to use such systems for location-aware service provision. For example, Carnegie Mellon University uses a campus-wide 802.11b wireless network to provide guided tours to visitors of the campus.[2] Visitors carrying handheld computers receive location-specific information as they walk from area to area around the campus. As more commercial 802.11 networks are rolled out in public settings, this may prove to be a low cost method for location based service provision.
Bluetooth	Bluetooth is a radio frequency standard for very short range (10 meters) ad hoc networking to support what are called personal area networks (PANs). Although mainly conceived for wire replacement (e.g. between headphones and a portable music player), such systems could also be used for proximity-based location services when a Bluetooth device comes within range of a service point.

As noted in Table 2, many of these approaches exist in campus or laboratory test environments, although wireless LANs, Bluetooth, and radio frequency ID tags (RFID) have been widely implemented for other purposes. Such systems, especially because they are largely operating in the unlicensed spectrum, can be quite low in cost since they are mass-produced and there is no cost to the "airtime."

---

[2] http://www.esite-cmu.org

A useful taxonomy of LBS technology attributes is given by Hightower and Borriello (2001). They note six attributes that can usefully distinguish techniques for determining location. These include:

- Physical versus symbolic location. Some systems, like GPS, provide a physical location in terms of latitude, longitude and elevation. Other systems offer a symbolic location, such as the target being in a particular room or in a certain neighborhood. Intermediate service providers can take the supplied physical coordinates and convert them into symbolic references that are more meaningful to users.
- Absolute vs. relative location. GPS, cellular systems and many indoor systems mentioned above provide an absolute location, either in terms of a common coordinate system (e.g. latitude and longitude) or a symbolic name. Other location systems are best considered to be proximity systems and report the relative location of people or objects compared with some reference (e.g. how far one device is from another). Again, location service providers might calculate proximity from absolute location data of different objects, enabling, for example, people to know who else from a set of contacts is nearby.
- Localized location computation. In some systems, such as GPS or the observed time difference approaches in cellular systems, the handheld device uses information supplied by the network to calculate its own position. This means that the network does not know where the subscriber is unless the subscriber is willing to reveal this information, affording more privacy protection. The alternative systems that rely on network-based calculations, such as the timing of arrival or multipath approaches automatically reveal a subscriber's location yielding lower privacy.
- Accuracy and Precision. The varying location systems offer different resolutions, ranging from the few centimeters possible with ultrasound to several kilometers in rural cell ID approaches. Precision refers to how often a degree of accuracy can be expected.
- Scale. This characteristic refers to the size of the area within which location of objects is feasible. GPS systems, for example, work worldwide, a cellular system might focus on a country or a city, an 802.11 wireless LAN network might locate objects in a campus or large building, and an infrared system might locate objects in a room or a building. Hightower and Boriello (2001) recommend assessing scale in terms of the coverage area per unit of infrastructure and the number of objects that can be located per unit and time interval.
- Recognition. This feature refers to the ability of the location system to recognize specific aspects or identities of the object being located. It involves more than knowing the location – it can include recognition of object data that will trigger specific actions by the system. Hightower and Boriello (2001) use the example of a baggage handling system that, upon recognizing destination codes on baggage, route bags to one place or another. GPS systems do not have this attribute, but cellular operators will likely want to be able to at least recognize valid LBS customers.

- Cost. Obviously, the various approaches all have quite different costs. A full assessment would examine how much infrastructure investment is required to implement the system as well as how much it would cost users to acquire the necessary handset equipment. Systems might also have quite variable maintenance costs, such as the database updating required by multipath systems.

Clearly there are a wide array of approaches, and many features upon which systems may be compared. This diversity, although good for innovation and choice, may actually be inhibiting LBS development, since there are not yet fully agreed upon standards. This topic will be addressed as one of the policy issues related to location-based services.

Applications

A wide range of services that rely on users' location information have been conceived, although the markets are not yet mature. The main point is to remember that location is simply a useful bit of data that can be used to filter access to many types of geographical information services (GIS). There are numerous ways to exploit location to provide more relevant information, or derive new services. It can be particularly powerful when combined with other user profile information to offer personalized and location sensitive responses to customers (Searby 2003). Van de Kar and Bouwman (2001) distinguish between emergency services, mobile network operator services, and value-added services (VAS), focusing on the latter category as the primary e-commerce opportunity. In the VAS category, they describe a number of different service areas, including information, entertainment, communication, transaction, mobile office and business process support services. Levijoki (2000) offers a simpler categorization scheme, distinguishing between billing, safety, information, tracking and proximity services. D'Roza and Bilchev (2003) classify services into two broad categories: those that are requested by users once their location is determined, and those that are triggered automatically once a certain condition is met (e.g. a boundary is crossed). We might consider the former set to be "pull" services and the latter to "push" services. In addition, D'Roza and Bilchev (2003) identify five groups of application areas: communication, fleet management, routing, safety and security, and entertainment. We can also classify services according to whether they apply to consumers, business customers, or employees in a firm. Some of the most commonly discussed services are briefly described below.

Emergency, safety and medical/health services

As noted earlier, many governments are moving to require cellular operators to develop the capability to automatically identify subscribers' locations in the event of an emergency. This data would then be forwarded to the appropriate public safety answering point (PSAP) to coordinate the dispatch of emergency personnel.

These are not necessarily revenue producing services in their own right, but it is possible to conceive of medical and safety services that would be offered on a commercial basis, particularly if LBS were combined with telemedicine techniques that would allow physiological data to be transmitted back to health care providers.

Information services

Mobile users can be provided with a wide range of localized information. Weather forecasts, tourist attractions, landmarks, restaurants, gas stations, repair shops, ATM locations, theaters, public transportation options (including schedules) are just a few examples of the types of information that would be more useful if filtered by the user's location. Gazetteer services link current and historic geographic names to spatial data. More sophisticated services will depend on the development of richer geographical information systems. For example, a query about local theaters might be extended to focus only on those playing a specific movie. Or, rather than look for particular types of businesses, a customer may input a specific product, and ask for all businesses in the area that carry it. If the database includes other product information, such as prices and other terms, then real time comparison shopping may be feasible en route or even inside stores.

Navigation/routing

In addition to identifying the location of various destinations, location-based services can also be employed to guide users along the best routes. Automobile manufacturers are already offering services such as GM's Onstar, using vehicle-based GPS receivers and mapping/route guide services in selected cars. Collectively these types of services are often referred to as telematic services and automatic vehicle location services by the automotive companies. If integrated with real time traffic data, such route guide services may also make routes contingent on current traffic conditions.

Transactions and billing

Cellular operators are beginning to offer different rates based on the location of callers (e.g. in a designated home area). E-commerce services might include use of the wireless device to make payments for tickets at theaters and on public transportation, vending machines, and for goods in shops to speed up checkouts. Often this capability requires that wireless devices exchange payment information with local POS devices. In the US, for example, a company called Merchant Wired is putting wireless LANs into shopping malls so that small stores can have this capability (Brewin, May 30, 2001).

Asset tracking and fleet management

Location services can be used to track the locations of people, pets, objects, vehicles, etc. Trucking companies are putting in their own systems, for example, that not only track the location of vehicles, but also the contents inside delivery trucks using an onboard wireless LAN. Last minute delivery changes can be made based on truck inventory and location (Brewin, June 11, 2001), enhancing efficiency and customer service. Tracking can also be combined with navigation services to help with route optimization for deliveries. Tracking services can also aid in preventing theft of valuable items, and even in locating people (e.g. lost children), or pets.

Mobile office

Many applications are targeted to employees that are out of their offices. In general, these will be internal information systems applications, but may involve partnering with location-based service providers for their implementation. Some applications have to do with the provision of location sensitive information, such as updates or changes to customer account information when field representatives are in proximity to specific customers. Given the limited screen space of mobile units, even emails might be filtered so that only those that are critical or relevant would be forwarded to a field agent, while others remain on the server. Scheduling applications might also take into account the location of workers.

Entertainment

There are many possibilities for location-specific entertainment services using a mobile device. One of the more well-known location services now in use is a game called BotFighters, developed by the gaming company It's Alive and offered by Telia Mobile (Norris 2003).[3] In this game, subscribers use the location determination capability of the network and SMS messages sent from their mobile phones to locate and "shoot" imaginary robots (other players). They must be close enough to the target to be able to "hit" them. New versions using Java-equipped handsets have even more functionality, and the game is spreading to other markets like the UK (Norris 2003). Other entertainment applications that have been discussed include dating services, DJ requests in clubs, person-to-person messaging in a closed setting like a concert.

Proximity services

Another category that overlaps with many of the above application areas is that of proximity services. These services inform users when they are within a certain dis-

---

[3] See http://www.botfighters.com and http://www.itsalive.com/ for more information.

tance of other people, businesses, or other things. Examples include those discussed in the information category, such as when users are informed of the closest desired business (e.g. in response to queries about the closest gas station or ATM), or the BotFighter game mentioned under entertainment. Other services have been introduced based on knowledge of the proximity to other mobile devices (and, hence, the people that are carrying them). For example, NTT DoCoMo offers a "friends finder" service on its iMode system (Levijoki 2000). Users predefine which friends are allowed to know their location.

The LBS value chain and LBS business models

There are many different players that may be involved in bringing location-based services to the market (Pearce 2001; Sadeh 2002; Spinney 2003a). Among the parties involved are:

- Geographic information service (GIS) and other content providers who offer a range of mapping services and geographically oriented content, often accessed via a server known as a geoserver.
- Service providers who aggregate GIS and other content to create services.
- Application vendors who package services for mobile operators.
- Location middleware providers who provide tools to facilitate mobile operators' use of various applications from different providers.
- Mobile operators who manage the infrastructure, collect the position data, offer the service to end subscribers, and perform billing and collection services.
- Location infrastructure providers who sell the mobile location centers and other hardware and software to network operators.
- Handset manufacturers who sell devices capable of interacting with location-based services.

Each of these parties stands to earn revenue from location –based services, but the whole chain requires standard data formats and interfaces to work effectively (Spinney 2003a). If each individual application has its own proprietary format, the costs to launch a suite of services for consumers would be prohibitive for mobile operators.

The business models for LBS will most likely vary considerably across services. Sources of revenue for service providers may include subscription fees for a bundle of service available via a portal, subscription fees for specific services, advertising, connection and airtime fees, fees for content, transaction fees or margins on the price of products ordered (D'Roza and Bilchev 2003; Sadeh 2002; Van de Kar and Bouwman 2001). In some cases, such as for emergency 911 services, the operators may collect revenue to pay for the services through regular phone subscription fees. Another source of revenue may come from businesses that pay a fee in order to be included in location-based business directories, even if the service does not include any push-based advertising. Indeed, many privacy advocates have expressed opposition to the use of advertising that is pushed to the client, rather than specifically requested, suggesting that this is unlikely to be a viable revenue stream.

Most likely, LBS will use various combinations of revenue models. For example, customers may be offered the choice between advertiser and non-advertiser supported services, with the former provided at no cost and the latter provided for a fee.

In addition, many location-based services will be offered as a business service to companies, targeting their employees. In these cases, the service will resemble something like a private network, with bulk or volume discounts offered to large business clients. Individual employees will not be charged. For firms, the motivation will be to enhance employee productivity and make particular business processes more efficient. Some analysts, in fact, believe that this will be the primary early market for location-based services (Economics Intelligence Unit, October 17, 2001; November 1, 2001).

LBS policy issues

The emergence of location-based services raises many important policy questions. We briefly highlight four issues in this section, including the potential dangers due to loss of privacy, the issue of who controls location information, problems associated with quality of service, and the need for standards.

Privacy

A great deal has already been written about the potential privacy problems of location-based services (Beinat 2001; Clarke 2001; Hamblin 2001; Levijoki 2000; Thibodeau 2000). One of the biggest concerns is that it can be possible to compile a very detailed picture of someone's movements if they are carrying a wireless device that communicates its location to network operators. The potential for abuse of this information ranges from the mildly irritating (a shop sends an unsolicited advertisement when a mobile user approaches) to the more serious (firms use location information on field employees to impose strict performance measures, or potentially embarrassing information is released) and even dangerous or repressive (criminals determining the right time to intrude on a subscriber's house, or an improper conviction based on circumstantial location information) (Beinat 2001; Clarke 2001). Firms may find themselves facing ethical questions when using location information of customers, such as an insurance company that charges higher rates for clients that drive in dangerous areas.

The industry response to these concerns has been to conceive of all services as requiring customer "opt-in." That is, location information would only be released to those service providers offering a service that a customer has chosen to receive. In the US, federal legislation considers location information to be customer network proprietary information (CPNI), and can only be released with prior customer authorization except for emergency situations.

Despite this general opt-in policy, the dangers to privacy and personal freedom remain, as noted by Clarke (2001). This is because users may not realize all of potential privacy implications at the time they consent to use such services. Moreover, even without consent, the transfer of such information to third parties or law enforcement officials may be forced through court orders or subpoenas.

The ownership of location information is also troublesome on systems that use WiFi or technology relying on unlicensed spectrum. The main problem is that normal methods of enforcement of good behavior by the service provider, such as licensing, may not be available.

To help deal with these concerns, privacy advocates have compiled a set of principles to guide the provision of online services in general, and LBS in particular. These principles, elaborated in Beinat (2001) and Langheinrich (2001) include:

- *Notice*. Users need to be provided with complete information about what information is to be collected, how it will be used, how it will be stored, who will have access, and what options they have regarding their location-based information.
- *Choice*. Users should be able to decide when information about their location and use of location-based services will be released, and whether they wish for it to be released or not. They should also be allowed to remove or change the information about themselves to maintain accuracy.
- *Consent*. An explicit written contract indicating consent to use location information should be signed, rather than an operator simply declaring that this information is being collected.
- *Anonymity*. If users' identities can remain anonymous, operators should be able to collect location information for statistical or planning purposes.
- *Access*. There should be enforceable controls over who has access to user location data, and third party service providers should only be able to access the data required to provide their service.
- *Security*. Information that is stored must be accurate, and users should be protected from loss, misuse or unauthorized access or alteration. In addition, the data should not be stored any longer than necessary, and if transferred to another party that is required for a service, it should be under secure conditions.

Economic control of location information

In the value chain for the provision of location-based services, depending upon which method of determining location is used, service providers may be dependent upon cellular network operators for access to customers' location data. If the network operator had a competing location-based service, then they may have an incentive to either not make this information available, or to make it available on terms that place the competing service provider at a disadvantage. Policy makers will need to make clear exactly what the obligations are for the provision of location data, in addition to ensuring that informed consent is enforced.

Analysts have also cautioned network operators to avoid the "walled garden" approach to location-based service provision (Economics Intelligence Unit, October 15, 2001). Operators might be lured by the opportunities for a larger share of the revenue if they provide their own restricted and branded set of services to users. Experience with WAP portals, and earlier generations of information services suggest that this strategy will fail. On the other hand, the fastest growth of wireless data services appears to be in Japan's iMode system, which does not restrict customers' access to third party services that are independent of the operator's brands (FCC 2001). I-mode also offers a full complement of location-based services known as i-area (Sadeh 2002).

Quality of service

Operators have chosen different methods for determining location, and with varying costs and accuracy. Some location-based services may require more accuracy than others (Fielt, et al. 2000). For example, driving directions may require an accuracy of 30 meters, while location-sensitive billing or mobile yellow pages may only need to locate a user within a range of 250 meters (Sadeh 2002). Moreover, if operators are using a GPS solution that requires a minute or more for the time to first fix, then such delays might result in quite inaccurate positioning in fast moving vehicles. Customers may not be able to obtain the requisite quality of service on a particular provider's network.

A more serious quality of service issue faces service providers who use the unlicensed spectrum. The introduction of wireless LANs in public settings, with fee-based access, creates an expectation for a certain quality of service. However, service providers might have little control over others' use of the same spectrum in that area, since it is unregulated and services might suffer from interference.

Another related issue is the extent to which location-based services will interoperate with different user terminal equipment. If a user roams, for example, to another state, region, or country, will their terminal equipment still be able to work with the available network infrastructures to determine location and provide LBS? Manufacturers and operators are working together in the Location Interoperability Forum to help avoid fragmented supply of services[4].

Standards

The ability to rapidly create and implement services, maintain service quality and enable roaming across different mobile networks depends on the development of industry-wide standards. The lack of standards, especially in positioning technolo-

---

[4] The Location Interoperability Forum is now a part of the Open Mobile Alliance. More information is available at http://www.openmobilealliance.org.

gies, is stifling industry development. This is especially a problem in the United States where there are many competing cellular networks using different air interfaces and network infrastructures with pockets of coverage on a market by market basis rather than with national licenses. In a report to the FCC on the status of wireless E911 implementation, Hatfield (2002) notes that such services require an unusually high degree of coordination among the stakeholders, and will depend on standards. He sees the lack of such standards as key problems likely to cause delays in meeting the commission's objective.

Many organizations are involved today in the development of location based services. The global Third Generation Partnership Project (3GPP), through which the various standards bodies around the world are attempting to create a smooth transition to third generation wireless networks, deals with location-based services primarily in its Services and Architecture Working Groups (Adams et al. 2003). The Location Interoperability Forum (LIF) is another venue where industry players gather to achieve consensus on technical standards in the location infrastructure. The Open GIS consortium focuses on standards for expression of geospatial data. They, along with the WAP Forum and LIF have now all joined together into a new association called the Open Mobility Alliance. Standards are required not only for the position determining technologies, but also for the services and interfaces among content and application providers, for privacy-related procedures, and for the testing of system accuracy (Adams et al. 2003; Hatfield 2002).

Future directions

It may seem a bit premature to discuss the future of the location-based service industry given its relative state of immaturity. Nonetheless, the extensive work in the computer science community on pervasive and context-aware computing further suggests that future systems will incorporate more than location information and data drawn from personal profiles in the provision of services. Rather, embedded sensors are likely to enrich the services with a wide range of additional context data. Additionally, the proliferation of unlicensed wireless and the rapidity with which both wireline and cellular operators have moved to integrate 802.11b options into their portfolio of services suggests that convergence across between indoor and outdoor systems is likely to occur.

Context awareness

Up to now, most service providers are focusing their attention on location as the primary type of information to use when customizing services for subscribers. However, researchers active in the area of mobile computing consider location to be only one aspect of a users' context. Over the past decade, computer scientists have been exploring a variety of ways to make computer-based applications sensitive to location as well as other contextual information (Abowd et al. 1997; Harter et al. 1999; Hightower and Borriello 2001; Schmidt 2000; Schmidt et al. 1999, 2000, 2001; Want et al. 1992). Context may include both user provided profile information, as well as other aspects of context that may be detected by the system. One trial WAP application, for example, involved the provision of a context-sensitive phonebook to users before they made a call. The system used certain icons to depict the status of names in a user's phone directory, such as whether a person's phone was on, whether their line was engaged, and so forth. With this status information, callers may decide to forego a call that will only result in a connection to a message system (Schmidt et al. 2001). Such information can be enriched with user-provided context information, such as "I'm in a meeting right now" or "I'm not busy and would be happy to take a call (Schmidt et al. 2000). While these are not e-commerce applications, per se, it is easy to imagine how interactions between customers and businesses could be enriched by such approaches.

Researchers also have explored the use of various sensors in mobile devices to provide other types of context data. Schmidt et al. 1999 define context as "that which surrounds, and gives meaning to something else." They developed a framework for considering various contextual features, including human factors and physical environment factors. Human factors include information about the user (e.g. habits, emotional state, biophysical conditions), social environment (co-location of others, social interaction), and the user's tasks (what they are doing at the moment). Physical environment factors include the physical conditions at the moment (such as light, temperature, noise.), infrastructure (surrounding resources such as computers or phones that might be used) and, of course, location (including absolute location and relative location). Applications of such data can range from changes in the system's output depending upon context (e.g. notifications or alerts may be contingent on whether others are around), to simple interface improvements (e.g. turning up the volume in noisy environments, or providing a backlight on the screen in low light conditions).

Some of the research on context-aware computing has quite direct implications for e-commerce. First, much of the research has been completed in indoor environments, using such location and context detection technologies as infrared, ultrasound, and low power radio (Schmidt 2000; Schmidt et al. 1999; Want et al. 1992). Hence, it has the potential to fill in an important gap in the coverage afforded by GPS and some public cellular network-based location services. Unlike straight wireless LANs, which generally do not determine the location within a building or room, these systems do provide precise positioning indoors. Retailers, for example, may be interested in helping shoppers find products once they are already inside malls or stores, and providing highly local navigation aides (Duri et al. 2001; Eklund and Pessi 2001). Depending upon the granularity of the position detection, as well as user preference information, changing information could be provided to PDAs as shoppers moved about a store or mall. Such systems have obvious application in museums and other tourist areas (Abowd et al. 1997).

Other types of context information may come from sensors deployed on machines. Automotive firms talk about "telematic services" as including data about the state of particular components on vehicles, such as their need for repair. This

information can be sent from vehicles to car dealers, setting up preventative maintenance appointments prior to breakdowns (Varshney and Vetter 2001).

Convergence between location sensing technologies

As WiFi systems proliferate, it is possible that they may supply many location-
based services simply by virtue of being able to assume that connected parties are
within range of a particular base station. This may threaten the viability of some
services offered by mobile operators, since increasingly, WiFi hotspots are either
free or very low in cost.[5] On the other hand, seamless provision of location and
context-aware services require a mix of technologies (Duri et al. 2001; Spinney
2003b). A consumer may initiate a request from his or her car for all businesses in
the local area using a GPS equipped PDA or cellular phone. The service provider
may provide navigational services to direct the consumer to the appropriate location. Upon entering the business, a local WiFi network may provide additional information, and guide the consumer to their desired product. Some method for
handover of such applications is needed, without requiring consumers to re-input
product preferences. Spinney (2003b) discusses handover methods that rely on
both the location of the mobile phone user and the location of the indoor "hot-
spot." He further sees future handsets incorporating both cellular and 802.11 capabilities. These connections need to be seamless and without effort, especially if
users are paying for access to services.

Many applications lose their value if customers, or business users are out of
reach once they enter indoor environments. For this reason, we may see greater efforts to integrate applications across the variety of technologies for location-based
services.

Conclusions

Our overview of location-based services reveals that the market potential is
thought to be significant, driven in part by the deployment of automatic location
identification systems for emergency response. There are, however, significant
barriers to overcome. Technological barriers result from the diversity and cost of
approaches to location determination, creating a complex set of choices for operators and potential interoperability problems that, if unsolved, are likely to stifle
development. There are many exciting services under development, and some
have been operating successfully in such markets as Japan for several years. Innovative applications such as location-based games have achieved a following in
Sweden and been introduced into other markets. Despite the promise of LBS for
consumers, however, privacy concerns, quality of service problems, fair access to

---

[5] For example, Verizon began deployment of 802.11 systems in payphones across Manhat-
tan in May of 2003. The access is free for Verizon DSL subscribers.

location information, and the lack of standards for technology and service providers may hinder market development and represent critical policy issues to be resolved. Finally, in the area of potential future directions, it is evident that location is merely a starting point for personalization and context-aware services that use other relevant information when constructing service offers. Moreover, the rapid deployment of alternative wireless technologies, such as Wireless Fidelity (WiFi or 802.11) is both a threat and an opportunity for cellular operators, and will likely shape the future development of LBS.

References

Abowd G, Atkeson C, Hong J, Long S, Kooper R, Pinkerton M (1997) Cyberguide: A mobile context-aware tour guide. Wireless Networks 3 (5):421-433

Adams P, Ashwell G, Baxter R (2003) Location-based services – an overview of the standards. BT Technology Journal 21 (1):34-43

Anckar B, D'Incau D, (2002) Value creation in mobile commerce: Findings from a consumer survey. The Journal of Information Technology Theory and Application (JITTA) 4 (1):43-64

Bakos JY (1997) Reducing buyer search costs: Implications for electronic marketplaces. Management Science 43 (12):1676-1692

Barnes SJ (2002) Provision of services via the Wireless Application Protocol: A strategic prospective. Electronic Markets,12 (1)

Clarke, I (2001) Emerging value propositions for M-commerce. Journal of Business Strategies 18 (2)

Beinat E (2001) Privacy and location-based services. GeoInformatics September

Brewin R (2001) Penske outfits fleet with wireless terminals. Computerworld June 11

Brewin R (2001) Merchant Wired rolling out 'wireless' mall for retailers. Computerworld May 30

Cairncross F (1997) The death of distance. Boston, Massachusetts, Harvard Business School Press

Clarke R (2001) Person-location and person-tracking: Technologies, risks and policy implications. Information Technology and People Summer:206-231

Djuknic G, Richton R (2002) Geolocation and Assisted-GPS. Lucent Technologies White Paper, accessed June 1, 2003, http://www.lucent.com/knowledge/ documentdetail/0,1983,inContentId+090094038000e51f-inLocaleId+1,00.html

D'Roza T, Bilchev G (2003) An overview of location-based services. BT Technology Journal 21 (1):20-27

Duri S, Cole A, Munson J, Christensen J (2001) An approach to providing seamless end-user experience for location-aware applications. IBM, Thomas J Watson Research Center

Economic Intelligence Unit (2001) A different way of working. The Economist, October 17, accessed June 1, 2003, http://www.ebusinessforum.com/index.asp?layout=rich_story&doc_id=4675

Economic Intelligence Unit (2001) Uncovering the real value of mobile computing. The Economist, November 1, accessed June 1, 2003, http://www.ebusinessforum.com/ index.asp?layout=rich_story&doc_id=4774

Economic Intelligence Unit (2001) Why mobile is different. The Economist, October 15, accessed June 1, 2003, http://www.ebusinessforum.com/index.asp?layout=rich_story& doc_id=4656

Eklund S, Pessi K (2001) Exploring mobile eCommerce in geographically bound retailing. Proceedings of the 34th Hawaii International Conference on System Sciences (HICSS-34), January 3-6, Maui, Hawaii

FCC (2001) Sixth annual report and analysis of competitive market conditions with respect to commercial mobile services, Federal Communications Commission FCC 01-192, July 17

FCC (2003) Enhanced 911. Federal Communications Commission, accessed June 1, 2003, http://www.fcc.gov/911/enhanced/

Fielt E, Bouwman H, Steinfield C, Adelaar T, Smit A, deLange E, Simons L, Staal, M (2000) Location-aware electronic commerce. PLACE Project Report D4.4: TI/RS/2000/144, Enschede: Telematica Instituut, December

Greenspan R (2002) Locating wireless revenue, value. CyberAtlas Wireless Markets, August 30, accessed June 1, 2003, http://cyberatlas.internet.com/markets/wireless/article/0,,10094_1454791,00.html

Hamblin M (2001) Privacy concerns mount over wireless location technology. Computerworld February 13

Harter A, Hopper A, Steggles P, Ward A, Webster P (1999) The anatomy of a context-aware application. In Proc. of the Fifth Annual ACM/IEEE International Conference on Mobile Computing and Networking , Seattle, WA, August:59-68

Hatfield D (2002) A report on technical and operational issues impacting the provision of wireless enhanced 911 services. Prepared for the Federal Communications Commission, accessed June 1, 2003, http://www.fcc.gov/911/enhanced/reports/

Hightower J, Borriello G (2001) Location systems for ubiquitous computing. IEEE Computer August:57-66

KRNIC (2003) Survey on the usage of wireless Internet. Korea Network Information Center, accessed June 1, 2003, http://isis.nic.or.kr/english/sub04/sub04_index.html?sub=01V&id=81

ITU (2003) ICT free statistics. International Telecommunications Union, accessed June 1, 2003, http://www.itu.int/ITU-D/ict/statistics/

Langheinrich M (2001) Privacy by design - principles of privacy-aware ubiquitous systems. Proc Ubicomp 2001, Springer-Verlag: 273-291, accessed June 1, 2003, http://www.inf.ethz.ch/vs/publ/papers/privacy-principles.pdf

Levijoki S (2001) Privacy vs location awareness, Unpublished manuscript, Helsinki University of Technology

Liete F, Pereira J (2001) Location-bases services and emergency communications in IMT-2000. ITU News 7, accessed June 1, 2003, http://www.itu.int/itunews/issue/2001/07/mobility.html

Millar W (2003) Location information from the cellular network – an overview. BT Technology Journal 21(1): 98-104

Norris A (2003) Hide and seek: Location-based services are heading for the UK. The Guardian, February 6, accessed June 1, 2003, http://www.guardian.co.uk/online/mobilematters/story/0,12454,889408,00.html

NTT Docomo (2003) Subscriber growth. NTT Docomo, accessed June 1, 2003, http://www.nttdocomo.com

Pearce D (2001) Location enabled content and applications. Mobile Location Services Workshop, Rome, June 19-20, accessed June 1, 2003, http://www.openmobilealliance.org/lif/presentations.htm

Priyantha N, Chakraborty A and Balakrishnan H (2000) The cricket location-support system. 6th ACM Conference on Mobile Computing and Networking, Boston, MA

Sadeh N (2002) M-Commerce: Technologies, services, and business models. New York, Wiley

Schmidt A (2000) Implicit human computer interaction through context. Personal Technologies 4 (2 and 3):191-199

Schmidt A, Beigl M, Gellersen H (1999) There is more to context than location. Computers & Graphics Journal 23 (6):893-902

Schmidt A, Stuhr T, Gellersen H (2001) Context-phonebook: Extending mobile phone applications with context. Third Mobile HCI Workshop, Lille

Schmidt A, Takaluoma A, Mantyjarvi J (2000) Context-aware telephony over WAP. Personal Technologies Volume 4 (4):225-229

Searby S (2003) Personalisation – an overview of its use and potential. BT Technology Journal 21 (1):13-19

Spinney J (2003a) A brief history of LBS and how OpenLS fits into the new value chain. Java Location Services Newsletter, accessed June 1, 2003, http://www.jlocationservices.com/

Spinney J (2003b) Cellular-to-WiFi handoff, micro-LBS, and the symbiotic power of location. Java Location Services Newsletter, accessed June 1, 2003, http://www.jlocationservices.com/

Steinfield C, Klein S (1999) Local versus global issues in electronic commerce. Electronic Markets 9 (1):45-50

Steinfield C, Adelaar T, Lai Y-j (2002) Integrating brick and mortar locations with e-commerce: Understanding synergy opportunities. Hawaii International Conference on Systems Sciences, Big Island, Hawaii, IEEE Computer Society

Steinfield C, Bouwman H, Adelaar T (2002) The dynamics of click and mortar e-commerce: Opportunities and management strategies. International Journal of Electronic Commerce 7 (1):93-119

Thibodeau P (2000) Huge privacy questions loom as wireless use grows, Computerworld, December 18

Van de Kar E, Bouwman H (2001) The development of location based mobile services. Edispuut Conference, Amsterdam, October 17

VanderMeer J (2001) What's the difference between m-Commerce and l-Commerce? Business Geographics, March/April, accessed June 1, 2003, http://www.geoplace.com/bg/2001/0401/0401wire.asp

Varshney U, Vetter R (2001) Framework for emerging mobile commerce applications. Proceedings of the 34th Hawaii International Conference on System Sciences (HICSS-34), January 3-6, Maui, Hawaii

Want R, Hopper A, Falcão V, Gibbons J (1992) The Active Badge location system. ACM Transactions on Information Systems 10 (1):91-102

Wireless Today (2001) Market snapshot: Worldwide wireless data market 2000-2004 TelecomWeb, Accessed June 1, 2003, http://www.telecomweb.com/reports/cotm/snapshot.htm

Employing mobile communities for marketing consumer goods

Peter Aschmoneit[1], Mark Heitmann[2], Johannes Hummel[3]

Institute for Media and Communications Management, University of St. Gallen, Switzerland

Abstract

Communities are a traditional concept to enhance customer attraction, loyalty and retention for consumer goods. These communities are supported through either companies or customers themselves. Companies that are able to encourage their customers to interact stimulated by their branded products could position their product as a link between their customers and employ the developing communities for marketing purposes. To stimulate this kind of interaction companies have increasingly used Internet functionalities in the past years. Drawing on the overwhelming penetration rate of mobile devices of over 80 percent in Europe, we propose to employ the mobile channel to support this kind of community building process. We derive four constitutional elements of communities based on existing research and develop a structured and theoretically founded four step method to analyze the potential of mobile services for specific community building purposes.

Introduction

On the internet communities were initiated by companies to gather a critical mass of people, to transfer a sense of bonding between community members to a company or to encourage interaction about corporate products. Communities related to a product or brand are a conventional concept for increasing consumer loyalty and attraction. Owners of a Harley Davidson-branded motorcycle are not necessarily riding it because it represents the best technology. They do so because it enables them to be part of a community collectively interested in a set of values, such as freedom and American pride (McEnally and de Chernatony 1999).

---

[1] E-mail: Peter.Aschmoneit@unisg.ch
[2] E-mail: Mark.Heitmann@unisg.ch
[3] E-mail: Johannes.Hummel@unisg.ch

Companies tried to make use of the new possibilities of the internet to gather a critical mass of people independent of their physical location to stimulate brand related interactions. While many of these efforts have failed to meet expectations some succeeded the dot com bust by understanding the technology as well as the social effects of communities at an early stage.

In addition to the Internet, the mobile channel seems to be another promising electronic platform for community building. Since the introduction of the global system for mobile communication (GSM) in Europe in 1992, the wireless market has grown rapidly. By the end of the year 2000, 781 million people globally and more than 252 million people in Europe were mobile phone users (Müller-Veerse 2001). Like the internet this area offers great new potential but also great risks for the establishment of communities. Companies able to differentiate themselves at an early stage by tying customers to their mobile communities can establish sustainable advantages towards competitors. Current research is just starting to tackle this area (e.g. Koch et al. 2002; Aschmoneit and Zimmermann 2002).

The aim of this paper is to theoretically explore product-related mobile communities as a way to profitably manage mobile communities and provide first insights on how they can be designed. For this purpose, we employ community research to identify four constitutional elements of a community, which are clearly defined group of actors, bonding among the members, interactions between the members, and the common space. While the characteristics of the mobile channel are used to identify new ways of supporting the development of bonding and common places, consumers cognition towards a product can be used to clearly define a group and the scope of desired interactions between them. We analyze how companies can make use of mobile communities with the aim of increasing consumer loyalty and attraction by placing their product as a link between customers, i.e. encouraging them to interact about it. We assume consumers already have a strong cognition towards a product and towards a particular brand. While brands can represent multiple products, e.g. corporate brands, for the purpose of this discussion we are referring to individual product brands. A specific product will be offered by multiple competitors who make use of brands carried by their products for differentiation. In this paper we will discuss how the association of a brand with particular consumer values can be used in building a community for further differentiation and how to make use of the new possibilities of mobility for that purpose.

Virtual communities

In this section we analyze research regarding virtual or internet based communities as a basis for exploring mobile communities. We describe virtual communities, their function, their role as a business model, and results of sociological research to identify four constitutional elements of communities.

Communities as sociological phenomenon

The first sociological definitions were created by Taylor and Licklider (1968), who discovered the community potential of electronic networks. They described their vision of a virtual community as follows: "... in most fields they will consist of geographically separated members, sometimes grouped in small clusters and sometimes working individually. They will be communities not of common location but of common interest (...)".

One of the best-known definitions of virtual communities is probably that of Rheingold (1993): Virtual communities are "...social aggregations that emerge from the net when enough people carry on public discussions long enough, with sufficient human feeling, to form webs of personal relationships in cyberspace."

It is believed that for community members in cyberspace the dream is not just owning a house but living in the right neighborhood. Jones (1997) even speaks of "virtual settlement". Figallo (1998) stresses the meaning of common values "(...) according to that definition, members of a community feel a part of it. They form relationships and bonds of trust with other members and with (...) the community host. Those relationships lead to exchanges and interactions that bring value to members."

From the perspective of computer-mediated communication, the most important elements of a virtual community are shared resources, common values, and reciprocal behavior. Whittaker et al. (1997) write "(...) members have a shared goal, interest, need, (...) engage in repeated, active participation, (...) have access to shared resources, (...) reciprocity of information, (...) shared context of social conventions (...)". Preece (2000) extends this view to include the necessity of common rules "(...) an online community consists of: People, who want to interact socially (...), a shared purpose...that provides a reason for the community, policies (...) that guide people's interactions (and) computer systems, to support and mediate social interaction (...)". Tonnies (1957) argued that the will to form a community (Gemeinschaft) is based on the essential will, i.e. the organic or instinctive driving forces.

Communities as socio-economic business models

Hagel III and Armstrong (1997) broke with the view of virtual communities as a sociological phenomenon. They consider virtual communities as business models which utilize the possibilities of communication on the internet to increase revenues. Referring to Rheingold, they define virtual communities as "(...) more than just a sociological phenomenon. What starts off as a group drawn together by common interests ends up as a group with a critical mass of purchasing power, partly thanks to the fact that communities allow members to exchange information on such things as a product's price and quality" (Hagel III and Armstrong 1997). Timmers (1998) considers virtual communities to be business models in which "the ultimate value (comes) from the members (customers or partners) who add their information (...)".

For Hagel III and Armstrong (1997) as well as for Timmers (1998) the emphasis in the socio-economic view on communities is the economic element of it. They favor models where community organizers manage communities to increase online revenues. Currently, virtual communities meet those expectations only in part (Hagel III and Bughin 2001). Today, the emphasis is again more on the sociological element. The Cluetrain Manifesto (Levine et al. 2000) emphasizes the social aspects in "markets to be conversations with a transaction being just an exclamation mark at the end of a sentence".

Thus, virtual communities provide the social environment for transactions to take place and community members to contribute, build value online and further strengthen the virtual environment. Over time, a number of communities have emerged, and they distinguish themselves not only by the actors and their roles, but also by their social environment. They range from communities of interest to communities of transaction or gaming.

Social profile

Virtual communities differ in their business purposes and their ways to create value. The previous section illustrates the wide range of perspectives on virtual communities. One of the main challenges for the management of those communities is the management of the social environment. As complex social systems communities must develop over time. This can only happen in an environment in which the participants feel comfortable and in which visitors eventually become active contributing members. Therefore, in order to create an environment which fits the needs of the participants as well as the economic aims of the community operator, the managers of virtual communities need to understand their underlying social aspects.

The need for social relations is common to both virtual and offline communities. We follow Wellmann (1992) and consider virtual communities as simply a type of (offline) community in which communication is enabled mainly by electronic media. The model of the social network of virtual communities originates in sociological research of traditional (offline) communities. In describing virtual communities, we follow the approach of Hammann (2000) and Hillery (1955). Four constitutional elements of a community are identified:

1. A clearly defined group of actors,
2. the interaction between the members,
3. the bonding among the members,
4. and the common space - the medium that facilitates interaction.

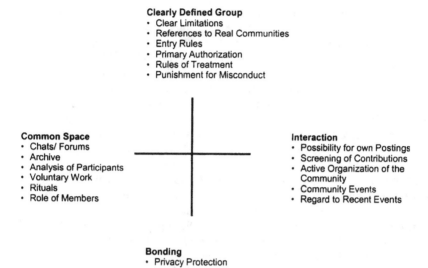

Clearly Defined Group
- Clear Limitations
- References to Real Communities
- Entry Rules
- Primary Authorization
- Rules of Treatment
- Punishment for Misconduct

Common Space
- Chats/ Forums
- Archive
- Analysis of Participants
- Voluntary Work
- Rituals
- Role of Members

Interaction
- Possibility for own Postings
- Screening of Contributions
- Active Organization of the Community
- Community Events
- Regard to Recent Events

Bonding
- Privacy Protection
- Personalization
- Sub-communities
- Identification of Organizer
- Identification of Members

Fig. 1. Community profile with four dimensions and features

In order for a community to develop, all four elements must be present. On the internet, each element can be supported through a number of features depicted in Figure 1. As an empirical study of fifty virtual communities (Hummel and Becker 2002) shows, different types of communities, e.g. related to gaming or interest, use these features in different ways.

It is essential for any kind of community to clearly define the audience it addresses (Turner et al. 1987; Kim 2000). Defining a group based on common interests and values alows for a precise characterization of the community for the potential participants. It enables them to evaluate a community on the basis of their ability to find interaction partners who reflect their interest. On the one hand a group has to be defined precisely for participants to engage in valuable focused interactions, but on the other hand the definition needs to be wide enough to attract a sufficient amount of members (Ostrom 1990; Kollock and Smith 1996).

The element of social interaction refers to the kind and quality of interaction between the members of a community. Due to social interaction, participants get to know each other, and, thus, bonding among them can develop. Even though interaction with others is regarded as a basic human need, it cannot be enforced, especially in electronic communities (Hummel and Lechner 2001). On the internet, interactions can be stored and participants are able to benefit from interactions in which they are not directly involved, making them potentially passive. This contradiction between collective and individual rationality can be found in virtual as well as other forms of communities (Kollock and Smith 1996). Nevertheless, interactions can be stimulated. For example, this can be done by ensuring that topics that are interesting to the defined group are constantly available.

Bonding among members is perceived to be the essential reason why participants stick to a community (McWilliam 2001; Preece 2000). Bonding is closely associated with trust between the participants. Bonding as well as trust must develop over time while participants interact with each other (Figallo 1998). Recent research shows that trust towards the operator of virtual communities can take the place of bonding between individual members (Döring and Schestag 2000). If the operator can be clearly identified and ensures that submissions to the community are actually relevant topics for the defined group, bonding towards the community as a whole is established.

The element of common space describes the space in which community members meet, e.g. chat forums, and how it is organized. Compared to traditional communities where members meet at certain physical locations, e.g. a sports club, the platform of virtual communities is detached from physical locations (Hummel and Lechner 2001). These platforms need to enable people with common interests to meet and start to interact (Turkle 1995). The operator of a community provides archives, enables participants to voluntarily work for the community or enables them to assume roles within the community.

From virtual to mobile communities

In this section we explore mobile communities in general as a basis for the analysis of product-related mobile communities. We describe the key characteristics of mobility and apply them to the two elements of communities, bonding and a common space, to depict new opportunities for mobile communities compared to virtual ones.

Mobile characteristics

In order to discuss mobile communities, one must first establish the characteristics that determine mobile interaction. Therefore, there is a need to analyze the phenomenon "mobility", and to identify the major differences between it and a fixed means of interaction. Some authors specify mobile characteristics as classified by the chronology of their realization, others arrange the characteristics by their assumed customer value, and there are also some who do not suggest any systematic order (Reichwald et al. 2002). Our interpretation of the existing literature and the attempt to cluster these characteristics into four classes will help to take advantage of the major innovations that new mobile technology is providing.

The following clusters can be identified from the existing literature: Location awareness, ubiquity, identification, and immediacy (see also Müller et al. 2002):

Location awareness

With the help of wireless technology every mobile device can be localized. It is easy to determine the physical location of the mobile terminal and with it that of the mobile user, as well as their movement as long as the device is switched on. The simplest cell localization takes place at the time the user logs on to a mobile network. But with new positioning technologies that are either network-based or device-based, exact localization up to a few feet will be widely available in the near future (Figge 2001). With the awareness of the position of the mobile terminal, a mobile (community) application can automatically consider the user's geographical context (location-based community features). The mobile community Friendzone is an exemplary use of the current localization technology. The Friendzone service was established by the Swiss mobile operator Swisscom in early 2001. Members of the Friendzone community are able to localize other members, receive an alert when members with similar profiles are in close range, and chat via Short Message Service (SMS), WAP, and the Web.

If location information is automatically combined and analyzed with other information like geodata, time, or personal interests, it is possible to create context sensitivity (Zobel 2001). Zobel (2001) differentiates between action-oriented context, where detailed geodata like public infrastructure is applied, time-oriented context, where the actual time is applied, and interest-specific context, where personal interests and preferences of the user are applied.

An example of a mobile community that is making use of combining location information with time and interests can be found in Sweden. Supafly is a location-based mobile soap opera that is offered by the start-up It's Alive. In Supafly the mobile user creates his own character which is associated with the mobile phone and – since the game is location-based – follows along wherever the user goes. As a trusty companion, the character will help the user to find nearby friends, or perhaps even to find a date. At close range, the user's companion can interact with those of other players in many different ways. For example, they can chat, quarrel or kiss. Supafly is licensed to mobile operators and service providers, who in turn provide the game to their subscribers.

Ubiquity

In addition to awareness of the user's location, mobile technology also helps to further reduce the need to attach certain services to a specific location. There are many services that have a high degree of location dependency, which means that the provision of the service must take place at a certain location (Reichwald et al. 2000). However, in cases where the location dependency is only factual, wireless technology can resolve the location dependency. While a bank transaction, for example, could in the past only be made at the branch or (with the help of the internet, phone, or fax) from home, current wireless technology abolishes this location dependency and allows the bank service to be provided ubiquitously. Wherever the user likes to make bank transactions, he can do so, no matter what location he is at. This allows users to reschedule certain activities to times that were previously unused.

For example, the Japanese I-Mode service is mostly used during commuting time to and from work, a time that was previously unused (Albers and Becker 2001). Now I-Mode users send emails, look at the weather forecast, load ring tones into their handsets, do online banking and stock trading, etc.

Closely connected with the reduction of location dependency is permanent availability. The user is able to use an interaction device regardless of his location, ubiquitously. The possibility to use different services through one device avoids media breaches. Thus, the interaction point with the customer always stays the same for a company.

Identification

Contrary to the existing internet most of the users are registered with one or more (virtual) mobile operators. Usually the identity of every mobile user is linked to the subscriber identity module (SIM) in the mobile terminal and the customer's master data is administered by mobile operators. While the household telephone and PC are typically used by different household members the mobile terminal is a personal item. Therefore, the technical prerequisites to individually target and interact with a segment-of-one are given.

Besides the technical dimension of identification, there is also a personal one. Like the owner's apparel, purse, wristwatch, or organizer, the mobile terminal usually belongs to his or her so-called personal sphere (Wiedmann et al. 2000). The personal sphere encompasses the direct ambiance of the individual. An individual has an intimate relationship with the objects of the personal sphere. Most of the time users carry their mobile terminals with them, and they often carry them as personal accessories (BCG 2000). Therefore, based on the personal dimension of identification, there is a huge potential for services that are built on the trusted relationship between the individual and the mobile terminal.

The German start-up Paybox is an example of a service that is using both the technical and the personal dimension of this identification. The start-up, which is half-owned by Deutsche Bank, is putting the mobile terminal to work as an electronic purse. Paybox customers can easily pay for their online and offline shopping, for taxis or restaurants, and can transfer money to accounts of other Paybox community members. Paybox users only need to enter their personal code into their mobile terminal to verify the intended transaction. The charge that the user has verified will appear as a deduction in the user's bank account.

Immediacy

Immediacy allows instant action and reaction to arising demand. To date, immediacy in the U.S. has been provided for voice and short message transmission. With the introduction of general packet radio service technology (GPRS) in Europe, permanent connectivity is an imminent feature. This is a step towards instant delivery of mobile services. With GPRS, the "always-on" mentality evolves on the customer side. Time-critical services like financial trading or emergency services are applications that receive a higher value and new features through immediate functionality.

Another aspect of immediacy is that the dial-in process that we know from PC internet use is put aside. This may lower the barrier for individuals to use electronic services at all. The ability to offer situation-specific services at the same time will on the other hand raise expectations regarding quality and speed of mobile services delivery as immediacy allows two-way communication and instant customer feedback.

Immediacy as a functionality is beneficial for instant messenger services that have been adapted for mobile devices such as those provided by AOL, Yahoo, or ICQ. The possibility to be always online further enhances the messaging functionality we know from SMS and Multimedia Messaging (MMS). Without any time lag, the user is able to see which of his buddies can be reached and react directly. When the user connects the instant messaging service with a mobile terminal, the conversational partner will see a small icon appear, indicating that this user might be a little slower in reactions (due to the simple keypad) or use more shorthand language.

New opportunities for communities in the mobile environment

For participants, mobile communities may have advantages in the four named areas over virtual or offline communities. Since there are also disadvantages, e.g. leaner communication due to limited I/O interfaces, mobile communities need to utilize the mobility characteristics in order to succeed. At the same time, the four constitutional elements of a community must be fulfilled. In the case of product-related communities, the elements *interaction* and *clearly defined group* should be determined according to the product itself. For the elements *bonding* and *common space* the characteristics of the mobile channel will be applied.

Bonding in mobile communities

In order for bonding between members of a community to develop, it is essential that the members trust each other as well as the operator of the community. In this case, trust is limited to the interactions between the members of the community. If participants feel that they are treated with honesty and without deception while they are interacting with others in a community, trust is built. Operators of community platforms are able to support this process by setting codes of behavior, specifying ways how these codes are determined (Döring and Schestag 2000), and also by helping participants to inform themselves of the interaction history of their interaction partners (Heintz 2000).

Using the location awareness of mobile devices, a common context of individuals can be detected and communicated. This in turn can increase trust and bonding, since participants will more frequently have common goals for the interaction and will be convinced of this commonality more easily. Sometimes the quality of information can be estimated by the location of the submitter. For example, in a community that provides customer ratings and reviews on movies, trust towards reviews can be increased by adding the information in which context the review was provided, e.g. before entering, shortly after leaving the theater or in some completely unrelated situation. Due to the potential physical interaction, location awareness induces more contacts with stronger bonding. Physical meetings initiated by location awareness are regarded as the spontaneous formation of a sub-community, which is also believed to increase bonding (Hummel and Becker 2002). The location-based soap opera Supafly is putting these principles into practice.

In many virtual communities, some members participate only casually whenever they have the time. At the same time, frequency of usage influences bonding. Communities that enable participants to share cartoons, ring tones or logos for their mobile phones, etc. are accessible to users at times that were previously unused, e.g. on the way to work. Like in the Japanese I-Mode service, bonding can be established around subjects that would have been unsuitable for that purpose on the internet.

If members of a community can identify each other on the community platform (according to other members settings), trust and bonding is positively influenced. On the internet, communities that incorporate stronger bonding offer the possibility to identify other members by their e-mail address. As the mobile terminal (and SIM respectively) is mostly used by only one individual, new ways of identification between community members are possible, to the extent of a telephone number that can be provided and controlled by the operator. On the other hand, as mobile devices themselves are a more personal item than a computer, identification and trust with the device and the network operator can be transferred towards the community. Integrating community services in network operator platforms or in the software of devices themselves, will blur boundaries towards the community and in turn increase trust.

Compared to virtual communities, bonding can be increased using the immediacy of mobile services. To give members of communities a feeling of constant potential attachment, and of not missing out on any kind of event, enhances the bonding towards the community itself and by extention also between its members. In addition, immediacy induces an increasing amount of direct reactions. Communities of interest that share information on common problems, e.g. using special features of a mobile phone, can benefit from this possibility. In virtual communities, users assist each other using forums, but also by making use of direct interactions on instant messenger systems. The potential to solve problems as they arise, e.g. how to take and transmit a picture with a mobile phone, increases bonding with the community. At the same time, immediacy increases the number of available partners for these kinds of problem solving processes and thereby improves the reliability for the user.

Common spaces of mobile communities

Common spaces need to enable people with common interests to meet and start interaction (Turkle 1995). On the internet, communities were detached from a common physical space to a common virtual space (Hummel and Lechner 2001). Mobile communities are able to define common virtual spaces, but there are opportunities to create common physical spaces as well.

Location awareness enables community operators to blur the boundaries between physical and virtual common spaces. Informing participants of nearby other members, enabling them to check places for others, or broadcast their own location to a subgroup within the community has been suggested (Koch et al. 2002). Participants do not have to physically meet to provide a virtual common space for a subgroup based on their context information. A car-related community can enable their participants to exchange information about traffic jams and possible free circumventions. In this case a virtual common space around the same physical context would be established.

Virtual common spaces of mobile communities can be strengthened by building on ubiquity. As described for a given common space, frequency of usage can be increased, in some cases enabling virtual common spaces that would otherwise not attract a sufficient amount of participants. In addition, certain interactions may be primarily interesting at specific spots, e.g. the submission of statements about a painting at an art gallery. Some places may also motivate people to try to physically meet others, increasing demand for location aware community services.

Due to the immediacy of wireless networks, different kinds of virtual common spaces, where participants never really leave, can be established. For example, using instant messenger features available on always-on wireless networks, participants are constantly able to check each other's status. This is especially useful when searching for a contact needed for an urgent issue, e.g. how to put on snow chains when the user is actually driving in bad weather conditions and wants to learn from other community members.

Not only can identification be used to increase trust and bonding between members, but also to form common spaces based on the personal information of individuals. For example, people from the same town may be interested in meeting each other while on vacation. By agreeing to share this kind of information, operators can be used as a trusted party to make it available to others. A virtual common space can be formed according to personal information and location information, enabling physical common spaces.

As shown above there are many new opportunities where the characteristics of the mobile channel can add value compared to wired electronic media. The bonding of a community can be enhanced by higher context awareness (e.g. location awareness), the high frequency of usage of the personal mobile media and the immediacy of mobile services. Common spaces can be strengthened by the ability to blur the boundaries between the physical and virtual spheres, by location awareness and by immediacy. It is essential to use these benefits when employing mobile communities for marketing consumer goods. However to design a mobile community all four constitutional elements of the social profile must be considered in the development process.

Community design and product link

In order for communities to develop over time, an environment should be provided in which participants feel comfortable to participate actively. For the design of virtual communities, only few generic rules are available; there are even fewer for mobile communities. Some authors state critical success factors with regard to community building (e.g. Panten et al. 2001), distinguish different phases in community building (e.g. Hagel III and Armstrong 1999), or neglect any possibility to create communities (Shafer 1999). Explicit methodologies are rare. This is partly due to the fact that community building is not only a task of providing a common space or virtual platform on fixed or mobile networks, where people are able to connect to one another. Instead, the other three constitutional elements of a community must also be addressed (Hammann 2000). In this section we discuss how a target group and their interactions can be derived from consumer cognition to increase consumer loyalty and attraction. This can be achieved by positioning the product as a link between consumers.

For our purpose we conceptually identify three elements of a product link between any two consumers. These are (1) relationships around a product between existing members of a group, (2) product-related relationships between consumers previously unknown to each other or (3) one time relations between consumers. Many products are bought not because they meet customer requirements best but because they enable customers to be part of a community collectively interested in the same set of values, e.g. Harley Davidson customers in freedom (McEnally and de Chernatony 1999). Interactions between existing members of a group of Harley Davidson riders can be identified around the physical presence of the product in the sense of social acknowledgement or just communication about the motorcycle itself. In addition, customers of Harley Davidson previously unknown to each other feel closer and have an easier time building up new relations. For many luxury goods and even for products like sophisticated magazines, one-time relations do not have to comprise communication, in order for the product to function as a link. For example, people reading National Geographic in a public place might feel that they are communicating a particular aspect of themselves (see also Goffman 1959; Grubb and Hupp 1968). Product-related communities will have the strongest effect on consumer loyalty and attraction when all three product link elements can be evoked by a company. Since elements (1) and (2) involve the direct interaction between consumers, mobile services can be designed to support the community building process around those two elements.

All three product link elements can be exploited based on the consumers' cognitive perception of a product. This cognitive perception is especially represented in values that consumers associate with this product. Values represent important beliefs about oneself and the reception of oneself by others. They are understood as universal, object-, or context-independent convictions about desirable end-states of life (Schwartz 1994; Gutman 1982). Rokeach (1973) defines values similarly: "A value is an enduring belief that a specific mode of conduct or state of existence is personally or socially preferable to an opposite or converse mode of conduct or end state of existence." Thereby values determine the personality and are believed to be relatively resistant against changes in the environment (Herrmann 1996b). It is believed that only a small set of values is relevant to behavior. Therefore, lists of values can be used to identify values of consumers (e.g. Kahle 1997; Mitchel 1983; Opaschowski 1993). Examples of these kinds of values include self esteem, security, enjoyment and achievement. Even though values are relatively resistant to changes in the environment, long term changes in the generic values of a society need to be monitored (Opaschowski 1993).

A group of common interest as a constituting element of a community (Hammann 2000) can be clearly defined around the same set of values. Products carrying brands that are intensely associated with certain values, e.g. Mercedes and security, are a good basis for identifying people sharing common interests. How companies can try to establish consumer-perceived associations with certain values following a long term process is an extensively covered subject in marketing (e.g. Reynolds and Gutman 1984; Gardner and Levy 1955; Kapferer 1997; de Chernatony and Dall'Olmo Riley 1997). For this paper we take existing associations as a given. Many companies already own strong brands with the potential of developing communities around a common set of values. In order to support community building processes with mobile services, they need to validate the desired values associated with their products and analyze the way they are associated to it from a consumer perspective.

For this purpose the means-end chain methodology is particularly useful. It is based on the traditional expectancy value model (Rosenberg 1956), assuming that the attitude of an individual towards an object is determined by the individual's cognitive structure. The means-end chain concept divides this cognitive structure into three levels, namely attributes, needs, and values (Gutman 1982). With the aid of personal interviews, in particular the laddering technique, data is collected to map these three levels. Content analysis serves as a basis for quantitative evaluation and graphical representation of the results.

In marketing-related research the qualitative means-end chain analysis has increasingly been an object of scientific debate (e.g. Herrmann 1996a, 1996b; Vriens and Hofstede 2000; Wansink 2000; Aschmoneit and Heitmann 2002). It has been successfully employed for over ten years for communications strategy as well as product design. The underlying means-end model for most of the work is the one presented by Gutman (1982). This model is based on two assumptions: (1) values, defined as desirable end-states of existence, are dominant in the formation of selection structures and (2) people deal with the variety of products by forming classes in order to reduce the complexity of the decision. For the formation of classes, consumers consult the consequences of their actions or purchase decisions. Consumers learn to associate positive consequences, namely the benefit derived from a purchase, with certain decisions, like the choice of a product (Reynolds and Gutman 1988). Personal values allocate a positive or negative valence to these consequences (Rokeach 1973). Thus, a correlation between the concrete and abstract characteristics of a product, the functional and psychosocial consequences and the instrumental and target values is assumed (Gutman 1997). Since consumers are believed to form classes to reduce complexity in their decision making process, a relatively small number of values is connected to a larger number of consequences and attributes. In this hierarchy the importance of values determines the importance of consequences and attributes (Rosenberg 1956).

To determine chains of attributes, consequences and values, the laddering technique (Reynolds and Gutman 1988) for personal interviews is applied. With the laddering technique consumers are asked for distinguishing product characteristics and to reason why these characteristics are important to them. They are then asked to justify their answer again. This process is continued until they cannot reason in any further detail. Laddering and the ensuing qualitative content analysis has been discussed in literature controversially (e.g. Grunert and Grunert 1995; Johnson 1989). The main criticism refers to the implicit assumption that consumers are able to express their cognitive structure. Therefore, interviewers must be experienced and thoroughly trained not to influence consumers during the process, especially when determining the value layer.

The resulting transcripts of laddering interviews are analyzed by dividing answers into attributes, consequences, and values, and by categorizing them further using content analysis (Reynolds and Gutman 1988). The absolute number of concepts and the number of linkages between concepts, the reasoning of the consumers, is counted to construct hierarchical value maps. They are used to summarize the main results of a laddering study and show the levels of values, consequences and attributes from top to bottom.

Besides the criticism expressed towards laddering, the means-end chain methodology should be critically considered. From a consumer research perspective, it can be classified as a partial model since it focuses exclusively on motivational and cognitive aspects of consumer behavior. Emotional, sociological, dynamic or perceptional aspects are not considered (Kroeber-Riel and Weinberg 1999). Even though it is reasonable to explain specific aspects of consumer behavior in more detail as opposed to using excessively complex total models, more work regarding the connection to other partial models would be desirable (Grunert, K.G. and Grunert, S.C. 1995). In our case consumers also derive a benefit if they can be part of a product-related community. The means-end chain methodology only focuses on vendor to consumer relations; it does not depict consumer to consumer relations as a source for product-related benefits. In addition, the means-end chain model assumes a hierarchical cognitive structure in consumers whereas more complex networks are usually assumed in cognitive research (Grunert 1991). Further theoretical gaps lie in the process of preference building. Since the underlying model is based on cognitive structure rather than on processes, it is not possible to analyze how the determined cognitive structures have been established or how they are influenced.

Therefore, the means-end chain methodology will yield information on how communities should be established to position a product as a link, but not on how this influences consumers cognition towards the product. In our case we can

loosen the restriction of the partial model by integrating it with community research to exploit consumer to consumer relations. For defining a group and determining desired interaction topics for communities, hierarchical cognitive structures are sufficiently accurate and can be interpreted in a straightforward manner
for community design. Figure 3 illustrates a hierarchical value map regarding
automobiles as a result of a study conducted in Germany.

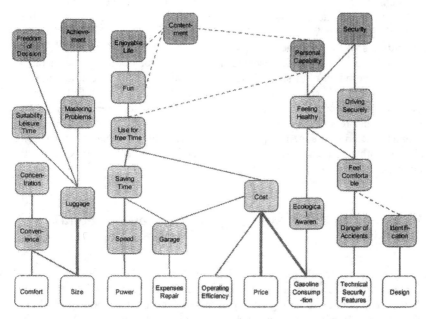

Fig. 2. Hierarchical value map regarding automobiles (Gaus et al. 1997)

When interpreting a hierarchical value map for mobile community design it is
important to focus on the linkages between concepts. The bolder the linkage the
more often it has occured in consumers' reasoning. For example, many respondents perceive it as useful to drive a larger sized car (attribute), because of greater
luggage space (consequence). Fewer respondents reasoned that being able to take
more luggage on a trip makes them free to decide wherever they want to go
(value).

For many brands associated values may be quite clear at a first glance, e.g.
Nike with winning or Marlboro with outdoorsmen or freedom. To design mobile
communities is has to be validated that consumers really associate the intended
values with a specific brand. In the automobile example five values generally associated with cars have been identified: "Freedom of Decision", "Achievement",
"Enjoyable Life", "Contentment", "Personal Capability", and "Security". Based
on this general cognition towards cars, the values associated with a particular
brand must be determined as an essential input to place the product as a link
within a product-related community. For example, if consumers mainly associate

the Mercedes brand with "Security", then this can be used to clearly define a group of Mercedes owners with a common interest in "Driving Securely" and "Feeling Healthy" while driving.

After clearly determining a group, product-related interactions must be defined. Hierarchical value maps also provide information on how consumers associate values with a given product. In the case of the association between "Security" and cars, "Technical Security Features", e.g. ABS or Airbags, are perceived to reduce the "Danger of Accidents", thereby enabling the driver to "Feel Comfortable" while driving, ultimately leading to the value of "Security". Keeping in mind that this cognitive structure is especially present to the consumer while driving a car, the structure should also be represented in the interactions between the members of the mobile community to strengthen the association between the community itself and the particular product as a carrier for a brand. As Figallo (1998) points out, interactions within communities can be stimulated by the operator. Since participants of a car-related community with the personal value of security are interested in associated consequences and attributes in the hierarchical value map, e.g. "Feeling Healthy", topics surrounding these concepts can be used to stimulate interactions, e.g. exchanging experiences on ergonomic sitting.

Approaches to the design of product-related mobile communities

Based on the social profile of communities, we identified the four elements essential for establishing a community: the clearly defined group, the interaction between the members, the bonding among members, and the common space. In order for mobile communities to succeed, each of those elements must be provided based on the characteristics of the mobile channel and by linking the product to the community. We propose a four-stage process for developing a consumer oriented concept:

1. Determining the hierarchical value map for a given product and the associations towards the particular brand.
2. Clearly defining a group based on validated values and the associated benefits.
3. Determining a broad subject for the community according to consumers' cognition towards the product.
4. Designing common spaces and identifying ways to support the development of bonding according to the group of people, the subject of the community and the characteristics of the mobile channel.

Following this process will increase the chances of positioning the product as a link between consumers, thereby enhancing consumer attraction and loyalty. The defined group and subject based on consumers' cognition towards a product predetermine which services can be used to increase bonding and which common spaces are suitable. Groups defined around the value of security associated with cars will want to exchange related subjects on different platforms and will feel comfortable with a different kind of bonding than groups defined around self respect associated with athletic shoes. While it is more appealing for a community related to athletic shoes to use location awareness for the creation of physical common spaces, virtual common spaces built around the same physical context are more interesting to a car-related community.

In Europe the mobile channel has been mostly used for direct marketing and the establishment of simple entertainment communities weakly associated with the product itself. The Nokia Game 2002 shows that support for product-related mobile interactions is picking up, but in terms of communities and positioning products as links, it is still in its infancy.

Nokia Game 2002, an interactive adventure provided by Nokia, was played from 11 to 29 November 2002 in nine languages across all 25 European countries simultaneously. The game was part of an ambitious branding project that aimed to increase awareness of Nokia amongst European countries and to bring life to Nokia's "Connecting People" brand claim. During the game, players received a mission that they had to complete within 20 days. Those players who completed the mission to the fullest (i.e. score the most points) won the game. Compared to previous versions of Nokia Game, the 2002 editionoffered both active and casual players the opportunity to play at their own level. Due to a new game concept, players could have the experience 24 hours a day, if they wished, and could upload and share their own created content to interact with, amaze and impress fellow players. In addition, players were challenged to create a new game identity and - using this game identity - experience the borders between fiction and reality. Close co-operation with the world's largest music publishing companies resulted in a game theme that taught participants the ins and outs of today's music business (Nokia 2002).

The Nokia Game used the Internet, SMS, chat, interactive voice response (IVR) calls and mini-movies distributed over the web to share information and provide clues and instructions to the players. To play, participants needed to have access to the Internet, an e-mail address, and a mobile phone with the capacity to receive short messages. At the end of the game, the top 10-100 players in each country each won a special new Nokia 3650 phone with integrated camera, video player and camcorder. The winners were among the first in their region to own and use this new phone (Nokia 2002).

The game featured multimedia messaging (MMS) and digital services. Operator logos, ring tones, and picture messages with Nokia Game themes were available from the Nokia Game site and Club Nokia, an online community loyalty program offering exclusive services to Nokia phone owners. The Club Nokia web and WAP services can be accessed once the Nokia phone is registered with Club Nokia.

The Nokia example shows that it is possible to stimulate interactions between consumers on mobile phones. To increase the effect on consumer loyalty and attraction, groups or subgroups need to be defined according to similar values and should be stimulated to interact about topics related to their cognition of a product. For this purpose, the described example can only function as a starting point.

Conclusion and future research

Based on theoretical considerations about virtual communities and the characteristics of mobility, the potential for mobile communities has been shown. Adding consumer cognition about specific products, ways of profitably making use of these communities for product-related communities have been introduced. By defining a group and introducing topics from consumer cognition, and by using the characteristics of mobility to support the other two constituting elements of communities, bonding and common space, concepts for product-related mobile communities can be derived.

At this stage, research regarding this topic remains theoretically explorative. The example of the Nokia Game illustrates how current mobile communities are built around the characteristics of 2G networks, employing multiple mobile technologies and involving participants in physical as well as virtual experiences. This has been proven to be a successful approach to attract participants but does not directly link products with the community itself. In view of the fact that consumer cognition about a product is especially present during immediate contact with that product, much of the potential of product-related mobile communities remains unexploited. It must be pointed out that there is very little practical experience with mobile communities. Until now there is not a single example of a mobile community which has shown stunning success in terms of building a tight product-link efficiently. We therefore advise companies to scrutinize the opportunities and risks of deploying mobile communities with the help of the methods we have provided.

Future theoretical research needs to address a number of issues. Due to the limitations of the I/O interfaces of mobile devices, the limited bandwidth of mobile networks, and higher costs of usage, many mobile communities will be nested within other kinds of communities. The interactions between those communities must be analyzed in addition to the dynamics of mobile communities themselves. Negative and positive effects between the elements of a mobile community itself and other types of related communities will have a strong impact on their long-term development. A related question is in what way communities might change consumer cognition of a product. Additionally, research is required with regard to which products and topics allow community building processes, especially for mobile communities. Products used by technology-affiliated consumers will be more valuable in this context. Furthermore, to date it is not certain which topics are suitable for communities - for example, whether or not it is possible to develop a community around security. Finally, the question of which additional goals product-related mobile communities may serve needs to be investigated, e.g. obtaining information about consumers and their experiences with certain products.

References

Albers S, Becker J (2001) Individualmarketing im M-Commerce. In: Nicolia A, Petersmann T. (eds) Strategien im M-Commerce. Stuttgart, pp 71–85

Aschmoneit P, Heitmann M (2002) Customer Centered Community Application Design. International Journal on Media Management 4 (1):13–20

Aschmoneit P, Zimmermann H-D (2002) Elements of a Mobile Community Business Model. In: Koshrow-Pour, M. (ed) Proceedings of the Information Resources Management Association International Conference, Seattle

de Chernatony L, Dall'Olmo Riley F (1997) The Chasm Between Managers and Consumers Views of Brands: The Experts Perspectives. Journal of Strategic Marketing 5 (2):89–104

Döring N, Schestag A (2000) Soziale Normen in virtuellen Gruppen. Eine empirische Untersuchung am Beispiel ausgewählter Chat-Channels. In: Thiedeke U (ed) Virtuelle Gruppen. Charakteristika und Problemdimensionen. Wiesbaden, pp 313–355

Figallo C (1998) Hosting Web Communities: Building Relationships, Increasing Customer Loyalty and Maintaining a Competitive Edge. New York

Figge S (2001) Situation Dependent M-Commerce Applications. In: Dholokai R, Kolbe L, Venkatesh A, Zoche P (eds): COTIM-2001 Proceedings: From E-Commerce to M-Commerce. Karlsruhe

Gardner BB, Levy SJ (1955) The Product and the Brand. Harvard Business Review 33 (9):33–39

Gaus H, Oberländer S, Zanger C (1997) Means-End Chains für Automobile – eine Laddering Anwendung. Workingpaper, Chemnitz-Zwickau

Goffman E (1959) The Presentation of Self in Everyday Life. Garden City, New York

Grubb EL, Hupp G (1968) Perception of Self, Generalized Stereotypes, and Brand Selection. In: Journal of Marketing Research 1 (5):58–63

Grunert KG (1991) Kognitive Strukturen von Konsumenten und ihre Veränderung durch Marketingkommunikation. In: Marketing ZFP 13 (1):11–12

Grunert KG, Grunert SC (1995) Measuring Subjective Meaning Structures by the Laddering Method: Theoretical Considerations and Methodological Problems. In: International Journal of Research in Marketing 12 (3):209–225

Gutman J (1982) A Means-end Chain Model Based on Consumer Categorization Processes. In: Journal of Marketing 46 (2):60–72

Gutman J (1997) Means-End Chains as Goal Hierarchies. In: Psychology & Marketing 14 (6):545–560

Hagel III J, Armstrong A (1997) Net Gain: Expanding Markets Through Virtual Communities. Boston

Hagel III J, Armstrong A (1999) Net Gain – Expanding Markets Through Virtual Communities. In: Journal of Interactive Marketing 13 (1):55–65

Hagel III J, Bughin J (2001) The Operational Performance of Virtual Communities – Towards a Successful Business Model? In: EM - Electronic Markets. The International Journal of Electronic Markets and Business Media 10 (4):237–244

Hammann RB (2000) Computernetze als verbindendes Element von Gemeinschaftsnetzen. In: Thiedeke, U. (Ed) Virtuelle Gruppen: Charakteristika und Problemdimensionen. Wiesbaden, pp 221–243

Heintz B (2000) Gemeinschaft ohne Nähe? Virtuelle Guppen und reale Netze. In: Thiedeke, U. (Ed): Virtuelle Gruppen: Charakteristika und Problemdimensionen, Wiesbaden, pp 188–220

Herrmann A (1996a) Wertorientierte Produkt- und Werbegestaltung. In: Marketing ZFP 18 (3):153–163

Herrmann A (1996b) Nachfrageorientierte Produktgestaltung. Ein Ansatz auf Basis der „means end"-Theorie. Wiesbaden

Hillery GA (1955) Definitions of Community: Areas of Agreement, Rural Sociology 20 (2):111–123

Hummel J, Becker K (2002) Profile virtueller Gemeinschaften. St.Gallen, forthcoming

Hummel J, Lechner U (2001b) The Community Model of Content Management - A case study of the music industry. International Journal of Media Management 3 (1):4–14

Johnson MD (1989) On the Nature of Product Attributes and Attribute Relationships. In: Advances in Consumer Research 16 (5):598–604

Jones Q (1997) Virtual Communities, Virtual Settlement & Cyber-Archaeology: A Theoretical Outline. In: Journal of Computer Mediated Communication 3 (3):35–49

Kahle L (1997) Values, Lifestyles, and Psychographics. Cambridge

Kapferer J-N (1997) Strategic Brand Management: Creating and Sustaining Brand Equity Long Term. London

Kim, AJ (2000) Community Building, Secret Strategies for Successful online Communities. Berkeley

Koch M, Groh G, Hillebrand C (2002) Mobile Communities: Extending Online Communities Into the Real World. In: Ramsower R (ed) Proceedings of Americas Conference on Information Systems, Dallas, pp 1848–1852

Kollock P, Smith M (1996) Managing the Virtual Commons: Cooperation and Conflicts in Computer Communities. In: Hering S (ed) Computer-Mediated Communication: Linguistic, Social, and Cross-Cultural Perspectives. London, pp 109–128

Kroeber-Riel W, Weinberg P (1999) Konsumentenverhalten, München

Levine R, Locke C, Searls D, Weinberger, D (2000) The Cluetrain Manifesto. The end of Business as Usual. Cambridge

Licklider JCR, Taylor W (1968) The Computer as a Communication Device. In: Science and Technology, pp 21–40

McEnally MR, de Chernatony L (1997) The Evolving Nature of Branding: Consumer and Managerial Considerations. In: Academy of Marketing Science Review [Online]: 11. Available: http://www.amsreview.org/amsrev/theory/holbrook11-97.html [August 2002]

McWilliam, G (2001) Online Communities geben Marken mehr Schub. In: Harvard Business Manager 8 (2):72–85

Mitchel A (1983) The Nine American Life Styles. New York

Müller C, Aschmoneit P, Zimmermann H (2002) Der Einfluss von 'Mobile' auf das Management von Kundenbeziehungen und Personalisierung von Produkten und Dienstleistungen. In: Reichwald R (ed): Mobile Kommunikation, Wiesbaden, pp 353–381

Müller-Veerse F (2001) UMTS Report – an Investment Perspective [online]. Available: http://www.durlacher.com [August 2002]

Nokia (2002) Nokiagame [online]. Available: http://www.nokiagame.com/ [November 2002]

Opaschowski HW (1993) Freizeitökonomie: Marketing von Erlebniswelten. Opladen

Ostrom E (1990) Governing the commons: The Evolution of Institutions for Collective Action. Cambridge

Panten G, Paul C, Runte M (2001) Virtuelle Communities. In: Albers S, Clement M, Peters K, Skiera B (eds) Marketing mit interaktiven Medien - Strategien zum Markterfolg. Frankfurt am Main

Preece J (2000) Online Communities. New York

Reichwald R, Meier R, Fremuth N (2002) Die mobile Ökonomie – Definition und Spezifika. In: Reichwald R (ed) Mobile Kommunikation, Wiesbaden

Reynolds TJ, Gutman J (1984) Advertising as Image Management. In: Journal of Advertising Research 24 (6):27–38

Reynolds TJ, Gutman J (1988) Laddering Theory, Method, Analysis, and Interpretation. In: Journal of Advertising Research 28 (1):11–31

Rheingold H (1993) The Virtual Community: Homesteading on the Electronic Frontier., Bonn

Rokeach MJ (1973) The Nature of Human Values. New York

Rosenberg MJ (1956) Cognitive Structure and Attitudinal Affect. In: Journal of Abnormal and Social Psychology 22 (5):368–372

Schwartz SH (1994) Are There Universal Aspects in the Structure and Content of Human Values ? Journal of Social Issues 50 (4):19–45

Shafer D (1999) The Responsibility - and Opportunity - of Community Builders in the New Century [Online] Available: http://www.onlinecommunityreport.com/features/newcentury [31 Mar. 2002]

Timmers P (1998) Business Models for Electronic Markets. In: EM - Electronic Markets. The International Journal of Electronic Markets and Business Media 8 (2):3–8

Turkle S (1998) Life on the Screen: Identity in the age of the Internet, New York

Turner JC, Hogg MA, Oakes PJ, Reicher SD, Wetherell MS (1987) Rediscovering the Social Group: A self-Categorization Theory. Oxford

Van Dusseldorp (2001) Cross Media Case Study [Online]. Available: http://www.vandusseldorp.com/publications/btb.asp [November 2002]

Vriens M, ter Hofstede F (2000) Linking Attributes, Benefits, and Consumer Values. In: Marketing Research 12 (3):5–10

Wansink B (2000) New Techniques to Generate Key Marketing Insights. In: Marketing Research 12 (2):28–36

Wellmann B (1992) Which Types of Ties and Networks Give What Kinds of Social Report? In: Advances in Group Processes (9:1), pp 207–235

Whittaker S, Isaacs E, O'Day V (1997) Widening the web. In: Workshop report on the theory and practice of physical and Network communities

Wiedmann K-P, Buxel H, Buckler F (2000) Chancenpotentiale und Gestaltungsperspektiven des M-Commerce. In: Der Markt 39 (153):84–96

Zobel J (2001) Mobile Business and M-Commerce: Die Märkte der Zukunft erobern. München

Part 5:
Policy challenges

E-commerce and Internet access in the European Union and the United States

Johannes M. Bauer[1], Michel Berne[2]

Michigan State University, East Lansing, USA
Institut National des Telecommunications, Évry, France

Abstract

Improvements in the availability and quality of Internet access are considered an important precondition for e-commerce. This paper examines public policies in the United States (US) and in the European Union (EU) towards communications infrastructures and their effect on Internet access and e-commerce. We update and expand earlier research, in which we found effects of public policies on Internet access, to study their implications for e-commerce. Whereas the EU as a region has been successful in closing the historical gap to the US in fixed and mobile communications, it continues to trail the US in advanced communications infra-structures. Large differences in the availability of access infrastructure (networks, terminals, and web servers) as well as e-commerce also exist between individual EU member states. The differing policies towards the development of fixed (wired or wireless) broadband and mobile telecommunications (2.5 and 3G) affect the means to buy online and shape e-commerce directly and indirectly. In the wake of the European 3G spectrum auctions and the collapse of major players in the broadband networking market, past policies have been revisited. In this chapter we examine important new initiatives and discuss the prospects for e-commerce.

Introduction

Although e-commerce is expanding steadily, most observers have recently scaled down their growth forecasts. One reason is the dot com bust, which revealed the weaknesses of some of the early business models and has reduced the funding for e-commerce. Sluggish growth in Internet access and insufficient bandwidth of ac-

---

[1] E-mail: bauerj@msu.edu
[2] E-mail: Michel.Berne@int-evry.fr

cess platforms are considered other culprits and are the focus of this chapter. Building on earlier work (Bauer et al. 2002) our goal is to analyze the factors behind the patterns of internet access in the member states of the European Union (EU) and the United States (US) and their effect on e-commerce. In particular, we are interested in the influence of public policy and regulation on internet connectivity. This task is complicated by rapidly changing technology, related changes in the legal and institutional environment, and the complexity of determinants of communications platform diffusion.

Section two of the chapter presents information on the availability of different internet access platforms in the EU and in the US. Section three develops a framework for the analysis of the heterogeneous pattern that we find and discusses important factors that shape the diffusion of internet access in more detail. Section three reviews public policies and regulatory measures adopted in the EU and in the US to foster internet access and e-commerce. Section four is dedicated to broadband access (fixed and mobile), which is expected to support enhanced e-commerce models. A synthesis and conclusions are presented in the last section. We find that the link between the availability of communications platforms, internet use and e-commerce is mediated by many variables, linked in a web of complex causation. No single "superior" but various "workable" configurations of technological, economic, policy and socio-cultural factors seem to co-exist. The EU and the US have adopted policy frameworks with many similarities but also important differences. While we find characteristic trade-offs between the two regions, overall it would be premature to claim that one model is more successful than the other.

Empirical evidence

Modern communications infrastructures can best be described as a network of networks, consisting of various wireline and wireless, fixed and mobile platforms. These platforms have different technological and economic characteristics. Voice, cable TV, and data networks historically provided largely complementary services. Digitalization and generic protocols such as TCP/IP increased their substitutability and allowed similar services to be configured on multiple communications platforms (e.g., broadband internet access via telephone loops, cable TV, or mobile phones). Even so, elements of complementarity remain and new ones emerged. For example, platforms continue to differ with regard to the degree of mobility and terminal equipment, applications, and content have become more important components of the value chain. Traditional comparative measures of infrastructure development, such as penetration rates of specific platforms, do not capture these aspects well and need to be broadened to reflect the overall mix of platforms.

The combination of technologies deployed in the communications infrastructures of the EU and US differs widely and reflects the specific historical evolution of the industries, public policy, entrepreneurial traditions, geographic factors, and socio-cultural factors (Table 1). Moreover, it differs widely among the member states of the EU and somewhat less dramatically among the US states. The US had a historical lead and continues to enjoy a higher penetration rate for fixed telephony. The evolution of mobile telephony is more varied and exhibits distinct phases related to the degree of standardization and the status of competition in the industry. In analog technology, the US, after a long struggle, adopted a common standard (AMPS, developed by Bell Laboratories) and established a duopoly market structure. In contrast, the EU market was fragmented with several co-existing standards and a monopolistic market structure. As a result, mobile service diffusion in the US exceeded its expansion in the EU. The situation changed in the second generation of digital mobile telephony, in which the EU adopted GSM as a mandatory standard and introduced a more competitive organization in the early 1990s. To avoid repeating the frustrating experience of the adoption of AMPS, the US decided to allow standards competition and did not license multiple service providers until the second half of the 1990s. During this period, mobile diffusion in Europe exceeded wireless growth in the US. As a result, until early in 1999, US mobile penetration was higher than in the EU, which since took the lead. The longer term outlook is not clear, however, and depends on whether the efficiency gains from standardization (e.g., economies of scale in equipment production, more intense competition) are higher or lower than the gains from standards competition (e.g., more efficiency technology such as CDMA) (Gruber and Verboven 2001; Gandal et al. 2003).

In terms of the total number of access paths (fixed and mobile), in 1991 the EU trailed the US by 26% but in 2001, the rapid growth of mobile users in the late 1990s, the EU was ahead of the US by 22.8%. This is remarkable, given that the GDP per capita in the US was US$ 33,000 compared to US$ 23,195 in the EU (measured at purchasing power parities). There are hints that platform diffusion in the two regions will eventually converge at similar levels (Koski and Majumdar 2000). It is likely that the EU will reach a saturation point in mobile service near 80 mobile subscribers per 100 population and in fixed service below 60. In contrast, the US will reach saturation levels near 70 fixed paths and mobile saturation at a lower level than the EU. This would imply that a different mix of access technologies prevails while the overall number of access paths becomes comparable.

Table 1. Penetration rates of platforms and applications (per 100 population, 2001)

	United States	European Union
Fixed access lines	66.5	55.6
Mobile subscribers	44.4	72.4
Access paths (fixed plus mobile)	110.9	128.0
Cable TV[a]	25.5	13.4
Satellite TV[a]	3.4	8.2
Internet users	50.0	41.6
Broadband subscribers	3.2	0.8

[a] Data for 2000. On a per-household basis cable penetration was 68% in the US and 31% in the EU; satellite TV penetration was 9% and 19%, respectively.
Sources: ITU 2002b; OECD 2001a; Deiss 2002.

Characteristic differences are also visible in cable and satellite TV, which can be used as platforms for broadband internet access. On average, the US has a much higher cable penetration rate, whereas the EU is ahead in satellite broadcasting services. One possible explanation is that cable TV evolved as a separate industry in the US, whereas in many European countries the incumbent Public Telecommunications Operators (PTOs) deployed it. PTOs may have had weaker incentives to invest in cable networks as they could not vertically integrate into content provision. Satellite communications was used in the US to develop a highly efficient wholesale distribution system to cable headends but not until the mid-1990s to deliver direct-to-home broadcasting service. In contrast, in many European countries, direct broadcasting via satellite was introduced in the 1980s and took a lead over cable TV. A gap between the two regions is also visible in broadband, where the number of subscribers was higher in the US (3.2%) than in the EU (0.8%).[3] The availability and mix of these narrowband and broadband platforms is one important component in explaining differences in the percentage of the population that uses the internet, which was higher in the US (50%) than in the EU (41.6%). However, other factors such as flat versus measured pricing, the diffusion of terminals, and the availability of content played a role as well and will be considered in section two.

In both regions, great diversity exists at the state level. For example, in 2001, household fixed telephone penetration in the US varied between 88.1% in Mississippi and 97.8% in New Hampshire (FCC 2002, p. 17-2). In the EU, it ranged from 90.6% in Portugal to 99.5% in Sweden (ITU 2002b, p. A-84). The heterogeneity is more visible for other communications platforms, such as cable TV. In 2000, in the densely populated Benelux countries, more than 90% of households were connected (compared to 68% in the US), whereas in Greece, Italy and Spain cable was only available to fewer than 5% of households. With the exception of basic telephone service, platform availability is more heterogeneous in the EU than the US. Figure 1 depicts Internet access in the EU and the US. Whereas numbers are converging within the EU, a clear "North-South" divide is evident.

---

[3] Broadband diffusion is growing swiftly. By September 2002, the EU average penetration was 3% and in the US it was 6.5%. See Broadband access in OECD countries per 100 inhabitants, September 2002, available at http://www.oecd.org/EN/document/0,,EN-document-13-nodirectorate-no-1-39262-13,00.html (last visited May 6, 2003).

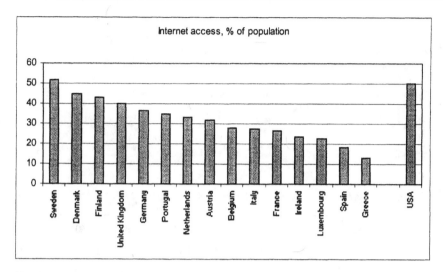

Fig. 1. Internet access in the EU and the US

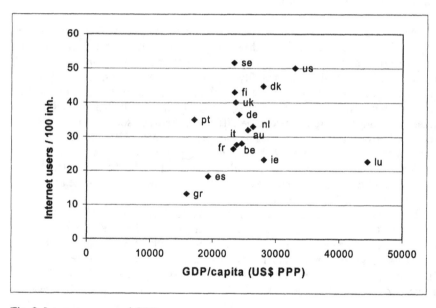

Fig. 2. Internet access and GDP

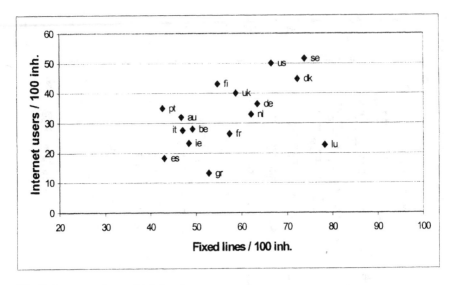

Fig. 3. Internet access and teledensity

Overall, three clusters become visible from this comparison. One is formed by the Nordic countries, which are ahead of other countries in fixed, mobile and internet use. The second area is the US, which is characterized by high overall communications platform availability, especially when it comes to advanced internet access, and of internet use. The third is formed by the rest of the EU member states, where internet use is lagging more substantially behind mobile and fixed penetration. There are also large differences between social groups. According to a Eurobarometer study, 73% of European students, 34% of the EU population, 28.5% of women, 10% of the low-income population and only 8.4% of retired people had internet access (Eurobarometer 2001). In the US, internet use similarly differs by age, income, race, and education, but it varies little according to gender (NTIA 2002, pp. 10–28).

It is interesting to note that in each of the three clusters one preferred technology seems to emerge at each point in time, perhaps reflecting a reluctance of users to adopt more than one technology simultaneously. In the US, the growth of internet access, beginning in the mid-1990s, preceded the expansion of mobile service. In most EU countries, the mobile boom came first (after 1995), followed by an expansion of Internet use in the late 1990s. In the Nordic countries, mobile service expanded rapidly in the early 1990s so that these areas were ready to embrace the Internet when user-friendly browsers became available. In all cases, it is obvious that the general preconditions for Internet access that is the availability of fixed (or mobile) lines were present. Therefore it is necessary to look for additional factors for an explanation of the differential developments.

Factors affecting internet access

The availability of an access path (fixed or mobile) and a terminal is a precondition for internet use. Moreover, access per se would not be useful without services. It is much less obvious to identify factors that are sufficient to explain the growth patterns of the internet and other communications platforms. Empirical studies all wrestle with the complexity of factors shaping diffusion processes. This means that different configurations of factors (income, pricing, policy, or cultural factors) can result in similar outcomes and that no individual factor is necessary and sufficient for internet access. Such complex causal patterns cannot be modeled with traditional econometric methods, which typically assume independent additive forms of causation. Methods like factor analysis or diversity analysis (Ragin 2000) can contribute to overcoming this shortcoming but they have other disadvantages. While we do not attempt a full-fledged statistical analysis, this section reviews the most important drivers of internet access and outlines some possible configurations that can accelerate its diffusion. Figure 4 represents the most important relations.

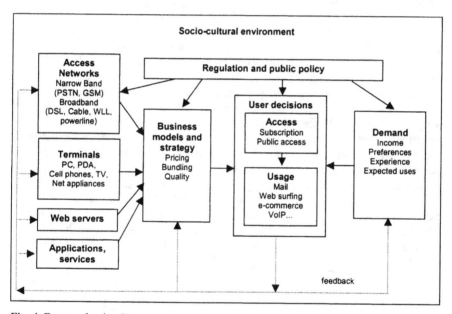

Fig. 4. Factors shaping internet access

Internet access and use are jointly influenced by supply-side and demand-side factors, both of which are affected by the industry-specific policy and regulatory framework of the industry. In turn, these relations are embedded in the broader socio-cultural environment of a country or a region. Most recent policy studies have focused on supply-side factors. For example, the OECD (2001a, 2001b) repeatedly emphasized the need for measures such as flat rate pricing or unbundling to accelerate the deployment of an internet access infrastructure. Comparatively less attention has been paid to the applications and services that are complementary to the infrastructure and an important precondition for user benefits. Demand-side and user-based factors, such as the specific communication or transaction needs of businesses and individuals or the skills in utilizing advanced communications technology, have also been studied less widely. Moreover, the interaction between these components is crucial for an understanding of diffusion patterns. There is mounting evidence that the bundling of network services, applications and content is an important factor explaining diffusion rates of advanced services. For example, the success of i-mode in Japan, Nate in Korea, or streaming services in Taiwan is driven by the unique bundling strategies pursued by the service providers and their attention to user needs.

Most users have a choice between several access network platforms. The narrowband public switched telephone network (PSTN) and digital mobile networks (GSM in Europe; iDEN, TDMA, CDMA, and GSM in the US) – often dubbed "second generation" or "2G" services – can deliver speeds up to 56kbps. Enhanced 2.5G mobile networks can increase transmission rates to just short of broadband. Broadband networks offer a wide range of upstream and downstream speeds and include various versions of Digital Subscriber Loop (xDSL), cable, wireless local loops, wireless local area networks (802.11b – also known as WiFi, 802.11a), satellite communications, and powerline communications. With regard to terminals, PCs and laptop computers continue to be the main access devices whereas NetPCs and Net Appliances have not yet had much success. Personal Digital Assistants (PDAs) are only emerging now, especially in the US, but the existing devices are still not able to exploit all internet services fully. 2G cell phones provide only limited access to the Internet using the WAP or i-mode protocols. However, evolutions to GPRS and 3G provide more bandwidth and may become serious competitors to the PC. Nonetheless, the PC is still a key factor in Internet access. PC diffusion per household varies more than telephone availability and is, like fixed access, strongly related to GDP (Figure 5). In the US, PC penetration exceeds mobile penetration; mobile internet access may therefore be more tilted towards WiFi, which is more effectively run from computers. On the other hand, in the EU mobile penetration exceeds PC availability, which might indicate a higher potential for mobile internet solutions based on 2.5 or 3G platforms.[4]

---

[4] As of 2001, 7.9% of American and 6.4% of West European mobile subscribers also accessed the internet via their mobiles (ITU 2002a, p. 64).

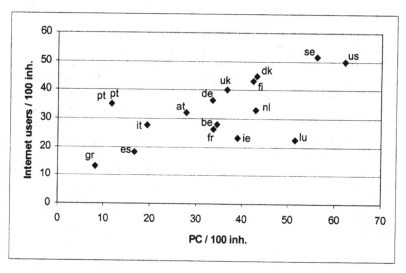

Fig. 5. Internet users and PC availability

The availability of terminals and platforms is no sufficient reason for consumers to subscribe to internet access. Complementary applications and services are needed to create value added that exceeds the incremental cost of becoming a subscriber. It can be expected that the minimal required complementary services depend on the access platform, as they are offered at widely differing prices and provide significantly different functionality. E-mail and applications that are not very information–intensive may justify subscription to dial-up narrowband access but perhaps not broadband access. Although broadband could be looked at as higher quality access platform, faster download speeds alone often will not suffice to induce subscription. Additional applications, such as more information intensive websites, music and video streaming, or interactive games, will be needed for widespread uptake. While advanced communications technologies would allow the customization of content, it is currently missing in the US and in the EU. Only a few Asian countries, most notably Japan and Korea, have had mass-market success with the commercial delivery of broadband-based content.

The pricing model and the bundling of services will be important additional factors that shape the subscription decision. Dial-up services enjoy a natural advantage in the US, where local phone service is typically priced at a flat rate. Users have to pay an additional monthly fee to their Internet Service Provider (ISP) but do not incur additional telephone charges. As a result, the average imputed dial-up charges per minute is decreasing with use. In the EU, local phone service is typically measured, implying a constant average charge per minute of internet use. For some time, this pricing model allowed ISPs to offer their service for free by sharing revenues with the telephone service providers. In the meantime, dial-up service is often priced at a flat rate or based on multi-part tariffs. Consequently, free services are facing increasing financial difficulty as the sharing model loses its appeal. Broadband services in the US and in the EU are typically offered at different download and upload speeds and at differentiated prices, giving customers broad choice options.

While uses, gratifications, and prices explain part of the demand for internet access, other factors, such as media habits and cultural factors play a role and are in part responsible for the different national diffusion patterns. One important set of contextual factors is related to the wealth of a nation, which creates a favorable environment for the use of advanced communications services. Wealthy nations tend to have more educated populations, are open to new ways of conducting business, and new lifestyles. They also have more disposable income and can afford terminals and Internet access charges. Another factor is market size, although its effects are not necessarily straightforward. Large countries benefit from economies of scale, as the development of services is largely a fixed cost. For small countries, the Internet provides a cheap and effective way to remain linked to the rest of the world (as the example of Finland shows). Despite rapidly growing content in other languages, English continues to be dominant on the web. Uptake in non-English speaking countries (or countries where English is not widespread as a second language) can therefore be expected to be slower. Another group of factors has to do with the propensity of the population (or groups of the population) to explore new technologies. Lastly, the presence of entrepreneurs and a willingness to take risks differ across nations but affect the diffusion of new services. These factors usually occur in clusters and different configurations may result in similar internet usage levels. For example, as the case of Korea demonstrates, a high propensity to adopt new technologies may compensate lower income per capita. Likewise, a missing entrepreneurial culture could be compensated in part by a concerted effort of the government to subsidize platform deployment or exert a demand-pull effect through accelerated e-government programs.

Communications systems and applications are durable investments into hardware and software. Despite rapid technological advances, the stock of infrastructure capital only reacts gradually. Decisions at any point in time may have repercussions long into the future, creating multiple forms of path dependence. Depending on the unique path and the set of contextual factors, different nations and/or regions may be first in deploying new applications and services. Early success may become a liability later on and delay the introduction of the next generation of technology. France offers a fascinating example of this interaction between legacy systems and emerging technology. The "Minitel" was a cheap, low quality videotext terminal that was widely distributed by the French PTT in the 1980s (and envied by many nations). At the peak of the system, 6.5 million terminals were active and could access around 36,000 different information services. The very slow decline of the Minitel, which is a partial substitute for present generation internet service, explains in part why France does not have higher Internet penetration rates. The US, on the other hand, with its open telephone network platform and relatively high PC diffusion, provided an environment conducive to rapid diffusion of dial-up access. Path dependency effects are also visible in the mix of technology platforms that are utilized to access the internet. For example, the US with its relatively high cable penetration rolled out cable modem service, whereas, on average, EU member states rely more on DSL for broadband access.

Several studies have attempted to investigate the determinants of communications platform diffusion with econometric means. Based on a set of panel data for the EU and the US for 1998–2000, Bauer et al. (2002) found that the number of internet hosts (corrected for global top-level domain name registrations) can be explained by the availability of PCs, the price of access, competition in the local market, and unbundling. Hargittai (1999) and Maitland (1999) found similar effects of economic and technological variables; in addition they identified effects of cultural and socio-economic variables, such as English language comprehension. Kiiski and Pohjola (2002) estimated a Gompertz model of technology diffusion for OECD countries for the years 1995–2000. They found a significant influence of GDP per capita and internet access costs but no independent effect of competition or investment in education (however, education becomes significant if developing countries are included in the data set). Although these studies shed light on some of the relations, they cannot fully reflect the complex causality patterns characteristic for the evolution of communications platforms and their use.

Public policy and regulation

Legal and regulatory framework

Although the internet per se is relatively free from direct government regulation, many policy and regulatory measures affect it indirectly. Relevant sector-specific regulatory measures include rules governing the different technology platforms (licensing regime, price regulation, interconnection and unbundling) and the provision of universal service. In addition, there are numerous policy measures, for example, in the realms of education policy or innovation policy that are not specifically designed to support internet diffusion but nonetheless influence it. Significant differences exist in the regulatory and policy mix between the US and the EU. Most importantly, since the 1980s, the US is driven by an increasing belief in unfettered market forces. Regulation and policy measures predominantly target areas with presumed market failure and focus on network access platforms (and more recently, network security issues). Very limited attention is directed towards applications, content and user skills. In comparison, while relying on competition, the EU, in line with its stronger industrial policy tradition, directs much more effort to stimulate applications and develop the knowledge-base required to use advanced communications.

Table 2 contrasts selected areas of regulatory policy. Important differences between the US and the EU exist in the scope and coherence of rules governing network platforms. In contrast to the US, the EU relies more on antitrust principles in delineating regulated from unregulated areas. This has to do with the unique historical and political environment in which telecommunications policy reform unfolded. In the US, telecommunications reform evolved gradually since the late

1950s. The Telecommunications Act of 1996 (the "Act") integrated many of the prior changes into a new legal framework. Even though it eliminated many specific rules that segmented the telephone, cable, and mobile communications industries and facilitated cross-entry between these sectors, it did not create a wholly harmonized framework. Therefore, significant differences continue to exist between telephone, cable, and broadcasting in important areas, such as interconnection, unbundling and universal service obligations. Moreover, the US does not apply principles of competition policy consistently when delineating regulated and unregulated areas.

Table 2. Internet regulatory framework

	United States	European Union
Overall framework	Heterogeneous regulation, reduction of cross-entry barriers since Telecommunications Act of 1996	Heterogeneous regulation, moving to technology-neutral regulation as of July 2003
Price regulation	Local voice regulated, cable, mobile and internet access unregulated	Local voice regulated in most countries, cable, mobile and internet access mostly unregulated
Interconnection	General interconnection obligation for all telecommunications service providers (telephone, mobile) but not cable and ISPs	Interconnection obligation for operators with significant market power (SMP)
Unbundling	ILECs need to unbundle local loop;(DSL platform prior to 2003); no unbundling obligations for cable service providers	SMP operators have to make full local loops, shared access lines, and bitstream access available on an unbundled basis
Resale	Resale obligation for LECs and ILECs, the latter at retail minus discount	Resale obligation for SMP operators
Universal service	Funding of basic voice, internet access for schools, libraries, and health care providers	Funding of basic voice service if net cost considered a burden on operators; new framework expands universal service principles to data communications at rates that are sufficient to permit functional Internet access

One of the goals of the 1996 Act was to allow the entry of local telephone companies into long distance markets, subject to certain safeguards. In pursuit of this objective, Congress adopted an asymmetric framework that differentiates telephone service providers' obligations based on their status. Regional Bell Holding Companies (RBHCs), the successor companies of the former Bell System, face the most challenging 14-point checklist (section 271 Communications Act). Incumbent Local Exchange Carriers (ILECs) – companies in the market when the Act was signed into law by President Clinton in February 1996 – are governed by more stringent rules than competitive Local Exchange Carriers (CLECs) (section 251 Communications Act). Telecommunications carriers[5] without a local presence

---

[5] The legal term "telecommunications carrier" refers to entities providing service for a fee directly to the public, regardless of the facilities used. According to current FCC rules,

are governed by very few rules, such as minimal interconnection obligations. Although there is some congruence, this legal design ties obligations of telephone companies to their status of rather than the competitive market situation. On the other hand, independently of the market situation, cable service providers do not have any obligation to make the cable modem platform available to third parties (some, such as AOL/Time Warner, have done so voluntarily to safeguard merger plans or avoid antitrust action). Overall, the framework reflects the unique fragmentation and decentralization of communications policy-making in the US.

The EU embarked on its telecommunications reform project much later than the US. The specific institutional framework of the EU, in particular the strong role of the European policy-makers, the predominance of state-ownership prior to reform, and the absence of a history of national regulation, was conducive to swift reforms (Cherry and Bauer 2002). During the 1990s, liberalization and harmonization of the patchwork of national approaches were on top of the agenda. The second phase of reform began with the 1999 Communications Review, which resulted in a new overarching framework, to be effective July 25, 2003 (EC 2002a, p. 47). The new model is designed in a technology-neutral fashion and deeply rooted in antitrust analysis. It adopts a horizontal layered approach by creating unified regulations for communications infrastructure and associated services. However, services provided over these networks are not covered by the new framework and will be treated by other policies at the national and EU levels. The new legal approach is built around five directives (on competition, authorizations, access and interconnection, universal service and user rights, and data protection and privacy) and a framework directive. It is too early to assess its impact on internet access, but it is likely that the framework will alleviate many existing conflicts about the appropriate regulatory treatment of new services while creating new unexpected issues.

Of particular interest for internet access are the provisions governing interconnection, unbundling, resale, and universal service. In the US, all telecommunications carriers are obliged to provide interconnection upon request (independent of whether they possess market power or not). However, LECs and ILECs are subject to more stringent regulatory provisions. ILECs have to unbundle local loops and also make unbundled network elements (UNE or UNE-P) available to requesting carriers, which then can combine them with their own equipment to offer services. Until February 2003, the ILEC's DSL platform was also covered by this unbundling obligation exists. Mobile service providers are not subject to unbundling or open access provisions. In the EU, only operators with significant market power (SMP)[6] are obliged to make a Reference Interconnection Offer (RIO) avail-

---

fixed telephone and mobile voice service providers are telecommunications carriers but cable and information service providers are not.

[6] According to the Interconnection Directive of 1998, a national regulatory agency (NRA) could designate an operator as having significant market power if it has more than 25% market share and entry barriers exist. The Market Analysis Guidelines of the new frame-

able; it is presumed that non-SMP carriers will negotiate interconnection among themselves as it is in their mutual interest. Operators that offer flat-rate narrow-band internet access, have to make a flat rate interconnection tariff available (FRIACO). Apart from single countries such as Sweden, mandatory unbundling requirements in the EU were only introduced as of 2001. Operators with significant market power need to make full loops and the HF portion of loops (shared access lines) available on an unbundled basis at non-discriminatory conditions and publicize the conditions in a Reference Unbundling Offer (RUO). In addition, they need to provide bitstream access – essentially a virtual loop – to requesting parties. Unbundling has contradictory effects on the incumbents (whose incentive to invest may be reduced) and new market entrants (whose incentive to invest may be increased) and the overall net effect is difficult to assess. Bauer et al. (2002) found a positive contribution of local loop unbundling on dial-up access. On the other hand, using mostly bivariate analysis, Howell (2002) did not find a link between unbundling and broadband diffusion.[7] Despite these challenges, unbundling is considered a cornerstone of EU policies to facilitate competition and broadband diffusion (EC 2002a).

Whereas both regions have a firm commitment to universal service, the scope and magnitude of programs is very different in the US and in the EU. In the US, two programs, one for telephone companies in high cost regions of the country and one for low income people, are intended to secure access to basic voice grade telephone service that is also sufficient to get dial-up internet access. The E-rate program subsidizes internet access for schools and libraries and a fourth program targets advanced communications services to rural health care providers. Overall, in 2001 the federal government administered programs over US$ 5 billion per year, 6.8% of the total interstate revenues upon which funding was levied (FCC 2002, pp. 165–169). In addition, state programs attempt to advance universality of access and many local initiatives are intended to quicken broadband diffusion. Compared to this broad universal service program, the EU approach appears slim. EU policy was inspired by the basic trust that competition would lower prices, which in turn would accelerate the diffusion of service. So far, this approach seems to have worked well, keeping the need for explicitly funded programs low. At the end of 2001, only two nations (Italy and France) had established a universal service fund to support the net cost of operators related to universal service goals. In all other member states the net cost were considered so low that the incumbent operators could fund them without constituting an unfair burden. As the market share of the incumbents continues to decline, it can be expected that additional requests for explicit funding will result in explicit national plans. In addition to these

---

work lift this threshold to 50% but introduce the concepts of joint dominance, collective dominance, and leveraging in addition to single dominance.

[7] The arguments pro and con unbundling are discussed in detail in Hausman and Sidak (1999), Bar et. al. (2000), Crandall and Alleman (2002), and Jorde, Sidak and Teece (2002).

limited initiatives, many policy programs exist to support the diffusion of internet access to schools and libraries, which will be discussed in the next subsection.

Broader policy initiatives

A significant difference exists in the importance of broader programs to build an information and knowledge-based society. The EU has a much stronger tradition of industrial and regional policy, of using the government to exert a demand pull effect, and of supplementary measures, for example, in the realm of education. In comparison, US policy, at least at the federal level, offers little by way of industrial policy. Many states have established programs but most of them focus on the support of access to advanced infrastructure.

The broadest EU initiative is eEurope. The Union vision of the information society is usually traced back to the "Bangemann Report" (1994). In the current framework of a market economy with widespread government budget deficits, it is difficult (and probably undesirable) to have heavy government intervention in the economy. Therefore, government policy within the eEurope program is directed to address the following issues:

- Passing of new regulations promoting innovation, both technical and economic (including technical standards)
- Coordination of member-states as regards regulations and policy decisions
- Promotion of best practices, information sharing, and benchmarking
- Funding of research and development through the EU framework programs
- Use of existing European structural funds for ICT development in the poorer regions
- Use of information technology in government functions (e-government)

Most European "summits" (held twice yearly) have addressed these issues. At the Lisbon summit in March 2000, the heads of state and government have set the goal for the EU to become the most competitive knowledge-based society in the world by 2010. To realize this vision, "businesses and citizens must have access to inexpensive, world-class communications infrastructure and a wide-range of services and that every citizen must be equipped with the skills needed to live and work in this new information society." It must be stressed that technology is only a part of the whole vision; the main emphasis is "to build on and strengthen the European social model including a high level of social protection [and] to preserve Europe's cultural and linguistic diversity" (EC 2002c). In November 1999, the European Commission launched the "eEurope" initiative. Its aim is "to ensure that everyone in the European Union – every citizen, every school, every company, every administration – has access to the new information and communication technologies and exploits them as fully as possible" (EC 2002b).

The second stage of the eEurope initiative – *eEurope 2005* – as explained in a Communication from the Commission (EC 2002b) aims at "modern online public services, e-government, e-learning services, e-health services, a dynamic e-

business environment." Means to achieve these goals are the "widespread availability of broadband access at competitive prices and a secure information infrastructure." In this respect, the succeeding telecom regulatory packages adopted by
the EU are a key component of the effort, dealing with licensing, access and interconnection, universal service, spectrum policy and of course competition policies.
A new regulatory package will be enforced mid-2003. Focussing on e-commerce,
the Commission can also build on a series of directives (electronic commerce,
electronic signatures, copyrights, protection of consumers, e-invoicing, value-
added taxation of digital supplies). eEurope 2005 guidelines require acting on:

- Legislation (basically, making sure that online and traditional commerce share
  the same "level playing field" by removing any obstacles to e-commerce)
- Specific actions for small and medium enterprise (SMEs), such as e-business
  support networks, innovation support, sharing of best practice
- e-skills
- Interoperability (for transactions, security, signatures, procurement and payments)
- Trust and confidence (in particular, on-line dispute resolution system)
- Establishment of the ".eu" domain name

eEurope 2005 also addresses infrastructure issues. It will "try to stimulate a
positive feedback between infrastructure upgrading, both broadband and multi-
platform and service developments." It will also enforce measures to promote security in ICT. Based on the experience with 3G licensing, it will review spectrum
use with respect to new developments like WiFi. Lastly, it will ascertain that less
favored regions of the Union participate in the benefits of new developments.
Moreover, the 6th Framework Program for Research and Development (starting in
2003) will devote 3.6 billion euros – that is about one-third of the funds allocated
to "priority programs" – to information technologies. Several research topics deal
with e-commerce issues like broadband for all, beyond 3G wireless and mobile
systems, networked firms, and multi-mode interfaces.

Compared to this rich panoply of initiatives, the US broader policy framework
is very limited. The vast majority of initiatives are intended to facilitate the more
rapid diffusion of access networks. In addition to the regulatory and universal service policy mentioned above, several states (e.g., Iowa, Oregon) have invested in a
state high-speed backbone infrastructure. The State of Michigan has established a
Michigan Broadband Authority to provide low cost financing to private investment in community networks. The State has also simplified the rights-of-way
patchwork created by a large number of municipalities, all pursuing differing policies. Many local communities have invested in community networks or at least
served as catalysts for the development of such networks (e.g., Blacksburg, Virginia). Moreover, the government provides information and training through local
centers of excellence to entrepreneurs willing to adopt e-commerce business models (Bauer 2002). While the government provides an indirect stimulus by providing many services via the internet, these efforts were downscaled in the wake of

September 11, 2001. However, no concerted efforts to pursue an e-commerce industrial policy strategy exist.

The future of broadband

The OCED (2000) claims that broadband has several technical features that will accelerate the growth of e-commerce. Telephone lines do not provide access at rates higher than 56 kbps. Although it is acceptable for simple web access or e-mail, this rate is considered too low for downloading of complex web pages and content (music, software, or video). ISDN is available in many EU countries (but less widespread in the US), providing 128 kbps just short of what is currently considered broadband. According to the OECD, broadband starts at 256 kbps downstream and 128 kbps upstream. The US Federal Communications Commission considers 200 kpbs broadband. The ITU has chosen 2 Mbps as the cutoff point. As applications change, it may be futile to define broadband once and forever. The most flexible definition was proposed by the Computer Science and Telecommunications Board (CSTB) of the National Research Council in the US. A technology is considered broadband if it has sufficient capacity not to limit state-of-the art applications. Moreover, the CSTB emphasizes that broadband services should provide sufficient performance and wide enough penetration to permit innovation in applications and services (CSTB 2002, pp. 78–81).

Broadband access should insure that e-shoppers' experience is faster, easier, less frustrating and possibly cheaper. (It also creates many new challenges for e-merchants, which we cannot discuss here in detail.) As an increasing number of websites offer users different access options depending on the speed of their connection, it is possible to view broadband as a higher quality type access. A key question is when consumers reach a quality/price ratio that warrants upgrading to the higher quality. It is likely that this threshold is different for various user groups. Broadband customers report three benefits according to a survey of European users. For 64% of adopters it frees up their telephone line, for 58%, it provides a faster connection, and for 49% the always on feature is important (although this could also be realized in narrowband networks). Deployment of broadband is a major challenge for all stakeholders and four majors issues have to be addressed: management of technology, policy and regulation, business models and strategies, and user needs and skills. We look into these issues briefly for fixed and mobile broadband.

Fixed broadband

E-commerce requires the integration of platform services, applications, and content. At the platform level, service providers have to cope with a complex and changing technology. At least half a dozen technologies compete on the market. They evolve very fast, some of them are unproven but others are widely available.

Two of them have taken a significant share of the market: DSL and cable modems. Which platform is utilized depends to a certain degree on the existing communications infrastructure. Where cable was widely available (as in the US, Belgium, and the Netherlands) it usually attracts the larger share of subscribers. Even though it is a shared medium, it provides high bit rates and is reasonably reliable. But for a variety of reasons (low population density, television media policy as in Italy or Spain, and cable operator strategies) cable is not available universally. In these areas, given the wider availability of telephone lines, DSL has taken the lead as a broadband access platform. DSL requires a simple upgrade of normal telephone lines, but does not deliver broadband rates when the local loop is longer than a few kilometers (5 km so far). Therefore, DSL is not yet a solution for rural areas. Other solutions exist or have been tried, from wireless local loops to satellites and powerlines (using electric lines for data transmission). Unfortunately, all these solutions appear to be expensive, cumbersome or not yet ready for residential customers. Thus, there is no obvious solution today for residential customers in sparsely populated areas (Table 3).

Table 3. Fixed broadband technologies

	Availability	Reach	Bandwidth
Copper pair (DSL)	OK	Urban	Up to 8 Mbps
Optical fiber	OK	Urban	Up to 1 Tbps
CATV	OK	Urban/some rural	Up to 560 Mbps
WLL	OK	Everywhere	Up to 155 Mbps
Satellite	OK	Everywhere	Variable
Powerline	LAN only today	Everywhere	Up to 2 Mbps

By mid-2002, about 50 % of Europeans had the possibility to buy broadband access (IDC research); in the US nearly 98% of the population were able to buy broadband (Pepper 2002). However, only 3.2% of Europeans and 5.6% of Americans had actually subscribed to it. A comparison between the regions shows that cable modems are more widely used in the US, while DSL is more widespread in the EU (Table 4). As discussed above, this mix reflects the unique conditions in each region. The gap between supply and realized demand is stunning and casts doubt on arguments that identify lack of access as one of the main problems of broadband policy.

This gap also hints at other issues that will deserve careful attention. One is the question of an optimal diffusion rate for broadband. Pepper (2002) argues that broadband access is expanding at rates that are comparable to the early stages of other communications technologies. In his view, it is too early to assess whether broadband exhibits sub-optimal growth. Probably the most pressing problem is the development of successful business models employed by service providers. The data seem to corroborate the view that – except for affluent technology-savvy users who consider broadband as part of their lifestyle – it is necessary to combine an access platform with applications and content. The value chain of advanced communications services therefore requires the combination of skills (network platform, applications, and content) that no single entity may possess. Businesses may hence have to collaborate more than in earlier generations of communications technology, such as the telephone. This is illustrated in the success of fixed broadband service in Taiwan, where the network service provider collaborates with television stations and other content providers to provide video streaming services. Many of the telecommunications incumbent service providers in the US and EU are used to control most of the value chain and may have difficulties adopting such a new business philosophy.

Table 4. Broadband mix in the US and in Europe

| | United States | | | | European Union | | | |
| | 2001 | | 2002 | | 2001 | | 2002 | |
	Million	%	Million	%	Million	%	Million	%
DSL	3.9	39.4	6.0	37.5	5.3	76.8	9.4	77.0
Cable modems	6.0	60.6	10.0	62.5	1.6	23.2	2.8	23.0
Total	9.9	100.0	16.0	100.0	6.9	100.0	12.2	100.0

Source : Idate 2002.

Apart from the intricacies of developing a new collaborative model, it is obvious that the ability of different players in the broadband market to forge or block successful coalitions differs significantly. New competitors have two principal ways to provide broadband access. It can be facilities-based (new networks are deployed) or service-based, using existing networks. Building new networks is expensive, so sharing existing networks seems a cheaper solution. A key question is whether sharing should be mandated (as expressed in the EU framework) or voluntary (as expressed in the US framework, at least since the elimination of DSL unbundling). Mandatory sharing has potential negative effects on the provider of network infrastructure and may reduce the incentive to upgrade. On the other hand, it improves the position of application and content service providers as it reduces their dependence on the incumbent. Whether the overall effect is an acceleration or deceleration of broadband diffusion is heavily contested and there is anecdotal evidence for both viewpoints. If access is voluntary, there is a risk that the incumbents will try to erect barriers to entry for new competitors, especially in markets where the incumbent offers internet access services to its own usually dominant, ISP. In this case, interconnection/unbundling agreements can be used as a weapon to prevent new entrants from reaching significant market shares. Therefore, new fixed broadband entrants are often very fragile (Covad and Excite in the US, German and French WLL providers in Europe are good examples). However, this outcome may not be inevitable as there are situations, in which it would be good business practice for the incumbent to share voluntarily (Farrell and Weiser 2002). This may happen if a competitor can acquire customers that the incumbent could not serve, perhaps because of brand name rejection. In this case, the incumbent would gain from offering a new competitor access to a network platform as it would generate additional wholesale revenues. Nevertheless, there are many situations in which this voluntary approach will fail, leaving policy makers in a quandary as to which course to pursue.

Given these comments, initiatives by countries to support broadband deployment with public funds need to be seen in a different light. Purely supply-side measures, such as subsidies, tax breaks, or the public roll-out of networks, can only provide a necessary precondition for access but are in most cases not sufficient to stimulate use. A wide range of approaches exists. For example, two Swedish bills of 2000 and 2001 provide incentives for broadband usage. On the other hand, the French government has been very hesitant to allow local authorities to build and operate public access networks. In the European Union, universal service obligations do not yet include broadband provision (although the new framework would in principle allow such measures). In the present fiscal situation, governments do not have enough money to subsidize broadband. Ironically, it seems likely that richer and eager local authorities will be able to fund broadband development; however, these are often communities with relatively high purchasing power, where commercial operators would be willing to supply broadband. Significant obstacles exist in communities with fewer funds and a lower level of demand. In these cases strategies of demand aggregation and measures to facilitate coordination between users and suppliers may be most successful (Bauer, Kim, and Wildman forthcoming).

Mobile broadband

The present mobile voice and data services can be used to provide narrowband access to the internet. Evolutions such as EDGE, CDMA2000 (US) or General Packet Radio Service (EU) allow higher transmission speeds up to 171.2 kbps. Third generation (3G) services, such as CDMA2000 1x EV-DO or W-CDMA promise transmission speeds of up to 384 kbps in a mobile and 2 Mbps in a stationary setting. However, the deployment of 3G solutions has met considerable difficulties, both technical and market-related. Europe has opted to deploy a community-wide Universal Mobile Telecommunications System (UMTS, which uses W-CDMA as technological platform), although no mandatory standard was adopted to avoid violating international trade rules. The US has studied possible frequency allocations for 3G services in the 1.7 and 2.1 GHz bands (NTIA 2002) as well as the 2.5GHz band. In November 2002, the FCC initiated a formal proceeding to define service rules for Advanced Wireless Service (AWS). Licensing for these bands was postponed several times and it now looks as if the respective frequency bands will be auctioned in 2004. Since 1999, the FCC has pursued a policy of flexible licensing. Therefore, present licensees in several frequency bands are free to use their spectrum to provide a wide range of applications, including 2.5 or 3G services. Several service providers are upgrading their networks to offer faster and more advanced services. Like in 2G services, it is likely that several standards will continue to co-exist. Present GSM/TDMA operators favor W-CDMA and the present CDMA operators favor CDMA-2000. Therefore, the US is unlikely to develop a nation-wide plan for 3G deployment.

In the EU, frequencies were allocated in the late 1990s and licenses were assigned between 1999 and 2002. Eight of the fifteen member states used multiple-round auctions and seven relied on more traditional methods such as beauty contests or sealed bids. In the UK and in Germany, winning bidders paid very high sums for the license (US\$ 600 and US\$ 560 per population, respectively) causing subsequent financial difficulties for several service providers. Especially in the countries where high license fees were paid, operators are not sure whether they will be able to recoup their investments. Standard microeconomic theory claims that license costs are irrelevant for the pricing of services, but this is only true if strong assumptions are met, such as that the demand curve is known, capital markets work perfectly, and the market structure will remain effectively competitive. As there are huge uncertainties regarding these factors, it is possible that operators will attempt to recoup their high license costs through higher service prices, adopt a slower roll-out path, or offer lower levels of service quality (Bauer 2003). These problems are aggravated by the attempt to allocate one more UMTS license than existing GSM licenses to allow awarding a license to a new entrant. Therefore, there are, in the "best" case, at least as many UMTS operators as they were GSM operators (e.g., France). In the "worst" case there are more UMTS operators than there are GSM operators (e.g., Germany, or the UK).

During the past year, a number of developments became visible. Several UMTS license holders gave up their very expensive licenses, including Quam, the Sonera-Telefónica joint-venture in Germany and mmO2 in the Netherlands. An increasing number of operators have entered network sharing agreements to decrease investment costs (Curwen 2002). With safeguards, regulators at the national and European level have generally allowed infrastructure sharing, although different approaches continue to exist. All operators have, sometimes very quietly and sometimes publicly, tried to delay the actual deployment of their networks. They hoped to reduce the inherent technical risks of deployment, to get a better visibility on marketing issues (as they have opened GPRS services) and to delay the impact of UMTS on their very profitable GSM networks. Therefore, in Europe, despite initial service offerings in more densely populated areas in Italy, the UK, and Austria, no national commercial launch has occurred for UMTS networks and will likely not happen until late 2003 and 2004.

In the US, and to a lesser degree in the EU, applications in unlicensed spectrum bands, such as wireless local area networks (802.11b also known as WiFi) are growing rapidly. Although the relation between 3G and WiFi is still evolving, the two technologies are in part substitutes and in part complementary to each other (ITU 2002a; Lehr and McKnight 2003). WiFi is capable of providing access speeds of up to 11 Mbps (802.11b) to up to 54 Mbps (802.11a) but over short distances. On the other hand, 3G will likely have more ubiquitous coverage but slower transmission speed. Recent experiments demonstrated that focused signals could travel over several kilometers. Access points are sprouting all across the US both in a grassroots movement that promises free ubiquitous access and by commercial service providers such as AT&T, which formed a joint venture with IBM and Intel to deploy 20,000 access points across the U.S. T-Mobile, the sixth largest mobile service provider, bought the assets of Mobilestar, a bankrupt WiFi service provider that had installed equipment in the Starbucks chain of coffeehouses across the U.S. The answer to several unresolved questions will affect the viability of WiFi and its relation to 3G. One issue is the problem of interference protection, although this is mitigated by the short reach of the signal and the ability to use real estate property rights, such as contracts with restaurant owners or airport operators, to protect against intruders. Another question is securing backhaul transportation capacity, especially for the many free hotspots. In addition, questions of mobility (which is better for 3G), ubiquity of coverage (potentially better for 3G), or security (better for 3G) will affect the mix. Given the higher availability of PCs in the US, WiFi may enjoy a higher share in the emerging mobile data market than in Europe, where mobile devices are more widespread. In the EU context, a risk of WiFi is that it might siphon off just enough revenue from the 3G market to undermine profitable business models. If this is the case, it can be expected that licensed 3G operators will attempt to secure a strong foothold in the WiFi market. The risk that WiFi may "balkanize" the advanced wireless services market is lower in the US, which pursues a more gradual path allowing carriers to incorporate the existence of WiFi in their spectrum bids.

Synthesis: internet access and e-commerce

This chapter started with the assumption that internet access was an important precondition for e-commerce. Previous sections reviewed the factors shaping internet access and illustrated the different national and regional paths that have emerged from their interaction. In closing, it seems appropriate to also revisit the starting premise. We emphasized that technological platforms and terminal equipment are necessary but not sufficient conditions for internet use. Likewise, internet access and use is only one among several necessary but not a sufficient condition for e-commerce to flourish. Any policy whose ultimate goal is to stimulate e-commerce will therefore have to pay close attention to other factors. Important complementary infrastructures need to be in place, including internet hosts and secure services. Additional preconditions include the existence of an electronic payment system, institutions that safeguard trust, in the case of physical goods appropriate transportation and logistics systems, entrepreneurs willing to offer goods and services on an e-commerce platform, and the cultivation of user skills.

To get a sense of the importance of the technological infrastructure on e-commerce, we studied the strength of the relation between these two variables. This task is complicated by the fact that standardized macroeconomic metrics to measure the level, growth and composition of e-commerce have only been adopted recently. Only a handful of countries have begun to report figures according to these definitions (OECD 2002, p. 61). Earlier reports therefore used the availability of secure web servers as a proxy for the e-commerce readiness of a country. This approach usually finds the US in a clear lead before other OECD nations. However, this approach presupposes that there is a clear relation between the number of secure servers and e-commerce. We subjected this claim to a test using data for the seven countries that report sales and revenue data for e-commerce using regression analysis. Seven OECD countries (Austria, Finland,

Luxembourg, Portugal, Spain, Sweden, and UK) have collected comparable data for the share of e-commerce sales in total sales for the business sector. In this – admittedly small and tentative set of observations – we did not find a statistically significant relation between the number of secure web servers and e-commerce. This is not surprising as the location of web servers is influenced by a number of other factors (e.g., the cost of domain name registration and web hosting) and is to a certain degree independent from e-commerce transactions. We also did not find a statistically significant link between e-commerce and the availability of communications access platforms. However, we found a strong and statistically significant relation between internet use and the number of secure web servers (Table 5). As this relation only explains 30% of the variance in the number of secure hosts, other important factors are likely present. We also found a statistically significant relation between internet use and e-commerce, explaining 60% of the variance in the seven countries for which data were available. Although these findings need to be interpreted with caution, they are compatible with our conceptual model. Figure 4 suggested a two-stage, recursive relation between access platforms, use, and applications: communications infrastructure is a necessary condition for internet use, which in turn is a precondition for applications such as e-commerce. It needs to be pointed out that this recursive relation prohibits establishing a direction of causality in the cross-sectional approach used in this chapter. Moreover, the small number of observations requires caution when extrapolating results to other nations. As more data become available, more sophisticated empirical research will be possible. With the help of panel data, an explicit time structure could be modeled to test the recursive relations in the observations.

This chapter has illustrated that e-commerce is shaped by a complex bundle of factors. The availability of access platforms, terminals, and server infrastructure is but one precondition for e-commerce. In all the countries reviewed, the supply of access options exceeds demand for them. Thus, other factors, most importantly, the bundling and pricing of access; the availability, quality and pricing of applications and services; user-based factors such as income, preferences, and lifestyle; as well as the socio-cultural context are important determinants of internet access and use. This complexity has several consequences for public policy. First, it implies that there likely is no "best" approach as different configurations of relevant supply and demand-side factors may allow similar outcomes. This most transparent in the case of access platforms, where – due to digitization and a more flexible legal framework – several fixed or wireless technologies are capable of providing substitutable services. Thus, as the capabilities of existing and new technologies evolve, the mix of access platforms available to a country or a region is likely less important than the overall diffusion of platforms.

Secondly, the increased number of links among stakeholders and the need to organize complex value chains imply that the government's ability to achieve specific outcomes is likely decreasing. Rather, it will increasingly have to focus on the framework conditions in which e-commerce unfolds and the creation of supporting legal and institutional arrangements. While public policy thus defines important conditions for e-commerce, it is doubtful whether it has sufficient influence to actually determine its overall trajectory. However, public policy has the important task to establish a framework within which welfare improving forms of e-commerce can be experimented with. Based on their respective socio-cultural and political backgrounds, the EU and US have chosen different paths. The EU pursues an approach that reflects a mix of liberalization, industrial policy, and auxiliary measures. The US has adopted a model with a much higher trust in un-fettered market forces. Both frameworks will allow e-commerce to develop but it is a priori impossible to say whether one will be more successful. At a high level of aggregation, a paradox becomes visible: despite the fact that the US does not have a clear lead over the EU with regard to its ICT infrastructure, it has neverthe-less managed to translate its services into significant productivity increases whereas the EU so far has not. This points yet to another set of factors that would need to be considered when assessing the effects of information infrastructure on e-commerce and related economic advantages.

Table 5. Network infrastructure and e-commerce

	Dependent variables		
	Internet users	Secure web servers	E-commerce
	Independent variables		
Fixed access paths	*0.485		
(dial-up and broadband)	0.021		
Internet users		*4.844	*0.338
		0.017	0.025
Prob > F	*0.0214	*0.0169	*0.0249
Adj. R^2	0.2754	0.2975	0.6010

* ... significant at the 95% level

References

Bangemann Report (1994) Europe and the global information society. Report by the High-Level Group on the Information Society to the European Council. Brussels
Bar F et. al. (2000) Access and innovation policy for the third-generation Internet. Tele-communications Policy 24:489–518
Bauer JM (2002) Regionale und lokale Wirtschaftspolitik und B2B eCommerce. In: Latzer M, Just N, Schmitz SW, Sint PP, Purschke I, Bauer JM (eds) Status und Dynamik des Business-to-Consumer eCommerce in Wien, Austrian Academy of Sciences, Vienna, pp 163–175
Bauer JM (2003) Impact of license fees on the prices of mobile service. Telecommunications Policy 27:417–434
Bauer JM, Berne M, Maitland CF (2002). Internet access in the European Union and in the United States. Telematics and Informatics 19:117–137
Bauer JM, Kim JH, Wildman SS (in press) Broadband deployment: toward a more fully in-tegrated policy perspective. In: Shampine AL (ed) Down to the wire: studies in the dif-fusion and regulation of telecommunications technologies. Hauppauge, NY

Cherry BA, Bauer JM (2002) Institutional arrangements and price rebalancing: empirical evidence from the United States and Europe. Information Economics and Policy 14(4):495–517

Crandall RW, Alleman JH (eds) (2002) Broadband: should we regulate high-speed internet access? AEI-Brookings Joint Center for Regulatory Studies, Washington, D.C.

Curwen PJ (2002) The Future of Mobile Communications: awaiting the Third Generation. Palgrave, New York

Deiss R (2002) The European TV broadcasting market. Statistics in Focus, Theme 4 – 24/2002, Eurostat, Luxembourg

EC (2002a) Eight Report on the Implementation of the Telecommunications Regulatory Package. COM(2002) 695 final, Brussels: Commission of the European Communities

EC (2002b) eEurope 2005 : An information society for all. June, COM(2002) 263

EC (2002c) Towards a knowledge-based Europe, October

Eurobarometer (2001) Les Europeens et la E-Inclusion, Eurobarometer 55.2, June, available at http://europa.eu.int/comm/public_opinion/archives/eb/ebs_157_fr.pdf

Farrell J, Weiser PJ (2002) Modularity, vertical integration, and open access policies: towards a convergence of antitrust and regulation in the internet age. Unpublished paper, University of Colorado, Boulder, CO.

FCC (2002) Trends in telephone service 2002. First Report, US Federal Communications Commission, Washington, D.C.

Gandal N, Salant D, Waverman L (2003) Standards in wireless telephone networks. Telecommunications Policy 27(5-6):325–332

Gruber H, Verboven F (2001) The evolution of markets under entry and standard regulation: the case of global mobile communications. International Journal of Industrial Organization 19:1189–1212

Hargittai E (1999) Weaving the Western Web: explaining differences in Internet connectivity among OECD countries. Telecommunications Policy 23:701–718

Hausman JA, Sidak JG (1999) A consumer-welfare approach to the mandatory unbundling of telecommunications networks. Yale Law Journal, 109:417–505

Howell B (2002) Infrastructure regulation and the demand for broadband services: evidence from the OECD countries. Communications and Strategies, no 47, pp 33–62

Idate (2002) Europe and Broadband. Idate News, no 33, p 6

ITU (2002a) Internet for a mobile generation. International Telecommunication Union, Geneva

ITU (2002b) World telecommunications development report. International Telecommunication Union, Geneva

Jorde TM, Sidak JG, Teece DJ (2000) Innovation, investment, and unbundling. Yale Journal on Regulation 17:1–37

Kiiski S, Pohjola M (2002) Cross-country diffusion of the internet, Information Economics and Policy, 14:297–310

Koski HA, Majumdar SK (2000) Convergence in telecommunications infrastructure development in OECD countries, Information Economics and Policy 12:111–131

Lehr W, McKnight LW (2003) Wireless Internet access: 3G vs. WiFi?, Telecommunications Policy 27:351–370

Maitland CF (1999) Global diffusion of interactive networks: the impact of culture. AI & Society, 13:311–335

NTIA (2002) A nation online: how Americans are expanding their use of the internet. National Telecommunications and Information Administration, Washington, D.C.

OECD (2000) Local access pricing and e-commerce. Organisation for Economic Co-operation and Development, Paris

OECD (2001a) Communications outlook. Organisation for Economic Co-operation and Development, Paris

OECD (2001b) The development of broadband access in OECD countries. DSTI/ICCP/TISP(2001)/2 final. Organisation for Economic Co-operation and Development, Paris

OECD (2002) Measuring the information economy. Organisation for Economic Co-operation and Development, Paris

Pepper R (2002) Competition, regulation and digital migration. Paper presented at the 14th Biennial Conference of the International Telecommunications Society, August 18–21, Seoul, Korea

Ragin CC (2000) Fuzzy-set social science. University of Chicago Press, Chicago

Privacy and regulation in a digital age

Abraham L. Newman[1], David Bach[2, 3]

Department of Political Science, University of California, Berkeley, USA

Abstract

Owing to the pervasiveness of personal data collection, transmission, storage, and analysis, privacy has emerged as a central public policy concern in recent years. The chapter explains the repercussions of the digital revolution for personal privacy, and situates the current debate in proper historical context. It shows that privacy expectations vary with the social context, and derives a framework through which to understand geographic, sectoral, and temporal variation of privacy protection. Privacy regimes in Europe and the United States are not set apart by profound cultural differences, as is often argued, but instead rely on distinct sets of enforcement mechanisms. After reviewing the respective role of the public sector, the private sector, and technology in enforcing privacy standards, the chapter concludes with a look ahead to new challenges.

Introduction

From mobile phones to the Internet, digital technologies generate vast amounts of personal data. People's locations, purchases, preferences, and even genetic susceptibilities can or will soon be tracked, processed, and stored. To industries such as insurance or marketing, personal data are information capital, enhancing product customization, market segmentation, and risk reduction. Unfortunately, the economic benefits of employing such "personal information capital" come at a potentially high individual cost: the progressive loss of personal privacy.[4] Governments

---

[1] E-mail: aben@uclink.berkeley.edu
[2] E-mail: bach@socrates.berkeley.edu
[3] The authors would like to thank Craig Pollack, Simon Stow, Almudena Villanueva, Sara Watson, the editors of this volume, and participants in the "E-Life after the dot com bust" workshop for insightful comments and suggestions on previous drafts.
[4] Privacy has many meanings, as we will argue throughout this chapter. In this general case, we view privacy as an individual's ability to control the access to and use of per-

have often found themselves in the difficult position of balancing market rational and economic opportunity on the one hand, and threats to personal liberty and human dignity on the other. In response, societies across the industrialized world have adopted distinct approaches to resolve this balancing act. What is the privacy debate really about? Why do privacy disputes appear to be coming to a head now? How do distinct privacy regulations affect business strategies and national economies? And what are the implications of cross-national variation among privacy regulations for global market integration and international trade?

Personal privacy has moved into public consciousness in close association with the Internet and e-commerce hype of the 1990s. Time and again, surveys have revealed that concern over privacy was the single most important reason that kept consumers from spending more time and money online.[5] As a result, the privacy debate in recent years has been framed in terms of "privacy on the *Internet*." Now, the dot com bubble has burst, the initial Internet hype is over and our expectations about the immediate impact of business-to-consumer (B2C) e-commerce are much more realistic. But are we hence to conclude that the salience of privacy concerns will similarly subside? We think not. In subordinating privacy issues to the newest technologies and commercial applications, the "privacy on the *Internet*"-perspective has obscured a public discourse over privacy that has stretched over several generations and continents. Concerns over privacy are not new, and neither are debates about appropriate public policy responses to emerging privacy threats. The articulation of a legal "right to be left alone" in America for example, dates to 1890, when it was first elaborated in a famous Harvard Law Review article by U.S. Supreme Court Justices Warren and Brandeis.[6] Already in the early 1970s, national legislatures across industrial countries discussed the need for action regarding personal information exchange. By reorienting the debate as one about "*privacy* in a digital age," this chapter moves beyond a narrow discussion of e-commerce and the Internet, and seeks instead to locate current privacy challenges and societal responses in a broader context of evolving technological innovation and deployment.

Over the last thirty years, industrial democracies have developed complex regulatory frameworks to deal with personal information privacy concerns. Responses have been plentiful and diverse, with considerable variation across societies. This diversity stems from the politically volatile character of privacy debates, the stakes involved, and the regulatory tools available to policy-makers. Far from starting with a blank regulatory slate, governments must mediate a wide range of consumer and industry interests, constrained by past policy decisions and institutional resources. This political struggle then produces regulatory compromises and shapes what can be called national "privacy regimes." These privacy regimes mix public sector, private sector, and technological governance tools to mediate pri-

---

sonal information about him or herself. See Schauer 1998. More generally, see Westin 1967.

[5] See, for example, Jupiter Media Metrix Press Release 2002. For a review of earlier surveys, see Kang 1998.

[6] Warren and Brandeis 1890.

vacy challenges.[7] Formal data protection legislation, trade association-sponsored self-regulation, and technological tools such as cryptography are all examples of privacy regime components. The character of privacy regimes assembled from these components and the overall strategies underpinning them have implications for individual protection levels, market opportunities, and societies' ability to deal with future privacy threats.

To illustrate the evolutionary and contingent nature of privacy regimes, this chapter is organized in the following four sections. The first section analyzes the inherently relative (as opposed to absolute) nature of privacy, and assesses the claim that Europe and the U.S. have fundamentally different approaches to privacy concerns based on differing cultural attitudes. The second section identifies some current privacy threats brought on by recent technological innovation. It illuminates why privacy has (re-) emerged as a central public policy concern in recent years. In the third section, we offer a lens through which to understand privacy regimes. This lens provides the basis for the geographic, sectoral and temporal variation of privacy regimes. The fourth and final section underscores the overall stakes by sketching out some future challenges to personal privacy. Examining "*privacy* in a digital age" reveals that, if anything, the privacy debate will intensify in years to come, as digital technology augments the types of information organizations may collect, as well as their ability to integrate diverse pieces of personal data.

The nature of privacy and the privacy debate

Many observers in recent years have identified the principal privacy battle line as running between the United States and Europe.[8] Americans and Europeans, it is often argued, have fundamentally different conceptions of personal privacy and how to go about protecting it. Many follow their intuition and claim that profound cultural differences set the two apart. Consistent with liberal ideals of personal freedom and individual responsibility, Americans are said to view personal information as a commodity that can be exchanged, traded, and sold. The state's responsibility in the protection of individual privacy is thus the creation of stable property rights for a market in personal data and to limit potential government excesses concerning government data collection. Europeans, it is argued on the other hand, cherish community values over personal freedom. Lessons from the Nazi period and totalitarianism more generally linger and facilitate government action on behalf of citizens' privacy. Rather than letting a market in personal data flourish by leaving it up to individuals to choose when to sell their information, Euro-

---

[7] Note that we employ public, private, and technological governance tools as analytic categories throughout most of this chapter to better dissect various privacy regimes. When referring to specific business firms or governments as purposeful social actors, we make it explicit.

[8] See Swire and Litan 1998. See also, The Economist 1999; and Tucker 1999.

pean governments have intervened and created standards approximating a de-facto "human right to privacy." Here, citizen protection extends beyond state data processing to the private sector.[9]

The alleged, culturally rooted contrast between liberal (Anglo-Saxon) and communitarian (European) notions of society on either side of the Atlantic is neither accurate, nor terribly useful for an understanding of contemporary privacy regimes. The culture argument risks inappropriately homogenizing European public policy, obscures enforcement and implementation variation across Europe, and ignores the set of common principles that underpin privacy protection worldwide. In this section, we seek to debunk the dichotomy and refocus academic attention on the actual implementation of abstract privacy principles. This section establishes a theoretical baseline from which a more nuanced discussion of privacy regimes and their components becomes possible.

As a matter of real-world implementation, liberal and communitarian ideals are often matters of emphasis, or even two sides of the same coin. Political theorists and legal scholars have long established that liberals invoke community standards to interpret rights.[10] Communitarians, on the other hand, frequently rely on legal rights and safeguards to protect and defend community values.[11] Privacy is not only no exception in this regard; as the following discussion will show, it is in fact a powerful illustration of the intertwinedness of individual rights and community values.

The development of international privacy standards demonstrates the need to move beyond a debate cast in terms of a cultural dichotomy. Starting in the early 1970s, pressure to safeguard personal information privacy began to rise in North America and Europe. With the rise of mainframe computers and large databanks, citizens, academics, and government officials began contemplating responses to the potential dangers of adopting powerful information technologies. The 1973 Swedish Privacy Act and the U.S. Privacy Act of 1974 represent first-wave data privacy policies that formulated and established basic privacy standards. These principles are known as the Fair Information Practice Principles (FIPP) and include the following concepts:

- *Notice* – data users should openly notify data subjects of privacy policies;
- *Consent* – data should not be disclosed or used for purposes without data subject consent;
- *Security* – stored data must be secure from theft or corruption;
- *Access* –data subjects should have access to stored data in order to verify accuracy;
- *Accountability* – a procedure must exist to enforce and punish breaches of the principles.

---

[9] See, for example, Singleton 2000.
[10] See, generally, Kymlicka 1989, 1995. In the area of privacy in particular, see Post 1989.
[11] For a discussion, see Taylor 1989.

These principles were later codified internationally by the Organization for Economic Cooperation and Development (OECD) in the 1980 *Guidelines on the Protection of Privacy and Transborder Flows of Personal Data*.[12]

On its face, the FIPP seem most consistent with the liberal approach to privacy and privacy protection. The FIPP are clearly based on the assumption that personal information is routinely collected and that this is even in a data subject's interest, as long as certain principles are guaranteed to protect the data subject from abuse. The spirit of the FIPP is therefore to enable a fair exchange of personal information between data subject and data user. To that end, the principles lay out the fundamental components of a property rights system in personal information.[13]

Yet privacy is an inherently intersubjective phenomenon.[14] It is intersubjective in the sense that questions about what is and what is not private only arise in relations among two or more individuals. Privacy does not make sense as an absolute attribute of individual social actors, and is not reducible to individual preferences or actions. Being the only citizen on his planet, Saint-Exupérie's Little Prince, for example, never had to draw a line between public and private.

The intersubjective nature of privacy implies that any privacy protection regime has a strong communal flavor. In order to actually implement the FIPP, decisions have to be made about what legally constitutes "fair" levels of *notice, consent, security, access*, and *accountability*. And what constitutes "fair" depends, of course, on the result of political battles over community norms and standards. It naturally varies considerably with circumstance. Rights created on the basis of the liberal-spirited FIPP cannot be implemented without invoking community standards. The U.S. as well as European nations thus generally base formal privacy protection on the assumption of a "reasonable expectation of privacy."[15] It is not the data itself that is protected; rather, privacy rules regulate the collection and use of data in particular contexts. Taking note of what an individual wears on the street, for example, is not objectionable; trespassing into her home to examine her closet is. Similarly, an individual might want a doctor to know that he has a certain disease; but he might not want his employer to have the same information. In short, the question whether a "reasonable expectation of privacy" exists in a particular context cannot be answered in a social void; it is highly contingent on the norms and practices that govern a particular community. And here we inevitably enter the world of politics.

---

[12] OECD 1980.

[13] Property rights, in this context, can be defined simply as "the social institutions that define or delimit the range of privileges granted to individuals to specific assets." See Libecap 1989, p. 1.

[14] On "intersubjectivity" and "intersubjective beliefs", see Lewis 1969 and Searle 1995. See Post 1989, for a similar discussion in the area of privacy.

[15] In the U.S., the particular phrasing is by Supreme Court Justice Harlan, concurring, in Katz v. U.S., 389 U.S. 347 (1967). Similarly, the German expert committee responsible for the development of the German Data Protection Act of 1977 determined that relative use ("Zweck") and not the data itself must be protected. See Bundesdrucksache 1971.

However, just as rights in personal data cannot be implemented and interpreted without community-derived reference frames, the creation of a property rights regime that enables a socially acceptable system of personal information exchange can be a political strategy to protect a community's privacy values. A clearly defined set of privacy rights and rules empowers consumers to individually defend and enforce collectively agreed upon community values. Casting the debate over privacy as one of (American) liberal versus (European) communitarian notions of society is thus not terribly useful at best, and misleading at worst. Cultural communities as diverse as Germany, Spain, Japan, and the U.S. use the same FIPP principles to guide modern data privacy laws. The interesting question is not whether contracts or absolute rights exist; instead we should ask how politics shapes the implementation of privacy norms and what means are employed by societies to guarantee a "reasonable expectation of privacy." In sum, privacy regimes are based on the ability of nations to mobilize distinct public, private, and technological resources to guarantee contextual interpretations of abstract privacy principles. Owing to the limited scope of this chapter, we focus on the implementation and enforcement side of privacy regimes in the following, particularly in light of recent digital challenges. However, we return briefly to the politics of norm development in the conclusion.

The digital dilemma

While the intersubjective nature of privacy has been established, the question remains as to why privacy issues have emerged as a central public policy issue in the 1990s. We argue that the development and spread of digital technologies has re-ignited and qualitatively changed privacy concerns and hence the privacy debate. In short, as suggested in the introduction, the diffusion of digital technology carries the potential for vast societal benefit as well as the possibility of grave harm. Four facets of new information technology can be isolated as having a profound effect on personal privacy concerns: greater amounts of data, different types of data, new data users, and international data transfers.

First, new data collection, processing and storage technologies have greatly augmented monitoring capacities. In the pre-digital era, data had to be manually collected, processed, interpreted, and physically stored, most commonly on paper. Digital technologies automate and seamlessly integrate these steps. The quantity of information that data collectors can thus accumulate and analyze according to sophisticated pre-programmed algorithms has reached staggering levels. The increasing use of credit scoring systems by credit agencies, financial service providers, and mobile telephone contractors is but one example of the explosion of automated decision-making made possible by new digital technologies.[16] Meanwhile, the cost of performing theses tasks is plummeting. The cost of data transmission over digital networks is already approaching zero at the margin; an in-

---

[16] See, for example, Australian Financial Review 2000, p. 21; and Singletary 2000, p. H1.

definite number of copies can be made at virtually no cost, with each copy as good as the original; and an end to the explosion in storage capacity is not in sight.

Secondly, new types of personal information have become "collectable," substantially transforming the quality of data collection. Information, according to Carl Shapiro and Hal Varian, is anything that can be digitized.[17] Any digital trail of individual behavior can thus be turned into personal information. Credit card records, shopping club cards, "click-trails" on the Internet, automatic toll-collection systems, and chat room transcripts are only some of the recent data sources that bring entirely new areas of human activity under public scrutiny. Integrated data banks and state-of-the-art data processing software enable the dissection and recombination of vast amounts of raw data from diverse arenas of personal activity into refined electronic profiles of individual behavior. Drawing from a vast array of distinct data sources, data processors can thus obtain a level of insight about a person that used to be the prerogative of only family and close friends.

Thirdly, a new agent of privacy intrusion has emerged over the last thirty years: the private sector. Initial privacy laws passed during the 1970s focused their attention on public sector threats. The Orwellian vision of Big Brother depicted in *1984* was long heralded as the ultimate justification for privacy protection. Large mainframe computers loomed behind government plans to rationalize social provisions like welfare benefits and increase efficiency in internal security and crime control. But the information technology revolution of the 1990s expanded access to powerful computing and empowered private actors just as much as public officials. Distributed networks and personal computers provide small- and medium-sized businesses with data processing capacities previously the prerogative of only the largest corporations and public bureaucracies.[18] In fact, privatization of public services and budgetary constraints increasingly force public bureaucracies to rely on private sector information gathering capacity. Recent government proposals to integrate private sector data collection and monitoring into anti-terrorism efforts typify this trend.[19] Even more important, new technologies facilitate the exchange of data across economic domains. Before the rise of digital information technology, only a limited number of companies, mostly direct mail marketers, collected, sorted, and sold information to companies from different sectors of the economy. A bank in New York in 1950 did not possess the know-how or tools to effectively and economically share information about its clients with an insurance company in California. The simultaneous advance of data collection, data production, and statistics programs permits firms to turn bits of data into information capital that can be used for in-house production as well as sale to third parties. While the original threat of an Orwellian government surveillance society may have been contained by initial legislation, individuals and communities must now reckon

---

[17] Shapiro and Varian 1999, p. 3.
[18] Cohen et al. 2001.
[19] The private sector is to play a critical role in the U.S. Department of Defense's new Total Information Awareness program, for example. See Markoff 2002.

with the possibility of something better described as an AOLian world where consumer monitoring expands at rapid speeds in the name of economic efficiency.[20]

Finally, enhanced data communications technologies have spurred a surge in international trade in services, giving privacy concerns an international dimension. Personal information about consumers provides the backbone of service industries ranging from finance, through retail, to marketing. As firms providing personal data-intensive services reach out across borders, privacy regimes of distinct jurisdictions come into contact. Transnational service firms with affiliates in countries with diverse data protection rules face increased regulatory burdens. At the same time, differences in data protection standards provide opportunities for regulatory arbitrage.[21] Citizens in a country with high privacy standards could fear the transfer of personal information to a company in a country with lower levels of protection. The most recent dispute between the European Union and the U.S. over the EU's Data Privacy Directive highlights the significance of this new dimension in the debate about privacy.[22]

The explosion in the quantity and quality of available personal information as well as the new users and internationalization of the issue confuse individual privacy expectations and thereby re-ignite a debate about appropriate privacy norms. Privacy principles focus primarily on how information may be collected and used. In both areas, collection and use, digital technologies blur and challenge existing boundaries between the public and private spheres. Are chat rooms public even though they are accessed from a private home? Does e-mail deserve the protection traditionally given to real mail? Is searching your hard drive through a network connection different than searching your home?

In sum, the rise and rapid diffusion of digital information and communications technologies has put strains on existing privacy regimes by greatly widening the scope and increasing the scale of data obtainable about individuals. Furthermore, existing regimes and privacy conceptions must reckon with the rise of private sector monitoring capacity and the increasing internationalization of privacy challenges. All of these developments predate the Internet and e-commerce. The EU's Data Privacy Directive, for example, was passed in 1995, and deliberations had

---

[20] In the aftermath of the terrorist attacks on the United States on September 11th, 2001 expansion of government surveillance privileges and capabilities in many industrialized countries may well shift the focus back on the public sector. At the time of writing, the medium- and long-run privacy implications of the most recent wave of anti-terrorism legislation could not be fully assessed. Early evidence suggests that law enforcement communities may increasingly seek routine access to data collected by the private sector, such as financial records and location-specific data obtained from mobile phones. The private sector's ability to monitor will thus not cease to be a matter of concern. The private sector's predominantly economic rationale of monitoring could be supplemented by security imperatives, however, and thereby fundamentally transform the debate over private monitoring once again. For early findings along these lines, see Reporters without Borders Press Release 2002.

[21] Froomkin 1997.

[22] See Swire and Litan 1998.

begun several years before. In many respects, however, the Internet has brought these distinct challenges together, greatly enhanced their overall visibility, and re-opened fundamental debates. As a result, privacy has become one of the top public policy issues of the digital age, both domestically and internationally.

Understanding privacy regimes

To gauge societies' ability to guarantee privacy in light of the challenges posed by the digital revolution, it is necessary to examine in more detail the three principal resources that interact to produce privacy regimes – public sector, private sector, and technological governance tools. We elaborate how these resources are mixed to provide context-specific "reasonable expectation[s] of privacy" and how these vary cross-nationally. We want to stress that countries do not have to employ one component at the expense of another. Rather, all three are employed to varying degrees given national incentives and constraints. Digital technologies have re-opened and recast the privacy debate, triggering political battles over such aspects of privacy regimes as the interpretation of "fair" levels of *notice* or *consent*, the appropriate role of industry self-regulation, or the desirability of private enforce-ment through technology. National contexts shape the interests of government, businesses, and consumers, and impinge on each group's ability to achieve their desired policy outcomes. The timing and sequencing of government and business decisions affect the control instruments available to public policy practitioners. Thus, a nation's capacity to mobilize public sector, private sector, and technologi-cal resources in response to new privacy threats depends in large part on the tools and strategies developed and employed to respond to previous privacy challenges.

Public sector tools

Public sector privacy protection efforts are multifaceted. They vary considerably cross-nationally and across sectors. Two aspects of government involvement seem particularly salient and account for much of the variation: first, the character and extent of conferred privacy rights in a given context; and secondly, the system of enforcement. We consider each in turn.

Privacy Rights - Governments create and back-up privacy rights. As business pressure increases to formalize the commodification of personal information, citi-zens and firms demand rules of exchange that guarantee the stability of an emerg-ing market. Yet, as elaborated above, these rules must be consistent with and are informed by community norms. Certain deals are not allowed, even if a buyer and seller could agree on a price. Just as individuals are barred from selling their or-gans, one could imagine rules in the future prohibiting the sale of ownership rights in personal genetic code. What specific privileges are formally granted to citizens and firms in conjunction with ownership of personal information is thus key.

When it comes to the specific rights granted, tremendous variation exists across countries and sectors. This should not surprise given that the social context and community values matter profoundly for privacy regulation. More specifically, public officials must broker deals and then translate the general FIPP concepts into coherent regulation that define and delimit rights associated with control over personal information. Implementing the FIPP principles of *notice* and *consent* into law in the United States provides a good example of the diversity of rights in personal information that have been created. At the least interventionist extreme, the direct marketing industry is left to pure self-regulation. No formal rules exist governing notice or consent. Citizens have no specific rights and firms do not have to account for their personal information collection procedures. The picture is very different in the financial services industry. Owing to the Financial Modernization Act of 1999, also known as the Gramm-Leach-Bliley Act, citizens and financial services firms confront a set of explicit rules of exchange. Financial institutions that share information with affiliates must give notice to their customers. This rule is meant to increase citizens' awareness of the activities of their financial service providers. Yet citizens are not given a right to prevent information gathering altogether or correct misreported information. Their only recourse is to terminate the relationship. For financial services firms that share information with third-parties, however, the Act provides an "opt-out" consent requirement. This policy mandates that citizens not only be informed of information collection, but in addition gives them the ability to request individually that information is not shared with third parties.[23] The Medical Privacy Rules, which came into effect in 2001, go even further in citizen empowerment by requiring an "opt-in" policy for information release. Without written consent by the patient, no medical information can be shared. The consent requirements have recently been adjusted by the Bush administration, but nevertheless maintain a high standard of protection for transfer to employers and law enforcement officials.[24] Additionally, patients have been given the right to review their health records and make changes if necessary, something to which physicians had long objected.

This brief overview of sectoral variation within a single country illustrates the context sensitivity of individual rights in personal information. Across the cases discussed, citizen rights continually increase. The direction makes sense, given that most people are much more concerned about somebody getting a hold of their medical information than their mailing address to send a catalog. It must be emphasized once more, however, that these rights are not static. As data mining software and data matching techniques improve across domains, individual sector rules may need to be reconsidered. The outcome will very much depend on the particular interests pitted against one another, and the political processes that mediate among them.

Enforcement – A second important dimension of government variation in privacy regimes concerns enforcement mechanisms. Once FIPP have been translated into specific exchange rules, nations must develop monitoring and enforcement

---

[23] For a review of financial privacy rules in the U.S., see Swire 2002.
[24] See Ladine 2002, p. A1.

systems. European countries have developed comprehensive statutory rules that govern the collection and transfer of personal information by both the government and private organizations. The implementation of these laws is typically coordinated through a national regulatory system that mirrors national regulatory structures. This means that unitary governmental systems like the U.K. have a centralized data protection authority while federal governmental systems like Germany rely on a decentralized network of regulators at the federal and state levels. The U.S., in contrast, has adopted a patchwork of sectoral laws. Lacking a central enforcement mechanism, non-governmental organizations and sectoral regulators play the primary enforcement role.[25]

By creating a comprehensive baseline statutory right, European countries have gone further than the purely sectoral approach in the U.S. In theory, this statutory right empowers EU citizens to enforce minimum privacy protection across all sectors and personal information trade across the sectors. This cross-domain protection is increasingly isolated as the main aspect of the European system from the U.S. point of view.[26] On the enforcement and implementation side, however, much variation can be found within Europe. The centralized French or Swedish monitoring organizations concentrate on databank licensing. The centralized system's focus on licensing becomes increasingly taxing as the number of organizations with databanks rises. This task also drains resources, hampering the organizations' ability to respond to citizen complaints and carry out audits. A central regulatory authority may prove advantageous when confronting large public sector projects like transportation or health care. In contrast, the decentralized networks of German or Austrian regulators are primarily engaged in advising legislators and the private sector. Privacy authorities provide advice and support private sector efforts to comply with data protection legislation or create self-regulatory solutions. Regulators in this system cannot impose fines for violations as easily as their colleagues in France, for example. Instead they rely largely on public "shaming" and reputational costs. The decentralized structure of the German system spreads out regulators, perhaps encouraging compliance among small and medium sized firms. An additional layer of enforcement is of course provided by citizens' ability to bring lawsuits against abusers, yet the extent of citizen rights in such proceedings also differs across European countries.

In the U.S., a baseline statutory legislation does not exist, leaving only a limited number of sector-specific laws. Furthermore, no federal privacy watchdog exists to date.[27] While sector laws such as the Gramm-Leach-Bliley Act for financial services are of course enforceable in courts, it is left up to market-pressure and the goodwill of companies in sectors without privacy laws to formulate their own rules. This incentive structure creates markets for private third-party protection

---

[25] For a review of U.S. regulation see Schwartz and Reidenberg 1996. European regulatory regimes are analyzed in Flaherty 1989.

[26] See, for example, Swire 1998.

[27] In recent years, the Federal Trade Commission (FTC) has tried to establish itself as a privacy watchdog of some sort. There are also efforts in several states to create statewide watchdogs, an example being California.

systems such as TRUSTe. TRUSTe, and also the Better Business Bureau, are both originally North American organizations that award seals of privacy standard compliance, offer dispute-resolution procedures, and serve as private-sector privacy watchdogs and auditors.[28] Yet companies in unregulated sectors that voluntarily provide privacy policies stand subject to Federal Trade Commission review under deceptive business practices legislation.[29] Paradoxically, then, this enforcement mechanism gives firms an incentive not to post privacy policies since they cannot be held liable if they never state principles in the first place.

Private sector tools

Private sector efforts to protect consumers' personal privacy can be divided in firm-level and industry-level initiatives. Both efforts witness private organizations in the field of privacy protection and provision. Entrepreneurs develop privacy enhancing technologies, taking advantage of new markets for personal information management. At the same time, business associations – often seeking to preempt the costly imposition of formal regulation – coordinate private sector activity to quell societal fears and to enhance consumer privacy protection.

Firm-Level – Individual firm activities manifest themselves in various business models. Anonymizer.com, for example, uses proxy servers to market anonymous web-surfing.[30] Customers can purchase an "add-in" for standard web browsers that ensure surfing is "privacy safe." Lumeria is developing a particularly interesting business model.[31] Its "Ad Network" replaces ads that would ordinarily appear on a user's browser with ads from areas previously chosen by the user. Lumeria's servers, in return, filter personally identifiable data out and only sell aggregate data about its users to data processors. Part of the money it receives is shared with its customers. Several other companies, such as Zero Knowledge, focus on developing so-called "Privacy Enhancing Technologies" (PETs) for both consumers and businesses.[32] We analyze the particular technologies in more detail below. Many established companies, lastly, seek to promote trust relationships with their customers, offering privacy management as an additional service. American Express, for example, provides its customers with one-time "Private Payments" numbers to be used for online purchases instead of the actual credit card number.[33] This not only enhances online privacy, it also reduces the threat of "identity theft," and providing the service free of charge is thus probably a good business decision.

Interestingly, pure PET providers have found it difficult to find a household consumer market in the U.S. Owing to the relative lack of consumer interest,

---

[28] www.truste.org and www.bbbonline.org
[29] This mechanism is also employed in the U.S.-European Safe Harbor agreement, discussed further below.
[30] www.anonymizer.com
[31] www.lumeriaadnetwork.com
[32] www.zeroknowledge.com
[33] www.americanexpress.com/privatepayments/

many technology companies have been forced to shift their product line over to corporate services. These products often relieve security concerns rather than personal privacy threats. The weak market for consumer PETs in the U.S. might result from the lack of a comprehensive legislative privacy statute, as discussed above. Without a positive legal right backing up claims to protection, individuals have little reason to purchase technology.

Industry-Level – Industry initiatives focus less on moneymaking activities than on the sector's reputation. Third-party non-profit organizations, industry associations, and quasi-public agencies offer self-regulatory certification and monitoring services. Fearing citizen backlash against information technology driven by privacy concern, private sector actors in many countries have attempted to quell discontent through self-regulatory systems. Among the best known are the previously noted TRUSTe and the Better Business Bureau online. One weakness of these programs, however, is that they are often funded and publicly legitimized by the organizations they are supposed to monitor. TRUSTe, for example, has earned considerable criticism over its decision not to pursue certain complaints against Microsoft, owing to the fact that Microsoft is one of its largest financial backers.[34]

Industry associations have played an active role in promoting privacy standards. The Canadian Privacy Standard, for example, was developed by the Canadian Marketing Association. It creates a clear baseline of behavior for firms within the sector and has been used as a model for other industries in Canada. Evidence suggests, however, that standards alone, no matter how comprehensive or how well intentioned, have little enforcement power in countries that lack comprehensive privacy statutes. It is also clear that sector organization plays a critical role in a country's ability to employ industry-level solutions. The German business community, for example, has leveraged its close-knit industry associations to assist the deployment and training of data protection officers in firms. Additionally, in European countries that have created public data privacy authorities, the state can play a facilitative role and help coordinate industry-level efforts. These regulatory agencies act as ombudsman for citizen concerns, giving self-regulatory standards "teeth", and thus enhance business compliance. It should be emphasized that the extent to which these agencies have been successful in coordinating industry-level activities varies considerably, even within the EU. Some, like the British or the German agencies, are perceived as vibrant and legitimate advisors to business communities. Others, like the Swedish, have gotten bogged down in bureaucratic wrangling and politicking.

Technology

Technology has always played an important role in privacy debates. The original Warren and Brandeis article declaring a "right to be left alone," for example, was a reaction to the rise of flash photography in mass distribution gossip newspapers. Just as technology threatens privacy, however, it also offers tools that can help

---

[34] Clausing 1999.

safeguard personal information.[35] The most recent incarnation of this role is seen in the previously noted Privacy Enhancing Technologies (PETs), which report to guarantee against digital threats to privacy. Two sets of innovations have gained particular attention. The first group includes technology that simply hides real-world identities. These "anonymizers" rely on encryption technology to erase electronic trails that would identify the user. Systems such as those by iPrivacy, for example, use proxy servers to generate fictitious one-time identities to keep the actual user's identity hidden.[36] Only a trusted third-party, such as a credit card company, can match the fictitious to the real identity.

A second group of data filters regulate the transmission of personal information and act as information intermediaries, so-called "infomediaries." Users select their own privacy preferences and then let their browser negotiate with the requested website's server. The best known of these systems is P3P, the Platform for Privacy Preferences, which is funded by the European Union and Microsoft among others, and developed by the World Wide Web Consortium (W3C).[37] P3P works by at-taching XML tags, so-called meta-data, to personal information. The tags ensure that the collected information can only be used according to the data subject's preferences. Data about how personal data may be used thus travels with the ac-tual personal data. The practicality of these technologies remains contested, but governments and business associations across the globe are looking to PETs as a vital mechanism in the protection of privacy in the digital age. Variation in the commitment of government agencies and industry associations to the development and diffusion of these technologies will no doubt affect PET deployment across countries.

This rough overview certainly does not do the variety and complexity of pri-vacy regimes justice. Yet it illustrates how all three elements – public sector, pri-vate sector, and technological tools – interact to form privacy regimes, and high-lights some dimensions along which regimes vary, cross-nationally as well as across sectors. As political scientists, we naturally view any particular mix as in large part determined by politics and political-institutional processes. While cer-tainly not everything governments do has the intended consequences, it is clear, for example, that the extent and character of privacy rights created on the govern-mental level provide incentives for the development of business models, industry self-regulation, and technologies.[38] Fundamental political-historical events such as the nation-building process, industrialization, and welfare state creation and ex-pansion have influenced the character of privacy regimes across generations. To illustrate, the role of businesses in a privacy system appears to vary significantly

---

[35] Lessig 1999, Chap. 11.

[36] www.iprivacy.com

[37] www.w3c.org/P3P/. Interestingly, Microsoft's new ".NET Passport"-system is seen by many in the industry as a direct competitor to P3P. Some observers have even gone as far as to suggest that Microsoft has deliberately slowed down the development of P3P to give its proprietary Passport system a boost. Be that as it may, it is an excellent example of the interrelationship of technological and business components of privacy regimes.

[38] The point is more fully developed in Bach and Newman (2003).

with industrial structures. All else being equal, countries and sectors with greater coherence and strong industry associations, for example, have greater capacity to organize industry-level initiatives.[39] Sector structures and the strength of industry associations, in turn, can often be traced back to the original national industrialization process.[40] Similarly, state structures born out of the nation-building process, such as federal versus centralized government, affect the character of enforcement institutions. Rules born out of previous historical moments have constrained or enabled specific uses of personal information. Interests and expectations have then evolved around these initial incentive structures. Over time, lobbies have formed to protect and defend regimes reflective of their preferences.[41] At the same time, what is politically possible may well depend on technological feasibility. Some privacy experts contend that compliance with the EU Privacy Directive requires technological sophistication beyond current levels. The lack of technology undercuts the implementation of the Directive, but simultaneously creates a market for PET innovation.

Citizens will want to make individual choices about their privacy and how to enforce their rights, in the digital age and beyond. However, much of this choice will be constrained by historical legacies, the terms of market competition, political bargains, and technological innovation trajectories.[42] Results will certainly vary across countries, as they have in the past.

The next round of challenges

Just as privacy regimes across advanced industrial countries struggled in the 1990s to cope with the implications of new digital technologies, privacy protection will continue to be confronted by new threats and challenges. Policy-makers, public interest activists, and business leaders must realize the evolving nature of privacy regimes and consider the next round of challenges, ideally before they arise. Three issues in particular deserve a brief introduction as a look ahead: first, yet again, new sources of data; secondly, emerging commercial markets for privacy protection; and thirdly, the centrality of regulatory interfaces.

---

[39] Streeck and Schmitter 1985. Similarly, the character of the "data protection advocate" shapes the character of privacy regulation. In the United States, mobilized non-governmental organizations leverage the media to focus the debate on integrating the individual into decisions concerning data processing. Legislative battles then focus on consumer notice and consent. German data protection officers, in contrast, work in highly technical legal environments to guide organizational behavior. They have attempted to integrate data protection principles into organizational decision-making. Recent reforms, which include the principle of data avoidance, demonstrate this trend.

[40] Gerschenkron 1962.

[41] This path-dependent logic in public policy is best explained in Pierson 1996.

[42] Zysman 1994.

New kinds of data

The next wave of technological innovation will produce new sources of personal information. Location-specific and genetic information are two prime candidates for emerging new privacy threats. Very soon, always-on wireless connections will become commonplace, creating a ubiquitous computing world. Internet access technology will be embedded in an increasing number of mobile devices, offering a tremendous amount of new commercial applications.[43] At the same time, however, they raise important question about who gets access to the location-specific data generated by these devices. Consider the following example: the U.S. government wants mobile communication service providers to rollout technology that can locate any user through triangulation of signal strength from three cell towers. Initially, the technology was intended as an emergency system that could locate car travelers involved in accidents. In the wake of the 2001 terrorist attacks on New York and Washington, however, the law enforcement community has shown tremendous interest in the ability to track potential terrorists, speeding up deployment efforts. But who should have access to location-specific data? Only law enforcement agencies? Or should mobile communication service providers, who are likely to bear the lion's share of deployment costs, be allowed to sell that data to third-parties such as marketing firms? It doesn't take much to imagine companies calling consumers or sending flashy messages to their screens as they stroll near a local store that has items on sale, creating a world of real-time "mobile spam." The insurance industry might also have an interest in location-specific data. How might location monitoring affect car insurance pricing if insurance firms can track individual driving patterns and reference them to regional accident patterns? Where do we draw the line?

Biological information, similarly, calls into question existing expectations of privacy. As genetic technology advances, it should soon prove feasible to determine any person's genetic risk for disease. While this information may permit early screening and genetic treatment, it also raises tremendous privacy concerns. Take the case of employment in the U.S., where companies are responsible for supplying health insurance. Employers would have an incentive to redline individuals using genetic information in order to contain costs. Should employers or health insurance companies have access to genetic information? Just as in the previously mentioned case of car insurance pricing, such schemes would technically enhance market efficiency and reduce deadweight loss. But at what cost to society and human dignity?

The Internet was not the first technology that opened the gate to a brave new world while also significantly affecting personal privacy, and it will certainly not be the last. New technologies will bring tremendous opportunities, but they will also permit the collection of entirely new types of data. Some future challenges can be anticipated, yet many remain opaque. Societies will have to constantly reassess values, reinterpret rights, and recombine tools to provide a "reasonable expectation of privacy," now and in the future.

---

[43] See chapters in this volume by Maitland, Steinfield, Aschmoneit/Heitmann.

The market for privacy protection

A second trend that will play an important role in the future of privacy concerns the marketization of privacy protection. Already technologies have emerged that seek to foster a reassertion of individual control over personal information management. As previously discussed, PETs will continue to evolve and their future in large part depends on the economic incentives provided by privacy regimes. At the same time, many companies are fashioning themselves into something that could be labeled Privacy Enhancing Businesses (PEBs). These companies strive to offer trust, security, and privacy as their product or as an added benefit of their existing product. Earthlink and American Express advertisement campaigns in the U.S. emphasize privacy protection as these companies' prime asset when compared to their competitors.[44]

As privacy regimes respond to new challenges, they will in turn affect the PET and PEB markets. Several important questions follow. Who will have comparative advantage in PET and PEB markets? How will different regulatory regimes shape the development of business models and firm competitiveness? The recent decision of the German state government of Schleswig-Holstein to buy privacy-enhancing software for its administrative apparatus, for example, highlights the potential impact public sector purchasing power might have on technological and market developments. Similarly, industry self-regulation in the U.S. has produced an impressive penetration of privacy policy statements on the Internet. But if private sector companies and technology increasingly provide privacy protection, who guards the guardians? As technology evolves, diverse players have diverse interests in setting the default rules for infomediary technologies such as P3P. Delegating choices about "fair" *notice* and *consent* in PET and PEB settings to the private sector carries its own risks. The market for these products and services will no doubt be huge. Nations will soon be asking how they can be competitive in them. At the same time, however, it is important not to lose sight of the normative implications raised by further privatizing privacy protection.

The need for regulatory interfaces

A third trend will matter regardless of whether markets for privacy protection will remain national or whether a vibrant world market will develop. In either case, international trade in services of all kind will certainly continue to grow rapidly. Because many service industries make extensive use of personal data, national privacy regimes will increasingly come in contact with one another. Although the FIPP are internationally recognized, nations have retained their own interpretation

---

[44] See Klein and Henry 2001; and Horovitz 2001.

of the rights conferred, as well as their own enforcement system. This means that regulatory variation will persist cross-nationally.[45]

To maximize the benefits of trade in services, regulators will need to ensure the interoperability of distinct privacy regimes. The development of "regulatory inter-faces" on all three levels of privacy protection – public, private, and technological – thus becomes crucial. Regulatory interfaces are tools, mechanisms, or principles that do not force convergence around one system of protection, but rather reduce friction at systemic connection points.[46] A variety of actors have already begun developing these interfaces for the different elements of privacy protection. The development of P3P and XML by international Internet development groups pro-vides an example of a technological interface that holds a lot of promise. On the firm-level, initiatives are underway to generate internal codes-of-conduct for mul-tinational so that subsidiaries in Europe and the U.S. can exchange data seam-lessly.[47] A recent alliance forged between TRUSTe and the Japanese Engineering Federation to implement TRUSTe's seal program in Japan demonstrates the cross-national adoption of industry-level solutions to facilitate cross-border exchange.[48] The Safe Harbor agreement between the U.S. and Europe, lastly, is an example of governments creating an institutional interface to reconcile distinct public poli-cies.[49]

These efforts are encouraging in that they suggest that privacy protection sensi-tive to local contexts and consistent with national preferences need not lead to im-penetrable trade barriers. Yet developing such interfaces is often cumbersome and time-consuming as demonstrated by the negotiation of the Safe Harbor agreement and the development of P3P. Furthermore, it is still not established that the Safe Harbor will work in practice. Few U.S. companies have signed up so far and the robustness of this particular interface is yet to be seriously tested. In either case, given that the persistence of regulatory variation in privacy protection is all but guaranteed, the quest for interfaces in all shapes and forms must continue and should be expanded.

---

[45] For a discussion of enforcement and implementation variation within Europe alone, see the results of the EU conference on the implementation of the Privacy Directive at http://europa.eu.int/comm/internal_market/en/dataprot/lawreport/index.htm.

[46] For a more comprehensive discussion of regulatory interfaces in transnational markets, see Newman and Bach 2002.

[47] DaimlerChrysler is an example. See the contribution by Alfred Büllesbach at the above-mentioned EU conference on the Privacy Directive.

[48] See TRUSTe Press Release 2001. The agreement makes TRUSTe Japan's preeminent self-regulatory seal program in the area of privacy protection.

[49] The Safe Harbor agreement, negotiated between the U.S. Department of Commerce and the European Commission, enables U.S. firms to get certified as compliant with EU rules despite being located in a country – the U.S. – whose privacy standards are considered as inadequate by the EU Directive. Firms operating in this "safe harbor" will not be cut off from European personal data flows. For an analyses of the agreement, see Farrell 2001.

Conclusion

In the wake of the dot com bust, it is premature to end societal discussions over privacy in a digital age. A series of continuing technological innovations are transforming the amount and type of information collected, the groups collecting information, and the geographical scope of information exchange. Owing to the intersubjective nature of privacy, these changes reopen debates about basic societal norms concerning reasonable expectations of privacy.

Although this chapter has focused primarily on the different implementation and enforcement components of privacy regimes, it is our hope that it will also encourage a dialogue over the norms that underpin privacy protection instruments. The debate over privacy is too often cast in defensive terms. Rather than thinking linearly about how to protect privacy we should begin the forward-looking process of "identity management," individually and collectively, as privacy guru Tara Lemmey has urged.[50] This view is motivated by the recognition that future privacy challenges are likely to make our current concern with e-mail spam, Internet cookies, and security cameras seem trivial. In the future, pharmaceutical firms will employ a different type of information capital – genetic information – to better target cancer cells and to customize drugs. But will they own this genetic information capital the way advertising firms own clickstream data today? Who owns cells reproduced according to my personal blueprint? Who will have copyright in my genetic code? And, if I don't own my own genes, am I really free? Most importantly, who gets to decide these fundamental questions?

The chance exists for a broad and inclusive public discourse over these and similar brewing privacy questions. Governments should play an important role in engaging these issues; but so must non-governmental organizations (NGOs), businesses, and individuals. Laws and their interpretation will continue to be based on a "reasonable expectation of privacy", but what that means in actuality is up to us. If we let invasive universal monitoring become commonplace, successive generations can no longer claim that certain expectations of privacy are "reasonable." Our decisions now will determine what will be a "reasonable expectation of privacy" in the future.

As the dust of the doc.com bust settles, we expect privacy regimes to continue to look differently across societies. In light of the range and diversity of players, stakes, and mediating political institutions, it is unavoidable that the mix of public sector, private sector, and technological tools employed to address privacy concerns will vary considerably across countries. At the same time, previously discrete regulatory jurisdictions will come increasingly in contact with one another as firms offer services across borders. These two trends – persistent regulatory diversity and transnational service markets – will require the continued development of creative regulatory interfaces to resolve market friction.

Digital technologies pose serious challenges to personal privacy, and these challenges will only intensify with the next round of innovation. Yet these drawbacks of new technologies should not be reasons to universally demonize techno-

---

[50] Lemmey 2000.

logical change. Societies have proven time and again that they can adjust laws and governing principles to new environments. The more proactively we engage new challenges while keeping the lessons from previous experiences in mind, the more digital technologies and whatever may come next will be sources of welfare and opportunity, not threats to personal privacy.

References

Australian Financial Review (2000) Home Loans: Just Give Us A Minute, Says Adelaide Bank. October 23

Bach D, Newman A (2003) Self-Regulatory Trajectories in the Shadow of Public Power: Resolving Digital Dilemmas in Europe and the United States. Under review

Bundesdrucksache (1971). Anlage 1. Grundfragen des Datenschutzes. VI/3826, July

Clausing J (1999) On-Line Privacy Group Decides Not to Pursue Microsoft Case. The New York Times, March 23

Cohen SS et al. (2001) Tools: The Drivers of E-commerce. In: The BRIE-IGCC E-conomy Project (ed) Tracking a Transformation: E-commerce and the Terms of Competition in Industries. Brookings Press, Washington, DC

Farrell H (2001) Negotiating Privacy Across Arenas: The EU-US 'Safe Harbor' Discussions. In: Heritier (ed) The Provision of Common Goods: Governance across Multiple Arenas. Rowman and Littlefield, Boulder

Flaherty DH (1989) Protecting privacy in surveillance societies: the Federal Republic of Germany, Sweden, France, Canada, and the United States. University of North Carolina Press, Chapel Hill

Froomkin AM (1997) The Internet As A Source Of Regulatory Arbitrage. In: Kahin and Nesson (eds) Borders in Cyberspace. MIT Press, Cambridge

Gerschenkron A (1962) Economic backwardness in historical perspective. Harvard University Press, Cambridge

Horovitz B (2001) Marketers tout consumer privacy. USA Today, March 1

Jupiter Media Metrix Press Release (2002) Seventy Percent of U.S. Consumers Worry About Online Privacy, But Few Take Protective Action, June 3

Kang J (1998) Information Privacy in Cyberspace Transactions. Stanford Law Review 50

Klein A, Henry S (2001) On Reflection, a Puzzling Ad Campaign; EarthLink's Restroom Mirrors Tout Online Privacy – or Try To. Washington Post, March 1

Kymlicka W (1989) Liberalism, Community, and Culture. Oxford University Press, Oxford

Kymlicka W (1995) Multicultural Citizenship: A Liberal Theory of Minority Rights. Oxford University Press, Oxford

Ladine B (2002) Medical Privacy Rules Are Relaxed – New White House Rule Drops Written Consent. The Boston Globe, August 10

Lemmey T (2000) Your Next Identity Crisis. Business 2.0, September

Lessig L (1999) Code and other laws of cyberspace. Basic Books, New York

Lewis DK (1969) Convention: A Philosophical Study. Harvard University Press, Cambridge

Libecap G (1989) Contracting for Property Rights. Cambridge University Press, Cambridge

Markoff J (2002) Pentagon Plans a Computer System That Would Peek at Personal Data of Americans. The New York Times, November 9

Newman A, Bach D (2002) The Transnationalization of Regulation. Paper presented at the 13th Conference of Europeanists, Chicago, IL

OECD (1980) Guidelines on the Protection of Privacy and Transborder Flows of Personal Data. Organization for Economic Cooperation and Development, Paris

Pierson P (1996) The New Politics of the Welfare State. World Politics 48, 2

Post RC (1989) The Social Foundations of Privacy: Community and Self in the Common Law Tort. California Law Review 77

Reporters without Borders Press Release (2002) The Internet on probation: Anti-terrorism drive threatens Internet freedoms worldwide. September 5

Schauer F (1998) Internet Privacy and The Public-Private Distinction. Jurimetrics 38 (4)

Schwartz PM, Reidenberg JR (1996) Data privacy law: a study of United States data protection. Michie, Charlottesville

Searle JR (1995) The Construction of Social Reality. Free Press, New York

Shapiro C, Varian HR (1999) Information Rules: A Strategic Guide to the Network Economy. Harvard Business School Press, Boston.

Singletary M (2000) Credit Rating: We Should Know the Score. The Washington Post, March 19

Singleton S (2000) Privacy and Human Rights: Comparing the United States to Europe. In: Competitive Enterprise Institute (ed) The Future of Financial Privace. Competitive Enterprise Institute, Washington, DC

Streeck W, Schmitter PC (1985) Community, market, state - and associations? European Sociological Review 1, 2

Swire P (1998) The Great Wall of Europe: CIO Enterprise Magazine, February 15

Swire P (2002) The Surprising Virtues of the New Financial Privacy Law. Minnesota Law Review 86

Swire P, Litan RE (1998) None of your business: world data flows, electronic commerce, and the European privacy directive. Brookings Institution Press, Washington, DC

Taylor Ch (1989) Cross-Purposes: The Liberal-Communitarian Debate. In: Rosenblum (ed) Liberalism and the Moral Life. Harvard University Press, Cambridge

The Economist (1999) Data dogfights. January 7

TRUSTe Press Release (2001) TRUSTe Launches Seal Program in Japan. March 19

Tucker E (1999) Data protection dispute exposes core differences, Financial Times, June 9

Warren S, Brandeis L (1890) The Right to Privacy. Harvard Law Review 4, 5

Westin AF (1967) Privacy and Freedom. Atheneum, New York

Zysman J (1994) How institutions create historically rooted trajectories of growth. Industrial and Corporate Change 3, 1

Cities, electronic commerce, and local policies

Gerhard Fuchs[1]

Center for Technology Assessment, Stuttgart, Germany

Abstract

This chapter analyses options that regional intermediary actors in the field of electronic commerce – focussing on the business-to-business sector – have at hand or
use to promote electronic commerce. Empirically the situation is examined in
three different regions of the state of North Rhine Westphalia in the west of Germany (Aachen, Dortmund and Bielefeld) and three regions in the southern state of
Baden-Württemberg (Ost-Württemberg, Karlsruhe and Mannheim). Specific supportive strategies are analysed in detail in these regions on the basis of extensive
questioning and secondary analyses. Experts from institutions for the promotion of
the economy, from chambers of commerce as well as chambers of artisans on the
one hand and selected managers responsible for decision making within enterprises of the goods production and information economy on the other hand are in
the centre of attention. A result of this analysis has been the development of a typology which allows us to distinguish between different types of activities and
promotion strategies.

Introduction

Hardly any other Internet-related application has attracted such wide attention as
the buzzword electronic commerce. In spite of the downfall of the „New Economy" electronic commerce and Electronic Business are still on virtually everybody's mind. They constitute fancy marketing concepts for software as well as IT
hardware companies. Visions of future data processing, trade, innovative applications in marketing, procurement, sales, in human resources development, and
training are linked to these concepts. And: Electronic commerce still looks like a
growing billion $ market for the crisis-ridden IT and telecommunications industry.
Not only companies are interested in electronic commerce, but also politicians,
economic development actors, and for some of them it is becoming a central field
of action.

---

[1] E-mail: gerhard.fuchs@ta-akademie.de

This chapter analyzes options that regional intermediary actors engaged in regional economic promotion activities have at hand or use to promote electronic commerce – focusing on the business-to-business sector. Empirical evidence is provided for three regions of the state of North Rhine Westphalia in the west of Germany (Aachen, Dortmund and Bielefeld) and three regions in the southern state of Baden-Württemberg (Ost-Württemberg, Karlsruhe and Mannheim). Supplementary case studies have been conducted for the cities of Munich and Stuttgart. Specific supportive strategies are analyzed in detail in these regions on the basis of extensive interviews and secondary analyses. Experts in institutions for the promotion of the economy, in chambers of industry and commerce as well as chambers of artisans on the one hand, and selected managers responsible for decision making in enterprises of the traditional manufacturing sector, and of the IT and the services sector on the other hand have been interviewed. This analysis has resulted in the development of a typology that we will present in this chapter. This typology allows to distinguish between different types of activities and promotion strategies.

The research was conducted in two stages. In 2000, the first three regions in North Rhine Westphalia were analyzed. The supplementary case studies as well as the second set of three cases were done in 2002. It has to be emphasized that the overall situation of the economy has changed drastically during these years as well as the evaluation of the importance of the "New Economy". Nevertheless the results are still valid and comparable in a number of ways.

The chapter will proceed in the following manner. Part two discusses the question, whether the concentration of economic activities in a region or a location is still a relevant category in the age of the Internet and electronic commerce. Part three presents a brief overview of the changing self-image and the instruments of economic development agencies. Different types of economic development promotion, implementation, financing and planning of electronic commerce related activities will be treated systematically in parts five to seven. The concluding part summarizes lessons learnt and develops recommendations based on the experience of cities and regions for the planning, conceptualization and implementation of e-commerce development strategies. In the following we will not make a systematic differentiation between "region", "city" or "community". The aim of this chapter is to identify policies developed at the sub-national level. These might be local policies, but also regional policies with a region encompassing more than one community or city.

The challenge of electronic commerce

Internet and its potential uses are linked to notions of globalization and international, boundless trade. Trade via the World-Wide Web – Online-Shopping – is supposed to mark the end of the importance of territoriality, the "death of distance" (Cairncross 1997). Thanks to electronic commerce everybody is now able to go shopping worldwide for the cheapest bargains and best deals. The locally based retailers are supposed to lose importance and are under growing competitive pressure, especially with regard to prices. One of the most often quoted examples and success stories for electronic commerce is the bookseller Amazon. This company succeeded in gaining world wide presence within a short time frame in the bookselling business. The company is now next to every customer with an Internet connection – without having to do large investments in local buildings, infrastructure etc. Theoretically the Web reduces transaction costs dramatically. High transaction costs previously might have been an impediment to penetrate a local market.

What might happen on the local or regional level as a result of such developments? Of particular importance at these levels are small and medium-sized companies (SME) . Most of these companies are ill prepared for a presence on a world-wide market. Their orientation is towards the local and regional market, where their customers are also located (see Läpple 1999). The example of amazon.com shows very vividly, how globally oriented companies succeed in penetrating local markets by using sophisticated (and expensive) marketing strategies. Web-based companies in many sectors can easily beat the prices of locally based businesses, which formally had to face hardly any competition. The attempt of a local bookseller to tie into the global book market on the other hand does not seem very promising. There are now a handful of Internet booksellers in Germany (3 big ones), but 4500 'ordinary' book shops (Riehm/Orwat/Wingert 2001).

How profound will be the changes on the local level? Let us look at a scenario developed by Steinfield and Whitten (1999). They ask what long-term effects electronic commerce might have on the local level if it spreads widely and quickly. Their answer highlights serious potential outcomes. A possible scenario could look like this: due to the impact of nationally or globally oriented suppliers on the net, the transaction volume of local businesses becomes smaller. There are increasing competitive pressures on the local businesses. The effect will be job losses especially among lower qualified employees. The declining volume of transactions might even force traditional shops to go out of business completely, which in turn leads to a decline in shopping options within the community as a whole. As a consequence,the attractiveness of the community deteriorates as well. The loss of shopping options is all the more dramatic, if these businesses were strongly oriented towards specific local needs and if they supported locally produced services and goods. For the local communities a reduction in revenues will follow. This again will make it more difficult for local governments to offer services for their citizens and to invest in the attractiveness of the community.

This is surely a one-sided worst case scenario, but it nevertheless highlights potential risks which should be taken under consideration. It should offer incentives to develop and to discuss strategies by economic development actors and local politicians alike. One potential strategy of companies as well as communities could be to use and emphasize the regional orientation of its businesses as an asset and to stress the local orientation with the help of the World Wide Web.

The idea that electronic commerce would create one global market and fundamentally change the rules of the game has indeed to be considered with some caution. It is true that for making a valid transaction buyer and seller do not need to meet physically. But still there are some restrictions. It cannot be the task of this chapter to comprehensively discuss this issue, but some reflections seem appropriate at this point. Four restrictions for a global Internet market place can be distinguished.

Communicative restrictions. The most important characteristic of a "real" market place is that people talk to one another in a given language or dialect, which usually will only be spoken within a certain territory. This implies that language barriers are still space and market barriers in spite of globalization and English as the lingua franca on the Internet. There are advantages for a seller, if he or she can advertise in the specific national or regional tongue and/or even cater to the specific regional/national tastes.

Institutional restrictions. Institutional rules remain important even for Internet based trade. The national rules and regulations are still the ones that are to be followed. Just imagine ordering wine at a German producer from Sweden or Switzerland. Or: sending a regular book from the U.S. to Germany. It will quickly become clear that national regulations (like customs regulations, national regulations concerning food and drink etc.) are still dominating the game and the global hunt for cheap bargains has to overcome many obstacles. Different currencies, monetary systems etc. are further examples for the prevalence of restrictions.

Distributive restrictions. The key to a successful transaction is a working logistics solution – especially for physical goods. For most goods the problem of logistics becomes more complex and transaction costs increase with the distance between buyer and seller. Furthermore certain characteristics of the traded goods or services have an impact on the cost increases – take for example certain quickly deteriorating food stuff.

Trust restrictions. Closeness creates trust which is difficult to establish at a distance. This simple formula, which reflects every day experience, is also important for Internet trade. Trust is diminished, if the complexity of procedures increases and the knowledge about persons, situations, brand names etc. decreases. In other words, trust as an important precondition for trade, increases, the better procedures can be controlled and understood. In the case of online-shopping, customers have to deal with geographical as well as with mental distance. It is not clear where exactly the seller is located and it is also difficult to understand all the digital and virtual procedures and their specific rules governing the Internet. Customers do not have the possibility to get to know the person on the other side, and they have no sensual perception of the traded goods or services.

Insofar there are a couple of restrictions that render it implausible that a totally new type of virtual trade will dominate in the future. Regional and local trade still makes sense, if e.g. the client prefers to go to a dealer whose language she speaks, and who is a person one can go to, if problems arise, and if the regulations by which trade progresses are clear to potential buyers,

The political relevance of electronic commerce

Before we look at the actual policies being developed, we need to define electronic commerce. We only talk about electronic commerce if real transactions are taking place. This means the distinctive characteristic in this project is that goods/services are offered as well as ordered over the Internet. One might add as further elements payment and delivery of the goods/services over the Internet, but this is not obligatory. Electronic commerce in this sense is more than just advertising one's company on the World-Wide Web. It is also not the same as work flow technologies or Customer Relationship Management (CRM) in general. Only policies aimed at promoting those types of interaction defined above as electronic commerce are addressed by our research.

The role of politics with respect to electronic commerce can encompass the whole spectrum of possible policy instruments – starting with regulatory policies, the promotion of specific projects or institutions up to persuasive policies. Governments and administrations use these instruments in a varying degree at various levels. In the regulatory arena the emphasis is without any doubt on the European/EU and national level or even on transnational initiatives in the form of public-private mixes. However, even here, there is room to maneuver for sub-national actors when it comes to pilot solutions (certificates, security measures etc.) or the implementation of directives or regulations. With respect to other types of political activity there is a large spectrum of possibilities available for sub-national actors.

First of all one can clearly state that many of the states ("Bundesländer") of Germany have attempted to bundle their respective activities in programs or initiatives. These are often based on activities which had begun already in the past with the aim to support the uptake of information and communication technologies. An example for this is the initiative media NRW (North Rhine Westphalia) or the media @ program by the state government of Baden-Württemberg. In the center of the NRW program is the support of projects involving SMEs. With the aim to help especially smaller companies to participate in the growth market electronic commerce, an Electronic Commerce Campaign NRW was initiated attempting to bundle all relevant competencies of the state. A large number of meetings in different locations of the state and addressing various subjects have been organized as part of the campaign. In addition, there is a so-called "Electronic Commerce Starter Kit", a CD-ROM for beginners with basic information about the Internet and electronic commerce as well as "useful software tools". Another product of the electronic commerce campaign has been the information platform ECIN (Electro Commerce Info NRW) which initially only issued a weekly newsletter but has expanded its scope substantially since.

What is happening on the level below the states? Is technology-oriented innovation policy a viable solution even for local and regional governments? In order to answer this question we need to briefly review the development of respective policies. Dedicated institutions for regional economic development are to be found in all larger communities across Germany. They take different organizational forms. These range from private companies to offices which are simply part of the public administration. Their tasks encompass a broad spectrum public administration. Their tasks encompass a broad spectrum of spatial management and infrastructure policies, location marketing and consulting services for resident companies as well as for companies that shall be attracted to the specific location. Since most communities develop similar policies, an already established strong competition between communities for business (re)locations has intensified in the last years. This is also due to the growing options for locating businesses (globalization, setting up production facilities abroad) as well as due to a certain leveling of basic infrastructural conditions of competing locations – at least in Germany.

As a reaction to these developments the conclusion has been reached that activating the endogenous potentials is becoming an ever more important part of the general strategy of local/regional economic development. Soft factors like the quality of living, environmental conditions, or the image of a region are important criteria when it comes to make location decisions.

As a relatively new approach in this respect we can observe the active support of innovative processes within a region, especially oriented towards SMEs. Many case studies and experience with policy programmes have demonstrated that coherent strategies for SMEs to support the development and operation of formal and informal business networks or clusters can make a major contribution to economic growth in local communities. There is evidence that one of the key determinants of dynamic local economies is the strength and effectiveness of their system of business-to-business networks (cp. Cooke/Morgan 1998).

SMEs are mostly firmly embedded in their local communities, and look to that community for the bulk of their work force, finance, sites and facilities, external services, information and advice, and external goods and services. In most cases, of course, a large share of a small firm's customer and supplier bases also resides in its local community. Activities designed to help such firms thus need to be fully aware of the diverse set of drives and motivations of the SMEs.

In this sense the promotion of electronic commerce can be seen as an attempt by local and/or regional actors to foster the existing potential and the existing resources of resident companies and to try to raise awareness for the importance of the subject.

The cases

In the following I will briefly characterize the regions which have been analyzed.

Aachen: Bordering Belgium and the Netherlands, Aachen features strong interregional cooperation structures and internationally oriented SMEs. It has 251,000 inhabitants, and the unemployment rate is close to the German average. Aachen is a strong research center with plenty of spin-off activities in new high-tech sectors.

Bielefeld: This is a medium-sized city of 322,000 inhabitants. The unemployment rate is slightly below the national average. There is a strong industrial presence: metal and machine tool industry, textiles, printing, food.

Dortmund is a traditional location for the coal and steel industry. It features all the problems of a declining centre of old industries. It has approx. 588,000 inhabitants and an unemployment rate well above the national average. For a long time, Dortmund has been trying to find new employment options in new industries, such as IT. These attempts were heavily supported by the state government.

Karlsruhe: The city of Karlsruhe with its 270,000 inhabitants is a service and research oriented location. Unemployment is below the national average and the region is largely considered to be one of the most important high-tech locations in Germany with the IT sector playing a very prominent role.

Mannheim is the second largest city in Baden-Württemberg with app. 323,000 inhabitants and an unemployment rate above average. Mannheim used to be a central industrial location (with a heavy emphasis on chemicals) and is meanwhile making the transition to a center for the service industries.

Ost-Württemberg: This region is usually treated as "peripheral". It has a strong industrial base of mainly small and medium sized companies. 47% of all employees work in manufacturing. Nevertheless there are no signs of a structural crises. Unemployment is modest.

Stuttgart is the capital of the state of Baden-Württemberg. It is the core of the most industrialized region in Germany. In spite of its concentration on the machine tool, automotive and electronics industries, it could avoid structural crises in the past. Stuttgart has close to 600,000 inhabitants and shows one of the lowest unemployment rates nationwide.

Munich is the IT location No. 1 of Germany. With a population of close to 1.3 million it is the third biggest city in Germany and features an unemployment rate well below average.

Regional promotion strategies

In all of the regions examined, electronic commerce was addressed in one way or another, and actors responsible for economic development considered it a topic of importance. Generally, the measures are oriented towards small and medium-Sized companies of a specific region. A special emphasis on an industrial branch could not be observed. It became very clear that larger companies should not be addressed by these measures, since it has been assumed that they have their own information base and resources at hand. Beyond this general assessment the differences between regions by far outweigh the common elements. Electronic commerce promotion strategies and the intensity of promotion in the different regions vary widely.

The aims of the different local entities are ambitious to a very different degree –moving up the ladder to Munich's aim to strengthen its leading position as an e-metropolis. All efforts mainly aim at a more rapid adoption of a promising, new technology which is supposed to strengthen regional competitiveness. This clearly explains the emphasis that is being put on raising awareness, to show options but also risks involved in an e-investment. This might also imply showing the way towards a cheaper access to the Internet.

Local promotion agencies or departments on the one hand and the chambers for commerce and industry or other (trade) associations on the other hand are usually the responsible actors for the promotion of electronic commerce. A specialty is to be found in regions which feature an Electronic Commerce Competence Center.

In all of the three examined regions in Baden-Württemberg as well as in Munich there are such centres. Having a Competence Center implies that the relevant actors have taken part in a federally funded competition, and it further implies that rather early reflections have taken place on the importance of electronic commerce. In this sense, an early commitment to the cause of electronic commerce was necessary to participate in the competition in a meaningful manner. All Competence Centers in the cases presented here are located at a chamber of industry and commerce itself or a dedicated subunit of it. Financing of the Competence Centers is provided by the Federal Government (80-90% of the expenses). The rest has to be covered by the chambers. An exception is the Mannheim center which is exclusively financed by the chamber.

The central task of the Competence Centers is to give advice to SMEs as well as to conceive and organize information meetings. The Competence Centers experiment with these aims in a different manner, which reflects the specific regional situation and strategies of the chambers and their clientele. E.g. a Competence Center which has to cover a large territory must think about other strategies than a chamber which is solely responsible for one city. One option for the first type is the organization of road shows to guarantee presence across the region.

Beyond the general wish to sensitize all SMEs of a specific region for the Internet and to guarantee access to this new medium, the Competence Center in Munich – ZEGO – has a more differentiated strategy. Their aim is not simply to bring as many businesses as possible into the Internet and make them fit for electronic commerce. Instead they provide more individualized consulting, which is supposed to assess the starting position, the aims and the available means within a company in a realistic manner. Based on these data it might even be concluded that being active on the Internet is not the most sensible strategy to pursue. However, after these initial questions have been discussed, the most appropriate strategy can be worked out based on an individual assessment of the business, and eventually its implementation can be supported.

Beyond these organizational questions there are further differences with respect to the aims pursued. While some centers clearly define their work only as providing information, others name (individual) consulting as their prime target. Part of this is the possibility to initiate pilot projects, which, however, is seldom used. Examples can be found in the cities of Munich and Dortmund.

Most of the Competence Centers concentrate on the task of information resp. information/communication and follow a (Pull-)Push-Strategy. Our survey has also shown, however, that the people interviewed think that concepts which are based primarily on information and information-sharing are meanwhile outdated. Companies in the last years had ample opportunity to inform themselves about the importance and the features of electronic commerce. Now it is time for the companies as well as for consulting institutions to take a further step. What is needed now is information on specific issues (like regulatory and safety issues, electronic money transfer etc.) and individualized consulting. It remains to be seen whether the existing Competence Centers, whose funding by the Federal Government is running out, can cope with this situation.

In our analysis we also found some important initiatives started by private associations or locally important entrepreneurs. This has been especially prominent in the region of Karlsruhe, in which associations like the CyberForum or KIK (Karlsruhe Informatics Cooperation) participate actively in the promotion of regional networks, of company foundations in the IT sector and information transfer for IT topics. These examples show that the personal activity of some eminent figures along with a receptive attitude on the side of public administration can help to build effective strategies. The cooperation with resident education and research institutions further supports the diffusion of electronic commerce. Insofar, the associations provide good examples of a public-private-partnership.

Next to information and consulting the financing and administration of portals constitutes an important aspect of promotion activities. This strategy is primarily followed by cities but also by other regional or supra local entities. There is a large variety in the realisation of regional portals. Some offer only information on the cities, some add special services for citizens and still others go all the way to provide links to commercial applications like a virtual (city) market place. Especially the last option can provide local SMEs with a chance to "play" and experiment with Internet applications. An attractively designed and well-visited portal can therefore be an essential part of a strategy to support local/regional electronic commerce application.

In all cases examined solutions have been worked out or are under discussion. Their actual realizations differ very profoundly and will be discussed later.

Another strategy pursued by municipal actors is to present a platform for the presentation of regional/local actors. This can take the form of Yellow Pages, specific data banks for industrial sectors or cooperation platforms, e.g. for the machine tool industry in Mannheim, which allows the participants to match free capacities.

Most cities have recognized the importance of cooperation and network building. Especially for the preparation of pilot projects usually a wide range of people and organizations are brought together in order to establish the best preconditions for a successful project. An example is the pilot project in the city of Munich, which is supposed to give especially SMEs and artisans the opportunity to get acquainted with the Internet. A consortium consisting of the department for Labor and Economics of the city of Munich, the Electronic Commerce Competence Center, the chamber of industry and commerce, and the chamber of artisans was created in order to link to the individual companies and to start a wide-ranging PR policy. In the pilot project magazine articles, newsletters etc. are used to motivate new companies to join the Internet. None of these actors alone, especially not the municipal department for Labor and Economics could have generated such a broad interest and publicity.

A similar strategy has been used in Mannheim with the construction of an interactive virtual cooperation platform. Again at the beginning there was a serious attempt to integrate all important stake holders like the chambers, banks, universities etc. in the project. Even now, after the project has been successfully launched, these actors are still working together within the project framework.

How are the activities evaluated by the target groups? Generally the measures (if known) are evaluated very positively. In various contexts it has been mentioned that the existing measures are lacking transparency and, thus, are difficult to tap into, especially for SMEs. This has not only been the result of our study, but also the result of a study by the German Institute for Urbanistics which analyzed IT-related promotion activities (Floeting/Grabow 1999). Many actors and departments, offices and what have you, are doing something, but the activities are not coordinated and synchronized. This creates a feeling of frustration and disorientation among the SMEs.

The question to what extent the aim of addressing the special needs of SMEs was actually achieved, which was asked in the case studies, has yielded conflicting answers. In general, for the Electronic Commerce Competence Centers which usually feature a type of strong cooperation between the chambers of Industry and Commerce, the problem to get access to SMEs is not a central one. Local agencies or other relevant institutions, however, reported difficulties in actually reaching their prospective clientele.

Regional economic promotion and local planning: portal solutions

The support of the development of portals and market places has to be treated separately. In most cases there is little or no overlap between the activities described above and the attempts to set up such platforms. Most of the analyzed entities are still at the beginning of their way towards offering fully fledged portals. But at the time of the interviews, they were all in a phase of pondering ideas, reflections and learning from past experiences. These considerations are mainly directed at the problem of financing such portals, especially for the phase once a portal has been initially launched. Who will actually run the portal and who will be responsible for further maintaining and developing it?

Actual analysis of territorially defined Online Markets clearly shows that administering a market place requires considerable work, resources and strategic considerations. Available knowledge (Brandt/Volkert 2000) also shows that at the moment these markets do not work profitably. Only those models "prosper" which have outside funding coming from dedicated political programs or sponsors (like the banking community).

One reason for this is that most market places suffer from poor planning and a lack of strategy. It can be shown that at the moment hardly any organizer of an online market cares about the economic feasibility and the economic aims of the market places. The question, how much turnover has to be generated before a market place turns profitable, remains mostly unanswered. Hardly any considerations are given to the question who might eventually use the market place, which should be the core clientele and what are their needs. What can be observed at the moment is a very colorful, not very systematic mess which very often is frustrating or even repulsive for the user. In addition only very few market places offer a real additional benefit which could convince the shopper to go online instead of staying offline (see Textbox 1).

Deficits of existing regional/local online markets
- Small turnover
- No business strategy
- No customer orientation
- No adequate selection of suppliers
- Small/deficient product portfolio
- Little support for suppliers
- Underestimation of required resources
- No dedicated selection of goods

Textbox 1

The suppliers are usually very inexperienced when it comes to electronic commerce. Consulting activities that help to ease this problem are hardly existent. Furthermore, it is not known which products are at all suited for sale over the Internet. The selection of goods offered is often very limited and arbitrary in its scope. The maintenance of the sites is sloppy.

All in all at present online market places are very unattractive for the average shopper. Hence, it is not surprising that they are hardly used. Here special demands for the actors maintaining such sites become visible: they have to make the market place attractive by targeting a specific clientele, by providing information and consulting, by offering special services, by offering a specific add-on that makes shopping online more convenient than other options, and by devoting more resources to the marketing of the sites.

These tasks pose severe challenges for the local/regional administrations. It must be clearly ascertained to what extent local administrations can fulfill these tasks and for how long. Already at the beginning of the planning process such questions should be taken under consideration.

It is quite clear that the most adequate option to pursue, if the communities want to stay in this 'business' is to engage in public-private-partnerships (see Stapel-Schulz/Eifert/Siegfried 2000). Public-private-partnerships are all kinds of formal or informal cooperation between public and private actors. The advantages for the cities in this cooperation are in the possibility to include expert know-how and to have potential private money available. Generally, the inclusion of private actors aims at reducing the financial risks. Also the enormous amount of content needed to make a portal running, speaks in favor of the inclusion of private actors. In spite of these obvious advantages, the cities are approaching the subject of private-public partnerships with great caution. A number of serious problems that new actors are hardly aware of are linked to such solutions. Which juridical form should be exactly used, how to conceive cooperation agreements etc. Very often cooperation is therefore limited to buying IT-services or to the outsourcing of specific tasks.

Regional strategies for the promotion of electronic commerce – a typology

In the following part a typology of promotion strategies will be presented. As argued before, since the late nineties a number of initiatives to promote electronic commerce can be found. Depending on the regional demand and regional economic structures, measures in a varying degree of intensity and breadth have been initiated. Attempting to classify the promotion activities one can distinguish between (a) measures aiming primarily at information, (b) measures trying to provide direction, (c) measures for developing instructions and (d) subsidies or investments (see Figure 1).

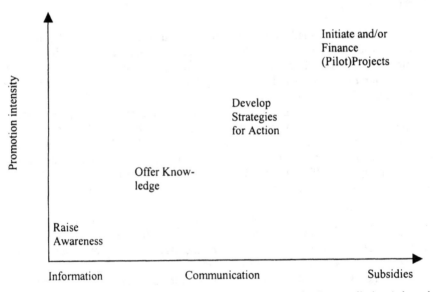

Fig. 1. Stage-model for the support of innovation processes by intermediaries (adapted from Michel et al. 2000)

(a) Raising awareness for the subject and its importance for the local/regional economy among decision makers. What is electronic commerce at all, which forms of electronic commerce do exist, what is the economic impact of electronic commerce, what is in line for the companies that plan to move into the Internet economy? Questions of this kind are addressed by the information activities of the local intermediaries.

(b) Offering knowledge means to address more specifically the needs of various economic sectors and types of companies. Very often best-practice examples are collected and presented. Next to the information by experts, communication and interaction among the companies becomes essential.

(c) The third stage is important for companies which have actually decided to implement electronic commerce. Now instructions and very hands-on recommendations are needed. What problems will I have to cope with, what technical solutions are best suited for me, what are the costs of the different solutions, how much training and consulting will be necessary etc. For discussing these types of problems working groups, study groups or other types of regular meetings are organized.

(d) Activities on the last stage imply a direct financial support of companies. Very often this comes in the form of (pilot) projects which are subsidized by public authorities or financial help for newly established or small companies.

Table 1. Measures for the promotion of electronic commerce (examples)

Information	Data Banks
	Electronic Commerce Information Day
	Information Meetings
	General Consulting
	Congress
	Exhibition
	Road Show
Communication	Working Groups
	Electronic Commerce Club
	Regional Networks
	Cooperation Platforms
	Workshops
Subsidies/Investment	Electronic Commerce Competence Center
	E-Commerce Incubator
	E-Lab
	Portals/Online Market Places
	Individual Consulting
	Pilot Projects

Based on this stage model we can distinguish between three different types of promotion strategies in the regional context.

Type 1: Pull strategy
The intermediaries set their activities in the framework of a demand-driven information concept. Within this concept general information for specific innovation processes is being prepared. Only on very specific demands further and more specified information resp. instructions for companies in the specific region are given. The aim of this type of promotion activities is to guarantee a sufficient awareness for electronic commerce in the region.

Type 2: Pull-and-push-strategy

Besides an information concept, which is supposed to offer companies a sense of direction, the promotion strategy aims at developing a regional platform for communication among companies and the passing on of existing practical knowledge. This can be done e.g. by initiating working groups and discussion fora. (Information and Communication concept). Intermediaries following this strategy convey a higher priority to electronic commerce than in Type 1 strategies.

Type 3: Push-strategy

In addition to activities, which serve the purpose of information transfer and the development of communicative/interactive structures in the region, more far-reaching measures are taken up, which aim at a comprehensive rooting of electronic commerce in the regional economy. Thus, a poignant supply-concept, which includes also the practical aspects of project promotion and/or the actual implementation of pilot projects, is pursued. Of course, the realization of a promotion strategy of this kind requires a much higher financial and long term commitment compared with the two previous strategies.

This typology of promotion strategies aims at giving a first overview of activities of intermediaries which have been found in the case studies. It does not aim at evaluating the efficiency or quality of the individual promotion concepts. On the contrary: each type of promotion strategy is to be seen within the framework of the specific regional structures and overall development strategies. Thus, it cannot be said: the more the better. In this sense one of the persons interviewed said: "Surely one can always demand and offer more man power, more consulting and more information; whether this optimizes the use of electronic commerce, is a completely different question."

Table 2. Characteristics of the regions examined

	Challenged by structural change	Importance of the IT-cluster	Unemployment
Aachen	+	+/-	+/-
Bielefeld	-	-	-
Dortmund	++	++	++
Karlsruhe	+/-	+	+/-
Mannheim	+	-	++
Ostwürttemberg	+/-	-	+/-
Stuttgart	+/-	+	-
München	-	++	-

- = small/little; +/- = average; + = high; ++ = very high

It is interesting to look at the question, whether there is a certain correlation between the type of strategy pursued and the socio-economic framework within which a regional government operates. To find a clear-cut correlation in our sample, however, is not easy. It is obviously not true that the higher the challenges posed by structural change, the more innovative the communities are with respect to electronic commerce measures. The two communities which practice most clearly stage 3 policies are Dortmund and Munich. Economically they are the two most extreme cases in our sample. The city with the greatest structural problems and the one with the least pressing ones are grouped together. What they have in common, however, is a strategic outlook that posits their communities as front-runners in IT-development. Little is done in communities in which the importance of an IT-cluster is low and challenges by structural change are not considered to be dramatic (see the cases of Bielefeld, Ostwürttemberg).

Experiences and future plans

The communities under scrutiny have meanwhile plenty of experience with promoting electronic commerce. Their clientele is broadly satisfied with the activities – provided they know that they exist. This, however, is a big "if". The trend of what is being offered moves away from fostering a general understanding about what electronic commerce and the Internet are all about to more dedicated, sector or even enterprise specific solutions. Communities which feature a strong cooperation between Competence Centers (if available), chambers and municipal institutions do better than isolated solutions.

The analytical stage model presented before can also be looked upon as a temporal phase model. In a first phase, in which the aim of the promotion agencies has been to get the message out to the companies of a specific city/region that the topics electronic commerce and Internet will be important for them, is now mostly over. In this phase general information material was produced and distributed, and general information meetings took place.

In a second phase the transfer of more dedicated knowledge is in the center of activities. In a third phase the demand for practical recommendations increases. The number of companies experimenting with electronic commerce has increased and for implementing solutions they want to have practical advice and support. In addition concrete pilot projects can be started and supported within or in addition to individual counseling.

Cities and regions which already offer all stages of support will just make a shift in emphasis. For other communities the question arises whether they are willing and able to move up the ladder of involvement or whether they opt out of respective activities or at least downscale their support.

Conclusion

Our analysis has shown that the promotion of electronic commerce has become an important goal for many an economic development actor. The survey among representatives of economic development agencies, chambers of commerce and industry as well as small and medium-sized companies has further demonstrated that a variety of promotion strategies is being used. These strategies can be described by using a stage model. The interviewed business people think that the scope of existing promotion and information programs is far too complex and intransparent. In order to optimize existing instruments (a) a clearer structuring and far more transparency of the measures seems to be necessary, (b) more public relations efforts for the information of business should be made and (c) a stronger orientation of the measures towards the immediate and very practical needs of the companies would help.

A more far-reaching reflection about the structural or regional economic relevance of electronic commerce hardly takes place. At first hand this is not surprising, given the strong identification of electronic commerce with intentions to enter and conquer global markets. The effects on the local/regional markets on the other hand have been largely neglected in these discussions and are beyond the intentions of most promoters. On the regional level, however, changes might take place, which, in a stylized version, seem to indicate a growing competitive pressure by virtual, not locally bound businesses, the expansion of local companies beyond their established markets as well as the support of new electronic commerce based business models. Applications on the regional/local level, such as the enrichment of traditional business relationships with electronic commerce elements, might induce a push of service innovations, which might influence the regional economic sphere much more intensively than the internationalizing tendencies of some single firms, a consideration which has so far not sunk very deep in the mind of regional/local development actors. Most of the present promotion activities still result from a gut feeling that something has to be done. Aim and direction are very often not clear. Insofar there is a policy oriented towards the promotion of electronic commerce, but no electronic commerce policy.

References

Brandt M, Volkert B (2000) Analyse regionaler Online Märkte. Arbeitsbericht der Akademie für Technikfolgenabschätzung Nr. 181, Stuttgart

Cairncross F (1997) The death of distance, How the communications revolution will change our lives. Harvard Business School Press, Boston

Cooke P, Morgan K (1998) The Associational Economy. Oxford University Press, Oxford

Delpho H, Todt J (2001) Zwischenevaluierung der Fördermaßnahme: Kompetenzzentren Elektronischer Geschäftsverkehr. Untersuchung der Prognos AG im Auftrag des Bundesministeriums für Wirtschaft und Technologie, Basel

Floeting H, Grabow B (1999) Information, Kommunikation und Multimedia in den Städten. Teil I: Die Fallstudien Braunschweig, Hannover, München, Nürnberg. Materialien des Deutschen Institutes für Urbanistik, Berlin

Fuchs G, Purschke I (2002) Potenziale der E-Commerce-Förderung auf regionaler Ebene. Arbeitsbericht der Akademie für Technikfolgenabschätzung in Baden-Württemberg Nr. 227, Stuttgart

Grabow B (2000) Information, Kommunikation und Multimedia in den Städten. Teil II: Die Handlungsfelder Wirtschaft/Arbeit und Infrastruktur. Materialien des Deutschen Institutes für Urbanistik, Berlin

Icks A, Richter M (1999) Innovative kommunale Wirtschaftförderung, Wege – Beispiele – Möglichkeiten. Deutscher universitätsverlag, Wiesbaden

Läpple D (1999) Die Ökonomie einer Metropolregion im Spannungsfeld von Globalisierung und Regionalisierung – das Beispiel Hamburg. In: Fuchs G, Kraus G, Wolf H-W (Hrsg) Die Bindungen der Globalisierung: Interorganisationsbeziehungen im regionalen und globalen Wirtschaftsraum. Metropolis-Verlag, Marburg, pp S 11–47

Michel LP, Burgdorff F, Heinze M (2000) Regionale Initiativen zur Förderung von Electronic Commerce in Nordrhein-Westfalen. Arbeitsbericht der Akademie für Technikfolgenabschätzung Nr. 168, Stuttgart

Riehm U, Orwat C, Wingert B (2001) Online-Buchhandel in Deutschland. Die Buchhandelsbranche vor der Herausforderung des Internet. Arbeitsbericht der Akademie für Technikfolgenabschätzung in Baden-Württemberg Nr. 192, Stuttgart

Schenk M, Wolf M (2001) Nutzung und Akzeptanz von E-Commerce. Arbeitsbericht der Akademie für Technikfolgenabschätzung Nr. 209, Stuttgart

Stapel-Schulz C, Eifert M, Siegfried Ch (2002) Organisations- und Kooperationstypen kommunaler Internetauftritte. Arbeitspapier des Deutschen Institutes für Urbanistik, Berlin

Steinfield Ch, Whitten P (1999) Community Level Socio-Economic Impacts of Electronic Commerce. JCMC (5)2